UNENDING CAPITALISM

T0373891

What forces shaped the twentieth-century world? Capitalism and communism are usually seen as having been engaged in a fight to the death during the Cold War. With the establishment of the People's Republic of China in 1949, the Chinese Communist Party aimed to end capitalism. Karl Gerth argues that despite the socialist rhetoric of class warfare and egalitarianism, Communist Party policies actually developed a variety of capitalism and expanded consumerism. This negated the goals of the Communist Revolution across the Mao era (1949–76) and down to the present. Through topics related to state attempts to manage what people began to desire – wristwatches and bicycles, films and fashion, leisure travel and Mao badges – Gerth challenges fundamental assumptions about capitalism, communism, and countries conventionally labeled as socialist. In so doing, his provocative history of China suggests how larger forces related to the desire for mass-produced consumer goods reshaped the twentieth-century world and remade people's lives.

KARL GERTH is Professor of History at the University of California, San Diego, where he holds the Hwei-Chih and Julia Hsiu Chair in Chinese Studies. His earlier books are *As China Goes, So Goes the World* and *China Made: Consumer Culture and the Creation of the Nation*.

UNENDING CAPITALISM

How Consumerism Negated China's Communist Revolution

KARL GERTH

University of California, San Diego

CAMBRIDGE
UNIVERSITY PRESS

CAMBRIDGE
UNIVERSITY PRESS

University Printing House, Cambridge CB2 8BS, United Kingdom

One Liberty Plaza, 20th Floor, New York, NY 10006, USA

477 Williamstown Road, Port Melbourne, VIC 3207, Australia

314–321, 3rd Floor, Plot 3, Splendor Forum, Jasola District Centre,
New Delhi – 110025, India

79 Anson Road, #06–04/06, Singapore 079906

Cambridge University Press is part of the University of Cambridge.

It furthers the University's mission by disseminating knowledge in the pursuit of
education, learning, and research at the highest international levels of excellence.

www.cambridge.org
Information on this title: www.cambridge.org/9780521868464
DOI: 10.1017/9781139025225

First published 2020

Printed in the United Kingdom by TJ International Ltd, Padstow Cornwall

A catalogue record for this publication is available from the British Library.

Library of Congress Cataloging-in-Publication Data
NAMES: Gerth, Karl, 1966– author.
TITLE: Unending capitalism : how consumerism negated China's communist revolution / Karl
Gerth, University of California, San Diego.
DESCRIPTION: Cambridge, United Kingdom ; New York, NY : Cambridge University Press,
2020. | Includes bibliographical references and index.
IDENTIFIERS: LCCN 2019049016 (print) | LCCN 2019049017 (ebook) | ISBN 9780521868464
(hardback) | ISBN 9781139025225 (epub)
SUBJECTS: LCSH: Consumption (Economics) – China – History – 20th century. | Consumers –
China – History – 20th century. | Communism – China – History – 20th century. | Capitalism –
China – History – 20th century. | China – Economic conditions – 1949– | China – Politics and
government – 1949–
CLASSIFICATION: LCC HC430.C6 G473 2020 (print) | LCC HC430.C6 (ebook) | DDC 339.4/
7095109045–dc23
LC record available at https://lccn.loc.gov/2019049016
LC ebook record available at https://lccn.loc.gov/2019049017

ISBN 978-0-521-86846-4 Hardback
ISBN 978-0-521-68846-8 Paperback

Contents

Figures

Acknowledgments

Over a decade of researching and writing this book, I would not have found nor made sense of many of the materials used here without the assistance of May Cao. And this book would not have been completed without the editorial help of Jeanne Barker-Nunn. Reading critiques of capitalism as part of the research for this book sensitized me to the structural inequalities on which capitalism depends. So I am fairly certain it is more than a coincidence that these two individuals whose wages do not approximate the value that good people create are women. It is to May and Jeanne that I dedicate this book.

Peter Carroll symbolizes my anxieties of forgetting to thank friends and colleagues who contributed directly and indirectly to the completion of this book. Although he was instrumental in encouraging me to explore an archive that proved critical to the completion of my first book, I forgot to thank him in that book (but did so in my second). I don't know who the "Peter" of this book will be. But the Peter possibilities are vast: a forgotten conversation at a conference, a book read long ago that contributed to my thinking but did not end up in the notes, or, most unnerving of all, someone as directly helpful as Peter. Thank you, "Peter," whoever you are.

The most obvious to thank are those who read all or parts of the manuscript. Before I name names, though, I must state that many of those who provided feedback did so, more often than not, by disagreeing with the arguments they encountered in my earlier drafts. Naming them, therefore, does not imply endorsement. Indeed, one should assume the opposite, starting with Andre Schmid, whose thoughtful disagreements and suggestions led to many improvements. I am particularly grateful to Sarah Schneewind for demanding logic and clarity across the entire manuscript. Many others gave feedback on specific parts, including Juliette Cadiot, Mark Hendrickson, Matthew D. Johnson, Fabio Lanza, Hyung Gu Lynn, Oscar Sanchez-Siboney, Dagmar Schäfer, Michael Schoenhals,

Stephen Sheehi, Lewis Siegelbaum, Aminda Smith, Felix Wemheuer, and Jake Werner.

A joy of academic life is having a large community of people to discuss ideas. Frank Trentmann provided the earliest feedback on my first book and has been a resource ever since. Similarly, Joel Andreas, Mabel Berezin, Chris Bramall, Archie Bryant, Linsun Cheng, Alex Day, Katherine Epstein, Antonia Finanne, Lisa Fredsti, Shang Gao, Jane Hayward, Bill Kirby, Greg Lewis, Peter Perdue, Shen Yu, Sun Peidong, Warren Sun, Patricia M. Thornton, Clint Twist, Hilde de Weerdt, Qitao Wu, and Yiching Wu all provided additional forms of assistance. For providing decades of intellectual engagement, institutional know-how, and friendship, Rana Mitter's help defies easy categorization in these acknowledgements.

At Cambridge University Press, Lucy Rhymer lived up to her stellar reputation as a commissioning editor. Among her many contributions was to solicit tough but fair anonymous readers for the press, whom I also thank. At the press, James Baker provided production assistance. In addition, I am grateful to Nancy Hearst for checking every footnote and improving the book on nearly every page and Dan Harding for his copyediting work. Isabella Furth provided additional help with writing and revisions. Mathilda Lieberman, the writing counselor at Grinnell College, was the first to teach me how to write academically – and, indirectly, taught me the importance of getting feedback.

One of my graduate advisors, the late Philip Kuhn, was fond of telling graduate students that we would learn more from each other than from him. What he did not say was that faculty learn just as much from their students. In addition to the students in the undergraduate course at the University of California, San Diego (UCSD), where I first tested this material, I am grateful to the Modern Chinese History graduate seminar participants, including our graduate students Peter Braden, Yupeng Jiao, Chuchu Wang, Matt Wills, Thomas Chan, Lin Yang, Ben Kletzer, and H. C. Leung. Both Thomas Chan and Matt Wills deserve added praise for reading and commenting extensively on earlier drafts and suggesting useful sources.

I am also fortunate at the UCSD to have a vibrant Chinese Studies community to share ideas and find new sources of intellectual inspiration. I thank in particular Susan Shirk, Lei Guang, Micah Muscolino, Samuel Tsoi, Victor Shih, Barry Naughton, Li Huai, and Jude Blanchette. In the wider Southern California Chinese studies community, I give thanks to Jeff Wasserstrom for making my transition to a new location much easier. The singularly indefatigable Paul Pickowicz continues (even in retirement) to share the secrets behind his and Joseph Esherick's successful graduate program – devotion and hard work.

The research behind this book spans my time at three universities. The University of South Carolina, Oxford University/Merton College, and now the University of California, San Diego have provided a steady stream of funding and administrate support. In particular, I wish to thank the funders of my Hwei-Chih and Julia Hsiu Endowed Chair in Chinese Studies at UCSD, the UCSD faculty senate, the warden and fellows of Merton College, the Fell Fund of Oxford University, the British Academy, the British Arts & Humanities Research Council, and the Blakemore Foundation. These institutions supported my research, but their people did the paperwork. The professionalism of the administrators at these institutions, particularly Susan Winchester, have made my life much easier.

During the 2018–19 academic year, I had the good fortune to complete the manuscript as the Starr Foundation East Asian Studies Endowment Fund Member at the Institute for Advanced Study in Princeton. Nicola di Cosmo cultivated the ideal environment for research, writing, and conversation. Additional support for that year came from a Frederic E. Wakeman, Jr. Fellowship in Chinese History of the American Council of Learned Societies.

Many opportunities for academic exchange improved this book. Jennifer Altehenger and Denise Ho not only read an early version of the introduction but also organized a multi-year series of conferences around the world that allowed me to present and solicit feedback on early versions of two chapters. I am grateful to the other participants, particularly Jacob Eyferth, Jie Li, and Cole Roskam. For inviting me to visit as a Senior Scholar at the Academia Sinica on Taiwan, I thank Wu Jen-shu. At Princeton University, Janet Chen and Sheldon Garon provided much collegiality during my year in their midst. I received early critical feedback from Thomas Gold, Wen-hsin Yeh, Kevin O'Brien, and Peter Zhou at a talk at the University of California, Berkeley. As part of the Modern China Seminar, Columbia University, Chuck Wooldridge, Robert Culp, and the other participants, especially Eugenia Lean, offered constructive criticism. I also thank Arunabh Ghosh for the opportunity to speak about my research at Harvard University. Yang Kuisong, Feng Xiaocai, Xu Jilin, Jiang Jin, Qu Jun, and Zhang Jishun, all of East China Normal University, have provided years of rewarding scholarly exchange. And Jin Dalu and Zhang Xiuli of the Shanghai Academy of Social Sciences allowed me to test the final thesis with a Chinese audience of specialists.

Vast improvements in research technology and new electronic sources and databases have made it much easier to challenge established interpretations of the Mao era, as have the countless testimonials in Chinese blog postings I used. Naturally, these and other resources would have been unknown or inaccessible to me without the aid of librarians, particularly Xi Chen at UCSD, Marcia Tucker at the Institute for Advanced Study, and Joshua Seufert at Princeton. In addition, I am indebted to the staff at these libraries, including Scott McAvoy and Kirk Wang for helping prepare the images.

I am grateful to those who improved my life beyond this project. My family, especially my parents Roger Gerth and Judy Valentine Gerth, long ago mastered the fine art of expressing interest and encouragement in my work without making me feel self-conscious of the glacial pace of its progress. Denise Demetriou read countless drafts and provided many happy diversions. Misty Gerth ensured I had many hours of carefree fun. Many friends also contributed to the quality of my life, especially Frank Bechter, John Carroll, Ken Chase, and Stacey Millner-Collins. Because my work–life balance centers around rowing, I am particularly grateful to members of that community, starting with Andy Dyson for convincing a middle-aged academic to join the college's rowing squad and my teammates for enduring life on the water with "the Gerthquake." Since then, many others have supported my efforts, including, most recently, Gary Ahrens, Chris Callaghan, Carl Douglas, William J. Manning, Patrice Rioux, and Joanne Stolen.

Last year, I had two reminders of the value people create that transcends wages and helps others. In Princeton, after hearing me describe my book, Amy Gottschalk, whom I had just met, ran to her car and returned with a fabulous set of Mao badges, a part of her collection she had given to her mother and had recovered after her mother's death. She insisted I accept them as a gift because, she determined, I would find them an appropriate home (some of them now live in these pages). Also last year, while preparing to move, I came across my elementary school graduation book in which teachers and classmates had written me farewell notes. In my final encounter with one teacher, Sister Mary Ellen, who on more than one occasion had punished me with good reason, found the compassion to write, "I believe in you." Without such instances of generosity over all these years, I would not have finished this book.

Abbreviations

CCP   Chinese Communist Party
CPSU   Communist Party of the Soviet Union
DGB SH   *Dagongbao* (Shanghai)
JFRB   *Jiefang ribao* (*Liberation Daily*)
NBCK   *Neibu cankao* (Internal reference)
NEP   New Economic Policies
NPM   National Products Movement
PLA   People's Liberation Army
PRC   People's Republic of China
RMRB   *Renmin ribao* (*People's Daily*)
SMA   Shanghai Municipal Archives
SRC   Shanghai Revolutionary Committee
WDGW   Song, Yongyi, ed., 中国文化大革命文库 (Chinese
             Cultural Revolution database) (Hong Kong:Xianggang
             Zhongwen daxue, Zhongguo yanjiu fuwu zhongxin, 2002)

Introduction
Consumerism and Capitalism

With the establishment of the People's Republic of China in 1949, the Chinese Communist Party aimed to end capitalism. Three decades later, however, capitalism appeared to have survived the Communist Revolution and even to have triumphed over communism as the driving force in China's economy and society. This book, the first history of consumerism during the initial decades after the Chinese Communist Revolution, offers a new explanation for the seeming failure of communism in China. As it demonstrates, the three central processes of consumerism – the mass production of consumer products, the proliferation of a discourse about these products in popular media, and the use of such products to create and communicate identities – were not only already underway in China by the time of the revolution but actually expanded through Chinese Communist Party (CCP) policies.[1] Beyond integrating consumerism into the history of the early People's Republic of China (PRC), this book argues that the party's self-defined socialist state represented not an antithesis to capitalism but rather a moving point on a spectrum of state-to-private control of industrial capitalism. As a result, the policies of the party continually negated the goals of its own revolution.

This attempt to integrate consumerism into the history of the Mao era, here defined as 1949–76, completes my earlier efforts to explore the history of consumerism in twentieth-century China.[2] In my first book, *China Made* (2003), I examined the emergence of nationalism in early twentieth-century China and the early spread of mass-produced products and the consumer culture that developed around them. Later, in *As China Goes, So Goes the World* (2010), I explored the history of consumerism since the end of the Mao era, during which the impact of consumerism was widely evident in China, as indicated by the creation of the largest market in the world for cars, the spread of global and national brands through advertising and mass retailing, and the resurgence of markets for everything from stolen babies to endangered species to second wives. These accounts of the

birth of Chinese consumerism before 1949 and its resurgence since the late
1970s led me to formulate the central question addressed in this book –
what happened to consumerism during the intervening Mao era? – and my
central argument about China's supposed movement toward communism
during that period.

The history of consumerism during the Mao era has remained a mystery
because few scholars thought there was any consumerism to study in a poor
socialist country.[3] Based on earlier research, I initially expected to find that
many aspects of consumerism that had developed before the founding of
the People's Republic – including advertising, branding, fashion,
and social differentiation through the consumption of mass-produced
products – had not disappeared but in fact had quietly persisted. And,
indeed, as I continued my research, I uncovered ample evidence that
"Communist China," despite its anti-consumerism rhetoric, had developed what it called its own socialist versions of consumer fashions, commerce, product branding and advertising, and all other aspects of
consumerism that are familiar in market capitalist countries. As these
attributes of consumerism spread, growing numbers of people in China
began to create new identities around the desire for and acquisition of
mass-produced goods such as bicycles, sewing machines, and wristwatches.
The abundant evidence and examples of consumerism included in the
following chapters reveals a history that is very different from that of
popular perceptions of this era, which tend to be dominated by Red
Guard rallies, economic experiments, policy disasters, mass famines, and,
above all, the power of one person, Mao Zedong.

Initially, I followed both the CCP's own terminology for its policies and
scholarly conventions by appending the label "socialism" to my findings.
Because the consumerism I had discovered was occurring in a socialist
country, I deemed it "socialist consumerism." But as I amassed more
examples, I began to wonder what it meant to find so much consumerism
existing under the control of a Communist Party whose stated goal was to
"build socialism" by eliminating the attributes of capitalism, including
their consumerist expressions.[4] As the number of exceptions to the party's
professed intention to transform China into a more equitable socialist
state, a working people's republic, became so abundant, it began to seem
that those very efforts, first, had created not less but more consumerism
and, second, this consumerism was in fact a structural consequence of the
state's social and economic policies.[5] Whereas the party predicted
that manifestations of capitalism would fade away over time as it "built
socialism," what I saw developing was a form of industrial capitalism on

a state-to-private spectrum that China's leaders, with varying levels of sincerity and success, attempted to justify, or to make more acceptable, through the use of socialist language and implementation of socialistic policies (Figure 0.1).[6]

It is hardly surprising that the history of consumerism during the three decades after 1949 has until now been largely unexamined. China was and remained a poor country throughout the Mao era. Only a minority of the population had access to consumer goods, and many fewer people created a culture of consumption around these goods. Accordingly, conventional histories of the era have focused on other aspects of the aftermath of the Communist Revolution. These include the party's struggle to establish a new state, form geopolitical alliances, reorganize rural labor, expropriate

Figure 0.1. Industrial consumerism. The Mao badge fad discussed in Chapter 7 illustrates all three defining aspects of consumerism: the unprecedented scale of industrial production of consumer products, the spread of discourse about such products in mass media that taught people to have new needs and wants, and the growing use of products, including badges, to create and communicate different, often hierarchical, identities. Source: All badge photos are from the author's personal collection.

the wealth of urban capitalists, industrialize the economy, experiment with social engineering, and initiate mass mobilization campaigns to garner support. Yet, as these chapters demonstrate, the spread of consumerism was both a vanguard of these transformations and also closely related to them. Interpreting the Mao era through the lens of consumerism thus offers a new framework for understanding the entire political and economic reorganization of China during the post-1949 period. The advance of consumerism has always been a correlate of industrialization and therefore always a part of the complete reorganization of society to facilitate mass production.[7] In the conventional view, the Mao era represents the party's boldest attempts to build an anti-capitalist, hyper-egalitarian, and anti-consumerist socialist alternative to industrial capitalism. But moving beyond the party's rhetoric to examine its policies and their outcomes reveals that consumerism during the Mao era was far from a remnant of pre-Revolutionary China that survived underground or an unexpected outcome of state policies. The expansion of consumerism across the entire Mao era was a predictable outcome that continually negated the central goals of the revolution itself. Rather than end capitalism, the CCP simply moved China, with fits and starts, toward the state side of the state-to-private spectrum of industrial capitalism. At all times, regardless of the specific institutional arrangements, the CCP was always developing one or another variation of industrial capitalism.

Therefore, this book is intended not only to illuminate the origins of the resurgence of consumerism in China that followed Mao's death but also to broaden the longstanding critique of whether China – as every other "socialist" country – should be considered a variety of a capitalist state by including consumption and consumerism in the analysis. The book argues that the Mao-era political economy can be better understood not as socialism but as what earlier scholars have described as *state capitalism*, that is, a variety of industrial capitalism in which state power dominates the accumulation and allocation of capital, usually through the institutions of central planning and state ownership.[8] The primary goal of the party was to use practices associated with capitalism to industrialize the country and to achieve pressing or longer-term economic, military, and political goals. Some communist leaders, such as Stalin in the Soviet Union, were willing to accept the resultant social inequalities as a stage of socialist development necessary to reach the goal of communism.[9] In contrast, while Mao and other party leaders followed the Soviet lead and acknowledged the necessity of an intermediate stage of socialism en route to communism, they were also often painfully aware of the contradictions between their stated aims and the policy outcomes and feared that these inequalities would undermine their revolutionary goals. Yet, to further expand capital, party leaders continually chose to experiment with shifts in the institutional arrangements toward greater use of markets, private property, and material incentives – all of which led to expanded consumerism.[10]

Mao regularly warned that these and other manifestations of capitalism would negate the Communist Revolution in China, the Soviet Union, and elsewhere. In Mao's pronouncements, the word "negation" (否定) is meant to invoke the process of dialectical historical materialism, in which one mode of production is negated by another (e.g., feudalism by capitalism and capitalism by communism).[11] Despite these fears, the overarching goal of industrialization and the resultant need to accumulate capital became a higher party priority than the long-term goals associated with becoming a communist country, such as creating an economy of shared equity and democratizing worker control over production. In short, party promises of communist ends justified its capitalist means.

At the same time, my focus on consumption and the allocation of the surplus – that is, what happens to what is produced – offers a new perspective on the history and politics of this era. Moving beyond the traditional emphasis on production and accumulation, I show in these chapters that the state's efforts to exert more control over industrialization also required greater control over consumption. The state's repeated decision to prioritize rapid industrialization over the socialist goal of transforming the social relations of production (from production controlled by capital to production controlled by labor) had a corollary on the consumption side. In a poor, capital-starved country desperate for resources, the state was forced to attempt to either suppress individual desires to consume or to channel these desires away from what it called "bourgeois" consumerism and in directions that would be more useful to it. This included what Mao referred to as the *social consumption* of collective goods, such as weapons and infrastructure and social programs intended to improve human capital (Figure 0.2).[12] Ultimately, the CCP failed to end capitalism, in large part because it chose instead to harness the practices of industrial capitalism and consumerism for larger or more immediate state goals. To be sure, the institutional arrangements of industrial capitalism differed between "capitalist" and "socialist" countries. But the presence of non-market distribution mechanisms, such as ration coupons and urban work units, and the unremitting party rhetoric about the establishment of a communist country have obscured underlying continuities in the development of capitalism and consumerism before, across, and since the Mao

Figure 0.2. Social consumption. Although the term *social consumption* comes from neoclassical economics, Mao and the party used the concept as integral to "building socialism," valorizing the social or public consumption of collective goods such as the Yangzi River Bridge at Nanjing (illustrated in a state poster here) as the opposite of private or bourgeois consumption. Source: The International Institute of Social History (Landsberger Collection).

era.[13] Admittedly, the work unit and some of the other institutional arrangements associated with Chinese socialism may have provided more opportunities for constructing and communicating identity than the consumption of mass-produced products. When examined through the concept of consumerism, however, they appear to be additional means of limiting consumption to facilitate faster industrialization and thus to have contributed to the structural inequalities manifest in consumerism.[14]

In short, the many manifestations of capitalism that developed in China during this era were not, as the party frequently told the Chinese people and the outside world, remnants of the "old society" that the state was in the process of eliminating. They were reflections of the coexistence of diverse arrangements of state-driven and market-driven capitalism on the same state-to-private spectrum, which shifted over time in response to economic and political exigencies. An economy routinely characterized as "planned" and "socialist" included not only diverse attributes of consumerism but also numerous institutional arrangements equated with "capitalism": private enterprises, underground and open markets, commodity prices, wage labor, and competition among firms.[15] The evidence of capitalist practices presented in these chapters does not merely challenge or complicate socialism by creating a "state" or an "actually existing" variety of socialism, as scholars have often suggested. Rather, such evidence reflects the flexibility of industrial capitalism during the era, a flexibility reflected in the periodic institutional shifts along the spectrum of capitalism toward the greater use of the institutional arrangements of private capitalism, particularly markets and private ownership, to aid state capitalist accumulation.

Naturally, the party attempted to control or limit the impact of such private capitalist arrangements in the economy. I coin the term *state consumerism* to refer specifically to the wide-ranging efforts within China's form of state capitalism to manage demand in every respect, from promoting, defining, and even spreading consumption of some things to eliminating, discrediting, or at the very least marginalizing private preferences for the allocation of resources (Figure 0.3). These efforts involved all three of the defining aspects of consumerism: the manufacture and distribution of mass-produced consumer goods, the proliferation of discourses about such goods, and the communication of identities through the consumption of these goods. The rhetoric of state consumerism was often superficially socialist and egalitarian, which I refer to as "socialistic." The party promised "building socialism" would negate the attributes of industrial consumerism, including what the party itself called the "three major inequalities" (三大差别): inequalities based on whether one lived in a city or in the countryside, whether one's work relied on mental or manual labor, and whether one worked in a factory or on a farm.[16] Its policies, however, sometimes by design and other times unintentionally, served to exacerbate these inequalities.[17]

The concept of state consumerism employed in these chapters helps extend the traditional focus on state-led accumulation in previous analyses of state capitalism to include the state's management of material desires. Under state capitalism, the Chinese state produced its correlate, state consumerism, by acting not simply as the chief appropriator of capital but also as the chief allocator of capital, suppressing competing demands for other uses of the surplus. In effect, the party not only made decisions about who would get what, but it also suppressed or discouraged uses of capital that were associated with socialism, including fulfilling the workers' desires for higher wages, additional housing, or a more equitable distribution of scarce consumer goods. Under state consumerism, individual choices were considered too important to be left in the hands of either

Figure 0.3. State institutions promoting consumerism. State consumerism included both the suppression and promotion of consumption based on state-defined priorities. The party conspicuously suppressed consumption through its budgetary allocations and its promotion of an ethos of "hard work and frugal living." But state consumerism also involved the promotion of some products and the creation of a nationwide infrastructure for consumerism, including department stores such as this one in Beijing. Source: 北京画册编辑委员会, ed., 北京 (Beijing) (Beijing: Beijing huace bianji weiyuanhui, 1959), 81.

"bourgeois" or "feudal" individuals – or even "the masses" of urban or rural workers.

As I argue, however, state consumerism was only one aspect of the consumerism during this era, and it failed to achieve near total control over material desires, much less over consumption, throughout the entire country. In China as elsewhere, it was impossible for the state to dictate individual desires; attempts to replace individual-centered "bourgeois" consumerism with total state control proved more aspirational than actual. The history of such consumption by the Chinese people is the history not of a rejection of the party's stated goals but a refusal to give the party monopoly power to equate socialism with the state-promoted ethos of "hard work and frugal living" (艰苦朴素). This book demonstrates numerous ways in which the Chinese Communist Revolution was negated "daily, hourly, spontaneously, and on a mass scale" not only by small-scale production, as Lenin had predicted, but also, as the party had feared, by the consumerism that is integral to all points on the spectrum of industrial capitalism.[18]

Viewed through the lens of the continuity of consumerist and capitalist development, China's seemingly sudden abandonment of its supposedly revolutionary socialist heritage after 1978 is more comprehensible. Deng Xiaoping and subsequent Chinese leaders did not end socialism as much as they reshaped (or, to appropriate their language, reformed) a variation of capitalism by shifting the country along the spectrum toward greater private capitalism and private consumerism. Thus, the history of the Mao era recounted here helps explain the revival of private enterprise, market capitalism, and unfettered consumerism in China in recent decades by showing that the "reformers" in the party who succeeded Mao did not reverse the efforts to end capitalism. Rather, they simply adjusted institutions to continue to accelerate the expansion of capitalism.

CHAPTER I

Self-Expanding and Compulsory Consumerism

Material desires for mass-produced commodities spread quickly during the Mao era. An increasing number of people began to learn about new goods, felt the urge to acquire them, and sought ways to do so, particularly in places privileged by CCP industrial policies, such as cities, state-owned factories, and administrative offices. The story of the spread of these desires, which had already begun to take hold before 1949, helps illustrate how the state both deliberately and inadvertently contributed to building consumerism and negating the Communist Revolution.

Two aspects of consumerism – its self-expanding and compulsory nature – are central to the analysis here. Consumerism begets more consumerism – that is, in China as elsewhere, consumerism, like capitalism, is *self-expanding*.[1] Products became prerequisites for both old and new social activities. To find a better job or a better marriage partner, for instance, Chinese people felt compelled to acquire a bicycle, a fashionable article of clothing, or other mass-produced items. To be sure, the spread of capitalism and consumerism in China encountered numerous obstacles, including a pre-existing cultural value of frugality and revulsion about identities communicated through commodities. Naturally, some people readily embraced the ethos of "hard work and frugal living" as promoted by the party during this period, not only because the mass media told them to do so but also because such an ethos already existed. During the Mao era, consumerism overcame obstacles to its continued expansion, including those erected by the party.

This chapter shows how luxury products became more commonplace and expanded both capitalism and consumerism in the Mao era. In the 1960s, millions of people felt *compelled* to acquire three luxury products in particular: wristwatches, bicycles, and sewing machines. By the end of the Mao era these were widely known and discussed as the Three Great Things (三大件).[2] Before the late 1950s, all three of these goods were difficult to acquire in China. They were usually imported or manufactured by foreign-owned companies in China and were found only in the homes of those who were well-off. But as domestic industries recovered from decades of war and the state expanded its control over both production and consumption, the Three Great Things became increasingly available throughout China's cities and towns, and even in some rural areas. By the end of the Mao era, production of these items had increased dramatically. In Shandong, for instance, production of the Three Greats approximately tripled between 1975 and 1980, allowing many people to fulfill their desire to own a wristwatch, a bicycle, or a sewing machine.[3] Demonstrating the correlation between the expansion of capitalism and consumerism, the policies and rhetoric of state consumerism shifted from an initial emphasis on thrift to promotion of consumption of the Three Greats.[4] As the original Three Greats gradually began to lose their elite status while spreading throughout the country, by the early 1980s they became known as the Old Three Great Things (老三大件).[5] They were replaced by a newer set of more technologically complex and capital-intensive consumer products such as televisions, washing machines, and refrigerators.[6]

Increased access to the Three Greats in the 1960s was viewed by both the state and the populace as a symbol of socialist success, offering tangible evidence beyond the boastful newspaper headlines that the country was industrializing and becoming wealthier. The party was starting to transform what before 1949 were urban luxuries produced by the imperialists into everyday desirables acquired by new segments of society, and to accumulate the human and industrial capital necessary to mass produce all three things domestically.

Although the ability of people to acquire such goods was cited by the party as an example of the shared prosperity that it touted as proof that it was "building socialism" on its way toward communism, an examination of the distribution of these symbols of economic success shows that in fact policies were introducing, elaborating, and manifesting new forms of social and economic inequalities. As suggested below, although the party made rhetorical and policy gestures toward its stated communist goal of preempting or ending the inequalities associated with industrial capitalism, such inequalities, including those targeted by the party, actually became worse.

Throughout the era, the party sent conflicting messages about consumerism. At the same time that it was reassuring the public that socialism included state-sanctioned inequalities, party rhetoric of "hard work and frugal living" was often equated with socialism. At times the state would attempt to vilify individual material desires as a threat to both national security and advancement toward the goal of communism. Yet it could not separate consumerism from industrialization, and for political reasons, did not always try. Party leaders understood that prioritizing the expansion of production as an end in itself was the best advertisement for what it would inculcate as "socialism." As Mao once told a visiting Polish delegation, "If China catches up in global industrial production with England and the US, then the majority of [domestic opponents] will consent to socialism."[7]

Just as the defining attribute of capitalism is a political economy – and society – dominated by the needs of capital to be reinvested to create more capital, the expansion of industrial production includes the self-expansion of consumerism. In China, consumerism affected even those without access to or the means to buy things. The discourse about consumerism became more complex as the party-led state capitalism developed new products and brands and state consumerism attempted to shape and control material desires. Living in the midst of a discourse of national backwardness and progress, people used consumerism to overcome a perceived personal backwardness. They began to desire products for both their practical applications and for their social value.

The Production and Introduction of the Three Great Things

The desire for the particular goods that became the Three Great Things was neither inevitable nor innate. Rather, the party focused on producing those consumer products that – like big technologies such as railways, bridges, and roads – it determined would further industrialize the country. The same state that wanted to limit its citizens' material desires also wanted its citizens to desire and to master everyday technologies, or to obtain products that extended to other technologies, particularly those associated with fossil fuel-enabled mass production techniques. I use the word "technology" instead of "product" in this context to underscore a critical element in industrial capitalism: continual, self-expanding compulsory change as a consequence of competition. Whereas a "product" appears to be a finished and end-of-the-road item, an "everyday technology" signals the process of one thing becoming something else, such as a bicycle becoming a better (or less expensive) bicycle or even becoming a car. Additional examples of everyday technologies not covered here include typewriters, radios, gramophones, cameras, rice mills, cigarettes, and many others. Even toothbrushes and toothpastes taught new perceptions of the body and hygiene (for example, that teeth required regular brushing) and of class and urbanity – that those who did not know to brush their teeth, much less actually brushed them, preferably with a brand-name toothpaste, were backward.[8] Although not included in this book, big technologies were considered critical to increasing productivity and lowering transaction costs; for instance, the way a railroad or bridge might move coal in the northwest to factories in the southeast or move rural crops to urban centers or export markets. Big technologies helped make things faster, better, cheaper, and more ubiquitous. Both before and after the establishment of the People's Republic, Chinese leaders felt compelled to acquire big technologies in order for the nation to survive and prosper.

The production and proliferation of such goods helped the party produce a population capable of competing in the world's new industrial economy, particularly in the context of Cold War rivalries. Chief among these mass-produced everyday technologies were the Three Greats, whose production and promotion increased the productivity of those individuals who possessed and mastered them. Indeed, the Soviet Union placed these three products (and several others) in a special category of mass-produced "cultured goods" and disseminated official statistics (as did the PRC) on the expansion of their production.[9] Through the consumption of these technologies, and often with state urging, such owners enacted an updated, no-longer-backward identity as useful participants in an industrializing country.

State policies and cadres both aided and altered – but could not arrest – the general spread of consumerism. The state's greatest direct control over consumerism was through directing production levels and prices, financing, and distribution policies, including extensive use of rationing throughout most of the era.[10] State policies meant that the availability of highly desired consumer goods varied by region, types of worker, and financial resources. The state also exercised basic control over institutions of consumerism that facilitated demand: advertising, mass media, propaganda campaigns, and other forms of social pressure. Yet, as demonstrated here, people perceived and internalized these messages and used these products in varying, changing, and unanticipated ways. While the state was attempting to shape demand, consumerism was expanding as part of capitalism.

The Three Greats were introduced to China in the late nineteenth century, when imperialism forcibly accelerated the integration of the domestic market into global capitalism and new forms of industrial consumerism. Factories set up in China under the auspices of the imperialist powers after 1895 introduced mass-produced products and made them less expensive and more accessible. These same companies also expanded the techniques of industrial consumerism that the capitalist firms had developed at home to stimulate material desires.[11] Industry leaders, including the US-based sewing machine company the Singer Corporation, British bicycle manufacturers BSA (三枪牌) and Raleigh (雷利牌), and Swiss watch manufacturers Selca (塞尔卡) and Roamer (罗马), fostered demand with innovative marketing techniques such as new forms of advertising.[12] This imposed industrial capitalism and Sino-foreign contestation over the domestic market, examined in Chapter 2 in greater detail, cast a shadow over all of the Three Great Things. Policies after 1949 intending to replace imported capital and technology and to exercise state control over the domestic market were not unique to the party; rather, they were continuing decades-long efforts that had begun during the Republican era (1912–49). Because the party's primary economic goal during this period was industrialization rather than meeting consumer demand, demand usually outstripped supply, thereby making the distribution of these products a useful tool for identifying state priorities.

The Wristwatch

Among the Three Greats, the one with the most far-reaching social value was the one with the simplest immediate use: the wristwatch. Although timepieces such as clocks and watches are unnecessary for production in pre-industrial agricultural societies, their application value is critical to industrialization. The proliferation of watches in China represented a small, everyday emblem of global competition that included the transformation, standardization, and internalization of time with the establishment of worldwide timekeeping.[13] In particular, soldiers were early adopters of watches, as it was necessary that they synchronize their military maneuvers.[14] Likewise, railroad workers had to adhere to accurate schedules, especially when trains going in opposite directions shared the same tracks.[15] Factory and office workers who relied on timepieces to coordinate labor shifts and schedules used – and felt compelled to acquire – their own watches to counter management control over their time.[16] For these reasons, by making and exporting clocks since the early twentieth century, domestic manufacturers had already responded to the demand for mass-produced timepieces. Although most of this industry was destroyed by the Sino-Japanese and civil wars, production resumed after 1949, and national manufacturing increased from 144,000 clocks in 1952 to over five million clocks by 1962. Domestic production soon included all manner of specialty timepieces, including clocks for planes, boats, and trains, and hundreds of varieties of decorative timepieces. Major brands known throughout the country included Yantai's North Star clocks, Shanghai's Sanwu and Jewel alarm clocks, and Tianjin's Golden Pheasant alarm clocks.[17] Each new brand expanded the range of products available and therefore the different tastes and identities one might express through their possession.

Watches, however, represented the further development of clock-making technology, and China initially lacked the skilled labor and technology to produce them domestically. Technically more complex than a clock, a wristwatch has more than a hundred parts and for assembly it requires more than a hundred procedures. For nearly a decade after 1949, the country relied on imported watches. To develop domestic production, in 1951 the Ministry of Commerce forbade private imports of wristwatches and it centralized all legal imports through Beijing, which then distributed the watches throughout the country via the head office of the state-run China Department Store Company (中国百货总公司).[18] Most (80 percent) of the imported watches during this period were Swiss (which carried the most prestige); China also imported Soviet, French, Japanese, and German watches. Imports in the 1950s fluctuated wildly, from a low of 36,700 in 1954 to a high of 1,341,800 in 1956, but then the number dropped off as domestic production began in the mid-1950s. Even after 1965 when China was producing over a million watches annually, it was still importing many millions more. Women's watches, with thinner bands and smaller faces, were more difficult to obtain because China did not begin to import them until after 1976.[19]

But as early as 1955, the state, which had been forced to compete with foreign manufacturers since the time of the National Products Movement (NPM) during the Republican era (1912–49), mobilized state resources to overcome the technological hurdles of manufacturing its own wristwatches.[20] It encouraged competition among cities throughout the country to compete in producing a working watch; Tianjin was the first to do so, with its Five Star brand watch (五星), which in 1957 was renamed the May Day (五一) brand.[21] Shanghai also competed in such watch-making. In the spring and summer of 1957, the Ministry of Commerce convened watch production research groups, such as a group of fifty-eight technicians from various factories who met in Shanghai in a joint effort to reverse-engineer a watch. Key to this effort were the country's experienced watch repairers, who were accustomed to working on imported watches and could provide engineers with knowledge about different kinds of watches and a chance to experiment with them. Among the one hundred trial watches that were assembled through this effort, only a dozen or so worked. Finally, by using a Swiss-made Selca watch as a guide, technicians produced a working model. Although the resulting watches were not completely "Chinese," as they relied on imported Soviet and Japanese components, they represented a major step forward in accomplishing the party's goal of producing domestic wristwatches. In 1958, an official state factory was established to mass produce watches, and in that year the new watches entered consumer markets under the brand name "Shanghai."[22]

The CCP's distribution of everyday technologies illustrates the relationship between the expansion of inequalities and industrial capitalism. Because there was not much initial production and imports were tightly restricted, watches remained rare luxury products in the 1950s. Production began slowly, with only 16,800 watches manufactured in 1958. But in that year and the following year, the state established additional factories in Beijing, Guangzhou, Jilin, and Dandong, and other brands soon followed, including the Forward (前进) in 1960, based on a Soviet model (and probably manufactured using Soviet machines), and the Red Flag brand in 1966 that used Swiss equipment. Despite the socialist rhetoric surrounding wristwatches, this first of the Three Greats to enter into domestic production expanded inequalities among the populace. The state regulated access to the purchase of watches to favored select members of society who constituted part of the state's industrialization priorities: workers in the metallurgical industry, shipbuilding, the military, and workers in other key industries, though only with a letter of introduction from their work units, a key institutional arrangement in Chinese state capitalism.[23] These distribution policies reinforced the emerging "three major inequalities" identified by the party itself as attributes of industrial capitalism: between mental/manual, urban/rural, and industrial/agricultural labor. And other forms of inequalities were reproduced anew by industrial capitalism, including inequalities based on gender, ethnicity, region, and one's relationship with the state.

The history of watch production and distribution also illustrates how the state's promotion of consumerism ebbed and flowed depending on its larger economic goals and commitments. As the state ramped up production of consumer goods in the 1960s to restore the economy following the late-1950s policies of rapid industrialization, it dramatically increased domestic production of watches (Figure 1.1). Production continued to expand even during the Cultural Revolution decade (1966–76), and surpassed thirteen million watches per year by 1978.[24] Nonetheless, even then

(a)   (b)

Figure 1.1. Two faces of progress. The proliferation of watches included a diversity of brands and styles to express different consumer tastes. Photographed here are two versions of the most prestigious domestic brand of watch of the Mao era, a Shanghai. The watch on the left is the original Shanghai with a black face and the original logo, modeled after a famous Shanghai building. The Shanghai on the right includes a logo written in Mao Zedong's handwriting, with the Chinese characters lifted from two of his poems. This watch also utilized the time-tested strategy of integrating political slogans into the brand. In this case, "Serve the People" was written below the center of the watch. Left: Author's personal collection. Right: Used with permission from the collection of Shen Yu.

only a small fraction of the country's 700 million potential purchasers owned a watch. Rather than becoming a product distributed to the masses, watches became a much more widespread marker of sophisticated identity, rural prosperity, or, as noted below, cadre status (and corruption). By following the Leninist lead of creating a "socialist" transition that included distribution based on work, the party openly prioritized industrialization over eliminating class differences. By distributing wristwatches to workers in selected jobs and industries, the party was introducing or widening the inequalities associated with industrial capitalism.

The Bicycle

Similarly, the production of bicycles reflected and advanced the state's commitment to industrial production rather than transforming social relations. Paralleling the imperialist-inflected history of wristwatches, mass-produced

brand-name bicycles also arrived in China in the late nineteenth century as
another imported everyday technology connected with global capitalist
competition.[25] People (especially in cities) had seen bicycles as a status symbol
since at least the Republican era, when sought-after British-made bicycles
became global brands.[26] Even before the founding of the PRC, owning
a bicycle was a critical part of some people's self-identification.
Industrialization focusing on workers and capital led to rapid urbanization
and an increased need for mobility and transportation. Bicycles were less
expensive and easier to operate than other modes of individual transport,
such as automobiles or animals. By the 1940s, bicycles had already become
a widespread mode of urban transportation and were a pioneering technology
of mobility. In 1949, for example, Shanghai alone had some 230,000 bicycles.[27]
The spread of bicycles allowed for personal mobility that lasted for some fifty
years until automobiles began to push aside bicycles in the 1990s.

The Three Greats spread a shared and expanding discourse of consumerism and branded hierarchies throughout the country. Consumer attitudes and popular discourse about bicycles, for instance, were already in
place and ready to expand after 1949.[28] In China, bicycles further helped
create a common discourse of consumerism that included a specific vocabulary related to both the general categories of the products ("bicycle") and
the branded subcategories (e.g., "Flying Pigeon bicycle"). Naturally, this
discourse of consumerism became more complex with the development of
industrial capitalism and led to the creation of brand and identity hierarchies. Factories contributed to the expansion of these competing consumer discourses by producing and differentiating their products through
unique branding. The subcategories of the Three Greats contributed to
brand-based hierarchies that further separated the meaning of commodities and their consumption from their production conditions, a process
Marx referred to as fetishization. As Marx observed, the products of labor
"appear as autonomous figures endowed with a life of their own, which
enter into relations both with each other and with the human race."[29]
In this way, branding further disguises the social relations of capitalist
production – that is, its fetishization – by helping products appear as
independent forces in society.

For Marx, commodity production is the foundation of capitalism, so
much so he begins *Capital* with a discussion of commodities as so complex
as to be "abounding in metaphysical subtleties and theological niceties."[30]
The CCP, by continuing not only to mass produce commodities but also
to brand them, further contributed to fetishizing mass-produced goods.
Brands enabled discourse about specific products and led to a compulsion

to consume newer, "better" products and to replace older, "backward" products. Consider the difference between the state-produced soap called No. 1 Soap Factory Soap versus the soap called Build the Country or Red Flag Soap. With the development of industrialization and consumerism, not everyone was satisfied once they possessed one item or even a generic item in a category. In the Lower Yangzi valley, one of the wealthiest areas in the country, for instance, by the end of the Mao era a young person sought to display her command over fashion by riding a specific brand of bicycle, i.e., the Forever (永久) brand, or by wearing a Shanghai-brand watch, or listening to a Red Lantern radio (红灯收音机).[31] Although the specific brands that were coveted may have varied, with the spread of industrial capitalism across the globe, within months, years, or several decades very different people throughout China (like others in the capitalist world) learned to desire the same kinds of things.

In China after 1949, the party expanded forms of competition. As with so many other consumer goods, China-made alternatives to imported bicycles sprang up during the Republican era. In the 1920s and 1930s, small "factories" assembled bicycles, using primarily imported parts.[32] As was often the case, inexperienced and less capitalized domestic companies competed at the lower end of the market. Although these companies (like Chinese manufacturers during the period) attempted to profit from patriotic consumer sentiments encouraged by the "buy Chinese" NPM at the time, they concurrently worked to reassure consumers that their products were equivalent to the high-quality imports by associating their products with imports and foreignness. Ironically, domestic producers reinforced consumer preferences for products and brands from the more powerful industrial capitalist countries, that is, those countries that were technologically more sophisticated. For instance, the top Shanghai bicycle maker, Tongchang Garage, which made the Feiren bicycle in 1930, advertised that its bicycles used British and German materials and were produced in a German facility.[33] In 1926 and 1927, Daxing Garage, Runda Garage, and others marketed their China-assembled bicycles as patriotic "national products," even though Daxing Garage had hired two Japanese technicians and used imported parts for its two bicycle brands, Red Horse and White Horse, and Runda Garage's Flying Dragon bicycle also used imported parts. Similarly, the rebirth and rapid growth of the bicycle industry following World War II and in the Mao era was based on expropriated former Japanese-occupied factories in the coastal areas that had better technology than those that had been destroyed during the war.[34] Two of these factories later housed the most coveted brands of the Mao era – the

Flying Pigeon (飞鸽), made at the Tianjin factory, and the Forever brand, made in Shanghai. The third top national bicycle brand of the era, the Phoenix (凤凰), emerged in Shanghai when, in the late 1950s, the state consolidated small shops into the No. 3 Bicycle Factory.[35] Due to these imported technologies, annual domestic bicycle production increased throughout the period, rising from a mere 80,000 bicycles by 1952 to more than 800,000 bicycles by 1957, 1.8 million by 1965, and 8.5 million in 1978.[36] Even during the Cultural Revolution decade, when production of some consumer goods declined or even ceased, the number of bicycle factories expanded from eleven to forty-six.[37]

As with the other Three Greats, the difficulty of acquiring bicycles and their association with the more technologically advanced countries meant that their acquisition represented additional cultural capital (Figure 1.2).

Figure 1.2. A slave to foreign fashions. These pages from a photo-story book suggest the persistence of both urban preferences for imported brands and the ongoing efforts by state media to fight those preferences and shape consumerism. The story centers on a young woman who "blindly worships foreign products." One day, while riding her British Raleigh bicycle she collides with another rider on a China-made Forever bicycle. Her bicycle is damaged but not his. She agrees to compensation but insists on only parts made by Raleigh. In the photo on the left, the woman states she "does not believe" Forever is China-made until she inspects the fork of the bicycle and its identifying nameplate. In the photo on the right, she says that "China-made products are simply not good" and the bystander scolds her by saying such assumptions exhibit "slavish foreign thinking." After others educate her on the vast improvements of Chinese industry, the young woman becomes convinced that Chinese bicycles, as well as other domestic products, are now as good as foreign ones and agrees to use Forever parts. Source: 气死英国蓝铃牌 – 上海跃进新气象之十 (Angry as hell at England's Raleigh brand – New Happenings in Shanghai's Great Leap Forward, Vol.10.) Shanghai: Shanghai meishu chubanshe, 1958.

The state mediated who would have access to this capital. In Shanghai in the late 1950s, for instance, the local government helped city residents secure better access to bicycles by implementing a registration system to ensure that bicycles were only sold to city residents. One measure of the impact of this preferential policy is that after the city eliminated this requirement, in 1960, an estimated 80 percent of the bicycles were taken out of the city.[38] Not only hard to come by, bicycles were also expensive. In the 1970s, the average price of a bicycle was RMB 159, or more than three months' salary for an urban worker. But among urban households, money was rarely the biggest obstacle; ration coupons (or connections to illegal ration markets to acquire such coupons) were even more crucial.[39] One Beijing cyclist, Zhao Shulan, recalled having a monthly income of RMB 47; even after she had saved enough money for a bicycle, rationing forced her to wait three years before she could purchase one.[40] Despite the wait people had to endure, urban bicycle ownership rose steeply. From 1949 to 1967, residents of Beijing added 50,000 bicycles a year to its streets. From 1967 to 1981, the number tripled to some 150,000 bicycles per year. By 1976, the city had 2.5 million bicycles for a population of 8.5 million.[41] Beijing was hardly alone. Bicycle ownership was nearly universal in Chinese cities by the end of the 1970s. But despite the Maoist rhetoric and the supposed rural basis of the Communist Revolution, by as late as 1978 less than a third of all rural households owned bicycles.[42] Inequality of distribution was a choice, including the state choice over what sorts of bicycles to manufacture. Although it was more difficult to use bicycles on dirt or non-existent countryside roads, the eventual introduction of sturdier bicycles with thicker rims that could be used under such conditions confirms that the state placed a priority on its urban-based industrial strategy over the people's desire and need for greater mobility in the countryside. Thus, even the types of bicycles that were developed focused on urban industrialization, further entrenching a pattern of urban/rural inequalities whereby products were first developed in cities and only later modified to appeal to the needs of rural consumers.[43]

The Sewing Machine

Sewing machines further strengthened the association of imported foreign products with superior technology. As elsewhere, sewing machines so effectively served basic needs in China that they became one of the first everyday machines to reach the Chinese market. In comparison with other labor-saving textile machines, treadle-operated sewing machines were inexpensive, efficient, portable, multifunctional, and as useful in villages as they were in cities.[44] The technology vastly increased the productivity of women and girls, who were the primary users, a process that reproduced the gendered division of textile production.[45] Although few households in late-industrializing countries, such as China and India, could afford sewing machines of their own during the first half of the twentieth century, knowledge of and a desire for such machines was widespread, setting the stage for their eventual place as one of the Three Greats.[46]

During the Republican era, Chinese private capitalists began to develop the technical expertise to build and maintain consumer sewing machines. As early as 1928, there were attempts to produce sewing machines domestically with the Conquer America brand (Shengmei 胜美), its name once again an attempt to pass itself off as both a patriotic product and an import to gain market share.[47] Even as the name appealed to the patriotic movement to replace foreign goods with China-made goods (as discussed in Chapter 2), the name of the China brand sounded similar to – and shared the first character in its name with – the largest international sewing machine manufacturer, the American Singer company, which was known in Chinese as Shengjia (胜家, or "Conquer the Household"). Emulating an established brand name was not enough to win market share, however, and this initial domestic attempt – like many others – failed. Domestic competitors built the majority of their sewing machines for use in textile factories rather than as consumer products, and they were large, inelegant, and expensive.[48]

After 1949, however, state consumerism put an end to the import of household sewing machines. China-made sewing machines became critical for meeting domestic demand and fulfilling export aspirations. Within three years, there were five state sewing machine manufacturers spread along the eastern coast, with three in Shanghai, one in Guangzhou, and one in Qingdao. These five exceeded earlier production, manufacturing 66,000 machines per year, or thirteen times more than the number produced by Chinese factories at the end of the civil war. By the end of the 1950s, the CCP had expropriated, reorganized, and added two more factories, making a total of seven factories, and by 1964 there were factories in twenty-eight cities throughout the country.[49] In the mid-1960s, domestic manufacturers produced more than one million machines per year, representing a huge state-funded expansion. From 1952 through 1978, or roughly during the entire Mao era, China produced some forty-seven million sewing machines.[50]

In addition to fueling people's desire for nicer things and better lives, sewing machines had a number of specific application values that helped create grassroots demand. For instance, sewing machines allowed households both to produce and alter their own clothing to make it more practical or even more fashionable. This created a feedback loop by which meeting the desire for sewing machines in turn created a greater desire for fashionable or simply better-fitting clothing. At the lower end of the economic ladder, sewing machines allowed families to stretch their limited incomes by repurposing old tattered clothing by stitching several pieces together, covering up holes, or making blankets out of scraps. Sewing machines gave the family, particularly its female members, a chance to make additional money or to accrue favors by sewing for others, creating even more fuel for the bottom-up demand.[51]

Sewing machines could have various practical applications for the same person. Wang Yushi, a woman born in 1955 and interviewed in 2014, reported that her mother, who had acquired a sewing machine several years after her marriage, had specified three reasons why the sewing machine was significant to her family in Ji'nan.[52] First, owning a sewing machine meant the family could do what nearly everyone then did: make their own clothing or alter what they bought. Wang's mother made clothing for her siblings and eventually for her daughter and son. Such clothing was both functional and fashionable, as she altered the hemlines, for example, to follow the fashions. Second, people during the Mao era often had a number of children so they had to economize and avoid spending the precious cloth rations by using hand-me-down clothing. Sewing machines enabled them to alter their clothing for the next child. Third, Wang's mother personally enjoyed making clothing; sewing gave her pleasure. The increased productivity and extra income generated by the use of the sewing machine then fed into another round of self-expanding consumerism that further separated the sewing machine haves from the sewing machine have-nots.

Popular linkages of sewing machines with an idealized vision of femininity also expanded material desires for them. Young women learned to use a sewing machine from a friend or a relative, creating a sense of communal identity. The sewing machine was so closely associated with femininity due to word-of-mouth, previous advertising, established tastes, and popular representations in the mass media such as films, that men using them were mocked.[53] Due to this social value, even if among the Three Greats a sewing machine was the hardest to acquire, it was probably also the most significant for a bride. A young woman who could attract a partner who was able to offer a sewing machine as one of the betrothal gifts gave her entire family "face," or cultural capital.[54]

Growing Inequalities

In mastering and making the most out of the Three Greats during the Mao era, people simultaneously expanded and strengthened inequalities. For example, as it became more critical for urban workers to regulate time, watches became increasingly necessary and common in factories and offices.[55] The growing popularity of cycling, both for transportation to work and for pleasure, helped popularize watches, which could be consulted much more easily than a pocket watch while riding a bicycle. The spread of the Three Greats accordingly highlights how one act of consumption, purchasing a bicycle, created a desire for another – a watch to tell the time while riding the bicycle.

The proliferation of the Three Greats did not affect the country uniformly. Consumption patterns varied by time and place (Figure 1.3). A factory manager in Shanghai – where there were over ninety well-known brands of products by the end of the Mao era – would have had very different experiences communicating identity through consumption than, say, a farmer in rural Guangxi province. They would also have a higher salary and more opportunities to acquire such products.[56] As the expanding social and economic inequalities during this period suggest, tens of millions of Chinese did not engage in much consumption. There were countless villages throughout China that had little exposure to the Three Greats, and they would not obtain them for years, or even for decades, after city residents had acquired them. Despite these local differences, however, consumerism continued to spread as more people used these technologies to compete with others. The use of a bicycle to bring crops to the market, a sewing machine to sell additional labor power, or a wristwatch to store and transport value were all instances of using the technology to compete. Consumerism and the desire for branded products affected tens of millions of urban and rural households. Increasing numbers of people came to know about, desire, and even feel compelled to acquire the Three Greats, even years before they might have the opportunity to do so.

Figure 1.3. Conduits of consumerism. The state rusticated these three young urbanites along with over twelve million others. The men, photographed around 1970 during a visit home, wore local brand Zhongshan watches on their wrists, trendy clothing (note the sailor t-shirt on the right), and a typical Mao-era gaze into the "brighter future." Their wristwatches and clothing symbolize the better access to better products available to urban rusticated youth, which set them apart from their rural hosts and taught them about the massive and growing inequality between urban and rural China. Source: The personal collection of Xi Chen.

The Proliferation of Reasons to Desire Commodities

By the 1960s, China was producing millions of these consumer products and had transformed what had been luxury goods for the wealthy into more accessible everyday items in the cities and parts of the countryside. At the same time, demand for these products as practical tools, social lubricants, and status symbols spread and intensified. People's recollections of the compulsion to acquire these things reflect how their social meaning and value expanded and deepened consumerism. Such memories of material desires and acquisitions offer a different perspective from histories focused on politics, transcending the previous focus on the era as a history of a procession of mass campaigns.[57] Many people vividly recall how they acquired the Three Greats and what the items meant to them more than they remember the mass campaigns of the Mao era.

The aspects of the Three Greats most recalled by people posting memories on blogs who lived through the Mao era are the challenges to obtain them, the pride in owning them, and their social value. These bloggers all described learning to navigate the complex social meanings that consumer goods could communicate. People who obtained watches during this period invariably had a story to tell about how exactly they acquired their watch and how they initially felt wearing a watch as well as about the identities, whether intended or not, the watches communicated to others. A middle-school teacher, for instance, recalled that he was the first person at his school to wear a watch. Rather than hide it, he proudly displayed it by alternating between a more discreet metal band for most of the year and a showy white canvas band that attracted attention to the watch during the summer. As proud as he felt about his watch, he recalled that when he wore his white canvas watchband to meet his girlfriend's parents for the first time, they regarded him as an inappropriate suitor because his conspicuous consumption indicated a lack of maturity rather than a status symbol.[58] Others encountered similar problems due to the conflicting meanings of their consumer products. A university instructor recalled that his top material desire when he began his first job was to buy a watch. After sending part of his salary home to his parents, he saved as much as he could, and after three years, he finally had enough to buy a top-of-the-line Enicar (英纳格) watch for RMB 148, or roughly three months' salary of the average factory worker. But when he finally bought the watch and had a chance to show it off at school, a cadre pulled him aside and asked him to consider the influence his watch might have on the other teachers and staff at the university who could not afford such an expensive possession. The cadre urged him not to set himself apart so conspicuously by wearing the watch.[59]

Most importantly, owning all Three Greats communicated a family's financial well-being. While a bicycle or a sewing machine had practical applications, a watch was a clear signal of above-average household wealth and a household's access to privileged products, particularly if the watch was a high-status foreign brand. Families regarded a top-brand watch as a precious item, almost as if it were an heirloom. Of the Three Greats, watches were usually the least functional, suggesting that they had the greatest social value. After all, there was no shortage of clocks and bells (and later loudspeakers) to indicate the time. Watches, unlike the other two items, had been communicating a high status since the Republican era.[60] Watches broadened or, to use the party's preferred term, "massified" (大众 化) the consumerism of a bourgeois status marker from the pre-1949 era. Ownership of a watch became increasingly compulsory for a growing segment of the population as a consequence of its practical application. However, a watch also carried bourgeois social connotations that some people (such as cadres) wished to avoid. At other times, however, the needs of the industrializing society carried the day, compelling people to seek ways to acquire a watch.

The desire for a watch undermined party efforts to promote a general ethos of frugal living. When courting, for instance, a watch was critical both as a status marker and as a gift. The popularization of watches fit into the long-existing material desires for betrothal gifts that the groom's family was expected to give to the bride's family along with the bride price – traditionally cash given in red envelopes. By the 1950s, even working-class factory women in Beijing had begun to gage a suitor's fitness by whether he owned a watch. At a Beijing cotton-weaving factory, for example, two women culled their dating pools by demanding up front that their pro-spective partners provide them with a watch and clothing, though they would return the gifts if the relationship ended.[61] Watches did more than signal financial success; they indexed an individual's social progress in overcoming backwardness. According to a study of marriage by the scholar Neil Diamant, "suburban women considered clocks and watches symbols of the urban modernity they lacked." Indeed, Diamant suggests, during these years many women cared more about finding a husband who could give them a watch than finding a husband who could provide a high political status.[62] The weight attached to material considerations is all the more significant given that women and their offspring acquired the political status of their husband's family, so a woman from a bad class background would generally seek to marry into a family with a better class background.[63]

The social value of sewing machines was vital for successful competition in the marriage market. Whereas a prospective groom might use a sewing machine to demonstrate to his betrothed's family his ability to provide for a family, a potential bride might use her possession of – and even her desire for – a sewing machine to convey her competence as a future wife, mother, and daughter-in-law. It was these social values that drove women's compulsion to obtain sewing machines. Despite their industrial associations, sewing machines were associated with femininity because of the preexisting gendered division of labor, advertising, and popular representations in the mass media. This social value meant that the sewing machine was also often the most important betrothal gift to a bride and her family.[64] The numerous connotations surrounding purchase and ownership of a sewing machine highlight how deeply consumerism shaped lived social realities.

As consumerism developed during the Mao era, products came to communicate different messages depending on the owner and the context. When eighteen-year-old Li Dong joined the air force as a mechanic for the J-6 fighter jet, for instance, he and the others from Shanghai were proud of the possessions they had brought to the base with them, including soap to wash their uniforms, heavier blankets, and scented lotions (which they would put under their noses to mask the smell of the latrine). Soldiers from smaller towns and villages either lacked or did not use any of these products. The commodities used by soldiers from Shanghai quickly attracted attention. Although the better possessions of these young men communicated urbane identities and superior educations, two forms of human capital, they drew criticism from superior officers who invoked the oft-promoted "socialist" ethos of hard work and frugal living and considered the nice shirts and wristwatches of the Shanghai recruits to be bourgeois extravagances. A superior officer informed Li Dong that if he continued to display these goods, he would not be allowed to join the Communist Party, which was the goal of every upwardly mobile soldier. Thereafter, Li Dong never showed his watch to anyone and he kept it in his pocket only to consult it on the sly.[65]

Even in the supposedly egalitarian military culture of the 1970s, a time when the People's Liberation Army (PLA) removed their rank insignia, the social meanings of watches grew. In the novel *Jiyi honghuang* (*A Flood of Memories*), loosely based on her military experience, author Xiang Xiaomi describes the military sumptuary regulations she experienced in the early 1970s: only officers wore watches, leather shoes, and four-pocket army uniforms. Even if the regular soldiers owned such things, they would not wear them until they were promoted. Because word of a promotion – and hence the right to display such items – might arrive before their new stateissued clothing, soldiers who were about to be promoted routinely purchased or received a watch as a gift so they could don it immediately after their promotion was announced. As Xiang recalled, watches further differentiated soldiers by origin, with rural cadres wearing the formerly fashionable Shanghai watches and urban cadres preferring the latest imports from Japan and Switzerland, signaling both one's standing as a cadre and one's family origins.[66]

Differentiating watches by gender was yet another way that social value was expanded, increasing consumer demands for updated products and thereby further expanding consumerism. For most of the Mao era, women's watches were rare, and therefore women, if they had a watch at all, wore men's watches with larger faces. Although women's watches were still rare in Ji'nan in the late 1970s, Feng Guoqing managed to acquire a smuggled imported Japanese Omega from a friend who had bought several watches on the state-tolerated gray market during a business trip to Shanghai, and he offered it to his future wife as an engagement present. It was the only thing she had requested, as she already owned a bicycle, did not want a sewing machine, and said that she wanted to go easy on Feng and his family in terms of wedding expenses. Accepting Feng's gift was the equivalent to accepting his marriage proposal. The women's watch cost RMB 60, which was less than the price of a bicycle or sewing machine, but it still represented roughly half of Feng Guoqing's disposable income for the entire year. (When asked why she remembers the price, she replied, "it would be impossible to forget it given the importance of the watch.")[67] Even though giving her a watch did not signal to her family or the broader community that he was wealthy, it did suggest that, in addition to being a thoughtful person, Feng Guoqing was capable of working the system to obtain critical, if difficult to acquire, items. The watch was evidence that the couple would have a minimum standard of living, especially as Feng's future wife estimated that at the time fewer than half of her friends and acquaintances had received watches as betrothal gifts.

Relatives also gave watches as gifts. When Ni Ping was preparing to leave Qingdao in 1976 to further her education at the Shandong Arts Academy, her mother wanted to buy her a watch as a going-away present. The local department store only had Shanghai-brand watches, which were not particularly feminine, with the "big round faces" that were favored by men. Showcasing how the desire for higher-status imported brands transcended generations, Ni Ping actually preferred her mother's watch, a Swiss Roamer, which was old but feminine and expensive. However, Ni Ping eventually agreed to accept a Shanghai watch, which, although fashionable, was less expensive than her mother's watch and therefore it would be less of a loss if it were stolen.[68] Depending on the style, brand, and design, watches communicated everything from one's gender identity to one's financial stability.

Changes in how people used the Three Greats created new social value for the products.[69] In the case of bicycles before 1949, physical exertion in public had lower-class associations, a social value that initially discouraged upwardly mobile men (much less women) from riding bicycles. After 1949, however, bicycles and working-class attributes, such as hard work, were equated with masculinity and positive "socialist" attributes. Simply knowing how to ride a bicycle became such an essential masculine skill that young men would not wait until they had their own bicycle to learn how to ride one. While young women learned to use a sewing machine by practicing with one owned by a neighbor or friend, teenage boys learned to ride a bicycle of a neighbor or a friend long before they could own one. During the 1970s, for instance, Cao Dongmei's two brothers, who grew up in the small Jiangsu town of Qidong, borrowed bicycles from their classmates and became competent riders years before their family could afford to buy even one bicycle.[70] Beyond expressing one's personal identity, people bonded and shared communal identities based on consumer goods. In addition, as women entered (or were coerced into) the formal economy at the end of the 1950s, they too needed a means of transport from home to work. Their entry into the labor force further heightened demand for – and increased the utility of – bicycles. Simultaneously, the increasing number of women riding bicycles spurred efforts to differentiate the types of bicycles by gender. Chinese society in the 1950s overcame earlier objections that the riding of bicycles by women was indecent, consequently doubling the potential demand for bicycles.[71] During the first decade of party rule, riding a bicycle lost its previous negative connotations for both men and women, thereby greatly expanding the application value and demand for bicycles – and the corresponding compulsion for new segments of the population to acquire bicycles.[72]

From the countless numbers of such stories, one theme emerges: people spread consumerism and demand for the Three Greats even before, and indeed sometimes without, actually acquiring them. Knowledge about and the desire for products spread faster than their acquisition. Even a very poor person with little chance of acquiring a Three Great might have seen a Three Great on a city street advertisement or in the thousands of state-made movies that were shown by traveling film teams that visited isolated villages. As a result, these products began to influence their lives. For example, they may have been told that their marriage prospects were bleak because their family could not acquire the Three Greats or because they may have seen the Three Greats owned by others, and they began to wonder how they could acquire them. In these and other ordinary ways, people learned about and perhaps began to feel compelled to desire these consumer products, thereby participating in, deepening, and expanding consumerism.

Gray Economic Activities and the Inability to Constrain Consumerism

The growing application and social values of the Three Greats and the accompanying shortages of all three further heightened desires for these everyday technologies. Such unmet and growing demands contributed to the development of an informal or gray economy of illicit consumption that was tacitly permitted by the state.[73] From the perspective of the state, both the unsanctioned desire for, as well as the unsanctioned means to acquire, the Three Greats threatened to undermine state control over the economy; people increasingly looked to the non-state sector of the economy to fulfill their material desires. Yet the more the state restricted consumption via production and distribution, the more it incentivized the non-state-controlled part of the economy, including state and collective factories that were operating without permission to fulfill such needs. When examined close up, the state economy appeared much less planned than it did on paper, as the expanding material desires created zones of gray economic activities.[74]

In an economy rife with fears of shortages and theft, some people turned to the gray economy to acquire the Three Greats as an alternative form of currency. Farmers, for instance, hoarded the Three Greats as a way to store value.[75] Likewise, because watches were small in size, high in value, and portable, they were favored by smugglers.[76] Most illicit activities were relatively minor. Jiang Yigao, a retired riveter at a factory outside of Chongqing, recounted how he helped his younger brother play the local ration coupon exchange market.[77] When Jiang's younger brother decided to escape the poverty of the Sichuan countryside by joining the army, Jiang wanted to help his brother find a safe and practical way to store and transport his modest belongings. After his younger brother exchanged his possessions with local farmers for 167.5 kg of grain rations, Jiang sold the ration coupons. Although technically illegal, such activity was ordinary. According to Jiang, industrial workers often discussed buying, selling, and trading ration coupons. They debated prices and attempted to maximize

profits by openly discussing how and where to get the best prices for extra
ration coupons. Jiang admitted to having sold 145 kg of grain ration
coupons for RMB 110, but he was apprehended in one of the periodic
police crackdowns before he could sell his remaining coupons. Because he
had a clean record and was a model worker, he got off by writing a self-
criticism, and although he was denied promotion and party membership
for one year, the police allowed him to retain his earnings. In the end, with
the RMB 110 and twenty industrial rations, Jiang had finally accumulated
the necessary combination of cash and rations to buy a much sought-after
consumer good for his younger brother – a Shanghai brand watch.

Due to persistent shortages, the numerous ways to present the Three
Greats as gifts, and the operation of the gray economy, people routinely
purchased watches and other high-value consumer products that they did
not intend to use themselves or did not need immediately. The social value
of the Three Greats and the compulsion to possess them worked against
the state ethos of frugal living, despite the state's focus on expanding
domestic production. Although watches were easier to acquire than
bicycles or sewing machines, depending on place and time the number
of those either produced or imported was usually insufficient to meet
demand. The scarcity of watches created an environment of opportunistic
shopping, whereby people were always on the hunt to prepare for future
needs. By the end of the 1950s, when the state fixed ration coupons to
specific locations and individuals could not easily travel without official
permission, business trips became ideal opportunities to learn about how
to acquire products from other places, particularly for those who did not
live in major cities. Serendipity played a critical role in such shopping, as
highly desirable products were seldom available; so those on business trips
headed to the main shopping thoroughfares, such as Nanjing Road in
Shanghai or Wangfujing in Beijing, without a specific shopping list but
just hoping to be lucky.

Such shopping was opportunistic in both senses of the term, as shoppers
took advantage of the opportunity to travel to acquire products that they
did not need but they anticipated would be much more valuable back
home. For Mr. Cheng, a manager at the Changzhi Iron and Steel factory in
Changzhi, Shanxi province, this sort of ever vigilant shopping became
a way of life.[78] The small city of Changzhi, while symbolically and
economically central to party policies, did not have as much access to top
consumer goods as the larger cities that Mr. Cheng frequently visited when
he traveled on official business. Whenever he traveled to major cities such
as Beijing or Shanghai, he would purchase whatever desirable goods he

could find, intending to give any he did not need as presents or finding other ways to later transfer their value. On a successful trip to Beijing in the late 1950s, for instance, he came across a used Swiss women's watch, a rare find. At the time, he did not know enough about watches to tell the difference between women's and men's wristwatches, but he thought the smaller watch was more stylish than the bulkier Chinese watches that had just begun to enter the market. He already knew that people considered Swiss watches to be the best, indicating that the discourse of consumer brands and their associated hierarchy had begun to spread throughout the country beyond the few major coastal cities. Because his monthly salary was less than half of the RMB 100 needed to buy a Swiss watch, he and a colleague decided to split the cost of the watch and trade off wearing it each month. Cost, however, was not the only obstacle. A letter from a work unit was also sometimes needed to obtain the most sought-after products. Fortunately, one of Mr. Cheng's contacts in Beijing agreed to write such a letter. Although Cheng and his colleague had no intention of selling the watch for a profit, they clearly believed that the social value of the watch was so great that they were willing to go to all this trouble. Their consumer instincts later proved to be correct. When it came time for Mr. Cheng to ask his girlfriend to marry him, his colleague agreed to let him give her their Swiss watch as a betrothal gift, which remained her cherished possession until the early post-Mao era when, heralding the accelerated consumerism, she took it to a local repairman who convinced her to trade it in for a newer watch as hers had already lost much of its original social value. In doing so, she inadvertently reaffirmed her compulsion to continue using an act of consumption to communicate social value.

People's material desires were so frequently filled via these indirect routes that they did not consider that obtaining consumer goods on the gray market was illicit. In the earlier story about Feng Guoqing's acquisition of a smuggled watch, only China's expanding contacts with international consumer markets enabled him to buy the watch. The watches Feng came across in gray markets could have been bought from smugglers or from people who had received gifts from overseas relatives, the two most common non-state-sanctioned channels. When asked about the dangers of owning an illicitly obtained watch, he responded that at the time he did not think of such products in terms of "legal" or "illegal," but rather as "available" or "unavailable." This was a widely adopted perspective that involved using extended networks to secure products that were only available in the major cities. Feng's uncle, for instance, regularly went to Guangzhou and always returned home to Ji'nan with smuggled goods, never worrying about being caught.[79]

Illicit economic activities aided the expansion of the state economy. Although party leaders expected that the cadres staffing the bureaucracy of the centrally planned state-owned economy would serve as socialist models for the rest of society, demand for the Three Greats was so widespread that local cadres found that the Three Greats and other consumer goods were more effective than cash to facilitate transactions with factories, work units, and even communes that were trying to obtain the necessary industrial products to fulfill state contracts. Products are universally used as a way to store and transfer value whenever money is an inappropriate or insufficient means of obtaining a desired good or service. But due to consumer shortages, as noted, one might additionally need ration coupons, a letter of authorization from a work unit, or political access to secure the Three Greats and other consumer products that were in high demand. All of which cadres were in a position to provide. In this way, material desires fulfilled through non-state channels contributed behind the scenes to the functioning of the planned part of the economy.

The norms propagated from on high ran into on-the-ground realities, revealing fissures between different levels of the state. On the one hand, Mao and party leaders understood the danger of cadres becoming an exploitative new class and thereby undermining public confidence in the effort to "build socialism." They further understood that business practices such as using the Three Greats to grease illicit business deals – practices they labeled "capitalist" – siphoned resources from the official planning goals, even when cadres did not corruptly take the resources for themselves but rather used them for purposes useful to the state. The Central Committee criticized the unexceptional practice of local commercial departments using high-end goods, such as watches and bicycles, to build business relationships among work units and to facilitate illicit trade. On the other hand, in a more localized version of the state logic guiding state capitalism at the national level, local cadres claimed that the economic development ends of their practices justified the supposedly capitalist means. For instance, the Central Committee circulated a report by local cadres in Guangdong province which argued: "Using gifts to build good business relationships may be a capitalist approach to business, but such practices have positive effects on the development of socialist business."[80] In response, the Central Committee insisted that the end of improved productivity did not justify the continued use of capitalist means, concluding that using the Three Greats to bolster social and business connections amounted to a "capitalist restoration" (资本主义复辟) within the society, a common term for the party to express concern over the negation of the revolution. Although such practices were so commonplace that the party felt the need to publicly admonish the local Guangdong cadres, punishment for these activities was typically not severe enough to discourage such behavior. At the top, the party, while it was ideologically opposed to it, tacitly accepted "capitalist" behavior that advanced its industrial goals, tolerating local cadre rule-breaking because it expanded capital. But the party would periodically launch campaigns to rein in the worst manifestations at the local level of the central contradiction between the espoused goals of building socialism and the widespread evidence of practices the party identified as capitalist.

The use of bicycles as an illicit form of payment clarifies the trouble work units went to in order to engage in illicit exchanges, creating a complex and deep gray economy in which consumer goods served many unsanctioned purposes. Indeed, gray market activity appeared so open and integral to local economies that it hardly appeared gray from the point of view of Beijing. In the capital of Shanxi province, the Taiyuan Market and Price Administration Committee recorded a series of illicit trades that began with the visit of four men from Dingzhou Commune, located in the neighboring province of Hebei. In February 1960, Ma Xifu, head of Dingzhou factory, Chen Shusen, the sales representative of another factory, and several of their co-workers arrived at the New People's Hotel in Taiyuan, laden with fourteen watches, four bicycles, three industrial cooling fans, RMB 4,200 in cash, and other industrial products. According to the report, their plan was to engage in the "illegal activity" of exchanging their goods for essential industrial materials. Ma Xifu began by contacting Mao Tongyi, who was from the same hometown and worked at the Taiyuan Water and Electric Installation Company. Through Mao Tongyi's various local contacts, Ma Xifu exchanged the watches, bicycles, and other items he had brought with him for seven motors, a bench drill, two winding machines, and 100 kilos of aluminum. This illicit "trade delegation" was also involved in smaller transactions. Chen Shusen used his own contacts to exchange two Flying Pigeon bicycles and other goods for four motors from several local factories. In all of these various transactions, bicycles and watches were used for direct exchanges as well as for gifts to thank the local contacts.[81]

Beneath such stories of illicit trade, the national and local goals of industrialization further intensified the desire to acquire the Three Greats so as to accelerate more industrialization. In its findings, the

Taiyuan Market and Price Administration Committee concluded that the desire of the Dingzhou Commune for these exchanges was admirable because the products that it received were critical for electrification. Nevertheless, the means of acquisition – illegally exchanging bicycles, watches, and other materials – was a "serious" infraction of market administration rules and of planned goods distribution. Consequently, the committee imposed on the two factories fines of RMB 1,000 and RMB 500 respectively, a total comprising less than half the amount the men had spent for their illicit purchases. Additionally, only one person was lightly disciplined. The committee recognized, as did so many cadres, that the commune – and more broadly, the state economy – could not operate without the aid of the gray markets and "capitalist" exchanges.[82]

Despite this widespread recognition, throughout the Mao era, cases of corruption – that is, the use of public power for private gain – tended to single out possession of the Three Greats, particularly high-status brands, as irrefutable evidence of graft. Possession of the Three Greats proved guilt by material association. Such cases can be found throughout the whole economy during the entire era. For example, the case of Zhang Zigang, who worked in the medical department of the Harbin railway, provides an ordinary and minor corruption case from December 1951. As part of the evidence against him, the court record noted that he owned five Western-style dress shirts, two Parker pens, an Enicar waterproof wristwatch, and a bottle of perfume. Specifying the brands added extra weight to the evidence against Zhang and provided evidence that brand hierarchies among consumer goods had become widely known and desired even in the early PRC, to the extent that they were admissible evidence in a court of law. Parker was the leading global brand of pen of the period, and the Swiss watch Enicar was particularly sought after among railway workers because it was not only a fashionable foreign brand but also had a reputation for keeping the most accurate time and having an especially easy-to-read face.[83] In another case, during a period of lenience toward consumerism following the Great Leap Forward, Liu Shaoqi antagonized local officials by suggesting that cadre ownership of highly desired products "stank of corruption." He asserted that "with a glance," one could identify corrupt local cadres by checking to see if they wore a watch, lived in a renovated house, or owned a bicycle or radio, luxuries that ordinary members of a commune could not afford.[84] The Central Committee, with the approval of the State Council, moved beyond the browbeating of local officials by demanding that the People's Bank forbid local-level cadres from using administrative credit lines to buy nice things for themselves.[85] But the compulsion to acquire the Three Greats continued to override state demands that cadres should seek to embody a state consumerist ethos of frugality.

Although using the Three Greats and other consumer goods to facilitate illicit trade between work units received only minor criticism, transactions for the purpose of a cadre's private enrichment were examples of the kind of capitalism and unbridled consumerism that the state wanted to quash. According to the vocabulary of the party, personal accumulation of such products by cadres signified "capitalist restoration" and the "restoration of an upper class," that is, cadres at the local level were becoming the feared exploitative new class that would negate the revolution. Consequently, public and internal party documents warned cadres within local commercial departments in places such as Shantou, the port city in Guangdong province, against demanding bribes in the form of watches and bicycles, which local cadres were using not simply to "open the back door" for illicit trade with other factories but also to enrich themselves and their families.[86]

Just as brand status could serve as evidence in a court of law underscoring the desirability of certain brands, so efforts to suppress private and personal consumption stimulated people's material desires. Zhang Huihu, for instance, recalled viewing a film when he was a child in the 1970s in which the villain was identifiable because he wore several watches on his wrists, which, Zhang's father had explained, indicated the man was guilty of corruption. Yet such state messaging inadvertently reinforced brand hierarchies, as Zhang learned that of all the watches, the Shanghai brand was the best. Thereafter, Zhang remembered, he had desired a Shanghai watch since the age of ten, and even when he later acquired a watch of his own he was not satisfied because it was not a Shanghai brand.[87] Zhou Baoxing, a watch collector, told the story of a classmate who, like millions of others, had been expelled from school in the city and sent to the countryside to engage in agricultural work. Most of the urban youth who were sent to the countryside wanted to return home, but they required official permission, otherwise they would have difficulty obtaining ration coupons and finding employment in the cities. Zhou's classmate met the qualifications to return to his urban home, but a local cadre blocked his return by refusing to provide him with the appropriate forms. Through a third party, the cadre suggested that if the student "gave the cadre a Shanghai watch," the cadre would "hand over the form" (decades later, Zhou remembered this request because the expression "fill out a form" [填个表] in Chinese is a homophone for "add a watch" [添 个表]). The student's parents, who were both factory workers, struggled but finally obtained a watch, which they exchanged for their son.[88] Beyond showing that watches had become a substitute currency that facilitated bribery, their story demonstrates that even the leader of a small rural village was aware of the hierarchy of watch brands and the top place in the domestic hierarchy held by Shanghai watches.

Conclusion

The small sample of stories included here, drawn from innumerable new experiences with commodities, begins to reveal the contours of how nascent consumerism began to encourage material desires. Far from disappearing as the party "built socialism" on its way to communism, the spread of material desires for these mass-produced items and the social values attached to them provide ample evidence of the deepening demand side of industrial capitalism. By justifying these inequalities as a necessary but temporary stage of socialism, the party tacitly endorsed the accompanying expression of these inequalities.[89] Facilitating the expansion of consumerism ultimately accelerated the negation of the Communist Revolution.

To compete socially in post-1949 China, it was not always enough to have one or all of the Three Greats. Rather, starting from a modest number of elites, an increasing number of individuals began to learn to differentiate themselves by acquiring knowledge of, desire for, and then possession of the trendiest brands. One such example is Chen Yilin, who began his odyssey as the proud watch owner of a regional brand, the Yangcheng (羊城), made in Guangzhou. His colleagues initially coveted his watch, so in addition to its practical value of telling time, it also had the social value of producing envy. But as more of his colleagues acquired their own watches and even the more prestigious Shanghai watches, the social value of Chen's watch declined. Chen began to feel self-conscious and the subject of the same compulsive force of envy he himself had earlier engendered, especially after a colleague told him directly that "no one wears a Yangcheng anymore." His once-smart Yangcheng, which still kept time, had become a marker of backwardness, and therefore he replaced it with a Shanghai watch. Thereafter, as industrial consumerism continued to exert coercive pressure on Chen to acquire consumer goods, he remained vigilantly brand-conscious, and when Japanese Citizen watches reentered the Chinese marketplace at the end of the 1970s, Chen was among the first to acquire this trendiest brand (Figure 1.4).[90]

The spread of consumerism reflects the party's prioritization of capital accumulation over eliminating inequalities and empowering labor. Rather

Figure 1.4. Shift in state consumerism. This photograph from 1975 captures the contending forces of social consumption and consumerism underlying state capitalism. On the one hand, the state wanted to limit consumer demand to reinvest in rapid production and promoted social consumption (in the background is an icon of social consumption of the late Mao era, the Nanjing River Bridge). On the other hand, as production increased, the state needed domestic consumers to want and acquire more mass products. The subject photographed here had recently upgraded his less expensive, less fashionable local Zhongshan brand watch to a new Guangzhou brand, one of many new brands of watches entering the market in the early 1970s. To earn the money needed, he had worked in an unauthorized factory and saved for half a year. The nicer watch gave him a sense of pride and accomplishment: "it showed that I had a job, could support myself, and could even afford to buy something nice." Source: The private collection of Xi Chen and interview by the same.

than focus on social transformation, the state tolerated corruption, backdoor trading, and the creation of new brand-based social hierarchies as long as they contributed to further accumulation. Furthermore, the spread of more complex mass-produced consumer products and greater desires among people to acquire them reinforced rather than diminished or weakened the social inequalities resulting from state industrial capitalism operating under the name of socialist construction. Despite its socialist rhetoric, the party's industrial priorities of rapid capital accumulation led the party to distribute social products unequally, as urban, managerial, and industrial workers received more desired goods, and this extended to the "three major inequalities" targeted by the government. Finally, the inequalities were reinforced through the use of state power to suppress all forms of consumption – even eating and housing – and to siphon the surplus from the countryside to further subsidize industrial capitalism. The everyday technologies discussed in this chapter reflected the more conspicuous and urgent forms of competition over the big technologies that will be discussed in Chapter 2. Together, the two forms of technological competition contributed to a compulsory self-expansion of industrial capitalism and consumerism, all under the banner of Maoist socialism.

Building State Capitalism Across 1949

Rather than negate capitalism and "build socialism," the initial policies of the party only gradually shifted the institutional arrangements of capitalism toward greater state control over capital and consumption. In the spring of 1949, as the PLA marched southward toward Shanghai, party leaders contemplated their options. They worried that if the army fought its way into Shanghai, looted factories, plundered personal possessions, and confiscated private property – as Nationalist propaganda had led people to expect – the new state would have a more difficult time controlling the population, winning support, and reviving the economy. The wealthy, in particular, needed reassurance that the party would accept them because its policies had initially regarded cities and towns as places where the rural and urban "exploitative classes," as wartime propaganda had said, stashed their "illicit" wealth.[1] But as victory now seemed imminent, the party hoped to rely on the resources and expertise of the wealthy to accumulate national capital. Put differently, the party prioritized accumulation and therefore paused its shift along the spectrum of capitalism toward greater state control.

Against the backdrop of urban fears and policy precedents, the treatment of Shanghai, the country's richest city, became a bellwether of the CCP's plans for urban economic elites under the new state. The party used Shanghai to broadcast an assuaging message to local, national, and international audiences. Led by Mao, it decided that the takeover of the city was not the time for class retribution or for transforming the social relations of production by placing workers in control of the means of production. Instead, the takeover would be an opportunity to reassure the urban middle and upper classes that party rule meant order, discipline, and the elimination of hyperinflation, in brief, a stable environment for private capitalism and the immediate revival of the economy.[2] Although the party formulated the justification described below, this early policy choice – to reproduce private capitalism rather than abolish it – created the central contradiction between the party's rhetoric of building socialism on its way to communism and its actual policies of building industrial capitalism. This contradiction would characterize the entire Mao era (and thereafter).

Party actions immediately began to allay the fears of Shanghai capitalists. Chen Yi and other generals who oversaw the takeover of the city implemented a policy of conspicuous self-control and non-consumption for the PLA. Their soldiers became walking billboards for the party-promoted state consumerist values of frugality, self-abnegation, and discipline, the opposite of the bourgeois values associated with Shanghai. When PLA troops filed into Shanghai in May 1949, they slept on the streets rather than requisitioning private homes. The party instructed the military to preserve private possessions, including the property of the wealthiest. In early June, for instance, the PLA returned to their original owners several thousand automobiles that had been commandeered by the Nationalists.[3] Once the fighting was over, all troops not assigned to maintaining control were ordered out of the city to prevent looting. The party forbade cadres from borrowing or renting civilian housing and from bivouacking in factories, hospitals, schools, temples, or churches. In sum, cadres in Shanghai had to embody the ethos of hard work and frugal living by having few valuable possessions and ensuring that public property remained public – and that the private riches of the wealthy remained private. This public relations offensive earned the party favorable press coverage at home and abroad, easing the concerns of many capitalists and helping persuade others to return to the city.[4] Even foreign enterprises, such as the British trading company Jardine Matheson, had positive initial impressions.[5]

The takeover of Shanghai introduced Chinese citizens to the contradictions between socialist rhetoric and capitalist policies. Whereas Chapter 1 examined why people felt compelled to participate in expanding forms of consumerism as a corollary of expanding industrial capitalism, this chapter examines the shift toward greater state involvement in the institutional arrangements of capitalism by addressing why the party decided that "building socialism" primarily meant facilitating the expansion of industrial production rather than doing so while concurrently transforming the social relations of production. Together, these first two chapters show how the party built on the pre-existing institutional foundations for the expansion of consumerism and prioritized the maximization of capital accumulation when deciding where and when to enact policies that would directly transform social relations. The examples discussed here explain why the party consistently – and explicitly – subordinated the transformation of social relations to the goal of amassing and controlling ever greater sums of capital.

The party enacted contradictory policies toward the capitalists and tolerated them as long as such policies facilitated its immediate goals. To that end, the two mass campaigns discussed below show how the party instrumentalized class struggle and used it for greater capital accumulation. Class struggle became a means to a state capitalist end rather than a socialist transformation in class relations. Because the party's class warfare was brutal when it came to urban–rural relations, the final section of this chapter returns to a basic inequality at the heart of the party's own Marxist analysis of industrial capitalism, that is, the urban–rural gap. The same party priorities of rapid industrialization over social transformation applied to the countryside, where the state sought to maximize rural extraction to facilitate urban industrialization and consumerism. As the focus of this book is urban consumerism, the countryside receives little attention. Nevertheless, underlying industrialization and consumerism are the crux of what Marx calls the "original sin" of accumulating the resources necessary for urban-based industrialization on the backs of those working in agriculture.[6]

Military Competition and Compulsory Capitalism

The life-or-death military struggles faced by Mao and the party forced them to support the state capitalism and state consumerism uncovered throughout this book, including the party's initial policies toward capitalists. Throughout the twentieth century, military competition, both domestic and international, had required ever greater concentrations of capital and state power. In the decades preceding 1949, invasions and wars had killed tens of millions of Chinese, destroyed the lives of countless others, and left an already capital-poor country destitute. Measures of production of consumer goods and agricultural products were both down by nearly a third from their pre-1949 highs.[7] Constant warfare had compelled first the Nationalists and then the Communist Party to turn to the global marketplace for the latest military technology or otherwise risk subjugation by a domestic or foreign rival.[8] In addition to inheriting a history of waging wars against better-armed imperialist powers, including the British, the Japanese, and the United States, the CCP had enemies – both internal and international – and had to consolidate control over its borders as well as conquer, or reconquer, contested areas such as Tibet, Taiwan, and Xinjiang.[9] China's entry into the Korean War (1950–3) further heightened the party's need for capital to manufacture or purchase weaponry.[10] Mao and the party leadership regarded developing conventional arms and a nuclear deterrent as essential to national independence and consequently it became China's primary goal.[11] Despite the party's oft-stated intentions of building a more equitable and democratic workers' state by transforming the relations of production, it keenly felt the compulsion to rapidly industrialize and to redirect resources and implement policies to catch up both militarily and economically with the capitalist countries that posed existential threats to the party's survival.[12]

Both sides in the Chinese civil war had used state-led, rapid capital accumulation in heavy industry at the expense of consumption. This was the tried and true strategy for late-industrializing economies facing similar threats, such as Germany, Italy, Japan, and the Soviet Union.[13] As Mao bluntly stated in 1945, "Without industry, there can be no solid national defense, no well-being for the people, and no wealth and power for the nation" (Figure 2.1).[14] Such massive allocations of capital – billions of RMB and millions of people – away from productive investments and to the military sector had cascading structural consequences for the nation and its citizens.

State consumerism was a consequence of the state's intense focus on accumulating more capital and funneling it toward key industries. The entire Mao era is rife with internal party discussions about how to balance the need to focus on accumulation at the expense of consumption, knowing well that too much focus on the former disincentivized labor and ultimately slowed accumulation. From the very beginning of its rule, the party tried to impose state consumerism by subordinating individual material desires to national goals, and by defining such subordination as part of the open-ended two-stage transition, starting with "building socialism" as part of the move toward communism. State consumerist discourses – repeated ad infinitum by the state media – differentiated party practices and intentions from those it labeled "capitalist," namely, people who favored individual or family-oriented consumption patterns over national interests. According to party propaganda, the consumer culture that would emerge from its policies would be a "massified" and therefore a "socialist" culture. The need to accumulate led the party to discourage all forms of consumption deemed excessive and wasteful, with Mao himself singling out a ban on gambling and requiring that weddings and funerals "be kept simple" (e.g., "make your own wine"). Furthermore, he admonished cadres to embrace "hard work and frugal living" with specific dos and

Figure 2.1. "Industry and Defense" (1956). State consumerism reflected party priorities over how to allocate scarce resources. The party determined that national survival and welfare depended on rapid industrialization and consistently allocated less to consumption than production, promoting an ethos of "hard work and frugal living." Below the title of this poster, an oft-quoted line from Mao underscores these priorities: "Without industry, there can be no solid national defense, no well-being for the people, and no wealth and power for the nation." To highlight the connection, the chart at the bottom explains how much steel is required to produce a tank and ship, aluminum to make an airplane, and cloth to make military uniforms. Source: The International Institute of Social History (Landsberger Collection).

don'ts, including, as he stated in a 1958 speech, that cadres "don't specialize in giving dance parties."[15]

The norms of state consumerism described in these chapters were always opaque and defined in terms of what the party sought to negate. The party popularized the idea of antithetical forms of "socialist" and "bourgeois" consumer culture. In policy statements, newspaper and magazine articles, advertisements, movies, propaganda posters, and at closed party meetings such as the one noted above, the party criticized "bourgeois" forms of consumption that communicated "capitalist" values of inequality, individualism, and exploitation through the desire for and acquisition of products and services. As noted, the catchphrase often used to express this ethos was "hard work and frugal living." This phrase was linked to the interests of the state in popular dictums, such as "build the nation through diligence and thrift" (勤俭建国). Additionally, party rhetoric linked the phrase to specific groups, such as housewives in "manage households with diligence and thrift" (勤俭持家) and professionals in "manage factories with diligence and thrift" (勤俭办厂), as well as a general call to "practice strict economy and combat waste" (厉行节约, 反对浪费).[16] According to this rhetoric, the only desire of the ideal socialist citizen was to work hard (and thereby generate more capital for the state) and to live a frugal life (and thereby reduce demand for and expenditure of state capital).[17]

Party calls to live a socialist life were part of the state's attempt to extract labor from "the masses" in response to industrial and military competition. The consequence was the central contradiction examined here: the party created a state capitalist political economy and culture to maximize labor's output and minimize labor's direct control over its products, the basic tenant of the party's own communist rhetoric. Promoted in the name of the eventual elimination of the inequalities symptomatic of industrial capitalism in communism, the actual practice of "building socialism" exacerbated the very inequalities and labor alienation that the party associated with capitalism.

Inheriting the Shift Toward Greater State Capitalism

Explanations have cast the party's move to exert more control over production and consumption as a radical shift in domestic political and economic policy, or simply as following the international playbook for "building socialism." But such explanations obscure the continuity with state policies that predated by decades the CCP victory.[18] From the NPM of the

Republican era, the party inherited the basic idea of state consumerism – that domestic consumption should further national capital accumulation rather than satisfy individual desires and priorities.

Both the NPM and the CCP urged people to buy China-made "national products" rather than "foreign products" in order to accumulate national capital by staunching the flow of imports into the country and the outflow of capital.[19] By the early twentieth century, China had begun to import and manufacture thousands of new consumer goods that created a nascent consumer culture and changed the everyday lives of millions of Chinese. Since its inception in the late nineteenth century, state consumerism in China faced the same challenges as state capitalism. Indeed, the challenges were always related: how to command consumption to serve production. Convincing people to distinguish between products by nationality and to prefer those labeled with the newly coined term of "national products" proved difficult, especially because a weak state could not simply control material desires by banning or restricting imports through the imposition of high tariffs.

Lacking a political fix such as high tariffs, promoters of national products were forced to attempt to introduce cultural constraints on consumption. Although the NPM had limited success in changing the behavior of consumers, it taught national leaders how the use of coercion could influence consumer patterns. The Republican era spread the NPM's name, slogans, and categories of patriotic consumption through state and non-state efforts, such as sumptuary laws mandating the use of China-made fabrics for clothing, frequent anti-imperialist boycotts, publication of *National Product Monthly* and other product-oriented magazines, state-sponsored propaganda campaigns, weekly newspaper supplements, fashion shows, and specially organized venues for display-ing and selling national products. State consumerism during the Mao era followed the NPM's premise that there were "right" and "wrong" products, and that a responsible state – and its disciplined, or "patriotic," citizens – should intervene to encourage, coerce, and enforce the consumption of good products and avoid the consumption of inferior products. NPM rhetoric, for instance, described imports as invading armies; therefore, choosing the wrong products was equivalent to aiding and abetting imperialism. The NPM legitimated private profiteering by demanding that acts of consumption be made in the name of the public good, but it allowed profits to remain private, free for capitalists to allocate as they saw fit. In doing so, the NPM prepared the way for the post-1949 shift along the state-to-private spectrum of industrial capitalism toward state capitalism by discrediting private capitalism and spreading the idea that private capitalists, in the absence of any state oversight, would inevitably profit from patriotism.[20]

Before 1949, a half-century of popular calls for state intervention into consumption and consumerism during the NPM established the foundation for state capitalism in the PRC. After 1949, the party was more powerful and better at implementing the NPM agenda. It was more effective in building and deploying what I term a "reserve army of consumers," a correlate of what Marx and Engels describe as the "industrial reserve army of labor," conscripted and regimented to help keep costs down and profits high.[21] Industrial capitalism throughout the world has always harnessed demand both at home and abroad to facilitate accumulation. Even though the Chinese reserve army of consumers had been growing decades before 1949, the party was much better at enlarging and deploying it. The metaphor of a reserve army of consumers expresses how seriously both the Nationalists and the CCP tried to militarize Chinese society.[22] The NPM provided the underlying state ideology that consumption should be a reserve army of consumers serving production and a population of "patriotic" consumers happily buying whatever domestic industrial capital produced rather than initiating production, as is routinely assumed under market capitalism (Figure 2.2).

After 1949, the party shifted the country along the spectrum toward state capitalism by building on the rhetoric, institutions, tools, and even scapegoats of the NPM to reduce the challenges to state accumulation and to manage the reserve army of consumers. The state used everything from tariffs, exchange controls, and countless other bureaucratic mechanisms of popular media to shape what people chose to consume. But as it did with the takeover of Shanghai, the party, in its shift toward state capitalism and state consumerism, had to compromise with the institutional arrangements of private capitalism and consumerism to accumulate faster and to broaden its political support. Internal discussions within the party confirm that the party understood the implications of its initial policies of reproducing the bourgeoisie after 1949, but that it had little choice. As Mao defended the policy in 1958: "Nationwide, there are 700,000 households of capitalists and several millions of bourgeois intellectuals; without them [we] can't run newspapers, engage in science, or operate factories. Some people say [you've] turned 'right.' Such a 'right' is necessary, [we] must transform [the bourgeoisie] slowly."[23]

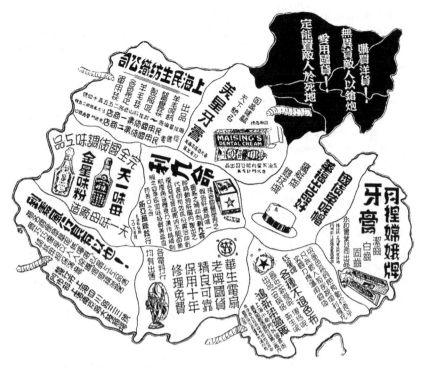

Figure 2.2. An army of consumers defends the country. State consumerism in the Mao era inherited and expanded the premises and institutions of the NPM of the Republican era. In this advertisement published regularly in the early 1930s, China is represented as an agglomeration of China-made products threatened by imperialist powers (the silkworms endangering the mulberry leaf that is China). The country's best defense: the domestic consumption of only China-made products, leaving the imperialists with no incentive to invade. The Mao-era state expanded the NPM by attempting to capture and reinvest a greater share of capital rather than allow only private (and state-connected) capitalists to profit from the mobilization of domestic consumers. Source: Karl Gerth, *China Made*, 16.

Expanding State Control Over Capital and Consumption

From the very beginning, capitalism triumphed over socialism. After 1949, the party did not, as many capitalists had feared, immediately expropriate all private capital or arrest or kill the country's capitalists.[24] Rather than eliminate what Marx had referred to as the "birthmarks" of capitalism after a Communist Revolution, it initially implemented pragmatic policies to consolidate control and revive the economy, allowing the vast majority of

private businesspeople to retain their businesses and capital. It also permitted the basic forms of consumerism associated with the bourgeoisie,
such as upscale nightclubs and mass advertising catering to middle-class
tastes, to continue. Although the party exerted more control over private
capital in the late 1950s, during the first few years of the PRC, the party,
including Mao, felt it had no choice but to continue to sanction manifestations of consumerism, such as buying fashionable clothing, eating at fancy
restaurants, or hiring maids, though these represented allocations of private
capital to what it considered undesirable, unproductive consumption.[25]

The party explained its concessions to existing capitalist practices based
on its policy of New Democracy. Formulated by Mao in 1940, New
Democracy was envisioned as the first of several transitional stages in
building socialism during the shift from the "old society" to communism
that would follow "liberation."[26] According to Mao, this initial stage of
development would explicitly prioritize strengthening the forces of production during a "transitional period of economic recovery" rather than
an immediate furthering of the goals of the Communist Revolution by
transforming the social relations of production. Whereas Marx and Lenin
had theorized that the emergence of a capitalist class and a bourgeois-
democratic revolution were necessary preconditions for the capital accumulation required for the inevitable Communist Revolution, Mao instead
argued that these two revolutions could be collapsed into one. He identified four progressive social classes to ally with the party and build the New
China – workers, peasants, petty bourgeoisie, and national bourgeoisie –
represented by the four smaller stars circling the one bigger star on the PRC
flag (the total of "five stars" is the reason why the first wristwatch manufacturer selected "Five Star" as its inaugural brand name, as mentioned in
Chapter 1).[27] According to Pavel Yudin, the Soviet ambassador to China
from 1953 to 1959, Mao told him that treating capitalists well at this stage
was essential to restoring production, and Mao criticized the "leftist sentiments" of comrades who sought to immediately confiscate private
enterprises.[28] The Common Program of September 1949, which served as
the country's interim constitution until 1954, further codified this compromise with capitalism, ensuring the continuation of private accumulation and consumerism even though it contradicted the public symbols and
rhetoric about the long-term goals of socialism to achieve communism.[29]

Between 1949 and 1956, the party explicitly characterized its political
economy as "state capitalism" (国家资本主义). It used the term to refer to
its efforts to consolidate control over private, industrial, and commercial
capital, leading up to its expropriation of private enterprises between 1953

and 1956 as part of the policies called the Socialist Transformation (I capitalize Socialist Transformation to flag it as the ubiquitous CCP term for a policy I would otherwise call "state capitalist expropriation").[30] To make the notion of state capitalism more palatable ideologically, it explained that unlike the state capitalism practiced by the Nationalists, whereby the bourgeois elites controlled the state and accordingly made state capitalism into an instrument of private accumulation, the party's form of state capitalism would operate for the betterment of the working classes on whose behalf the party claimed control. In its formulation of state capitalism, the state stood in for all of China's workers and controlled capital on their behalf. According to the party, this meant that no "surplus labor" was extracted from the workers. Yet even as the state gained greater control over the economy, four different institutional arrangements for owning capital persisted – state ownership, cooperative ownership, foreign ownership, and private ownership. These four types of ownership indicate an ongoing series of party efforts to accommodate its priority of controlling capital and allocating it to rapid industrialization. Throughout the Mao era, the party adjusted institutional arrangements of ownership – including markets and private ownership – as a means to facilitate faster state capital accumulation.[31]

As it began to build state capitalism, the new state's immediate concern, as stipulated in the interim constitution, was to assume state ownership over all enterprises considered to be "vital to the economic life of the country."[32] These enterprises were concentrated in capital-intensive industries such as mining, transportation, steel and chemical production, and banking. The resulting state-owned enterprises formed the backbone of state capitalism. As discussed in the Introduction, party leaders and their Cold War rivals unequivocally differentiated capitalism from socialism by focusing on the specific institutional arrangements of privately owned versus state owned and markets versus planning. In so doing, both sides shifted attention away from examining who produces the surplus to who appropriates and distributes the surplus.[33] By drawing attention to the visible differences in institutional arrangements, leaders on both sides of the Cold War obscured the similarities in their attitudes and treatment of the surplus.[34] Early in the twentieth century, foreign companies had owned the most technological and capital-intensive aspects of China's economy. During the Second Sino-Japanese War, these enterprises fell under the control of the invading Japanese, German, and Italian forces and were then confiscated by the Nationalists after the defeat of the Axis powers in 1945. Following its victory in the civil war, the party simply expanded state ownership by confiscating the capital of those who were deemed to be collaborators with the Nationalists and then, later, the capital of the remaining capitalists leading up to the Socialist Transformation.[35] Through these state-owned enterprises, the state immediately took possession of the capital of the most industrialized, or capital-intensive, parts of the economy, comprising 35 percent of China's total industrial output.[36]

A second and more common institutional arrangement complicating control over capital exercised by the party was collective enterprises (集体 企业). This arrangement included agricultural supply and marketing cooperatives organized by the state, and factories run by communes and local organizations in a quasi-state, quasi-private form of ownership.[37] Although collective enterprises may appear to be an institutional arrangement of ownership that most closely resembles basic definitions of socialism – as they allow workers to collaborate and exercise some direct control over the fruits of their labor – the party interpreted them as a transitional stage between private and state ownership. In its parlance, collective enterprises were "semi-socialist" and an "immature form of socialist public ownership" that presaged their eventual transition to "ownership by the whole people" (全民所有制), a phrase the party used synonymously with "ownership by the state" (国家所有制). The state, however, was reluctant to implement even its own version of socialism – namely, "ownership by the whole people" – because doing so would have entailed unacceptable costs. Greater state ownership would have required greater state allocations of capital to wages (that is, consumption) at the expense of faster industrialization (that is, accumulation). Non-state-run agriculture and enterprises would find themselves with little or no support from the national government. Like the communist ideal of "to each according to his needs," direct state ownership of most of the economy was seen as a noble aspiration but an impractical and expensive policy, especially compared to more limited state control and extractions of capital through local ownership and responsibility. From the point of view of rapid industrialization, the advantage of collective ownership helps explain why the party expropriated rather than nationalized most of the economy. The persistence of collective ownership provides another example of the state's repeated determination that addressing the inequalities arising from industrial capitalism was less urgent than rapidly accumulating state capital by keeping state costs low. Consequently, the party's low priority of employing greater numbers of workers exacerbated the inequalities between the urban workers in state enterprises, who were paid nationally set wages, versus those working in collective enterprises or in the countryside. Put differently, there were vast variations in the "socialism" one experienced in Mao-era China as a consequence of state capitalist priorities.

Likewise, private ownership of capital continued in various forms throughout the entire Mao era, ebbing and flowing according to the state's responses to political and economic contingencies. The history of foreign ownership of capital in the PRC, the third institutional arrangement of ownership, further demonstrates the state's various compromises. This example clarifies why outside observers labeled growing state control over capital as "communism" – that is, noncapitalist rather than, as I argue here, a state-led variety of capitalism that still exploited labor and sowed the inequalities of industrial capitalism. After World War II, neither the Nationalists nor the party completely drove foreign enterprises or their proprietors out of China, nor did it expropriate all their capital. At the end of the Second Sino-Japanese War in 1945, foreigners – bankers, traders, factory owners, officials, doctors, and teachers – expected to rebuild their lives and businesses in China, but the civil war and the accompanying economic turmoil destroyed these hopes and ended a century of growing influence of foreigners in China from market capitalist countries.[38] Even before 1949, many capitalists had left of their own accord, taking as much as possible with them, selling the remainder at a loss, blaming the Communists for the civil war and the economic disruptions, and becoming vocal anti-Communists in their own countries.[39] To slow the repatriation of capital out of China and minimize the costs of acquiring control over it, over the course of several years the party expropriated foreign enterprises. By 1953, half of the 1,000 foreign enterprises active in 1949 had folded, and only 23,000 of 126,000 foreign employees remained. The number of British enterprises dropped from 409 to 223, and the number of employees dropped from 104,000 to 15,000. As their assets became less valuable, business owners were keener to sell, an approach one observer called "hostage capitalism."[40] As one British businessman writing in Shanghai on February 26, 1952, concluded, "Surely the picture is very clear for all to see and the writing is on the wall even in braille for the blind. . . . British China trade has had it."[41] Unsurprisingly, by spring 1952 most British companies had decided to cut their losses and terminate their operations in China.[42] The conditions of their exit from China reinforced in these capitalists' minds that "communist China" was hostile to all arrangements of private capital, not only their own.

In addition to state, collective, and foreign capital, domestic private ownership continued to exist throughout the Mao era as a fourth type of institutionalized control over capital. During its early years in power, the party worked to "encourage and foster" two types of private capitalists it considered useful for a rapid economic recovery: national (large) capitalists and petty (small) capitalists.[43] To win over these groups and broaden its political base, the party cast itself as the savior both of the working classes oppressed by capitalism and imperialism and also of national capitalists who were unable to compete successfully against foreign competition.[44] Most of the businesses owned by national capitalists were in light industry and textile manufacturing, required little technology, and did not represent large amounts of fixed capital. Initially, the party allowed these capitalists to control their enterprises and to consume as they saw fit.[45] The second group of capitalists, petty capitalists, were proprietors of mom-and-pop shops and other small or household-based businesses who, before being herded into cooperatives in the mid-1950s, were allowed to retain the meager capital generated by their businesses. In addition to these sanctioned capitalists, the party tolerated a greater number of very small private capitalists who operated in the full sight of the state, within what I call the "gray economy" that existed throughout the era. Following 1949, the state began to lay the groundwork for expanded control over all private enterprises to facilitate state accumulation of capital. In the early 1950s, for instance, the state gained control over wholesale distribution, provided raw materials, and placed orders for finished products that, in the words of state economist Xue Muqiao, "guided [capitalists] onto the road of state capitalism." According to Xue, this "elementary form of state capitalism" ensured that private capital would support state-determined goals and permit capitalists to make a "reasonable profit" but not "reap fantastic profits through speculation."[46] The institutional arrangements of the private side of the spectrum of industrial capitalism – legal or gray – largely disappeared, especially in the cities, with the completion of the Socialist Transformation in 1956. However, their persistence during this period, re-emergence in the early 1960s, suppression at the start of the Cultural Revolution, and then their rapid spread thereafter confirms that the party never managed to attain comprehensive state capitalism. In fact, it did not even try.

By initially allowing the institutional arrangements of private capitalism to continue operations, the party accepted the capitalists' power to allocate capital as they wished, including to maintain luxurious lives. For the very rich among these business owners, this meant buying big homes and private cars and hiring servants. For most, their more modest bourgeois consumption styles included going to the movies, eating out, or purchasing one or more of the Three Greats. Naturally, however, the resulting social inequalities, however small, soon became visible to others. *A Small Town Called Hibiscus*, a popular novel by Luo Hongyu (known by his pen name Gu Hua), suggests the visibility of the mom-and-pop stores. Based on the author's extensive research, the novel tells the story of a small-town proprietress of a tofu shop whom at one point locals cherish for providing a vital service but at another point attack as a "tail of capitalism" whose profits allow her to enjoy a better life than that of her neighbors.[47] In Shanghai, the lifestyles of national capitalists were considerably better. Even after the state expropriated their businesses, they could continue to lead more comfortable lives due to the fixed payments they received from the state and their accumulated wealth.[48] They lived in mansions, threw lavish parties, dined out at one of the scores of prominent restaurants that still flourished, and played mahjong (despite the ban imposed by the party).[49] These people remained living symbols of the central contradiction between the party's rhetoric of "building socialism" and the evidence that state capitalist policies were building capitalism. Unsurprisingly, such (former) capitalists would become a major target of the Cultural Revolution.[50]

While there were many initial exceptions to state ownership of capital, throughout the 1950s the state continued the shift in the institutional arrangements toward greater state control over capital, that is, greater state capitalism. By the end of 1952, the state controlled more than a half (56 percent) of all industrial output and another quarter (27 percent) of the emerging category of joint state–private ownership. By 1953, the state appeared to be sufficiently confident to announce that the period of "economic rehabilitation" had reached an end and the start of Socialist Transformation had begun. During the next three years, power over capital swiftly shifted from private capitalists to the state as the party forced private capitalists to "partner" with them in what they described as joint state–private enterprises. Such "partnerships" meant that the state provided the former enterprise owners with a fixed percentage of the assessed value of their enterprises and often titular positions, while cadres took control of the businesses.

Despite the party's authorization of very limited forms of private capitalism even after the completion of the Socialist Transformation, the terms "capitalist" and "capitalist roader" remained pejorative terms of abuse used by critics within the party toward leaders and cadre managers whom they accused of favoring economic development (that is, increasing the forces of production) over class struggle (or equalizing the relations of production).[51] Their accusations suggest that at least some members of the party – and presumably their targets – understood that the party was building something more akin to capitalism than a socialism en route to communism. Subsequent chapters will reveal how time and again people inside and outside the party expressed similar concerns that the party's "socialist" means were negating its professed communist ends.

Deploying the Army of Consumers in the Battle for State Control

The beginning of the Korean War in June 1950 confirmed party fears of military competition, increasing the compulsion of party leaders to accumulate capital. The party launched two mass campaigns that expanded state control over capital. The first, the Resist America and Aid Korea campaign (抗美援朝), aimed at shaping the attitudes and behavior of consumers (the demand side), and the second, the Three/Five-Antis campaign (三反五反), aimed at gaining greater control over the owners and managers of private capital (the production side). These campaigns provided a template for the state's methods of accumulating capital by attempting to control consumption throughout the Mao era.[52]

Launched in 1950, the Resist America and Aid Korea campaign attempted to control the culture around specific forms of consumption. Previous scholarship has described how, in order to strengthen loyalty to the new PRC and purge all American values and perceived imperialist influences, the party included in its boycott of American products institutions such as Christian missionary schools, hospitals, orphanages, and other charitable institutions.[53] However, the scholarly focus on ideology, influenced by the party's own rhetoric, overlooks the longer history of attempts to discourage people from diverting capital from China based on their behavior as consumers. For instance, the campaign targeted Hollywood movies, which at the time attracted the lion's share of the domestic market.

Following the model developed by the NPM, the CCP used the Korean War and the threat of American imperialism to link the consumption of American products to treason. Campaign activities began in Shanghai in mid-November 1950 with the formation of an organization to coordinate the campaign's mobilization activities, the Chinese People's Association for the Preservation of World Peace and Opposition to American Aggression. About 10,000 primary school teachers who formed 600 teams made up the backbone of this organization. The teams of teachers visited factories, neighborhoods, teahouses, and theaters to disseminate anti-American ideas.[54] Within a month, work units in Shanghai held over 8,000 meetings to identify and criticize various forms of American aggression, culminating in a mass rally attended by more than 100,000 student representatives, another 100,000 merchants and businesspeople, and thousands of teachers, doctors, lawyers, and other professionals from throughout the city to protest against American influences. During the following months, millions participated in other anti-imperialist rallies, including protests against America's rearming of Japan. Half of the 300 national magazines circulating at the time published articles tying America's actions in Korea to its earlier military and economic imperialism in China. Such articles echoed the party's argument that a preference for American products was tantamount to welcoming imperialist domination.[55]

"Parker Ink Runs Amok, China-Produced Ink is on the Verge of Death." With headlines such as this one, state media in November and December 1950 repeatedly attempted to rally the reserve army of consumers by reminding readers that American economic and cultural imperialism worked hand in glove with the military invasion.[56] State media argued that American influences on consumption damaged the country's ability to industrialize and, consequently, to defend itself. Such articles warned people to ferret out and resist imperialist influences. Headlines trumpeted ways that American products threatened China's survival: "American Imperialism: The Deadly Rival of Our National Industries"; "The Streets Are Full of American Canned Goods and Our Canned Goods Industry Is Gasping for Air"; and "Destruction of the Machine Tools Industry Is Under American Imperialism."[57] These polemics invoked death and dying to heighten the stakes of consumer choices. Furthermore, they explained the more day-to-day impacts by accusing American manufacturers of forcing Chinese companies out of business or into the lower end of the market for leather shoes, cigarettes, liquor, clocks, watches, and various other consumer goods, thereby undermining the growth of domestic industries and tarnishing the reputation of China-made products.[58] One story in the national newspaper *People's Daily*, for instance, quotes the director of the Chongqing Dairy Farm, who claimed that after the anti-Japanese war, "U.S.-manufactured KILM milk powder monopolized Chongqing's milk market, leaving two-thirds of Chongqing's dairy farms unable to sell their milk. Farmers had no choice but to kill their cows in exchange for money. More than forty cows were killed on our family farm." Another article in the same issue of the newspaper points out that the arrival of US plastic toothbrushes in the domestic market caused sales of national toothbrushes to plummet from 840,000 to 96,000 per month.[59] Collectively, readers learned the same lesson promoted by the NPM: consumer choices had life-and-death implications for the nation.

A second major domestic mass campaign during the Korean War targeted those in charge of production. In 1951, the war effort led to shortages of everything, from basic consumer supplies to materials needed for combat. The party blamed these shortages on corrupt cadres and craven capitalists who exploited the scarcity by raising prices and refusing to fulfill state purchase orders as a way to rake in higher profits in the markets. The discursive relocation of responsibility for wartime shortages to the twin scapegoats of corrupt cadres and greedy capitalists established a foundation for the party to appropriate more private capital. In 1951–2, the party launched its greatest effort to restrict private capitalism and consumerism during the New Democracy period (1949–53), that is, during the Three/ Five-Antis campaign.[60] While stopping short of outright expropriation, this state-led, top-down campaign evinces the state's efforts to wrest control over capital from private capitalists.[61]

During the early stages of the campaign, the party targeted corrupt cadres, not the capitalists. By December 1951, to save money for the war, the party pushed for increased production on the part of management and workers and for more thrift on the part of consumers. This began with the lauch of a nationwide Three-Antis campaign against "corruption, waste, and bureaucratism" within the government itself.[62] Within a month, preliminary investigations had uncovered 1,670 offenders in twenty-seven central state organs. Discoveries of widespread problems surfaced quickly. In the Beijing tax bureau, for instance, out of 1,750 staff members, over 900 confessed to accepting bribes.[63] In cities throughout the country, the party identified wasteful spending practices, such as building extravagant offices, schools, and entertainment facilities.[64] Such evidence of widespread corruption and waste led to the removal of untrustworthy cadres from party, bureaucracy, and military positions.[65]

Even at this early stage, the Three-Antis campaign targeted both kickbacks to cadres overseeing private businesses and the widespread forms of consumerism among cadres. The better lifestyles of such cadres proved to the party that these cadres had been corrupted by placing their own and their family's material interests ahead of the nation's interests. As a result, seemingly minor misallocations of capital in the campaign became evidence of ideological impurities. The implication was that any cadre not living a frugal life was living a capitalist life. Foreshadowing later mass campaigns, the party denounced signs of "extravagance and waste," including the use of state funds to host parties, hire servants, tour the country, and purchase automobiles. Such "extravagance" undermined the state ethos of hard work and frugal living, which aimed to limit or direct consumerism into the proper channels rather than doing away with it.[66] Again invoking earlier NPM targets, the party labeled imports from the imperialist countries as wasteful and even treasonous, singling out the ostentatious use of British- and American-made automobiles by cadres in the northeast city of Shenyang as egregious.[67] But the campaign also attacked excessive cadre consumption of everyday items, such as cigarettes, alcohol, and food.[68]

In fact, the party policies of state capitalism created a new class of surplus-appropriators – cadres either directly or indirectly controlling what workers produced, and boldly using public resources to pay for private consumption. Until the Cultural Revolution, the party did not want to publicly admit this, and many party members may not even have believed it. Yet in obscurity, the party created new inequalities and soon shifted the focus of the Three-Antis campaign from the growing cadre appetite for bourgeois material goods to the corrupting influence of private capitalists and their fraudulent business practices: problems left over from the Nationalist state.[69] Shortly after the start of the Three-Antis campaign, as officials began preparations for the Five-Antis campaign, Zhou Enlai suggested that the campaign should redirect its focus from "corrupt officials" to "law-breaking merchants." By mid-1951, a full six months before the formal launch of the public campaign, the party forced all businesspeople and merchants to join a trade or industrial association. Once they entered these associations, they were urged to confess their complicity in cadre corruption and waste, and they were divided into "small study groups" that met nightly to examine various didactic documents relating to the Three-Antis campaign and socialism. These sessions justified state policies that placed much greater state control over capital. At the end of January 1952, the party began using the results of state investigations into the Three-Anti crimes, investigations that built on the small-group confessions, to support its public claims of a vast capitalist conspiracy within the country. According to these findings, "the corrupt elements [within the state] not only include a large portion of personnel taken over from the old regime, but more than 80 percent of the corrupt elements have connections with industrialists and merchants." Mao had shortly before this concluded that capitalists were engaged in all manner of corrupt business practices that, he claimed, collectively posed "an even more dangerous and serious threat than war."[70] What had begun as an internal party purification campaign using capitalism rhetorically and asking the capitalists for information about the cadres had changed to attacks on those who still held capital that could be expropriated.

Public discourse regarding capitalists shifted dramatically to classify capitalists as national enemies (Figure 2.3). State media ran articles blaming the lifestyles and business practices of the capitalists for corrupting party members, cadres, and the military. Under the headline "Resist the Attacks by the Bourgeoisie Class, Uphold the Leadership of the Working Class," for instance, party theoretician Yu Guangyuan informed readers of the influential *Xuexi zazhi* (*Study Magazine*) that capitalists had launched a "fierce attack" against the working class and the leadership of the party that was weakening the economy and the nation's ability to resist US imperialism in Korea.[71] Reinforcing official justifications for expanding state control over private capitalism, Yu Guangyuan argued that the party had given the capitalists an opportunity to help build the New China under the policies of New Democracy. But the capitalists had remained true to their own interests and had opted to pursue personal profits instead of national interests. Now the survival of the Communist Revolution required that the party and the masses strike back. Yu Guangyuan identified five activities that the state should outlaw: bribery, tax evasion, theft of state assets, failure to conform to contract specifications, and theft of economic secrets. All five consisted of misallocations of capital and encompassed practices commonly used by businesspeople. These recommendations to strike back included educating the masses about the capitalist threat, preparing them for class struggle, and forcing the capitalists to sign a "patriotic contract." In the contract, each "capitalist" would acknowledge personal guilt for past wrongdoings and promise to cooperate with the authorities, who would inspect and supervise their enterprises. Furthermore, Yu Guangyuan called for inspection of the accounting records of all businesses, in effect endorsing state penetration into the inner workings of increasingly less-than-private enterprises. The state adopted all of Yu's measures, thereby launching the "Five-Antis" campaign.

The combined Three/Five-Antis campaign of 1951–2 transformed the lives of capitalists more profoundly than the events of 1949. After 1949, urban capitalists had continued to engage in the same business practices as before, even as they began to work with state organs. Although new taxes, inflation, and the growth of state control over distribution and retail threatened private accumulation, enterprises often kept two sets of books, falsified receipts and orders, converted earnings into gold and

(a)   (b)

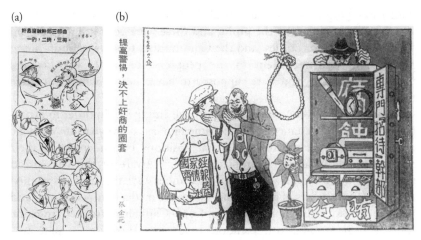

Figure 2.3. Vilification of capitalists and consumerism. Here are two examples from the Three/Five-Antis campaign's attempt to popularize the notion that bourgeois consumerism threatened to corrupt the revolutionary spirit of the party. In 2.3a, "The three steps used by treasonous merchants to corrupt cadres: fishing, handcuffing and digging" (*Manhua*, February 1, 1952, 9), the illustration metaphorically describes how a private businessman works a cadre who is, we are told with the script above his head, "insufficiently determined to maintain his willpower." The businessman "fishes" by using "bait" such as a cigarette to establish a friendly relationship. Next, the merchant "handcuffs" the cadre by putting an expensive watch on his wrist as a gift. And, finally, he "digs" into the cadre's outfit to bury a stack of banknotes into the cadre's inner pocket, which the illustration likens to putting a dagger into his chest. In 2.3b, "Be vigilant and never fall into the trap of the treasonous merchant" (*Manhua*, March 1, 1952, 7), a cadre (in a cadre's outfit) carries a briefcase labeled "national economic intelligence involving the people's interests." He receives a warm welcome from a businessman dressed in a Western-style jacket. The contents of the vault include many of the most desired products in the 1950s: a fountain pen, a wristwatch, a clock, a radio, and two boxes of money labeled as "special treats for cadres." The words "corruption" and "bribery" are printed on the vault to emphasize that the goods and money are traps. Besides the products and money, the cadre faces two other dangers: sexual temptation in the form of a beautiful woman and the potential for blackmail by a gangster, who lies in wait behind the vault.

foreign currencies, and devised other methods to hide capital from prying state eyes, as they had done under Nationalist rule. By the time the Three/Five-Antis campaign began to crack down on these activities, most enterprises were in fact guilty of such practices, a vulnerability used by the party to extract revenue from them. As one Shanghai businessman described it, "In fact, if you made a decent profit, this meant, by definition, that you had done something illegal in the eyes of the Communists. You revealed the ways in which you made the profit, and these were your crimes. . . . You then confessed your crimes, and the Communists took away your 'illegal profits' and returned them to the people – or rather the People's Government whom you were supposed to have cheated when you made the profits."[72]

As well as effectively criminalizing private enterprise, in order to expropriate capital, the state used the campaign as a crowbar to dislodge capitalists from their privileged social positions by undermining their authority and social and workplace status.[73] Aware of the widespread practice of double bookkeeping, in December 1951 the state dispatched auditors to enterprises of all sizes and used mass media to urge relatives and friends to pressure the capitalists to confess.[74] Capitalists, isolated from one another, were exposed to tremendous psychological stresses, as state propaganda targeted them by, for instance, posters denouncing them that were placed throughout the cities, demanding that they confess and urging that their employees supply incriminating evidence.[75] In Shanghai, the local government, using the new tools of mass communication, set up loudspeakers on commercial thoroughfares directing pedestrians to urge shopkeepers to confess.[76] The state not only sought alleged back taxes, as it claimed, but also expanded its control by facilitating the extraction of capital. This marked the further ascendancy of state capitalism, the state as the primary appropriator and distributor of capital.

Alongside the enrichment of the state, the Five-Antis campaign amplified the socialist rhetoric of capitalist–worker class conflicts in the workplace. Through mass rallies, the state mobilized hundreds of thousands of people to criticize private capitalism, thereby bolstering mass support for the social, financial, and symbolic weakening of the private capitalist class and the corresponding centralization of state control. During Guangzhou's Five-Antis campaign, for instance, 10,000 individuals entered factories and shops to organize mass denunciations of the capitalists.[77] In Shanghai, more than 80 percent of the workers and shop attendants participated in "speak bitterness" mass meetings, during which the employees recounted their mistreatment at the hands of the capitalists.[78] The attacks on and public humiliation of the capitalists weakened or severed the ties of loyalty between employers and workers by using the rhetoric of class conflict and deflecting attention away from the state as the new extractors of labor power and controllers of the surplus.[79] As Liu Changsheng, chair of the Shanghai General Labor Union, put it, "In the past, employers had a bad attitude toward workers; now workers are reversing the roles."[80] Moreover, the campaign popularized a fundamental premise of state capitalism and state consumerism: whereas private capitalism exploited labor for private accumulation, state capitalism and state consumerism demanded "hard work and frugal living" on the part of everyone in the name of benefiting all.

By late March 1952, the state had all the incriminating material it needed for the official campaign. Agents of the state had obtained confessions, exacerbated tensions between owners and workers, and divided and demoralized the capitalists. All that remained was for the capitalists to make public confessions, representing a humiliating acceptance of the party's narrative of class exploitation that thereafter gave the state greater latitude in treating the capitalists and their capital. The pressure was so great that it set off a wave of suicides by business leaders.[81] The public phase of the campaign proceeded swiftly in the urban areas. Although the starting date of the campaign differed by city, it followed the same pattern throughout the country.[82] In Guangzhou, for example, the local government tested its procedures during the first week of April by targeting a single industry: pharmaceutical manufacturers and merchants. In "struggle sessions" with Five-Anti work teams as well as workers and clerks, capitalists ritualistically confessed to the crimes that the preceding months of investigations had uncovered. The state then meted out various types of punishments, including fines.[83] The next stage began with a citywide rally. During the following fortnight, the campaign's scope broadened to some 200 industries and trades. In the final stage of the campaign, which took place during the first three weeks of June, all the cases were settled.[84]

The Five-Antis campaign reduced the amount of capital funneled into private consumerism. After the campaign began in the spring of 1952, most capitalists discontinued or reduced their use of automobiles, stopped buying jewelry and other luxury items, avoided conspicuous markers of bourgeois status such as Western-style business suits, and cut down on the giving of gifts at Chinese New Year. The result was a dramatic drop in business at the top department stores that catered to the affluent, and which at that time were still privately owned; for instance, sales at Shanghai's Yong'an Department Store, considered one of the most elite department stores in China, as discussed further in Chapter 5, dropped by two-thirds within a single month.[85]

The campaign placed massive amounts of private capital under greater state control. After investigating almost a million businesses and imposing penalties, the state gathered nearly 30 trillion RMB (roughly US$1.25 billion) in fines and taxes, forcing the capitalists to turn over or to sell their hard currency, precious metals, merchandise, and equipment. By one estimate, the total amount of capital extracted equaled more than half of China's military expenditures for the entire three years of the Korean War.[86] By pressuring the capitalists to overstate their crimes and, consequently, to increase the amount of back taxes and fines they owed, the campaign had long-term ramifications for the expansion of state control over the economy and capital. To survive, the capitalists had to liquidate an increasing amount of their businesses and personal assets, and over the course of the campaign many – such as the patriotic industrialist Wu Yunchu, a leader of the prewar NPM – gradually surrendered their enterprises to the state.[87] The state used the techniques developed in the campaigns, such as enacting regulations and internal monitoring by workers, to gain control over nominally private industries and to become further involved in all aspects of their operations, from the hiring of workers to the fixing of prices.

In a pattern repeated throughout the era, however, the party had to back-track a little from its efforts at maximum capital extraction in early June of 1952, when the resulting damage to the country's economy forced the state to temporarily revive private enterprises by extending loans, reducing their back taxes, and providing state contracts.[88] Nevertheless, over the course of the Three/Five-Antis campaign, the party destroyed the social standing, absorbed much of the personal wealth, and discredited the capital-intensive lifestyles of the capitalists. The campaign thus paved the way for the shift along the state-to-private spectrum of industrial capitalism toward greater state capitalism and the confiscation of private capital during the Socialist Transformation, and the periodic discrediting of anyone or any activity labeled "capitalist" throughout the Mao era. The Three-Antis demonstrated the party's preferred strategy for dealing with corruption, waste, inequality, and their manifestations in conspicuous consumption, both then and now: attack their manifestations and blame a few selected targets rather than address the structural and institutional contradictions of inequality created by state capitalism. While private capitalists would virtually disappear as a class by 1956, the problems identified by the party as the new appropriators and allocators of capital – the cadres – only grew more conspicuous.[89]

Appropriating the Rural Surplus to Pay for Urban Production and Consumption

Although expropriation of the capital of the urban capitalist class through the Three/Five-Antis campaign provided an initial boost to state control over capitalism and consumerism, the state demands for "hard work and frugal living" were felt much more acutely in the countryside. In the countryside, where 80 percent of the population resided, the party created or expanded forms of state control over the surplus and its allocation in ways that enabled the party to extract as much as possible and as quickly as possible. The party's "building of socialism" in the cities – with rapid industrialization facilitated by better-paid urban workers with "iron rice bowl" job security in state enterprises – relied on policies of population management and labor extraction bordering on feudalism in the countryside that heavily suppressed rural consumption so as to aid urban industrialization.[90]

As noted in Chapter 1, the party's state capitalism, like all varieties of industrial capitalism, expanded and spread those inequalities that it claimed "building socialism" would address, including urban–rural, mental–manual, and factory–farm inequalities. In addition to the extraction of the surplus from the countryside, countless other policies favored urban accumulation and allocations so that those in the cities prospered despite the party's hostile rhetoric about cities being emblematic of imperialism and consumerism. After 1949, for instance, the party shipped in supplies and shipped out over 400,000 refugees from Shanghai to favor long-term urban residents.[91] A series of policies that tied rural residents to the fewer opportunities and lower incomes of rural life culminated in the household registration policy of 1958. Party policies favored cities because of their potential as centers of industry and capital accumulation. At the same time, however, these policies delayed and undermined not only the transformation of the social relations of production in the cities but also expanded the urban–rural divide.

Capitalism required capital. The party rationalized its abandonment of rural workers in favor of the urban bourgeoisie and urban workers by following the Soviet template for justifying urban industrialization by rural expropriation. In 1926, Stalin endorsed the work of leading Soviet economist Yevgeni Preobrazhensky, and later enshrined forced industrialization and collectivization as the foundation of "building socialism."[92] Preobrazhensky defended brutal rural extractive policies that created and spread the inequalities of industrial capitalism by simply applying the word "socialism" to the policy, as the leaders in "socialist" countries repeatedly did to institutions and policies otherwise associated with capitalism. Preobrazhensky's "primitive socialist accumulation" was meant to contrast with the "primitive capitalist accumulation" discussed both by Adam Smith as the "original accumulation" and by Marx, who, as noted, likened it to the theological "original sin." Other Soviet party members – for instance, Bukharin – knew the "sinful" implications of an urban "socialism" built on rural extraction and challenged such policies. But, as was the case in China, the Soviet leadership concluded it had no better option – no foreign peoples to enslave, colonies to exploit, or foreign loans to provide the capital necessary for the industrialization and military improvements; the key goals, as indicated earlier in this chapter, that the party leadership had determined the country most needed.[93] In his "Speech to Industrial Managers" in 1931, Stalin defended expedited extractions from the countryside as necessary for national survival in military competition: "We are fifty or a hundred years behind the advanced countries. We must make good this distance in ten years. Either we do it, or we shall be crushed."[94] Two decades later, the CCP followed the same path. In urban centers, the rhetoric of war and survival justified state consumerism; in the countryside, the rhetoric justified nearly anything the state did to the already impoverished population.

As with other forms of primitive accumulation in the early days of industrial capitalism, such as the enclosure movement in England or slavery in the United States, "primitive socialist accumulation" in the Chinese countryside was both ruthless and central to commencing industrial capitalism. The state used a diverse and effective range of tactics to accumulate rural capital. It began by taking a larger share of the harvest and then exploiting the low-cost labor power of those whom it forced to remain in the countryside through the household registration system. Finally, the state engaged in rampant and unsustainable extraction of environmental resources. State capitalist policies extracted as much as possible while minimizing reallocations into local consumption – to the point of starving millions of farmers. Indeed, the countryside can be described as the least "socialist" sector of the economy, leaving aside the few policies often associated with socialism but that also served capital accumulation, such as improved health care, the provision of education, small-scale rural industrialization, and the establishment of communes that facilitated low-cost capital extraction. As in the Soviet Union, China under the CCP saw rural areas as a piggybank: the original (or "primitive") source of capital to finance the largely urban industrialization.[95]

State capitalism exerted maximum control over the extraction of the agricultural surplus. It allocated this surplus not to the original producers of that capital – the farmers – but instead to the capital-intensive, mostly urban, heavy industry. These policies reduced the already low rural incomes and paved the way for a much more austere consumer landscape in the countryside. Because extraction of the surplus removed income from the countryside, the state also sought to eliminate the ability of people living in the countryside to allocate the non-state surplus. This meant that the state took as much grain, vegetables, cotton, and other products as possible – to the extent that farmers had practically nothing to wear or, worse, nothing to eat. Less grain remaining in the countryside meant less capital for rural people to acquire bicycles, wristwatches, and sewing machines (then spreading to the countryside as essential betrothal gifts, as discussed in Chapter 1) and, therefore, less capital to devote to the possibility of marrying off a son to a good partner. Little wonder locals responded to the realities of the extractive central policies by seeking to retain more of the surplus for themselves.

The concept of state capitalism captures the three forms of capital the party attempted to extract from farmers: labor power, land and livestock, and tools. As this form of "primitive socialist accumulation" has always been a critical dimension of scholarly understandings of the party's developmental strategy, how the state gained much greater control over the agricultural output – the harvest – in the 1950s is well documented.[96] To put it briefly, after redistributing the land of the landlords in the early 1950s, the state first cajoled and then later forced almost the entire rural population into a series of progressively larger state-controlled (but rarely state-owned, thereby minimizing the costs to the national government) agricultural institutions that facilitated maximum capital extraction, culminating with the people's communes at the start of the Great Leap Forward in 1958, which was heralded as a "bridge" to communism and the elimination of the "three major inequalities" of industrial capitalism.[97] The household registration system kept rural labor costs low by disrupting the labor market and barring rural people from finding higher-paying jobs in the cities. In effect, the household registration system minimized the costs of state services to an otherwise larger urban population by creating an almost indentured labor class living in the countryside.

Rural land-ownership patterns resembled the types of capital ownership found in the cities and they similarly served state capitalist accumulation. State-owned farms were the rough equivalent of the work units in the state-owned enterprises because farmers working in the state-owned farms experienced the most stable conditions, including guaranteed wages. But, like their urban state enterprise counterparts, state farms employed only a small percentage of rural labor and produced only a small percentage of the total harvest.[98] Cooperative farms and communes were the equivalent of the urban cooperatives and communes. That is, they were useful to the state to facilitate capital extractions, but they were expected to survive with little or no state support. Finally, there was private land, which (like the urban private capital equivalent) persisted despite the popular Cold War image in the market capitalist countries that the "socialist" countries had confiscated all private land and businesses. Even after the state expropriated nearly all land by 1956, the party continued to debate whether allowing small private plots would increase production. Regardless of national policy and similar to the situation of the private enterprises persisting in cities, the countryside had significant private farming beyond what was officially permitted by the state. Such private or semi-private farming existed throughout the entire Mao era, not merely at its end.[99] And, once again in parallel with the urban private capitalist activity, state policies attempting to maximize rural extractions incentivized these private activities.

When the state took more, city workers ate more, and rural people ate less and bought less. The policies of state consumerism in the countryside meant reduced rural incomes and rations at subsistence levels or below, that is, the suppression of the first defining aspect of consumerism – circulation of mass-produced goods – much less communication of identity through consumption.[100] In addition to an acquisitive state, the party incentivized its local cadres to overreport crop yields, which allowed the state to take even more.[101] Institutionally, taxation, price-fixing, and monopolies on essential goods enforced state consumerism by giving the state additional control over incomes and leaving rural residents with little to spend on essentials, much less on consumer products.[102] First, agricultural taxes were an obvious, though minor, form of direct extraction. Second, the state profited by making agricultural products cheaper and industrial products more expensive (an institutional arrangement known as the "price scissors").[103] The state bought agricultural products first from farmers and then from cooperatives/communes at low prices and sold necessary industrial products – foodstuffs, clothing, and fertilizers – for a handsome profit. Third, the state reduced competition for industrial goods by establishing a monopoly over industrial products sold to the farmers. This eliminated competition for industrial products (and for other uses for rural labor) by banning private rural handicraft industries that previously had supplied farmers with most manufactured goods. In addition, during times of shifts toward greater state capitalism, such as in 1959, the state closed the private rural markets that had provided opportunities for farmers to sell and barter independently processed (or stolen) goods, thereby preventing farmers from accumulating capital that the state wanted to capture. Finally, during the First Five-Year Plan period (1953–7), high state investment in urban-based heavy industry meant low investment in agriculture.[104]

The party classified rural denizens in different ways, and the different groups owned capital in 1949 in distinctive ways. The most numerous rural "capitalists" – and those whose capital the state would extract – were not labeled "capitalists." They were called "landlords," the exact definition of which the party shifted to suit its objectives. In contrast to the cities, where the capitalists survived 1949 and continued to enjoy some degree of consumerism, the state immediately targeted the rural landowners. Unlike the capitalists, the landowners did not necessarily know more than other rural people about farming; and, in any case, they were unlikely to be able to flee abroad and take their capital with them. During the "land reform" of 1950–2, the state took their land, thereby eliminating control by "unproductive" landlords over the surplus and reducing inequality based on income derived from land ownership rather than from labor. Those who had land, worked some of it, and hired labor were labeled "rich farmers." At first, they avoided expropriation. The party compromised with them for the same reasons they did with their urban counterparts: to win their political support and to take advantage of their skills as both farmers and potential literate cadre recruits.[105]

But the bulk of the various state compromises with private control over land critical to reviving the rural economy did not last long. In 1955–6, during the "high tide of socialism," as the party was completing the Socialist Transformation of urban enterprises, the party took land from a wider catchment of people, expropriating the "middle peasantry" almost overnight through the coerced formation of collectives. With the formation of collectives, the party forced (slightly) wealthier farmers who had more land and better equipment to share with those who had less. By sharing land and tools, the party's stated goal was to reward labor more than those who already had the possibility of additional income derived from even the smallest forms of capital: a bit more land, an ox, a solid mattock. As with its other policies, the party rhetorically advertised the policy of first creating collectives and then massive communes not for intensified state extractions but rather as the next stage in "building socialism." The party went so far as to float the idea during the "Communist Wind" of 1958 that people's communes were the precursor to the imminent realization of communism and "ownership by the whole people."[106] Rather than workers controlling the fruits of their labor, the policy of pooling capital facilitated greater state extractions and thereby the transfer of capital from the countryside to the cities.

Public challenges to the party definition of its extractive policies as "socialism" were rare. However, there were criticisms of those policies that led to famine, most prominently by Peng Dehuai in 1959.[107] There were also more modest signs of dissent. In 1958, for instance, Wang Wenchang, a lieutenant at a military academy, wrote an article to a military magazine criticizing the grain requisition policy because it enriched cadres at the expense of rural workers.[108] However, there was no shortage of implied dissent. Scholarly interviews with people who left China during the Mao era consistently revealed that rural residents did not always surrender their capital and labor power to the state. Because state extraction was unrelenting, there were countless grassroots efforts, forms of "everyday resistance," that formed the "weapons of the weak" to preserve more capital locally.[109] Farmers engaged in – and the state responded to – countless strategies to retain greater control over the fruits of their labor. They would hide, eat, or steal grain. They conserved their labor power when working and engaged in gray and black economic activities on the sly. State extractive policies even led to the destruction of capital so as to block its confiscation. During the Great Leap Forward, farmers slaughtered cattle en masse rather than turning it over to the collectives, a semistate instrument of extraction. Because they offered no incentives (or, rather, increased incentives to hide agricultural yields), the policies led to smaller total yields. As in the aftermath of the Three/Five-Antis, the state responded to the economic setbacks in the countryside by backtracking from its direct extractive policies to sanction limited private accumulation to incentivize more labor. And it sought other means, such as direct taxation, to gain more control over the agricultural surplus.[110]

State capitalism authorized better standards of living in the cities than in the countryside. In addition to the price scissors that created cheap agricultural products and expensive industrial products, rural China paid the highest price during Great Leap Forward famine. Rural people constantly faced death due to starvation, the sale of children, cannibalism, and other unspeakable actions in times of desperate famine, while the state ensured that the city dwellers did not starve.[111] When grain capital dried up, humans became monetized as items for sale or trade, while others were turned into "food capital" in the form of cannibalism.[112] To maintain urban standards of living in times of rural economic slowdowns, the state dumped surplus laborers in the countryside to fend for themselves. For instance, from 1962 to 1979, the state rusticated nearly eighteen million junior and senior high-school graduates because it could not find urban jobs for them.[113] Following the Great Leap Forward, the state banished twenty million industrial work-ers to the fields.[114] Beyond these numbers, perhaps most telling of all the abuses of the countryside to solve the state accumulation problems was that rustication was an inexpensive (for the state) solution for what to do about urban criminals.[115]

By 1956, China had moved significantly along the spectrum of industrial capitalism away from markets and private property and toward total state capitalism. The four types of ownership of capital were largely (but not entirely) reduced to cooperative and state ownership.[116] Even this seeming advance toward total state control, however, contained elements of private capitalism. If one excludes the extreme experiments during the Great Leap Forward, when everything other than housing, bedding, and clothing was required to be turned over to the communes, farmers still owned or controlled various amounts of "capital" in different forms: private plots, equipment, animals, and, most importantly, unequal shares in the output of the cooperatives. The state never eradicated these inequalities. To the contrary, such inequalities grew.

The central contradiction between the party rhetoric of socialism and the realities of capitalist practices makes more sense when we see the political economy and society of the time for what they were and how people experienced them rather than for what it was not. Rather than a failed attempt to "build socialism," the policies of the 1950s selectively endorsed the socialist goal of transforming the relations of production, but only when it facilitated the state's broader compulsion to accumulate more capital. What people experienced stemmed from this concerted – and effective – effort to construct a form of state capitalism that maximized the extraction of labor and goods from the countryside to build industry in the cities.

Conclusion

Before 1949, a half-century of popular calls for greater state interventions in consumption and consumerism on behalf of one ideology (nationalism) helped lay the foundations for greater state interventions on behalf of another ideology (socialism) in the PRC. After 1949, the party became more powerful and better at implementing the pre-existing agenda of state consumerism to serve state capitalism. Party leaders felt compelled to intervene in both sides of capitalism – production and consumption – in order to industrialize as rapidly as possible to meet military and other demands.

Early party policies in the PRC shifted the institutional arrangements toward greater state capitalism and state consumerism, despite occasional halts and reversals. The need for capital accumulation repeatedly trumped even the desire for greater state control over production and consumption. The histories of the four institutional arrangements of ownership during the Mao era as outlined above – state, collective, foreign, and private ownership – all demonstrate the party's privileging of capital accumulation, even when that priority meant "postponing" the basic tenets of socialism or delaying shifts toward greater state control. Because each arrangement contributed to building state capitalism, not socialism, each revealed the central contradiction between the party's rhetoric of building socialism on its way toward communism and its capitalist policies. The party looked for ways to accumulate more and faster, including in the shift toward greater state capitalism in the crackdown on unauthorized cadre and capitalist allocations of capital during the Three/Five-Antis campaign. This campaign helped the state penetrate private enterprises as never before and also generated nearly RMB 30 trillion from fines and taxes that the state claimed had been evaded. However, as with the subsequent expansion of state control and extraction, the result of the economic downturn accompanying the Three/Five-Antis campaign was a slowing of the party shift toward greater state capitalism.

Finally, although this book focuses on urban consumerism, all urban consumption and consumerism depended on the state's rural expropriations. Ancient, feudal, capitalist – whatever the forms of rural production, appropriation, and distribution – they were organized and authorized to facilitate state capitalist accumulation that expanded the inequalities of industrial capitalism. The party's rural policies of extraction – however quasi-feudalist or socialist they may appear – were designed to serve urban-led industrial capitalism. The policies of state extraction in the countryside enabled the expansion of industrial capitalism and all its attendant inequalities, including inequalities of consumption and participation in consumerism. As subsequent chapters will show, the party had a much easier time facilitating the state and non-state expansion of capitalism than it did limiting or controlling the corresponding expansion of consumerism.

CHAPTER 3

Soviet Influences on State Consumerism

In the spring and summer of 1949, while the CCP was compromising with the capitalists, it was simultaneously building its credentials as a socialist party. Months before the formal establishment of the People's Republic on October 1, Mao declared that the Soviet Union had created a "great and splendid socialist state" and was "our best teacher."[1] After 1949, state media routinely referred to the Soviet Union as China's "Elder Brother," "Our Tomorrow," and "Our Model."[2]

The party's geopolitical situation meant it initially had little choice but to foster close relations with its Elder Brother. China's relative backwardness and the military threats the CCP faced from the Nationalists and their ally the United States compelled the party to import industrial and military technology from wherever it could, which meant replacing American and other market capitalist sources of military and industrial capital with other suppliers. On February 14, 1950, the party formalized its relations with the Soviet Union and announced the signing of the Sino-Soviet Treaty of Friendship, Alliance, and Mutual Assistance.[3] The treaty provided the party with political legitimacy, economic aid, and critical military supplies. Throughout the 1950s, the Soviet Union remained the PRC's main political ally and its largest trading partner.[4]

As discussed in Chapter 2, the import and manufacture of weapons to defend the new state was an urgent capital requirement for the party and a key driver behind its shift along the state-to-private spectrum of industrial capitalism toward greater state control over both accumulation and consumption. Public knowledge that the country needed military imports from the Soviet Union spanned 1949. In February 1948, rumors circulated in different regions of the country that the party, still deep in the civil war with the Nationalists, had agreed to exchange Chinese children for Soviet weapons. Such rumors resurfaced in the spring of 1950 in the northwestern city of Lanzhou, where hundreds took to the streets to protest what they had heard was a secret deal between Chairman Mao and the Soviet Union to exchange 100,000 Chinese children for Soviet weapons. In June 1950, after the start of the Korean War, another rumor circulated that China needed ammunition so desperately that it would exchange human testicles for bullets.[5]

But even before the start of the Korean War, without the military support provided by the Soviet Union, the party would not have been able to launch its strategy of rapid industrialization. By March 1950, for instance, the Soviets were providing Shanghai with air force advisors, radar, and searchlights, allowing the PLA to repel Nationalist air raids. In mid-May, the PLA took the Zhoushan Islands near Shanghai from where the Nationalists had launched its raids. Due to imported Soviet military supplies and personnel, China's light industrial and commercial hub resumed its industrial development.[6] The underlying compulsion to rapidly accumulate capital, here in the form of weapons, could not have been clearer (Figure 3.1).

Beyond turning to the Soviets for essential military and economic assistance, the party leadership also imported from the Soviet Union the institutional arrangements associated with countries that in the twentieth century were labeled "socialist." As noted in the Introduction, the most advantageous political import was the use of the concept of socialism as a transitional stage to reach the goal of communism, which included as its defining attributes the institutional arrangements of state planning and state ownership as a replacement for allocations via markets and private ownership. This critical Soviet ideological import was not only the abstraction of an indeterminate socialist stage but also a specific and elaborate justification for the persistence of many of the other attributes of capitalism, including commodities and wage labor.[7] In the political and social spheres, Soviet institutions that were associated with "socialist" countries included a highly centralized state ruled by a single party, a lack of independent media to express political dissent, and state control over mass organizations, including labor unions, the media, education, youth organizations, and women's groups. Rather than simple hallmarks of "socialism," however, these institutional arrangements facilitated state capitalism's faster accumulation of capital by structuring large parts of the economy – especially the countryside – with noncapitalist relations of production.

In addition to institutions and ideological specifics, during the opening years of the PRC, the party promoted all things Soviet.[8] By endorsing the Soviet Union as a model, including all of its material and cultural manifestations, the party was approving the expansion of consumerism and helping to

在蘇聯偉大的援助下，我們將盡最
大的努力，逐步地實現國家工業化！

Figure 3.1. Elder Brother. This poster was part of a nationwide effort by the CCP to promote the Soviet Union as "China's Tomorrow" and underscores the highest priority China attributed to the relationship. "Elder Brother" was not a model of "socialism" as much as a blueprint for rapid, state-led industrialization. The caption reads: "With the great support of the Soviet Union, and our own greatest strength, we will realize the industrialization of our nation step by step!" Source: The International Institute of Social History (Landsberger Collection).

popularize Soviet styles. Soviet films, art, novels, and its political ideology that explicitly called for rejecting capitalism and bourgeois values helped buttress the Chinese version of state consumerism, including through the specific Soviet imports examined here – clothing, fashion, and model workers.[9] But over time, during the 1950s and early 1960s, criticism emerged at both ends of the social hierarchy. Mao and other Chinese leaders became disenchanted with Soviet-style policies and economics, and ordinary people both noticed and criticized the implicit endorsement of consumerism behind Soviet fashions and products. The state attempted to counter such criticism by disseminating justifications for fashion as not being bourgeois but rather being fully compatible with socialism, including by importing Soviet opinions on the matter.[10] Inside and outside the party, the growing criticism culminated in outright public accusations by the party that the Soviet Union – as demonstrated by its rampant corruption and consumerism – was negating its revolutionary heritage and becoming capitalist. In contrast to the many histories on the Sino-Soviet split that focus on elite politics and, for instance, emphasize that the split originated in a rivalry between Mao and Khrushchev for leadership of the socialist world, this chapter focuses on the everyday, incremental doubts sowed through ordinary interactions that something was amiss on the "road to socialism."[11] However, as Chapters 6 and 7 will reveal, the eventual rejection and conscious turn of the party away from the Soviet model in the 1960s were insufficient for China to avoid confronting the same expanding inequalities created by industrial capitalism elsewhere. After all, the turn away from Soviet economic policies – and stigmatizing them as capitalist – did not result in socialist policies leading toward communism. Rather, the years following the split witnessed state capitalist policies that continued to expand capitalism.

Adopting the Soviet Model of State Consumerism

There was no simple, fixed Soviet model to export to China. By the 1950s, the Soviet Union had already experimented with various institutional arrangements to reach its goal of urban-based industrialization. In the end, the experiments yielded arrangements that included limited markets, private ownership, and greater material incentives. These arrangements, in turn, translated into the inequalities associated with consumerism, but they were recast as temporary problems of a socialism en route to communism.[12] Nevertheless, when China looked to import a model to build a socialist country, it encountered a Communist Party of the Soviet Union (CPSU) that had been experimenting, notably in the 1920s, with reductions in state control over capital in exchange for immediate economic gains and faster capital accumulation. The Soviet state determined how much to produce, where to market goods, and how to price them, as it tolerated the basic inequalities of industrial capitalism generated through scaled wages and bonuses, and even encouraged forms of private capitalism and consumerism.[13] The CCP initially saw the entire Soviet model as sacrosanct, the prototype of how a country should go about building socialism.[14] Because the Soviets saw no contradictions – only tension requiring periodic policy adjustments – between its version of building socialism and the accompanying inequalities, the model was also adopted in China.

The party's initial tolerance of capitalism and consumerism following 1949 thus paralleled the Soviet model of "building socialism" both during its earlier New Economic Policy period in the 1920s as well as during the policy experiments of the 1950s. The Soviet model reflected its longstanding incorporation of consumerism into the economy (Figure 3.2).[15] As early as the mid-1930s, following the period of revolutionary Stalinism, the CPSU had made what appeared to early scholars of the Soviet Union to be a "Big Deal" and, more pointedly, a "Great Retreat." They saw the policies that implicitly endorsed bourgeois values, including consumerism and its associated inequalities, as part of an exchange for the political loyalty of the segment of society that was needed by the Soviet leadership for faster industrialization, namely, educated urbanites.[16] Regardless of whether such policies were adopted purely to buy political support, the Soviets backed away from strict distribution of food and consumer goods through rationing and from its earlier condemnations of asceticism and its endorsements of egalitarianism as the defining characteristics of a socialism-en-route-to-communism governing ideology. The increased presence of fashion, dancing, and leisure activities, such as carnivals and holidays, all reflected the policy shift toward embracing consumerism in concert with – rather than in contradiction to – building socialism. Consequently, the images of the model Soviet citizen of the period, in posters, films, and literature, often appeared to be more bourgeois than proletarian in both dress and activity.[17] The Soviet Union's open embrace of consumerism as evidence of building socialism grew even stronger after World War II.

Khrushchev's rise after Stalin's death in 1953 included a continued move toward expanded consumerism, including the compulsion to acquire ever more mass-produced products.[18] The CCP's later assessment had a factual foundation. In Ozersk, the small Russian city that benefited from its role

Figure 3.2. "What do Soviet women wear?" These pages from the Chinese edition of the magazine *Soviet Woman* illustrate how the Soviet Union promoted consumerism, including fashion, as compatible with socialism to Chinese audiences. The Soviet author of the article claims that socialist fashion conforms to human nature and emphasizes convenience and beauty, unlike capitalist fashion, which seeks to maximize profit. Source: *Sulian funü*, no. 4 (April 1956), 46–7.

producing material to build atomic weapons for the Cold War arms race, one historian observes that party members feared that the "conditions of advanced socialism were creating citizens who were entirely unsocialist."[19] Its residents not only wanted more but they also became increasingly discriminating in their material desires, demanding, for example, that their clothing come only from Moscow or from abroad. Their purpose in life, according to one party activist in 1960, was to acquire "a car, a suite, television, rugs, while work and social responsibilities became secondary affairs."[20] While the Chinese looking to the Soviet model would have seen signs of growing material abundance and industrialization, they would have also viewed the similar forms of inequality that are associated with capitalism.

The ongoing Soviet shift in the 1950s included a redefinition of products that had been castigated as bourgeois luxuries unsuitable for the ascetic, self-sacrificing Soviet worker: jewelry, cosmetics, trendy clothes, permed hair, manicures, and patent leather shoes. Whereas in the past lipstick might have led to a young woman's exclusion from the Communist Youth League (*Komsomol*) on the grounds of moral degradation, in the 1950s red lips were de rigueur.[21] By the time Soviet advisors and aid began streaming into China after 1949, material cravings had, according to the scholar of Soviet literature Vera Dunham, "engulfed postwar [Soviet] society from top to bottom."[22] However unlikely consumerism was to have "engulfed" the entirety of Soviet society, the Soviet case did illustrate the reciprocal relationship between industrialization and expanding consumerism that China had also begun to experience.

The Soviet endorsement of consumerism – with all its accompanying inequalities – as compatible with socialism became evident to residents of Chinese cities that hosted large numbers of Soviet experts. Totaling more than 18,000 by the end of the 1950s, these experts, presumably representative of those most benefiting from the inequalities associated with expert-led urban industrialization, arrived in China ready to consume.[23] According to one Soviet advisor who lived in China between 1958 and 1960, although the numerous mom-and-pop shops in Beijing were in poor condition and bereft of quality goods, the main state department store on Wangfujing Street still sold luxury items to tourists and Soviet advisors. He was happy to discover a wide variety of products that were scarce in Moscow, including furs, watches, jewelry, and especially enamelware. Custom-made suits were much less expensive and easier to procure in Beijing than they were in Moscow, so he and other advisors availed themselves of the opportunity, generating so much business for local tailors that many posted store signs in Russian.[24] Although the spectacle of avaricious Soviet consumers eager to snap up anything and everything that the limited marketplace and the gray and black markets had to offer seemed to provide an official stamp of approval for such consumption, some Chinese were critical, or at least envious. As one observer in the industrial city of Wuhan noted, "They spent great quantities of our People's money on such things as clothes, pens, watches, and jewelry, [all of] which had come from the hated Western industrialized society."[25] Urban Chinese could see that the representatives of their socialist "model" country were buying the imported products, and enjoying the bourgeois Western culture, such as jazz music and dancing, that the party was telling them to reject as remnants of imperialism and capitalism. To make matters worse, some Soviet advisors were condescending toward their Chinese hosts as they violated the spirit of socialist internationalism.[26]

Soviet-style consumerism thus communicated inequality and implied competition both within and among the nominally socialist countries. Soviet experts earned salaries at least ten times higher than their Chinese counterparts and, because they received both their original salaries from home and their special pay in China, they had much more disposable income.[27] While in China, their spouses and children filled their free time with shopping. Indeed, the experts and their families might have spent even more on Chinese products had the Soviet authorities, anxious not to lose capital to Chinese competitors, not made special arrangements to sell them the then Soviet equivalents of the Three Great Things – televisions, refrigerators, and cars – at favorable exchange rates that they could pick up when they returned home. Among these, cars were the biggest draw, as obtaining a car in the Soviet Union required years on a waiting list. Few, however, managed to save enough money to purchase such goods because, as one Soviet advisor recalled, most of their disposable income went to Chinese products like "cheap furs, china, silks, [and] dresses."[28] Soviet demand for consumer goods, however limited by policies back home, created doubts among some Chinese observers: just how good was the quality of life – including the consumer goods – in the country that represented the promise of "China's tomorrow"?

The encounters between Chinese and Soviet experts left lasting impressions both of the cooperation but also of the implied competition measured by consumption between the two. Some sixty years after working among Soviet experts, for instance, Wang Mingrong, who worked in a shop serving Soviet experts at a metal manufacturer in Lanzhou, recalled the special perks provided to Soviet experts. Her shop provided immediate access for the experts working in her factory to the cigarettes, candy, tea, and alcohol on offer in her shop. In addition to living in nicer buildings with full-time service staff, the experts received much better food. A colleague of Wang's traveled the country to find special food for them, which always included fresh vegetables and meat. Wang further recalled the pressure to keep up with the Soviets in dress and appearance. Sometimes the pressure was direct. One day her boss requested that all women working in the office who interacted with the experts perm their hair and dress fashionably. She felt uncomfortable but "for the party and the job, I permed my hair."[29]

During the 1950s, in addition to the observed habits of its experts, Soviet exhibitions exposed millions of Chinese to Soviet-style consumerism. For instance, during the last three months of 1954, nearly three million people attended the "Exhibition of Soviet Economic and Cultural Achievements" at the new Soviet Exhibition Center in Beijing, and millions more attended in other cities as the exhibit toured the country.[30] These displays echoed earlier NPM exhibitions of China-made products intended to spread awareness of and consumer preference for these products. In this case, the Chinese state hosted the Soviet exhibitions to present the results of the Soviet Union's form of industrial capitalism as a vision of "China's tomorrow," a visible goal that allowed people to see themselves as worthy of the sacrifices demanded by the CCP. But the visitors sometimes came away with unintended impressions. The exhibits – and the food on offer – contributed to skepticism about the Soviet model, its applicability to China, and even the global competitiveness of its technology.[31]

A third channel through which Chinese people learned about Soviet-style consumerism as part of its version of socialism was Soviet mass media, which in the 1950s poured into China in the form of novels, movies, magazines, and pictorial magazines with photographs of Soviet life.[32] Articles in the journal *Xin Zhongguo funü* (*New Chinese Woman*) renamed *Zhongguo funü* (*Chinese Women*) in 1956, for instance, disseminated Soviet ideas of gender equality in all areas of life – from work and education to vacation and pay. Chinese leaders were eager to demonstrate that they were catching up by touting female political participation at all levels of Chinese society.[33]

Making Fashionable Socialism

The Chinese state imported a Soviet version of socialism that strengthened its citizens' identification with its political and economic goals through self-expanding and compulsive forms of consumerism linked to clothing and fashion. Globally, including in the countries of Eastern Europe, mass fashions helped spread all three aspects of industrial consumerism: mass production, distribution of discourse on fashion, and communication of hierarchical social identities through the consumption of fashionable clothing.[34] During the entire Mao era, party-led industrialization relied on the spread of consumerism, and especially its specific manifestations in mass fashions. Like Paris and Moscow, the PRC had its own national variations of fashion.[35] Fashion in the PRC created, reflected, and sold a variety of different social and political identities.

The party used mass media messages and the example of cadres to promote the ethos of hard work and frugal living. It popularized simple, inexpensive outfits easily identifiable as proletarian.[36] Their durability, functionality, and working-class orientation made these fashions socialistic – that is, fashions purporting to advance the goals of socialism but operating according to a consumerist logic – in three ways.[37] First, socialistic fashions created new hierarchies and subcategories of social and political identity that people could communicate to others through consumption. Second, fashions created social pressure to compete, adding to the compulsion to consume that continued to expand consumerism and capitalism. People who did not pay attention to or keep up with the latest socialistic fashions risked being seen as out of step with the political times. Socialistic fashions, as with any styles, created a new set of rules to pursue cultural capital in the 1950s. Rather than eliminating the pursuit of unequally distributed cultural capital through clothing fashions, fashion built consumerism.[38] Third, in the final analysis, despite state efforts to impose a norm of uniformity among categories of workers, the primary contributor to differences in dress during the era were precisely the inequalities that the Communist Revolution sought to target.[39] Mass-produced fashion expressed, reproduced, and deepened the inequalities manufactured by industrial capitalism.

After 1949, many young urban women with the means to do so soon joined the new fashion trends by replacing their bourgeois body-hugging *qipao* dresses (also known as *cheongsams*) and high heels with loose-fitting cadre uniforms and simple cotton shoes. Some went so far as to adopt men's clothing styles, in particular checkered shirts and working-class overalls with chest pockets; others embraced the clothing preferences associated with farmers and the countryside, such as shirts in floral cotton prints.[40] Urban men often opted for blue workers' outfits topped off with blue caps, or for PLA uniforms, a socialistic style that by the start of the Cultural Revolution in 1966 would become unisex fashion orthodoxy. Likewise, Liberation shoes, the green canvas shoes with rubber soles and toecaps that the PLA troops had worn during the civil war, became fashionable because of their association with the hardworking and frugal peasant-soldiers. In addition to the general shift toward working-class fashions, there were subfashions that communicated social and political prestige depending on the situation. For instance, the color white was the color of choice to convey that one engaged in mental rather than manual labor, doctors and scientists providing the best examples.[41] Socialistic fashions, despite their superficial differences, operated according to the same basic principles as all fashions under industrial capitalism, visibly differentiating people according to profession, age, gender, identity, and class.

In addition to personal identity, people communicated their support of or participation in the Communist Revolution through fashion. For example, Su Xiu, the voice-over star of countless foreign and domestic films, recalled that immediately after the conquest of Shanghai she felt intensely envious of the female cadres arriving with the PLA, who had bobbed haircuts and wore blue hats and blue cadre outfits. She envied such cadres because their genealogy could be visibly traced back to the army uniforms of the CCP's Soviet sponsors. Although no one would have stopped her from adopting the style, she considered that doing so would be presumptuous until she became a cadre, which she soon did.[42] Likewise, business elites in prosperous cities such as Hangzhou switched from Western-style suits into the fashionably socialistic suits worn by cadres. Tellingly, even under the auspices of a Communist Revolution, people with more money communicated their socialistic identities sooner than many workers, peasants, and soldiers. Those unable to acquire the latest styles but wanting to demonstrate their support might do so through smaller acts of fashion consumption, such as wearing red armbands, a fashion accessory symbolic of the revolution that later would be revived by the Red Guards during the Cultural Revolution.[43]

The state both directly and indirectly promoted fashion. First, the state's dictates to civil servants regarding appropriate choices of clothing reveal its role in popularizing socialistic fashions and thereby expanding consumerism. The state issued male cadres with the four-pocket cadre suit, which also became known as the Sun Yat-sen suit, and female cadres received the double-breasted suit that was referred to as the Lenin jacket. State media encouraged people to emulate these Soviet-inspired styles through features such as a 1950 documentary showing Chinese movie stars wearing these suits as they purchased savings bonds to support the Resist America and Aid Korea mass campaign (see Chapter 2).[44] Second, the state responded to the ensuing demand for similar clothing by making versions of these styles available for ordinary people, including the "people's outfit," "student outfit," and "youngster's outfit." These pocket-heavy outfits facilitated a holdover fashion accessory from the Republican era, sporting a fashionable fountain pen or two in the breast pocket. Due to expanded domestic production and state promotion, these styles democratized a trend previously regarded as a symbol of urban education and culture.[45] A third state influence on fashion was through the political elites and their spouses. In the spring of 1950, for instance, after Mao's wife, Jiang Qing, hosted a group of celebrities from film and theater circles with whom she had worked twenty years earlier, her gray-blue Lenin jacket was soon copied by the urban population.[46] Likewise, Vice President Song Qingling, the widow of Sun Yat-sen, long known for her fashion sense, began to wear the Lenin jacket.[47] Fourth, the state mass media, like the mass media in market capitalist countries, through films and newspaper articles informed potential consumers about what to wear to communicate an identity. For instance, the legendary female spy character in the movie *Guards on the Railway Line* (1960) (铁道卫士), Wang Manli, became an overnight fashion icon by wearing a railway crew suit, a style similar to a Lenin jacket, with a fountain pen in her breast pocket.[48] Young women encountered similar variations of socialistic chic through new role models featured in state media, such as the first female tractor driver, Liang Jun, whose image in overalls later adorned the 1 RMB bill, and the first female train driver, Tian Guiying, who was pictured wearing a Lenin jacket.[49]

The Sino-Soviet alliance contributed to the spread of new fashions. As noted above, by labeling such capitalist practices as "socialist," the Soviet model legitimized consumerism and provided political cover for the desire to acquire consumer goods, including fashionable clothing, to express variety and personal expression.[50] In addition, the CCP's embrace of consumerism extended to encouraging women and men to expand their wardrobes beyond basic worker and cadre outfits by adopting middle-class Soviet styles, for example, the mid-1950s state-supported fad of wearing clothing crafted out of colorful fabric, colloquially referred to as "Soviet large floral cloth" (苏联大花布). In particular, the cloth was used to make the one-piece style of dress known as the *bulaji* (布拉吉), a transliteration of the Russian word for "frock" (Figure 3.3). The history of the fabric highlights the specific role of the state in promoting the consumption of fashion. Throughout China, the fabric soon appeared in the wardrobes of males and females from various urban social strata, the latest way for those lucky enough to have access to communicate a new hierarchy of socialistic fashion.[51] This Soviet fashion was initially spread by its use in military and other uniforms and then through coverage in the state media by Soviet advisors and their spouses on the streets of major cities, and by the influx of Soviet pictorial magazines and films into China.[52] From the start of the Sino-Soviet Alliance until 1966, some 750 Soviet films were shown in China, accounting for nearly half of the total number of films during the period.[53]

State efforts to promote consumerism had an immediate effect. In Nanjing, a railway worker witnessed the transformation in the summer of 1951, when young people suddenly started wearing brightly colored

(a)   (b)

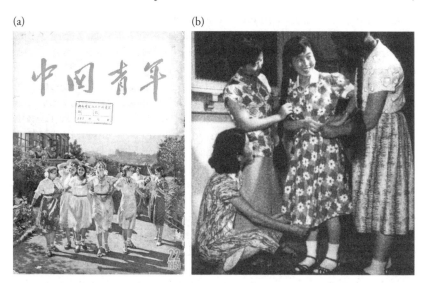

Figure 3.3. Promoting Soviet fashions. State consumerism encouraged frugality but at other times also encouraged the consumption of specific products. With this magazine cover for *Chinese Youth* (3.3a), state media promoted the adoption of the *bulaji*, the Soviet one-piece dress worn by the young women. The stamp on the cover identifies the subscriber as the library at the Lanshan County Number Two Middle School in a rural, mountainous part of Hunan province, suggesting just how widely such images of "China's tomorrow" were distributed. Figure 3.3b (courtesy of Shen Yu) shows women wearing a variety of dress styles helping the one in the center try on a *bulaji*.

checkered shirts. Shi Shenglin, then a teenager, recalled that the state prompted the change by having leaders of work units instruct their subordinates to adopt the new Soviet-influenced style.[54] Professor Wu Yiye similarly recalled that "the first boy to show up at his middle school wearing the new fabric was called up to the front of the class to model."[55] Young women embraced the styles they encountered in films and magazines from the Soviet Union. When the fabric was made into a simple one-piece *bulaji* style, it quickly displaced the *qipao* as a more formal outfit for females. Chinese state media urged young women to adopt the style, describing the current fashion of wearing only blue, the color of worker outfits, as drab, and encouraging them to "dress a bit more beautifully."[56]

Confirming the power of the state to shape consumerism, the *bulaji* style – an outfit quite different from the initial austere socialistic chic – soon became the way to communicate a personal commitment to the ideals of socialism. Although introduced years earlier, the dress became popular after the 1957 release of the popular Chinese film *A Nurse's Diary*, which not only depicts women working in Lenin jackets but also features the *bulaji* style among the protagonist's numerous outfits. In fact, the costume changes in the film are so frequent and conspicuous that critics blasted the dozens of outfits worn by the protagonist for promoting fashion more than the socialist values that the film ostensibly illustrates.[57] As scholar Zhu Dake notes, although the style was considered risqué because it highlighted female curves and exposed legs, China's socialist Elder Brother gave the style legitimacy as socialist.[58] Indeed, on May 17, 1955, Shanghai's *Youth News* (青年报) published an article written by someone using the pseudonym Qixin ("Begin anew"), who cited the Soviet example to argue for more variety and fashion in young women's styles, rather than dressing head to toe in the drab blue color worn by workers.[59] Indeed, an official from a state women's organization argued that women had a duty to make socialism look good by dressing well.[60]

As the foregoing confirms, state consumerism included promoting consumption useful to state capitalism. CCP dependence on the Soviet Union for military and industrial capital meant that promotion of this Soviet style was not voluntary. Overproduction in the Soviet Union meant the country wanted China to desire its cloth, and the Chinese state promoted wearing what it called "patriotic clothing" made from "patriotic cloth" as a way to communicate the proper political stance. Once again, state promotion of fashion worked.[61] As a tailor from Nanjing recalled,

> A lot of printed cloth was purchased from the Soviet Union. Because there was too much, the state persuaded people to buy the cloth. The party expected its cadres to set an example. One type of printed cloth was covered with big peony flowers, a style incongruous with what people were wearing at that time. But people wearing clothing made of this cloth no longer felt shy about it.[62]

Recalling a specific moment when state consumerism urged people to embrace Soviet fashions, Guo Yuyi reported attending a meeting at his school shortly after 1949 when students were instructed that "everyone should wear clothing made from imported Soviet printed fabrics. Doing so strengthens the relationship of our two countries and is a sign of patriotism."[63] As this anecdote suggests, the state once again was asserting the right to define patriotic consumption – in this case, not by buying China-made products, as had been promoted during the NPM, but by encouraging people to wear specific fashions that would allow the state to sell otherwise useless cloth and to profit off its investment. In this way, state consumerism became the demand tool of state capitalism.

The state sanctioning of consumerism shaped fashion trends throughout the country. As Guo Yuyi recalled, female students quickly embraced the new "patriotic" change to androgynous and masculine fashions. The new fashions were more conducive to work than the *qipao* and therefore expressed women's greater utility for work and dislike for useless fashion. The patriotic connotations of fashion made boys and men keen to participate, and many switched from blue and black uniforms one day to colorful Soviet fabrics the next. Guo recalled that even older teachers – a demographic not known for their fashion sense – made quite an impression by changing into the new style. One male student who led this change was the son of a manager of a big state-owned enterprise whose father, Guo suspected, gave him a colorful shirt to help introduce the new fashion. It worked. The first time the young man stepped into the classroom wearing the shirt, everyone "stared at his shirt with admiration, so much so he blushed."[64] The writer Shen Kun notes that these fashion changes spread even to his small hometown in Shanxi province. Shen noticed that after 1949 men quickly abandoned the traditional style for cadre suits and then, at the state's urging, changed to wearing clothes made of the Soviet large-patterned cloth. "When I was still in elementary school," he recalled, "after being ordered by my teacher, my family made me a short-sleeved shirt with the printed cloth. At the school both boys and girls wore colorful clothes."[65]

Others confirm Shen's experience of a far-reaching state-led campaign to promote the consumption of Soviet fabric. When Zhang Quanqing was a secondary-school student in the Shandong city of Liaocheng, Soviet large-patterned cloth suddenly appeared everywhere. His female teachers led the way, using the cloth to make summer dresses and skirts. Soon male teachers also had clothing made from the fabric. But, once again, consumerism revealed its links to inequality. As Zhang recalled, poor rural students could not afford cloth that cost 20–30 percent more than the domestic alternatives. Nevertheless, pressure to change grew, as newspapers promoted the shift with slogans, articles, and photos of local leaders donning the new fashion. Furthermore, the state soon used its control over stores in cities and towns to ensure they were stocked with the Soviet fabric, leaving those who could not afford new clothing fewer alternatives.[66]

A Model "Socialist" Consumer

To promote the consumption desired by the state, party officials imported a propaganda tool associated with the USSR – model workers. One celebrated worker of this kind, Huang Baomei (黄宝妹), became both a national and an international exemplar of the goals of state consumerism (Figure 3.4). Initially

Figure 3.4. Fashioning a model consumer. The party used model workers not only to encourage greater work but also to shape consumption. The model worker Huang Baomei, here shown wearing a *qipao* and wristwatch, for instance, expanded consumerism by democratizing fashion to new social classes. Source: "一位劳模的美丽记忆" ("The Lovely Memories of a Model Worker") in the TV documentary series *Shanghai Stories*, a documentary produced by Shanghai Video Studio.

presented as a model of Sino-Soviet amity and the ethos of hard work and frugal living, Huang Baomei later became known for her wardrobe and lifestyle. By extension, she became a model of the consumerism and material desires that both furthered the goals of the state and extended beyond state control. Huang helped create the model of an ideal consumer who, unlike before 1949, was not a rich capitalist but rather was a worker. Through this use of model workers, the party expanded consumerism by democratizing fashion to new social classes and contributed to the compulsion among members of the new classes to participate by learning about the latest fashions, seeking to acquire them, and communicating identity through their consumption.

Huang Baomei would have been an unlikely candidate to become a fashion icon in China before 1949. She was born in 1931 on the outskirts of Shanghai, never attended school, and in 1944, at the age of thirteen, started working in the Japanese-owned Yufeng Cotton Mill, which in 1948 became the No. 17 Textile Mill. Her ascent from obscurity began in August 1953, when, as a twenty-two-year-old, she was named a National Model Worker in the Textile Industry by the Ministry of Textiles. She earned the award both for her outstanding performance in quality and production competitions and for her political study, including "learning from the Soviet experience."

But Huang illustrates the centrality of the state in expanding consumerism after 1949. What set Huang apart from the thousands of other model workers was the way she dressed and the way she was covered in the state media. In 1954, when she made her first of three visits to the Soviet Union to attend May Day celebrations, she encountered a Soviet Union that had further relaxed its cultural policies after the death of Stalin in 1953. What impressed her about what the party billed as a more advanced socialist country were the fashionable Soviet female workers who wore beautiful dresses with colorful flowered patterns. Upon her return to Shanghai, she changed her own image dramatically by perming her hair, sporting two Soviet-style *bulaji*, and learning ballroom dancing.[67] The state's promotion of Huang by sending her on tours and featuring her in mass media stories had an immediate impact on other workers. As she retold her story, "After I returned from visiting the Soviet Union, I started to wear *bulaji*; workers in my factory thought that I looked good, so they started to wear *bulaji* as well. We also sang the song sung by Wang Danfeng: 'Little swallow, dressed in flowered clothing, flying back here every spring.'"[68] The reference to the song, sung by Wang Danfeng in *A Nurse's Diary*, demonstrates how the mass media proliferated a discourse about products and reinforced the state's call to adopt Soviet styles of consumerism.

In a 1956 newspaper article, Huang described the impact that her trip to the Soviet Union had on her thinking about fashion and lifestyles and their compatibility with socialism.[69] She reported that she had taken a very beautiful silk *qipao* with her to the USSR but still felt ordinary when compared to the women she encountered, all of whom, "even older women," wore makeup and dressed in beautifully flowered patterns. They "really broadened [her] outlook."[70] Even the female workers at a Soviet sock factory dressed better than she did. According to her account, Soviet workers appeared to enjoy life more, as though they "had something to celebrate every day." Huang (and, by extension, the cadres who published stories about her in the state-owned media) felt that the drab Chinese styles reflected poorly on socialism, further justifying Huang's decision to embrace Soviet styles. In 1956, media stories featuring Huang promoted leisure and fashion-related businesses, such as hair stylists and barbers. One article, for example, showed Huang complaining to officials that the workers in a factory district did not have access to barber shops, which led to the transfer of skilled barbers to a local shop.[71]

Huang's path to consumerism through fashion suggests how she – and other consumers of fashion – had to overcome her pre-existing ideas of how she should appear. Although Huang was promoted as a model worker, she soon became more useful to the state as a propaganda tool than as a worker and, like other model workers, she did not return to full-time factory work. The state sent Huang to various places where she wore brightly colored *qipao* to promote Sino-Soviet friendship. At first, she later admitted, she had worried about her bold choices, even wearing a dark blazer or coat to reveal only a hint of her Soviet tastes. But the positive feedback encouraged her to wear the styles more openly, and she soon began wearing *bulaji* as everyday wear. The state then helped others transition to fashion. Media coverage of Huang spread her image across the country and turned her into an object of romantic interest for men and a tastemaker for young women, helping others embrace the pursuit of fashion.[72] The state media that covered Huang's official duties as a model worker depicted her efforts to promote Soviet fashions as her own individual initiative, perhaps to provide some political distance should the state declare that her specific fashion – or even the pursuit of fashion itself – was unacceptable.

In addition to model workers, state media encouraged regular workers to diversify and spruce up their fashion choices. On the eve of Women's Day in 1956, for instance, the labor union at Huang's textile mill called on female workers to celebrate the holiday by wearing Soviet flower-patterned clothing. Even the chair of the union, Wu Xiuzhen, began wearing the style, thereby providing a strong signal to her subordinates to follow suit. Qi Gendi, secretary of the factory Youth League committee, reportedly stated that "sister workers" wore the flower-patterned clothes on Women's Day that year. Wu predicted that the style would become ubiquitous in the future and thus urged department stores and designers to pay more attention to workers' preferences for sophisticated and colorful but not "gaudy" clothing.[73]

Such fashions were "socialistic" because they promoted the idea of equality yet actively undermined its actual practice by doing what all fashion does, that is, creating and accentuating distinctions and hierarchies among people and thereby contributing to the self-expansion and compulsory nature of consumerism. Not everyone who wanted Soviet-style fabrics could afford to acquire them, and many only wore them for special occasions, such as photo shoots.[74] Articles featuring Huang justified her fashion choices, highlighting that Huang, readers, and the state were all aware of the potential contradiction between fashion and the socialist rhetoric of overcoming the inequalities of industrial capitalism. According to newspaper reports, when other female workers initially challenged her decision to dress so fashionably, she replied, "we must learn from the Soviet people and wear more beautiful clothing," thereby using the Soviet example of building socialism to justify her potentially objectionable "bourgeois" behavior. Consequently, the state's promotion of Huang as a role model provided explicit political cover to fashion-conscious women who, due to the post-1949 fashion trends and state promotion of frugality, began to feel uncomfortable following the "bourgeois" fashion trends emanating from market capitalist countries.

Throughout 1956, state media endorsed Huang's choices and her vocal support of fashion as a source of pleasure and beauty. But, in 1957, due to the changes in the political climate discussed below, fissures over the place of fashion in a country "building socialism" began to appear. The media backed away from overtly endorsing consumerism, particularly women's fashions, with earlier advocates such as *Youth Daily* even publishing self-criticisms. Likewise, state organs such as the Shanghai Federation of Labor Unions criticized the bourgeois "tendency to pursue luxury and enjoyment." The party began to express its doubts about the Soviet example by criticizing young female workers known as "fashionable misses," who were always on the lookout for the latest trends and used their salaries to engage in the conspicuous consumption of the latest fashions. Nonetheless, the shift in state policy away from fashion was not absolute. For example, Huang escaped criticism and became a "working-class film star" during the Great Leap Forward. Her image continued to appear in both domestic and foreign mass media. In 1958, she starred in her own biopic, "Huang Baomei," which was voted the year's best domestic film in a competition hosted by *Beijing Daily* and *Beijing Evening News*.[75]

Clearly, the lack of a consistent party position on the utility of fashion, what was fashionable, and material desires made it easier for people to ignore state admonitions to participate in building socialism by simply working hard and living frugal lives. The state ambivalence clarifies how industrial capitalism relied on consumerism and the resultant inequalities. The same state that rebuked consumerism continued to circulate new discourses on fashion when it wanted the population to consume more, as in the case of the Soviet cloth, highlighting the extent to which the state relied on the use of fashion consumption to generate state capital.

Rejecting the Soviet Model of Building Socialism

Throughout the 1950s and into the early 1960s people at all levels of Chinese society, from Chairman Mao to ordinary individuals on city streets, increasingly doubted whether the Soviet Union was an appropriate model for "building socialism" or, indeed, in extreme examples, whether the Soviet Union was genuinely "building socialism" at all. The growing disagreements between the CCP and the CPSU and the popular disillusionment about Soviet-style policies and products reflect the development of different conceptions of what "building socialism" entailed, including how much private economic activity or expressions of inequalities through forms of consumerism such as fashion should be tolerated. Varying expressions of identity resulted from and manifested in people's doubts about the Soviet model. In 1957–8, divisions at the top emerged. Some in the party leadership, such as Zhou Enlai, Chen Yun, and Bo Yibo, wanted to continue emulating Elder Brother and continued calling such emulation "building socialism."[76] But others, led by Mao, saw in the Soviet model evidence of consumerism that was symptomatic of the restoration of capitalism that should be attacked.

Although China needed Soviet assistance, members of the party leadership always harbored doubts about the Soviet model. Party leaders chafed at the terms under which Soviet aid was offered, which they believed undermined the Soviet rhetoric of socialist solidarity.[77] Stalin's Soviet-first policies had forced China to pay a high price for critical technology and to sell grain, its only available export, at low prices.[78] Furthermore, by providing loans rather than outright aid, the Soviets forced the CCP to divert scarce human, material, and financial capital to military expenditures and costly loan repayments, especially during the Korean War, thereby sowing early doubts about the meaning of socialist solidarity.[79] To add symbolic insult to economic injury, the Soviets initially refused to turn over to China a naval base on Chinese territory at Lüshun at the tip of the Liaodong peninsula, a strategically important harbor for control over China's northeast seaboard.[80]

Contrary to what scholars often argue, geopolitics provided only the conspicuous evidence of much deeper Chinese misgivings created by ordinary impressions. The doubts created by the ostentation of Soviet experts residing in China's cities have been described above. Prominent people in China who had experienced firsthand life in the Soviet Union expressed serious misgivings about the appropriateness of the Soviet model to build socialism in China. Several years after 1949, for instance, Mao's wife, Jiang Qing, spent a year in the Soviet Union, where the Soviet preoccupation with consumerism appalled her. The Soviets, she told her biographer, seemed "obsessed" with money. Elites not only had special perks but were outright wealthy, such as one Russian writer who was a millionaire and whose wife had a fondness for expensive jewelry. Jiang Qing was also disturbed by the presence of French-speaking "aristocrats," who dominated the society culturally and criticized her for "not keeping up with latest fashions." An obsession with overcoming individual backwardness by pursuing wealth and consumer products appeared to pervade both the state, with cadres demanding gifts and tips, and Soviet society more broadly.[81] Unlike Huang Baomei, Jiang criticized ordinary women who wore cosmetics for not being "revolutionary." Jiang Qing's nurse at a spa wore jewelry and told an incredulous Jiang that it did not have negative political implications. According to Jiang, the problem was that the Soviet leadership offered no genuine alternative socialist values to the consumerism permeating Soviet society. Nor was Jiang Qing alone in her concerns about the Soviet model. Vice-Chairman Liu Shaoqi, who had studied in the Soviet Union, concluded that the risk of the potentially corrupting influences of Soviet life was still worth the rewards of sending his children to the Soviet Union to study.[82] But he warned a group of students departing for the Soviet Union that the country still had class differences exemplified by "women wearing necklaces and rings with precious stones."[83]

While cultural contacts slowly introduced doubts, after the start of the Great Leap Forward in 1958 Sino-Soviet relations deteriorated much more quickly. The party rejected the Soviet economic model of concentrating on rapid growth and the development of urban industry run by a technocratic elite. Rather, the party sought to, as Mao put it in 1958, "walk on two legs," or to balance urban and rural, and national and local, industry, and other aspects of development.[84] At one level, the Great Leap was an attempt to escape the consequences of Soviet-style industrial capitalism, with its priority on rapid accumulation, including the creation of a privileged urban class that was the functional equivalent of industrial capitalism's bourgeoisie. In allowing for the expansion of such inequalities, the Soviet model was openly subordinating the communist goal of negating capitalism to the more immediate goal of rapid urban industrialization.

Whereas the party's discomfort with outcomes of the Soviet model contributed to the break with the Soviet Union, the Great Leap policies contributed to building a different version of state capitalism. As discussed in Chapter 5, Great Leap policies, both urban and rural, relied on the massive mobilization of unremunerated laborers to facilitate rapid accumulation. The Leap, as discussed in Chapter 2, exemplified in horrific terms the urban and rural inequalities by starving tens of millions of the rural population to save the urban centers of industrialization. This was, as predicted by one observer, the outcome of the state capitalist search for renewed accumulation after the Soviet model had reached its limits.[85] The capital to purchase technology to contribute to urban heavy industrial development had to come from somewhere. Rather than using technocratic elites to drive further development, the party leadership envisioned a decentralized industrialization that took advantage of the country's rural population to engage in less capital-intensive industries that relied on labor rather than on technology. Rural industrialization utilized what China had in abundance, a vast reserve army of labor to generate more "primitive socialist accumulation."

The Great Leap, however, was overly ambitious and overly extractive, becoming another policy that reflected the party's compulsion to accumulate as rapidly as possible, even at great human cost. State policies transferred one-fifth of the agricultural workforce to rural industry and demanded unrealistic agricultural gains to feed the urban and rural industrial workforce, while continuing to repay Soviet loans with grain.[86] The consequence was a famine of nearly unimaginable proportions that killed tens of millions, discrediting both the agricultural and the rural industrialization policies of the Great Leap.[87] To revive accumulation, in the early

1960s the party once again allowed greater private capitalism and consumerism to incentivize labor, thereby sanctioning another round of visibly
inegalitarian material outcomes. Despite its attempts to break away from
the Soviet model, the party continued to struggle with the central contradiction between its stated ambition of building socialism leading to
a negation of capitalism in communism alongside the inequalities arising
from rapid industrialization.[88] Even in its attempts to break from the
Soviet model, the party deepened, rather than negated, the inequalities
arising from the entire state-to-private spectrum of industrial capitalism.

"Phony Communism"

Between September 1963 and July 1964, the CCP published nine
scathing and lengthy commentaries, also known as the "polemics,"
on the Soviet Union.[89] Drafted by a team of party researchers and
propaganda officials, the commentaries reflect both theoretical and
mundane doubts that the Soviet Union was a country building socialism. The party disseminated the commentaries both nationally and
internationally to map out what the party and the Chinese people
would have to do to remain "on the socialist road."[90] These commentaries, especially the final one, confirm that the CCP at this juncture
would have understood my central thesis: on-the-ground realities, such
as the spread of consumerism, demonstrate how policies deemed to be
part of "building socialism" were negating the revolution by building
a state-led variety of capitalism.

Official Chinese worries about the "restoration of capitalism" in private
economic activity had much evidence to draw upon. By all accounts, there
remained a vast number of what the state labeled "underground factories."
The state never had total control over industrial production and distribution, not even after the Socialist Transformation. These "factories" were
more like workshops employing fewer than ten people, and only a handful
employed more than fifty people. Although the state acknowledged the
usefulness of such factories in the gray economy for producing needed
products, it also saw them as a competitive threat for skilled labor, raw
materials, and ultimately revenue. Moreover, Mao and like-minded leaders
feared that such factories were a harbinger of a larger trend for greater
private economic activity and wealth. They also signaled a lack of control,
especially as many "underground factories" existed within state enterprises,
including over 1,100 in Shanghai alone toward the end of 1956.[91] One year
later, Suzhou authorities identified over 7,000 such factories, a situation so

serious that the media accused state factories of "practicing socialism by day and capitalism by night."[92]

Mao and other cadres worried about what they referred to as the "spontaneous forces of capitalism." Those reading the cadre-only circulated news digest, *Neibu cankao*, would have been aware of the widespread problems of the gray economy and private production. Reports poured in from around the country. A report on Sichuan, Zhejiang, and Guizhou provinces, and Shanghai, for instance, recounted how in Chengdu alone, 455 households were participating in underground factories. The factories lured state workers to labor for them, purchased raw materials using the name of state enterprises, and thereby "deprived the state of resources and revenue."[93] A report on Dalian identified twenty-six factories with over 400 employees engaged in work such as construction and truck repair.[94] *Neibu cankao* also recounted rural "profiteering" in Shandong, where farmers were sold fake fertilizers. An investigation revealed thirty-three out of thirty-seven shipments of fertilizer sold to Linqu county were counterfeit, depriving the state of over RMB 100,000 in sales.[95]

Thus, when Chinese leaders favoring greater state control over capital looked to the Soviet Union, they worried not only about the future of state control there but also its future in China. For the party leaders under Mao, behind the nine commentaries the Soviet model of building socialism was a cautionary tale for both international and domestic audiences.[96] The polemics accused the CPSU of being "counter-revolutionary" and "revisionist" (the latter is a term that appears 400 times in the commentaries).[97] Furthermore, Khrushchev was a "phony communist" leading the Soviet Union to a "capitalist restoration." According to the CCP critiques, Soviet policies had popularized capitalist culture, disparaged socialist culture, and transformed the Soviet Union from "a dictatorship of the proletariat into the dictatorship of the bureaucratic bourgeoisie and its socialist public economy into state capitalism."[98] These accusations further splintered the Sino-Soviet alliance, heralded the global dissolution of a hegemonic Soviet model of building socialism, and presented "Maoism" and the PRC as an alternative model that claimed to reject the Soviet shift toward greater market capitalism and the associated expansion of social inequalities.[99]

Although it may not have been the party's intention, at least in the early 1960s, the nationwide and global articulation and dissemination of its argument that the Soviet Union was not truly socialist raised similar questions among many people about what the party was building in China. The CCP leadership and others would have been aware of the criticism of "socialism" from the left. For instance, Djilas Milovan's *The*

New Class: An Analysis of the Communist System had been translated in 1957, and was reissued in 1963.[100] For those in the domestic audience without access to such criticism, these very detailed nine commentaries explained how to detect a "capitalist restoration" through the daily activities of the people around them, and in that way they acted as a mirror for the Chinese themselves. The party used these commentaries to crack down on capitalism in China itself, implementing policies to counteract the implications of its critiques of the Soviet Union. These policies included a series of mass campaigns that foreshadowed the Cultural Revolution: the Socialist Education Campaign to eliminate corruption in the countryside, a new Five-Antis campaign in the cities, a mass propaganda campaign to emulate the spirit of hard work and frugal living embodied by the soldier Lei Feng, and in September 1963, the purge of Sun Yefang, labeled "China's Liberman" after the Soviet economist whom Khrushchev had relied on to justify using greater material incentives and profits in economic management as fully compatible with socialism.[101]

These policies reflected the same critique leveled against the Soviet Union: that "capitalism" was occurring at all levels of Chinese society, including inside the party and the bureaucracy. Furthermore, they highlighted that seemingly trivial transgressions of "socialist" norms – such as cadres taking small gifts, factories producing outside the plan, and men and women pursuing fashion – were everyday manifestations of capitalism that threatened the future of socialism and the possibilities of achieving communism. Although undoubtedly bound up in elite power politics, these party policies countering a Soviet-style slide toward a capitalist restoration were also a genuine attempt to discourage consumerism and increase direct state control over accumulation and consumption, that is, an attempt to shift the political economy away from the post-Great Leap policies of tolerance for private capitalism and consumerism of the early 1960s and back along the spectrum toward greater state control over capital. In contrast with the analyses by scholars of the Sino-Soviet split cited here, which focus on elite power struggles and attempts by Mao to take leadership of the International Communist Movement abroad and to solidify his leadership over the party at home, I embed the polemics in the political economy and therefore also see them as either a genuine concern about the compatibility of the Soviet model and fulfillment of the basic aim of socialism to negate industrial capitalism or, at the very least, a threat to state control over capital.

The party went to great lengths to ensure that cadres and people throughout China learned the "lessons" of the commentaries.[102]

Although these texts were abstract, to maximize comprehension a specially assembled team 400 to 500 strong crafted them in straightforward prose and in the voice of the common person engaged in class struggle against the privileged. For cadres, they were published on the front page of the must-read publications, *People's Daily* and the party's theoretical journal, *Red Flag*. Major newspapers and journals reprinted and discussed them, and state radio broadcast them throughout the country to China's vast semi-literate and illiterate population. The commentaries and other compositions by the assembled team were also printed in the form of pamphlets and stocked by the state distribution network of the New China bookstores. These bookstores, present in cities and smaller towns across the country, facilitated the dissemination of the books and magazines that the party wanted people to have access to. To maximize readership, the team also translated and printed the commentaries in non-Han ethnic minority and foreign languages.[103]

The CCP's most thorough articulation of what capitalist restoration looked like at the grassroots level of everyday life was the ninth commentary, "On Khrushchev's Phony Communism and Its Historical Lessons for the World" (hereafter "Phony Communism," 假共产主义).[104] The text informed readers that during the "very long" transition from capitalism to socialism to communism, socialist countries would face constant pressures to decide between "the road of capitalism and the road of socialism." Invoking the authority of Lenin, "Phony Communism" identified four ways that people should guard against capitalist restorationism. First, they should be on the lookout for the "thousand and one" subtle tactics that "overthrown exploiters" would use to recover their lost wealth and power. Second, they should be aware that the battle would be ongoing because new elements of capitalism would be generated "constantly and sponta-neously." By renewing Mao's 1958 call for a "permanent revolution" against capitalism, the commentary reiterated Mao's rejection of the Stalinist position that the revolution was over and class struggle was no longer necessary in a socialist country already moving toward communism.[105] Third, the people must be on the alert against "new bourgeois elements" arising even within the state and the working classes. Finally, "Phony Communism" reminded readers that the threat of armed intervention remained constant, and that the need for rapid industrialization and, implicitly, state consumerism was even more urgent now that China was facing "encirclement by interna-tional capitalism."[106]

"Phony Communism" provided numerous Soviet examples of the "bourgeois ideology" that the party was trying to address in China through the Socialist Education, Five-Antis, and Emulate Lei Feng campaigns. It cited Soviet examples of private capitalism in factories that had "fallen into the clutches" of "degenerates" and had become "socialist enterprises only in name." Instead, the commentary charged, these factories were "capitalist enterprises by which these persons enrich themselves. The relationship of such persons to the workers has turned into one between exploiters and exploited, between oppressors and oppressed." Examples included underground factories that sold their products illegally and then divided up the profits among the managers; state employees who misused state assets to privately produce and sell fountain pens and other consumer goods; and the re-emergence of labor markets for those wishing to work in such factories. The text cited instances of cadre control over the surplus and its allocation to personal consumption and consumerism as evidence of bourgeois ideology, such as one manager who secretly set up a clothing workshop inside his state furniture factory and made so much money he "had several wives, several cars, several houses, 176 neck-ties, about a hundred shirts and dozens of suits." Throughout the country, the commentary asserted, such people were turning "socialist collective economic enterprises into economic enterprises of new kulaks."[107]

In the two years between the publication of this commentary and the start of the most conspicuous popular attack on "capitalism" with the launch of the Cultural Revolution, the evidence continued to mount that Soviet-style policies permitting greater private capitalism created wealthier private capitalists and corrupt cadres. Irritated by the levels of corruption manifest in material desires, Mao suggested at the depths of the anticorruption campaign in the summer of 1964, "At present, you can buy a branch secretary for a few packs of cigarettes, not to mention marrying a daughter to him."[108] By the mid-1960s, Mao clearly feared that large parts of the party and society had forgotten his 1962 admonition that the country must "never forget class struggle." The party's preoccupation with the specific manifestations of private capitalism highlights that the party was aware of the problems brought about by those economic policies that it had been emulating for close to a decade.

Conclusion

The state helped to propel the expansion of consumerism by promoting Soviet styles, but then tried to stop doing so. When Sino-Soviet relations deteriorated toward the end of the 1950s, Soviet styles faded once they became politically passé or risky. By the early 1960s, a tailor from Nanjing later recalled, no one dared to wear Soviet styles – neither the colorful fashions made from imported Soviet fabrics nor the Lenin jackets that had been popular for even longer and were more widely worn. Even the word *bulaji*, which sounded foreign, was discredited and replaced by the more Chinese-sounding *lianyiqun* (连衣裙), or "one-piece skirt." Ironically, by the time the party had exposed the dangers to the revolution posed by the Soviet model, the damage had already been done within China. The widespread attacks on the cultural manifestations of "capitalist restoration" during the early Cultural Revolution were symptomatic not of China following too closely in the footsteps of its erstwhile Elder Brother and its failure to "build socialism," but rather China's successful expansion of industrial capitalism and its correlate in consumerism.

Although the Soviet Union changed from a model to a cautionary tale that party leaders such as Mao sought to avoid, party leaders could not escape its shadow, as will be demonstrated in Chapter 4. Avoiding the Soviet model did not leave any good alternative models to accumulate capital for industrialization and militarization, especially given China's few domestic sources of capital and the hostility of the market capitalist world led by the United States. Even after China officially broke ties with the Soviet Union in 1960, its influence persisted. The party then faced not one but two superpowers with which to compete, compelling the party to allocate even more capital to military preparedness and consequently to look for new ways to accumulate capital. To solve the capital dilemma, the Chinese state once again turned to expanded control over consumerism, including through the discourses of advertising, propaganda, and films.

CHAPTER 4

State Consumerism in Advertising, Posters, and Films

State consumerism sent mixed messages. Whereas the Soviets provided justification for policies that expanded consumerism, the CCP used its control over public discourse surrounding consumerism to concurrently promote restraint. These forms of discourse included advertisements for products, mass propaganda efforts such as political posters, and cultural products such as films. All attempted to subordinate people's material desires under a blitz of messages proclaiming the importance of hard work and frugal living. Thus, the party's brand of consumerism often attempted to castigate individual material desires as "bourgeois" and to celebrate collective social consumption in its place. Those collective achievements benefited the entire nation by expanding production of goods and the building of infrastructure, including nuclear weapons, bridges, electrification, railways, parks, fertilizer and farm equipment, public education, collective dining, childcare, and health care.[1] But this message was undermined by others.

The party used its growing media apparatus to promote consumerism even as it attempted to shape – and at times to suppress – consumerism's self-expanding, compulsory nature. This chapter examines the evolution of three forms of economic propaganda – advertisements, posters, and films – to reveal the move toward greater state consumerism and the ways the party navigated the central contradiction between its socialist rhetoric and its capitalist policies.[2] Under state supervision, newspapers and periodicals continued to contribute to the fetishization of commodities – the systematic masking of capitalist social relations of production – with print advertisements, including in the party's own mass media.[3] In the early 1950s, during the era of New Democracy discussed in Chapter 2, readers continued to see advertisements for products and movies that were similar to those viewed in the pre-1949 era.[4] These images included refrigerators packed with food, toothpaste endorsed by a racist caricature of a black man, cigarette smoking presented as a complement to a bourgeois domestic life, and women shown with permed hair, high heels, and form-fitting dresses touting cosmetics. Readers of newspapers and magazines throughout the country thus encountered advertisements side by side with political propaganda in the form of photographs of parades, public celebrations of "liberation," and texts of political speeches hailing the advent of socialism.[5]

As the CCP's economic and political agendas advanced throughout the 1950s and into the 1960s, the party placed restrictions on advertising and films to reduce customer demand for consumer products and to downplay the inequality of distribution implicit in bourgeois advertising and screen depictions.[6] New, widely distributed films, advertisements, and posters taught the state's valorized version of consumerism – social rather than individual consumption to build the shared prosperity of socialism. Each of these three forms of economic propaganda, however, communicated mixed and even contradictory messages about the party's plans for material life in New China. Despite the increasing control over the media and the hundreds of advertising agencies, advertising and films continued to generate controversy as state policies and rhetoric about consumerism shifted throughout the era.[7] The proposed solution to the central contradiction was to replace the conspicuously bourgeois aspects of consumerism with a more socialistic, state-endorsed consumerism, and to use propaganda to channel consumer demand in the desired direction.

Advertising Industrial Consumerism

During the early years of the People's Republic, the party's advertising policies revealed how its New Democracy policy prioritized the forces of production over transforming social relations. For example, the party allowed advertising to continue because it helped the party finance the production of newspapers, a key tool for political communication that the party would soon take over.[8] Readers noted the incongruity. Letter writers complained that "obscene advertising" undermined the CCP cause and socialist journalism. In response, the editors of the *People's Daily* assured its readers, including cadres throughout the country seeking guidance on the official party line, that advertising was merely a temporary necessity.[9] Business models could not change instantaneously. Just as the party justified New Democracy as a temporary expedient to persuade capitalists to cooperate until the state established sufficient control to take over private capital, so too the party permitted advertising, which implicitly reassured more affluent readers that "liberation" would not end their privileged access to consumer goods and services.[10] Although the internal party debates discussed below confirm that the controversy over whether advertising was compatible with socialism persisted throughout the entire Mao era, the party attempted to harness advertising by implementing policies that appeared to endorse socialism, including by reducing the amount of product advertising. Nevertheless, people used other means to continue to learn about and acquire products, thus communicating and reinforcing inequalities and social differences.

Advertisements for middle-class products in the early 1950s demonstrate the party's compromises with capitalist practices and the contradiction between socialist rhetoric and advertising policy. The new state wanted to help private companies survive and recover. In the case of Heiren toothpaste (黑人牙膏), this undermined the party rhetoric of solidarity with oppressed African Americans by allowing the company to use a racist name and racist imagery to market its brand.[11] This well-known brand of toothpaste, initially made in Shanghai and later in Hong Kong and Taiwan, was known throughout much of Asia by the English name "Darkie," which appeared in English on its packaging and its logo along the Chinese name "Heiren" – literally, "black man."[12] Like countless other China-made "national products," this brand had carefully chosen its name and marketing materials to lure customers by implying an international reputation. The company's name, Hawley, which was printed in English on its packaging, sounded British, even though four brothers from Ningbo had founded the Haolai/Hawley Pharmaceutical Company in Shanghai's British Concession in 1933. Like countless other "national products," Heiren tried to pass itself off as a slick import. Imitating the internationally adopted American practice of using black figures to sell toothpaste, the Yan brothers chose a jarringly racist name and logo for the product that featured a dark black man (or a man with a blackface) dressed in a black tuxedo and black top hat, grinning ostentatiously with brilliant white teeth shining against the contrast of his black face.[13]

From the toothpaste's first advertisement in the Shanghai-based newspaper *Shenbao* on November 14, 1936, advertisements for the product used common brand-building techniques by making dubious claims, using racial stereotypes, and inventing personal deficiencies to teach people they were backward in terms of hygiene in order to sell the product. Furthermore, advertisements disseminated the idea that people who used Heiren could distinguish themselves from those who lacked the knowledge or the money to overcome their hygiene problems.[14] According to the company's advertising copy, the company had discovered the secret to the supposedly whiter teeth of black people – a cleaning agent hidden in a twig that black people allegedly chewed – and that the company had incorporated it into its toothpaste. In addition to brightening one's teeth, the advertisements claimed, the toothpaste could keep one's mouth fresh for twenty-four hours and ward off diseases originating with bad oral hygiene. By inventing a solution to the "problem" of inadequately white teeth and juxtaposing real people against the impossible standard of their racist caricature, these advertisements planted doubt in readers' minds about whether their own teeth were sufficiently white. These ads thus demonstrated how manufacturers attempted to create an awareness of a personal deficiency, such as body odor, wrinkles, cellulite, unpermed hair, blemished faces, unfashionable attire, or non-white teeth, to sell a mass-produced solution to a previously unrecognized problem.[15] After 1949, the presence of such advertising continued to spur sales and reproduce the culture of consumption-based social hierarchies surrounding the acquisition and use of such products.

One month after the conquest of Shanghai, an advertisement for the toothpaste appeared in the June 10, 1949, issue of the party's own newspaper, *Liberation Daily* (*Jiefang ribao*), which had merged with the popular newspaper *Shenbao*. The Chinese-language advertising copy reminded readers of the brand's long history, high quality, and broad distribution, and, despite the use of a non-Han person as its symbol, it invoked the NPM slogan that "Chinese people should use Chinese national products" (Figure 4.1a). This combination of image and text surprised some readers, judging from a letter sent to the *People's Daily* by Zhang Yi, a cadre in the Inner Mongolia Commercial Bureau. Zhang complained that the package's foreign script and logo had misled him into believing that the product was an American import and he urged that the branding be changed to make clear that Heiren was a China-made brand of toothpaste.[16] In a response, Baichanghang, the private distributor for the product, justified the mismatch by referring to the toothpaste's export market, countering that the product's association with America had helped the company establish its brand in China and throughout Southeast Asia – thereby fulfilling the popular NPM aspiration that domestic products could be sold wherever ethnic Chinese people lived and could contribute to nation-building back home. Nonetheless, the distributor reluctantly promised that "once stocks were depleted," the company would discontinue the logo and the use of English for the domestic market, though not for exports.[17] Yet two years after 1949, advertisements for Heiren had not changed. In an advertisement for the toothpaste appearing in the more

(a)   (b)

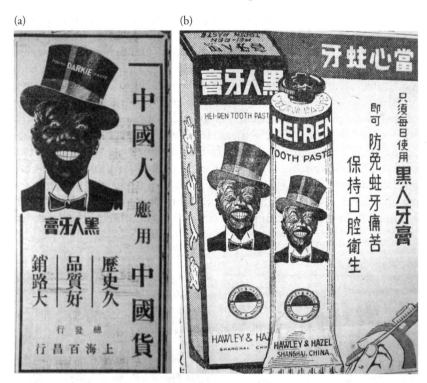

Figure 4.1. Heiren toothpaste advertisements. In this advertisement for Heiren toothpaste in a June 10, 1949, issue of the Shanghai-based party newspaper *Liberation Daily* (Figure 4.1a), the advertising copy reminds readers of the brand's long history, high quality, and broad distribution, and invokes the NPM slogan that "Chinese people should use Chinese national products." Two years later (Figure 4.1b), advertisements for Heiren and similar products indicated that brands targeted at middle-class readers still wanted to associate themselves with the products of imperialism through the use of English text. Note in *Dagongbao* (Shanghai edition) on May 5, 1951, the English print on the packaging receives greater prominence, with the company's name and Chinese location (Shanghai) printed in English.

commercially focused newspaper *Dagongbao* (Shanghai edition) on May 5, 1951, for instance, the English print on the packaging is given even greater prominence (Figure 4.1b).[18] After years of exposure to party discourse, including the Resist America campaign in the ongoing Korean War, Heiren and similar brands targeted middle-class readers who still wanted to be associated with the imperialist products through the use of English texts.

During the seven years between 1949 and the expropriation of private enterprises during the Socialist Transformation completed in 1956, many advertisements retained their pre-1949 branding and marketing strategies. Perhaps reflecting discomfort with the racist logo and its association with the United States, given the Resist America and Aid Korea campaign then underway, in a Heiren advertisement from early 1951, the size of the image of the black man is decreased, flipped sideways, and demoted to the bottom of the frame (Figure 4.2a). Instead, the advertisement features the image of a woman who retains fashionable pre-1949 bourgeois urban markers.[19] This woman, who is wearing lipstick and nail polish, and has plucked eyebrows, long eyelashes, and permed, wavy hair, is shown holding up a mirror to confirm that her smile is brilliantly white and her breath presumably fresh. Advertising here clearly lagged behind other state-led

(a)　　　　　　　　　　　　　　(b)

Figure 4.2. Women sell. In this Heiren advertisement from *Liberation Daily*, February 19, 1951 (Figure 4.2a), the size of the image of the black man is decreased, flipped sideways, and demoted to the bottom of the frame. Around the same time, the party began disseminating images of new forms of femininity associated with hard work rather than consumption, as in Figure 4.2b, a poster from 1954 entitled "We are proud of participating in the founding of our country's industrialization." Source (Figure 2b): International Institute of Social History.

shifts in visual culture during the period, as this woman and her obvious attention to her appearance are the antithesis of the New Socialist woman portrayed in the state posters of the period (Figure 4.2b). Although both women appear to be happy – and both appear to have white teeth and reddened lips – one woman derives happiness from consumption and the other woman – a cheerful young woman with a ready-for-factory-work bobbed haircut and worker pants and shirt, wielding a blowtorch at a construction site – from labor.[20]

Readers of nationally distributed magazines and newspapers, such as the *People's Daily* and *Dagongbao*, and local papers such as the *Beijing ribao* (*Beijing Daily*) and *Ningbo shibao* (*Ningbo Times*) encountered innumerable similar advertisements featuring bourgeois subjects that were directed to better-off consumers. They demonstrate a seamless continuity between pre- and early post-1949 advertising. Take, for example, an advertisement for Ganlu, a product for skin ailments, published in *Liberation Daily* just one day after the formal declaration of the founding of the PRC on October 1, 1949, featuring an attractive woman with long, curly hair wearing earrings, her back arched and chest foregrounded (Figure 4.3).[21] An even more extreme contrast between the stated ideals of the Communist Revolution and the content of an advertisement appeared in an advertisement in the Shanghai edition of *Dagongbao* in January 1951, featuring a woman in high heels standing at an open, full-sized refrigerator and choosing from among its packed contents – at a time when only the wealthiest people owned refrigerators, or had even seen one. The continuity of these advertisements with the pre-1949 examples highlights that, at least initially, the party followed the Soviet lead discussed in Chapter 3 and had few qualms about perpetuating consumerism through product advertisements to serve its more immediate goals.

As the state expanded control over the economy between 1949 and the completion of the Socialist Transformation, advertising agencies and their clients faced the conflicting demands of winning customers as well as the approval of an increasingly interventionist state. Several years after 1949 such advertising shared space with advertisements representing the working-class men and women celebrated in other state media. Although smoking was initially associated with a pre-1949 bourgeois lifestyle, the self-interest of cigarette companies led them to include both bourgeois and working-class subjects in their advertising.[22] An advertisement for Brandy cigarettes published in *Liberation Daily* during the first month after the founding of the PRC depicted an obviously upper-class couple relaxing.[23] Several years later, in 1951, an

Figure 4.3. Advertising bourgeois lifestyles. This advertisement for Ganlu, a product for skin ailments, published in *Liberation Daily*, October 2, 1949, features an attractive woman with long, curly hair, wearing earrings, her back arched and chest foregrounded. Years later, readers continued to encounter such bourgeois advertisements in leading newspapers.

advertisement for My Dear (Meidi) cigarettes featured workers unloading a truck (Figure 4.4a), and an advertisement for Rat cigarettes featured farmers and urban steel workers with the slogan, "Our quality is high and our prices are low. We are geared toward the needs of the working masses."[24] An advertisement for Rat cigarettes in the same year mixed politics and commercial advertising even more explicitly, showing a cadre indulging in a smoke; the text above him reading, "Extremely satisfying."[25] Within two years after 1949, advertisements still sold the same products, but state attempts to make consumerism appear socialist were much more visible.

(a)   (b)

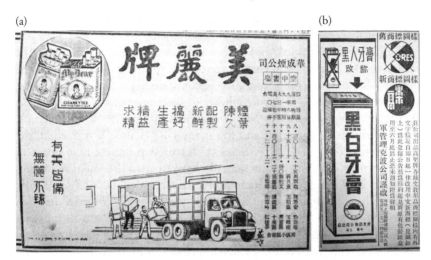

Figure 4.4. Socialistic changes. Although advertising continued throughout the entire Mao era, it did take on socialistic attributes, including the use of working-class subjects in Figure 4.4a unloading the truck (*Liberation Daily*, March 20, 1951) and the elimination of "bourgeois" and "feudal" words and images. An advertisement in *Liberation Daily* from June 23, 1952 (Figure 4.4b) informed readers that Heiren toothpaste had been renamed Heibai ("black white"). As further evidence of the new restrictions on advertising, an adjacent advertisement for the Kores brand of stationery announced, "henceforth our company has removed the foreign text from our logo and will exclusively use the Chinese name, Gaole ['high pleasure']".

The party increased pressure on advertisers to adjust to the prevailing political priorities. By the summer of 1952, the Resist America and Aid Korea campaign and the Three/Five-Antis campaign against cadre corruption and business malfeasance discussed in Chapter 2, and new state-mandated efforts to eliminate racist, imperialist, and bourgeois symbols, affected advertising. The party promoted anti-imperialist movements and attacked the poor treatment of African Americans as part of its Korean War propaganda, and newspapers promised to expunge American film advertisements and products from its pages.[26] Reflecting these changes, an advertisement in *Liberation Daily* in the summer of 1952 (Figure 4.4b) informed readers that Heiren toothpaste had been renamed Heibai ("black white"). The company's racist logo was deemed inappropriate for advertisements, although thereafter it may still have been printed on the packaging.[27] Advertisers replaced this and other newly discredited images with symbols of industrial advances, strong-looking working-class women, and other representations of social consumption that appeared on the propaganda posters of the era.[28]

As the 1950s unfolded, newspaper readers regularly pointed out the contradiction between the party's rhetoric of building socialism and the capitalist-style advertising that they encountered. In 1954, for instance, a reader named Chao Qi wrote a letter to the editor of the *People's Daily* criticizing advertisements for being too similar to capitalist advertisements, with too much exaggeration and too many false claims. Worst of all, the letter writer continued, advertisements featured products that stores or government producers did not actually have in stock, stimulating desires the state could not meet. Such problems extended beyond consumer goods. Chao claimed, for instance, that in order to advertise its own construction crane a company in Dalian had used a photo of a Soviet product, which it had not yet successfully produced and therefore could not be sold. The transgression, Chao asserted, was more egregious because a state-owned enterprise committed the deception and should have "opposed this kind of bourgeois advertising technique."[29] In 1955, another *People's Daily* reader, Wei Baoxian, complained that the state used scarce capital for advertising to attract customers rather than for improving product quality. In his hometown of Jilin, for instance, Wei had counted seventeen "eye-catching advertisements" by a state-owned manufacturer which had signed a contract with the Shanghai-based advertising agency Yongli for more than 500 oil-painted advertisements that it posted on the walls of sixty cities. Although Wei agreed that it had a place in New China, he thought it was a wasteful capitalist practice to spend so much money on advertising.[30] These and other similar complaints demonstrate that the state continued to use capitalist practices to promote consumerism. These may have been genuine letters from concerned citizens or – more likely for the letters to the *People's Daily* – letters from cadres. It is also possible they were manufactured by the newspaper's editors. Nevertheless, here and elsewhere, publication of such letters in a national newspaper confirms that open doubts circulated about the compatibility of "building social-ism" with the spread of advertisements.

State-owned media companies continued to print advertisements and thereby contributed to the expansion of consumerism. After 1956, the state assumed control over all advertising agencies and publications, and accord-ingly over all media discourse about mass-produced products. Yet adver-tising companies continued to use advertisements that contained images associated with the bourgeois lifestyles of China before 1949. In the April 21, 1958, issue of the *People's Daily*, for example, a Heiren/Heibai advertisement from the now state-owned Hawley Pharmaceutical Company printed the image of a woman wearing lipstick and sporting brilliant white teeth (Figure 4.5).[31] The advertisement not only shows that the state continued to use bourgeois tropes and messages from the pre-1949 period to sell products, but also how, in doing so, the state reinforced the inequalities arising from industrial consumerism. Such advertisements implied that women should know how to use the appropriate consumer products to portray a sophisticated, urbane identity – an identity that included lipstick and white teeth. Products such as toothpaste – and the incomes to afford even modest goods such as these – were more available in cities and towns than they were in the countryside. Advertising – and the state policies of income and product distribution – reinforced the growing gap between consumers in cities and people in the countryside. Far beyond expanding a simple notion of inequality based on income, industrial consumerism demonstrated through advertising how those who had (and understood the importance of having) clean teeth could be separated from those who did not.

By the time China completed the Socialist Transformation in 1956, advertising accommodations with capitalist practices had become increasingly subject to criticism. Critiques of the compatibility of advertising and socialism were a longstanding part of the Marxist tradition. According to the orthodox Marxist view, advertising was a symptom of the irrational and excessive competition among capitalist manufacturers. It created false needs and facilitated the further masking of social relations in fetishized commodities. Moreover, advertising expenses took from the working classes' share of the surplus and manufactured these false needs as a way to sell products to the middle classes, reinforcing a major inequality (mental versus manual) by transferring capital upwards, similar to the rural–urban transfer of capital discussed in Chapter 2. In this view, capitalist enterprises used advertising to gain control over the behavior and financial resources of individuals. Such control compelled people to participate in capitalist commodity exchange – they had to earn money to buy those items that advertising claimed they needed.[32] Furthermore, according to orthodox theory, advertising is unnecessary in planned, centrally controlled, and production-oriented socialist economies because production decisions are based on a rational central plan rather than on material desires manufactured and manipulated by profit-seeking private companies. Socialist production aimed to meet genuine human needs, not to generate profits by fulfilling false needs. Under this theoretical framework, the mere existence of advertising in a socialist country was

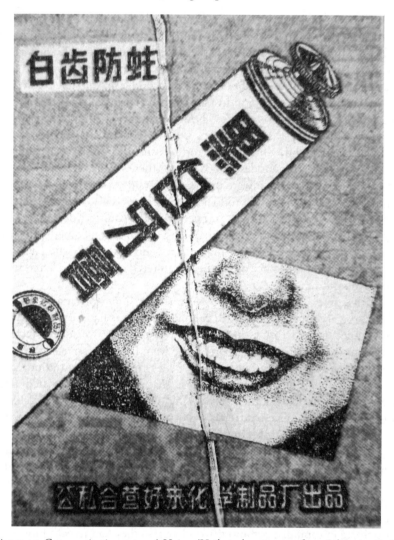

Figure 4.5. Communicating status. A Heiren/Heibai advertisement from *Liberation Daily* on April 21, 1958, demonstrates how a state-owned company also published advertisements that used the image of a woman wearing lipstick to communicate the message that the more advanced women in cities knew how to find and use commodities to compete socially.

potentially a tacit admission that something was wrong with the state plan, and even with the basic economic system. Indeed, the continual critique of advertising both inside and outside the party reiterated this charge.[33]

Critics argued that the persistence of advertising in China in the 1950s corrupted the mass media and the larger public by generating profits through the creation of false needs, teaching people to want things they did not need and constructing bourgeois identities and social differences based on consumption. Such criticisms in the "socialist" countries were longstanding. As Soviet writers Ilya Ilf and Eugenii Petrov observed in descriptions of their travels through Depression-era America,

> the more widespread the advertising the more trivial the object designated in it. Only the sale of utter trifles can pay for this mad advertising. The houses of America, the roads, fields, and trees are mutilated by the boresome billboards. It is the purchaser who pays for these billboards. We were told that the five-cent bottle of "Coca-Cola" costs the manufacturer one cent, but that three cents are spent on advertising it. Where the fifth cent goes there is no need to say. That is quite clear.[34]

According to such a critique, advertising promoted the attributes of bourgeois culture that were decried by the party and undermined the ethos of hard work and frugal living by promoting individualism, indulgence, class distinctions, and inequalities associated with industrial capitalism.[35]

Even after the completion of the Socialist Transformation in 1956, commerce and industry officials repeatedly reformulated advertising policy to eliminate the worst of pre-1949-era modes of advertising, and to create "socialist commerce" rather than eliminating advertising altogether.[36] They shared this project with the ruling parties of other nominally socialist countries that together publicly claimed to create in their economies a distinctly "socialist" form of advertising while privately debating the issue among themselves.[37] At a 1957 conference on "socialist advertising" in Prague, for example, representatives of the Soviet Union, Poland, Hungary, Yugoslavia, and China debated how best to use advertising to create a more "socialist" version of consumerism.[38] A report by Shanghai's Commercial Bureau addressed the conference's discussion about whether advertising was irredeemably capitalist or might serve socialist purposes, and came to much the same conclusion: China's socialist advertising was not the same as pre-1949 capitalist advertising, which it described as having been dominated by "compradors, colonialism, rip-offs, and excessive market competition."[39] Reflecting an unstated recognition that even the nominally socialist state had to control the consumptive behavior and financial resources of individual consumers, the report concluded that it would be a mistake to eliminate all forms of advertising simply because of earlier excesses and, in fact, it recommended that China expand its venues for advertising and put more "socialist advertising" on trains, buses, and other public facilities. Again, following the Soviet example, the report favorably quotes Soviet Minister of Trade Anastas Mikoyan's 1953 defense of advertising as essential to promote trade that was critical to improve the quality of life under socialism.[40] Unlike capitalist advertising, according to Mikoyan, good socialist advertising improved the consumers' understanding of a product, expanded awareness of new products, and cultivated desires for those goods that the state wanted them to purchase. Here Mikoyan provides the clearest example of a definite shift along the state-to-private spectrum of industrial capitalism toward greater state capitalism and the use consumerism to allocate the surplus. To Chinese observers, the Soviet example demonstrated beyond any doubt that consumer demand could drive production, and that advertising, by shaping and directing material desires from the top down, was essential to allocate the surplus back to the state.[41]

The report elaborated on how the state could use advertising and consumption patterns to allocate the surplus. First, advertising should reinforce rational, top-down production decisions based on central determinations of society's needs rather than stimulating irrational material desires from below in the interests of expanding capital. Second, advertisements for products in short supply should emphasize how to use them to extend their lifespans, while advertisements for more widely available and commonplace goods should, as in capitalist advertising, foster desires to expand the market for those goods. Third, advertisements for new products should emphasize their quality, uses, and special characteristics. Following these recommendations, the party engaged in a much more restrictive use of advertising. Readers noticed the smaller number of advertisements and that they were restricted to limited spaces. In contrast to the didactic content of articles in Chinese newspapers, which disseminated the party line, advertisements rarely engaged in the hard sell. Instead, the usual advertising format in state capitalist countries such as China included only the product brand, a basic illustration of the product, and a list of locations where it was available.

The state's compromise with advertising created more work for the party as the state monitored advertising to make sure advertisers did not artificially stimulate demand by exaggerating, or even lying, about a product or its availability. Cadres in the Bureau of Industry and Commerce, for instance, refused to believe that any product could cure a stomachache in five minutes and consequently forced the Shanghai manufacturer of the "5 Minutes to Cure Stomach Aches" brand to change its name to one that implied an hour-long cure.[42] The bureau forbade use of the description of children's baby food as made of "milk and dough" because it did not contain milk powder and it instructed advertisers to call such products "nursing infant pudding," even though such a term did not feature in everyday speech. Similarly, advertisers could not claim that products that were not widely available were "sold everywhere," and the bureau instructed them to sparingly use the ever present advertising phrase "inexpensive but very good quality."[43] Concern with the truth for its own sake was one part of the state's rationale.

The gap between unlimited supply as suggested by advertisements and actual shortages created tensions between using advertising to increase sales and the state's fear that stimulating unmeetable demands would expose the state's placement of accumulation above consumption. In 1959, during the Great Leap Forward and the accompanying massive shortages of products and food, the Ministry of Commerce and other departments ordered local offices to stop advertising products that were not locally available, stating that such advertisements undermined the state's credibility: "When an order is placed for goods in a socialist country and the goods are not supplied, this has a major influence on faith in our country."[44]

The ebbs and flows of advertising underscore the party's prioritization of capital accumulation over elimination of social hierarchies. Although advertising declined throughout the 1950s, the state still tried to find a place for it. In 1959, for instance, the Ministry of Commerce convened a Conference on Commercial Advertising in Shanghai for representatives from twenty-one cities to reaffirm the importance of advertising.[45] When state accumulation flagged, as it did in the aftermath of the Great Leap, the state again sanctioned advertising and other institutions of consumerism.[46] The rationale behind this shift was explained in a 1961 report by the Shanghai Advertising Agency, the source of most national and international advertising copy and images. This internal government report on the recent history and national conditions of advertising congratulated the industry for having eliminated the worst capitalist advertising practices, particularly those that made exaggerated claims and used degrading images, but it warned that the "residual influences of capitalism" on advertising remained. In particular, the report noted that socialist advertising was insufficiently socialist.[47] It criticized, for instance, medical advertisements that displayed images of people suffering, arguing that socialist advertising should show only positive images, and the frequent use of beautiful women who, although dressed in working-class clothing, still struck poses and exhibited facial expressions that "lacked the spirit and emotions of working people." Although the report supported the policy that claimed that good socialist advertisements should emphasize the uses of products and should replace "Western-style" advertisements with ones featuring a Chinese "national style" (民族形式), it noted that attempts to eliminate capitalist boasting made political slogans, such as the Great Leap vow that China would "surpass Britain and catch up with America" in production, appear to be exaggerated when included in a restrained socialist advertisement.[48] Moreover, it noted that designers had a difficult time identifying the national style that cadres demanded, frequently confusing it with traditional ("feudal") images, such as dragons, pavilions, and figures from the past that indirectly advertised traditional lifestyles rather than properly branding socialism with images of workers, peasants, and soldiers.[49] As the report confirms, those overseeing advertising attempted to sell to state cadres a vision of socialism that was compatible with advertising as long as the content appeared to be more socialist.

The proposed solutions in the 1961 report reveal the pressure on advertisers to abandon even modest socialistic restrictions, especially when doing so contributed to state coffers. The report proposed loosening regulations on advertising content, including reducing the use of political slogans and giving designers greater autonomy to create more appealing advertisements. One driver behind these recommendations was the need to increase foreign trade. Citing the example of a high-end export-oriented candy company that had failed to secure new markets, the report concluded that exports suffered because the decline of bourgeois advertising practices at home had made it difficult to create effective advertisements that promoted Chinese products abroad. Designers, it claimed, had become too cautious and unsure about what they could include in their advertisements, and too worried about the political risks at home of making advertisements that could stimulate material desires among customers overseas. The report declared that designers should not fear political retribution for taking their clients' preferences into consideration, and should not worry about things such as setting people in scenery that made them appear to be at leisure rather than "working hard for socialism."[50] This report suggests how the compulsion to compete through products, as discussed in Chapter 1, included the compulsion to keep up with the latest best practices in advertising.

While accepting these recommendations, the state continued its earlier efforts to make domestic advertising more socialist. Advertisers were encouraged to tout the nation's collective accomplishments as a form of social consumption, but within limits. Regulators simultaneously fought ongoing attempts by manufacturers to inappropriately co-opt national symbols for commercial gain. In the spring of 1964, for instance, the Central Propaganda Department ordered a crackdown on the widespread local misuse of Chairman Mao's image and calligraphy in product advertisements and trademarks (as his calligraphy had been co-opted in the redesigned logo for Shanghai-brand watches in Figure 1.1b).[51] That same year Shanghai's Bureau of Industry and Commerce similarly instructed manufacturers not to use national symbols, including the flag or rockets, on "superstitious goods" or other "inappropriate things" such as toiletries.[52] The existence of these debates and regulations illustrates how the state continued to incentivize manufacturers to ignore or skirt regulations and to expand the use and content of advertising – even deceptive or politically suspect advertising – to advance its own economic interests.

Propagandizing State Consumerism Through Posters

As consumer product advertising decreased in China throughout the 1950s, the state vastly increased the production and distribution of posters, a second form of economic propaganda associated with the visual culture of the Mao era. Tens of millions of posters printed in hundreds of designs communicated party-approved messages to advance the goals of state capitalism and state consumerism.[53] These posters preached the gospel of social consumption that lay at the heart of state consumerism – that socialism could be built only through hard work, frugal living, and consuming those items decided by the state. The rhetoric of social consumption informed people that although they might not currently own many of the things they desired, they were now "the owners of the new society" and the masters of the society's collective achievements, including bridges (see Figure 0.1), hydroelectric dams, A-bombs, conventional weapons (see Figure 2.1), and bumper crops.[54] These posters, in effect, enlisted people into the reserve army of consumers, whose members were to be ever eager both to help produce capital through their labor and to accept state dictates about the allocation of capital.[55]

The visual culture of the Mao era and its propaganda posters promoted the overriding goal of accumulation at all costs, and advocated social rather than individual consumption of the surplus. The model for this form of economic propaganda was Soviet socialist realism, which extolled the social consumption of public achievements and cooperative problem solving.[56]

Socialist realist themes of social consumption included, for instance, images of people gathered around a shared radio, rather than an individual listening to a radio on their own. In China, as in other state capitalist countries, advertisements and posters served state capitalism by promoting national accomplishments, such as the Soviet Union's Sputnik or China's new bridges crossing major rivers, thereby reminding viewers that they consumed capital as a nation, not as individuals.[57] Likewise, these countries used posters to popularize socialist holidays, including honoring labor on May Day, recognition of women's rights to equality on International Women's Day (March 8), and country-specific holidays commemorating their respective Communist Revolutions, such as October 1 for the PRC.[58]

Designers intended these posters to viscerally appeal to viewers.[59] Illustrations of economic progress and success included bumper crops, new infrastructure such as trains and bridges, and electrification – all delivered, in contrast to black-and-white newspaper advertisements, in eye-catching color. Posters reinforced the party line with slogans such as "Exert the utmost effort, aim high, and build socialism in more, faster, better, and cheaper ways." Other posters publicized the Great Leap's goal of overcoming China's relative backwardness in capital accumulation by "Surpassing Great Britain's industrial production within fifteen years" (1958).[60] As in "socialist advertising," the subjects in economic propaganda posters tended to be healthy and happy workers, farmers, and soldiers, whom the state urged to work ever harder (see Figure 4.2b). Working harder did not mean sacrificing one's health; most figures – male, female, children, and babies – appear plump and well. Posters thus packaged and sold an idealized vision of socialism, where, contrary to reality, working harder and longer hours without additional pay had no effect on one's health or well-being.

The overwhelming focus of these posters was on production. Even the rarer images that included consumption tended to depict production nearby, reminding viewers that consumption relied on production. Sometimes this economic propaganda was related to a specific mass movement, such as promoting government bonds in the Resist America and Aid Korea campaign during the Korean War, or learning how to industrialize faster by following the industrial model of the oil-producing site of Daqing. Posters unapologetically stressed the need for individuals and state policies to be as productive as possible. A poster from 1960, for instance, featured a rural woman threshing grain and it included the line, "Every single grain is yellow like gold."[61] Economic propaganda posters urged people to expend ever greater amounts of labor power so that the state could allocate "every last precious grain" while trying to limit and direct their desires – their demands for the surplus – to state-approved social consumption.

The number, variety, and placement of such posters skyrocketed during the Mao era, penetrating every corner of the country.[62] As the party took control of the country's commercial publishing industry, it used the power of the presses to advance its political and economic agendas.[63] Posters appeared everywhere: in homes, offices, factories, hospitals, meeting rooms, railway stations, on city streets, and at locations throughout the countryside. The state-run New China bookstore chain, as well as book-stalls, sold such posters throughout the country. Some even appeared on stamps.[64] In the decades before the Cultural Revolution, printers in major cities produced tens of millions of copies and hundreds of designs. The material designs of the posters also reflected the state consumerist emphasis on frugal living that they were meant to communicate: they were durable, inexpensive when produced in large quantities, and multipurpose, useful as decorations in homes, offices, factories, and schools. Posters therefore represented a massification of home decoration, even as they facilitated the further penetration of propaganda into private spaces.

Posters advertised the party's goal of negating capitalism by showing workers of all types and in all regions standing side by side, equally sharing both the burdens of building socialism and the fruits of their labor. The posters were intended to reach not only the literate and affluent middle classes but the entire population, particularly the illiterate, who could "read" the images in posters even if they could not read state messages in newspapers.[65] These images sometimes had the unintended consequence of serving as a striking counterpoint to the lived inequalities of actual life in China. Art historian Shen Kuiyi, for instance, has described how, as a child growing up in Shanghai in the 1960s, he read stories and sang songs that reinforced the idealized poster images of China as a land of happy, prosperous people. But when he was later relocated to the countryside as part of the policy of rusticating millions of urban "educated youth," he landed in rural Anhui province, where the rampant poverty shocked him out of his propaganda-induced naivety about a shrinking urban–rural gap.[66] The memoirs of many educated youth describe a similar shock at the extreme poverty they encountered in rural China.[67] Such memoirs provide first-hand accounts of the exact moments of encounter with the central contradiction between socialist rhetoric and the present reality.

The omnipresence of propaganda posters during the Mao era did not eliminate bourgeois consumerism. Rather, it attempted to sell to the general public a specific, idealized vision of socialism. Posters propagated new specific forms of consumerism to channel material desires and expenditures of capital into channels deemed useful by the state, while also facilitating the extraction of excess labor. Simultaneously, posters allowed the party to sell itself to all sectors of society – even the illiterate could make sense of a colorful poster celebrating the latest harvest. Consumerism and advertising techniques did not vanish during the Mao era; rather, the state reappropriated them to extract more labor and capital from an already overworked and underfed population.

Contesting and Spreading Consumerism Through Films

Well before the Communist Revolution, the Chinese state sought to transform public culture – including its bourgeois aspects – by controlling the media and regulating its content.[68] Similar to political parties in states throughout the world, the CCP saw cultural productions – especially film, a primary form of urban mass entertainment in the decades before television – as a critical medium for inculcating new norms.[69] As Mao Zedong outlined in his 1942 Yan'an Talks, literature and art should serve politics.[70] The party took a two-pronged approach to controlling the kinds of films moviegoers would be exposed to: restricting the supply of and interest in US and non-socialist bloc European movies, and increasing the supply of and appetite for domestic and other movies.[71] In this area of state consumerism, the party was particularly effective, as the state eventually controlled film import, production, distribution, and screening venues.

Alongside its other policies during the New Democracy period, the party initially permitted a more tolerant environment for cultural productions that catered to middle-class market preferences. As long as films did not attack the party or the Soviet Union, promote imperialism, or "support feudalism and bureaucratic capitalism," the party did not require them to serve the new political objectives. Mirroring other aspects of consumerism in the early 1950s, these compromises with respect to content meant that the film business continued much as usual. Even cadres in charge of cultural productions, who had begun their careers in the austere Yan'an days and understood Mao's position on art, tacitly accepted the economic and political needs for such temporary concessions.[72] Like the department store owners discussed in Chapter 5, owners of movie theaters in the big cities did not openly challenge the state's division of products into acceptable or unacceptable, socialist or bourgeois, but rather they pleaded for time to first lure customers back with those films that their customers enjoyed, and then to shift to more ideologically correct films that would promote "socialist" values – and state capitalist accumulation.[73]

Chinese movie directors, stars, and scriptwriters, however, lobbied the new state to immediately ban Hollywood films to aid the struggling domestic film industry.[74] Their efforts, yet another manifestation of the legacies of the NPM, put considerable pressure on the party to live up to its patriotic, anti-imperialist rhetoric. The pressure became so great that moderates in the party, understanding the popularity of American films and reluctant to alienate people newly brought under party rule by forbidding a favored leisure activity, enlisted professional film critics to write articles arguing that the showing of foreign films was compatible with building socialism.[75]

Beyond simply allowing movie houses to continue showing bourgeois films, the state tolerated the use of Hollywood marketing techniques to promote domestic films. For instance, in 1951 the *People's Daily* criticized the capitalist marketing techniques used by private movie companies and theater owners in China to dupe customers, including giving Soviet films titles that made them sound American, releasing the same film under different titles to trick people into buying multiple tickets, and using ads to suggest a film was full of sex and violence when it was not.[76] Rather than eliminating these techniques, at times movie companies and theaters tried to emulate them in the name of socialism. An advertisement for a Soviet film in Shanghai's *Wenhuibao*, for example, highlighted its violence and sex, and numerous Soviet films were retitled to suggest that their contents catered to Chinese tastes. A Soviet film called *Iron Will* (钢铁意志) about a Soviet war hero, which was also shown under the title *Real Human Being* (真正的人), was renamed *Flying General Without Legs* (无腿飞将军) to sound more like a martial arts film, while *The Peddler and Young Lady* (货郎与小姐) was renamed to suggest a melodramatic love story, *The Lovers Who Finally Got Married* (有情人终成眷属).[77] These examples highlight how, by arguing that one could use the tools of capitalism to defeat capitalism, officials introduced and legitimized capitalist practices under the banner of building socialism.

Newspaper and periodical readers once again noticed the contradictions between the omnipresent socialist rhetoric and these ordinary market capitalist practices. From 1949 to 1953, letters from readers complained about such practices. At the end of 1953, four years after the victory of the revolution, the state-run movie magazine *Dazhong dianying* (*Mass Films*) responded to such letters by demanding that theaters not use multiple names for the same film. Attentive filmgoers also denounced the continued practice of entertaining moviegoers with unsocialist content. As one customer complained in the *People's Daily*, "When I went to Daguangming cinema to watch a Soviet movie, ten minutes before the start of the film, American music was played. During the intermission, two fascist German military songs were played, thereby ruining the atmosphere."[78] Even after the Socialist Transformation, critics continued to note the widespread use of bourgeois content in movies and movie-related cultural products. They noted, for example, that *Shang ying huabao* (*Shanghai Film Pictorial*), which was launched in the summer of 1957, had a subscription base of nearly half a million within a single year, in part by pandering to bourgeois tastes with photos of beautiful, buxom "film-workers," as the state now called movie stars. The magazine sometimes did not even bother with the socialistic cover and instead included gossipy coverage of movie stars' family lives and bourgeois appetites, such as photos of their homes and leisure activities like raising fish.[79]

Domestic criticism that the movie industry was too capitalist became more vociferous in the context of the Resist America and Aid Korea campaign that accompanied the start of the Korean War.[80] The movement targeted films: between August and September 1950, members of the movie industry gave lectures to tens of thousands of students at schools throughout Shanghai denouncing "American imperialist films" as "poisonous tools of American cultural aggression."[81] In the autumn and winter of 1950, workers at movie theaters took matters into their own hands and refused to play the offending films; by November, forty theaters in Shanghai vowed not to show American films.[82] Newspapers and periodicals that had already framed America as a land of "false freedom" and "false democracy" clarified the reasons for the boycott: "Friend! Are you still unable to part with American imperialist films? In a time when American imperialism insanely expands its aggressive war, in a time when the people of the world roar, are you still so clueless? Wake up, friend!"[83] Likewise, newspapers ran articles describing the "poisonous" content of American films, warning readers that such films whitewashed the atrocities of American imperialism and squandered resources. To promote support for the ban, one article clarified the state consumerist link between such consumption and costs to national security by claiming that the tens of millions of US dollars consumers had spent on these films in the years prior to 1949 had subsidized the planes and weapons used by US ally Chiang Kai-shek to kill Chinese people and to seduce domestic consumers into buying American products dumped into Chinese markets.[84]

Nevertheless, people expressed ambivalence about state consumerist rhetoric and policies. On September 11, 1950, a weeks-long heated public discussion on American films appeared in *Wenhuibao* when the newspaper published a letter from a certain Chen Cangye, who admitted he had mixed feelings about American films. Chen wrote, "I have always been fond of American movies. After 1949, I began to change my views about watching such films after learning about socialism. But I still have my doubts about the extreme attacks on American movies in the newspapers." Chen pointed out that some "American imperialist movies" also spoke up for the proletariat, citing *How Green Was My Valley* (青山翠谷), the 1941 John Ford film about a Welsh mining family, and he argued that American films were better in areas that had nothing to do with capitalism – they simply had better sets, directors, acting skills, and dancing. Chen further claimed that domestic films should not avoid these features only "because [the capitalists] are our enemy" nor should they emulate the "shapeless" actors and actresses and "unrealistic" scripts of Soviet films just because they were made by socialists.[85]

Chen was not alone in expressing ambivalence about eliminating films the state labeled "imperialist." Another reader, identified only as a Mr. Chen, suggested that newspapers greatly exaggerated reports of fading demand for American films. Citing a news account that claimed audiences for American movies had dropped from 80 percent to 52 percent of moviegoers, he reminded readers that very few American films were still available during this period and he argued that demand for even dated American movies managed to attract more than half of all box office sales. As evidence, he reported that "I recently went to the Meiqi Movie House to watch the American film *Dark City*. The house was full even before the start of the film." In contrast, when he went to watch a Soviet movie with his brother and sister, the audience was much smaller.[86] Such endorsements of American films continued to pour in, leading a *Wenhuibao* editor to comment that "we have received more than ten letters supporting Chen Cangye's position, which means people remain fond of American imperialist movies."[87]

The state made several efforts to dislodge popular preferences for films from market capitalist countries because they sent capital overseas and undermined state consumerism by inculcating bourgeois values. The Movie Administration Office, for example, mandated higher ticket prices for films from capitalist countries to encourage consumers to "voluntarily" choose the less expensive Soviet and Chinese "progressive films." Middle-class filmgoers, however, could afford to pay more (and often did), so the office also required private theaters to limit the number of showings of American and British films and to show Soviet and Chinese films at least one out of every four weeks. The office also limited advertising for American and British films, raised taxes on such films to make admission more expensive and financially risky for movie house managers, and created bureaucratic obstacles, such as introducing a mandatory movie registration system (thereby cracking down on movie smuggling from Hong Kong). These market controls reduced consumer access to imported films from market capitalist countries, cutting ticket sales from nearly 800,000 in April 1949 to fewer than 450,000 by the end of May 1949.[88] By November 1950, a state-mandated boycott all but ended the public showing of American films. By December, with little hope of improving relations with the United States, the state formally forbade the import of new American films.[89]

Meanwhile, officials promoted the Soviet and Chinese films that filled the void left by the decreasing number of films from market capitalist countries. Between 1949 and 1953, China officially imported 234 full-length films, first from the Soviet Union, but later from Czechoslovakia, Hungary, and Japan.[90] In contrast to American films, one film magazine argued, socialist films were "people's movies" intended to inculcate socialism and promote "working-class thinking." To encourage demand for such films and make movie theaters more attractive to working-class audiences, the Movie Administration Office, in a massification of the movie industry, dispatched representatives to schools and factories to urge students and working-class people who had never attended movies to visit en masse. These representatives used sales tactics otherwise forbidden to advertisers, such as offering discounts to groups and anyone subscribing to *Mass Films*, a new film magazine designed to promote film consumption, and encouraged the establishment of film clubs and film lecture series. The office also attempted to attract people who would otherwise not see a film by establishing new theaters in working-class neighborhoods, abolishing toilet fees, replacing the English-language signs "Enter" and "Exit" with the Chinese equivalents, making it easier to buy tickets, and introducing a phone reservation system, a ticket-delivery service to factories, and even traveling ticket booths.[91]

Efforts to attract new viewers extended to the deployment of thousands of traveling film-projection teams that brought state-designated films to audiences in smaller venues such as schools, smaller towns, and the countryside.[92] Members of these factory worker and rural audiences reported being bored and confused by the new heavily didactic movies, especially by the Soviet movies, so the film teams were instructed to explain the meaning of the films beforehand.[93] Despite such efforts, progressive Chinese and Soviet films struggled to attract the same number of moviegoers as Hollywood films. In 1949 the mere rumor that American films would be banned set off a minor frenzy of fans attempting to catch one last American film. Foreshadowing a pattern seen throughout the Mao era, state consumerist efforts to reduce demand backfired by making bourgeois products scarcer and thereby increasing their desirability and market value. Even after the ban on the import of American and other films, state media continued to encounter resistance. In particular, many avid filmgoers did not like Soviet films. Sometimes viewers became so bored that they would leave the theater early, prompting newspapers to publish articles stating that it was inappropriate to leave movie theaters before the end of a film.[94]

In addition to increasing the marketing of ideologically useful films, the party also attempted to increase the number of politically acceptable movies to help fill the gap and keep movie theaters afloat. Although Chinese filmmaking in Shanghai had undergone what became known as a golden period in the 1930s, Chinese filmmakers had fled the city during the 1937–45 Japanese invasion. Production resumed following the war, and after 1949 the party encouraged private studios in Shanghai to make new films. In 1951, however, the government banned pre-1949 Chinese films as well as imperialistic foreign films, and formed a Film Steering Committee to "re-educate" workers in the private studios. Not content with these efforts, the state in 1953 incorporated private studios into the state-run Shanghai Film Studio. By 1954 the state had taken over foreign- and Nationalist-owned studios, claiming they enriched officials and their cronies at the expense of the people, labeling them bureaucratic capitalist enterprises. The state-run National Film Distribution Company further controlled cultural consumption by monopolizing the distribution of all foreign and domestic films.

Movie theaters – the point of contact with consumers – were the last businesses in the supply chain that the state expropriated and converted into joint state–private enterprises during the mid-1950s Socialist Transformation.[95] The last link was completed in the state capitalist chain connecting state control over film production with state control over the options presented to consumers as choices. In brief, all films produced during the Mao era – more than 600 feature movies and more than 8,000 documentaries and newsreels – were made, distributed, and marketed as part of party efforts to sell its policies as "building socialism."[96]

These state-produced films supplied countless examples of "socialist" values of hard work and frugal living. Tractors became heroes, symbols of the virtues of collectivization; women protagonists championed gender equality by operating heavy machinery and trains in films such as the 1950 *Female Locomotive Driver* (女司机).[97] The protagonists of these films demonstrated these values by sacrificing their own interests and personal comfort for national goals; the antagonists exhibited capitalist values by lusting for material goods and individual distinction. Above all, the heroes of these films cooperated and struggled for the common good, while the villains displayed individualism, hedonism, and a desire to enjoy life without labor, all basic attributes of that capitalist society that the party claimed the Communist Revolution would negate. Movies with these often heavy-handed and didactic themes were viewed billions of times throughout the country.[98]

In 1964, the same year as the party's dissemination of the ninth commentary, "On Khrushchev's Phony Communism," condemning the restoration of capitalism in the Soviet Union, the well-known film *Never Forget* (千万不要忘记) spread the state consumerist message that the desire to distinguish oneself through personal possessions undermined socialist values. The film's title was meant to remind audiences to abide by Mao's admonition that one should "never forget class struggle" (千万不要忘记阶级斗争). Otherwise, material temptations would seduce them, as they did the film's protagonist, a model worker named Ding Shaochun. Set in a residential complex for workers, the film follows the young adulthood of Ding, who grows up in a comfortable working-class family and has a job at his father's factory. After Ding marries the daughter of a former private store owner, he begins to want nice things. On an outing with his wife to a department store, the couple spot a nice blue outfit, but they leave disappointed because they do not have the RMB 148 (roughly the price of a bicycle) to pay for the suit. Later, his new mother-in-law (reviving the NPM-gendered trope of women as particularly decadent and unpatriotic consumers)[99] begins to debase his proletarian attitude by hatching plans, including borrowing money to buy the suit and selling the ducks Ding hunts on gray markets, to make money so the family can enjoy nicer clothing and better food. Soon Ding turns into a dandy (Figure 4.6), and his sideline work and preoccupations with consumption distract him from his primary job, a job contributing to the building of socialism for the nation. One day he loses his key in a giant generator. If the machine had been turned on, it would have exploded, threatening the entire production line and the lives of those who worked around the

(a)   (b)

Figure 4.6. Class struggle forgotten and remembered. In 1964, the same year as the dissemination of "On Khrushchev's Phony Communism," the CCP's condemnation of the restoration of capitalism in the Soviet Union, the hit film *Never Forget* spread the state consumerist message that the desire to distinguish oneself through personal possessions undermined socialist values. In the film, the model worker protagonist is seduced by his desires to acquire nice things after encountering an expensive suit at a department store. To pay for such things, including the suit that he eventually buys (4.6a), he diverts his labor power into illicit activities such as hunting (note the rifle on the hook in the background). His appetites for nice things grow. Figure 4.6b shows him, with his mother-in-law's approval, trying on a leather jacket he borrowed to impress a visiting superior. Source: 千万不要忘记 (*Never Forget*), Beijing Film Studio.

machine. But the workers and the plant narrowly escape disaster when a co-worker finds the key. Chastened, Ding learns his lesson to "never forget" the insidious way bourgeois material desires undermine the building of socialism.

State media coverage of the film reinforced its central message. Local newspapers printed letters from moviegoers that were intended to teach readers how to search their own lives for signs of incipient bourgeois tendencies, something they were meant to do by keeping diaries.[100] In one such letter, Zhou Wenlin, a PLA soldier stationed in Hangzhou, confessed to having succumbed to pervasive bourgeois thoughts, similar to those of Ding Shaochun. Once, when he observed someone wearing a wristwatch, he felt the compulsion discussed in Chapter 1 to buy one for himself. He borrowed RMB 40 to acquire it, which later led his superior to chastise him.[101] In another case, Li Arong, a production team leader at an automotive parts factory, confessed to failing to warn his children of the seductiveness of material goods. When his eldest son, a cadre based in the countryside, asked to buy a wristwatch, a bicycle, and some nicer clothing,

Li did not like the idea but concluded the money was his son's to spend. His son's desires to acquire, however, did not end there, as he later borrowed RMB 200 from his collective farm to build a house, a flagrant example of using the surplus for private consumption rather than for state reinvestments in production. That was the final straw for Li, who called a family meeting to discuss the film and the errors of forgetting to struggle against bourgeois thoughts and actions. Disgraced, his son promptly sold his wristwatch and bicycle and repaid his debts.[102]

Yet the party could not force filmgoers to desire their state-produced films, much less learn their intended lessons, any more than it had been able to convince them to enjoy Soviet movies. In a futile attempt to win over these moviegoers and gain new audiences, domestic movies both directly and indirectly borrowed strategies they had earlier castigated as bourgeois in foreign films. Chinese films thus provided viewers with what they expected to see in a film, even if they held it up for criticism – bourgeois fashionable dress, hairstyles, home and office furnishings, and other scenes of urban consumerism. Products such as fountain pens, wristwatches, household furnishings, and other luxury products had near-supporting roles in films, like the leather jacket in *Never Forget*, and the multiple costume changes in *A Nurse's Diary* mentioned in Chapter 3. Moreover, onscreen consumerism influenced more than the moviegoers, as advertisements and popular discussions of these films spread their influence far and wide.

In spite of state efforts, audiences often took different messages from these films than the state intended them to receive. Like the critics who saw the tale of self-sacrifice and dedication presented in *A Nurse's Diary* but also noted the film's fashion sensibilities, urban viewers studied films for the fashion and consumer tips they provided rather than for their party-approved messages (Figure 4.7). Rural residents, for their part, often received unintended messages or no message at all. State films that promoted the values of social consumption in a clumsy way did not always do well in the countryside, as Meng Liya discovered when he went to Fenyang county with two other cadres to investigate the reception of the movies of New China. While there, the cadres played four films – *Bumper Harvest, A Wave of Unrest, Summer Story,* and *Spring in the Marshes* – for 800 primary school teachers and local cadres, and conducted two forums about "rural films" (农村电影), the genre of film that depicted agricultural production.[103] The results were overwhelmingly negative: the audience dismissed them as "propaganda films" (宣传片) filled with "narrow themes, boring stories, and dull characters." In the next village, Meng planned to play two rural films, but the film squad informed him that

(a)

(b)

Figure 4.7. A nurse's fashion sense. Films such as *A Nurse's Diary* promoted self-sacrifice as a defining attribute of socialism. However, as illustrated by the screen shots, the same films also promoted consumerism by indirectly advertising consumer goods. In the film, the protagonist wears multiple watches and many different outfits, including a *bulaji*-style nurse's uniform.

audiences hated this genre and that if he screened two, no one would come to watch. When evening arrived, the cadres screened just one such film along with a war movie. Half the audience left in the middle of the rural movie, and the rest remained only to view the war movie.[104] Finding a balance between "socialist" messaging and popular preferences proved difficult, mirroring the state's difficulty in balancing its rhetoric of "building socialism" with its policies of extracting surplus labor.

Audience reactions to Hong Kong films highlight the state's failure to limit consumerism. When Chinese theaters stopped showing Hollywood films, Hong Kong films became a politically acceptable alternative until the early 1960s, even during the height of the Great Leap Forward's emphasis on production and anti-consumerist propaganda. In Shanghai, for example, between 1959 and 1962, twenty-nine Hong Kong movies were screened, nearly all of them to sold-out audiences. In contrast, during the Great Leap Forward showings of Chinese movies, such as *Evergreen*

(常青树) and *Steel City Tiger* (钢城虎将), two films about workers overcoming obstacles to increase steel production, recorded far smaller audiences; one theater with 1,230 seats reported selling only about a fifth of the available tickets.[105]

The popularity of Hong Kong films presented several problems for the state. Ticket sales for Hong Kong films represented a waste of hard currency, and the desire to see these films subverted the state's ability to command the economy and drive capital toward state accumulation. In the early 1960s, rumors that the new Hong Kong film *The Lady Racketeer* (美人计, 1961) would soon come to Shanghai's screens led to a huge rush to buy tickets, with people queuing for up to six days and causing several fistfights. A gray market soon sprang up, further siphoning consumers' discretionary capital into non-state ventures. More egregiously, the bourgeois content of these films drove much of the demand for tickets. According to studies by Shanghai's Propaganda Ministry and Youth League, viewers found Hong Kong films appealing because of the bourgeois lifestyles on display, including the fancy dress parties and dancing.[106] Even the more didactic Hong Kong films that focused on the lives of the poor influenced consumers' tastes in hairstyles and clothing, leading to the "Hong Kong style" coming under direct attack during the Cultural Revolution (see Chapter 6). Young urbanites throughout the Mao era emulated these images of bourgeois Hong Kong lifestyles. As soon as new clothing, hair, or shoe styles appeared in Hong Kong movies, copies could be found on the streets of Shanghai. Others participated by trying to learn English on the off-chance of one day being able to visit Hong Kong. One female apprentice admitted to stealing cash from her workplace to buy the clothes on display in a popular Hong Kong movie, *The Beggar Girl* (垃圾千金, 1958).[107] The filmic juxtaposition of Hong Kong and Shanghai in the viewers' eyes undermined faith in China's progress in building socialism by showing how much better the alternative appeared to be. Indeed, the party's own surveys discovered that young filmgoers compared their material circumstances to those portrayed in Hong Kong films and concluded that ethnic Chinese in Hong Kong – even under imperialism and capitalism – had better lives. After seeing *The Lady Racketeer*, a young worker concluded that, "In Hong Kong, life is free and there is everything that you need, unlike here. We need a ration coupon just to eat."[108]

Finally, Hong Kong films underscored the failure of state consumerist policies in all three areas that define consumerism: urban sophisticates' procurement of tickets to Hong Kong films (a mass-produced good); watching Hong Kong films meant participating in a discourse around that good; and being overheard talking about the films became status markers, a way of communicating identity through consumption that is fundamental to consumerism. This use of Hong Kong films spread despite state attempts to produce domestic substitutes and to limit the popularity and influence of imports, or at the very least to present films from market capitalist countries as cautionary tales of bourgeois indulgence. Labor unions, the Communist Youth League, and work units largely replaced individual filmgoers as the primary purchasers of tickets to such movies. Despite being bombarded with warnings that such films were ideologically incorrect and promoted "petty bourgeois" values, these groups openly and consistently sought to watch them.[109]

At times, the authorities tried to harness the popularity of Hong Kong films for state capitalist ends. In 1959, for instance, the Shanghai Film Bureau decided to issue more licenses to more Hong Kong movies to increase municipal revenues, but such efforts led to a frenzy of interest and even violence. At the Daming Cinema, people smashed exit doors and seats, and at least ten people climbed in through the roof to get tickets. At the Huaihai Cinema, some queued for six days and nights to buy group tickets. At the ticket office in Culture Square, 3,000 to 4,000 people crowded for tickets, and policemen and members of the Communist Youth League were sent to the square to maintain order. In response, the state, as was its wont, attempted to implement more socialistic distribution regulations. In 1960, for instance, the Shanghai Film Bureau imposed greater controls. On the supply side, it imposed only light oversight of Hong Kong films that highlighted the evils of capitalism, but it limited distribution and ticket sales of films glorifying bourgeois lifestyles. On the demand side, the bureau criticized Hong Kong films through articles in state media, including newspapers posted around the city in public display cases, that explained how to interpret and critique such films.[110]

In 1962, during the shift in the institutional arrangements of capitalism away from state capitalism and toward greater use of markets and private accumulation following the Great Leap, yet another "fad for Hong Kong films" began, with even longer queues for tickets, even worse disorder, and rampant ticket scalping. Police responded with more crackdowns and the Shanghai Film Bureau imposed new rules intended to restrict people's ability to procure and to sell tickets on the gray market. Although these actions did reduce the more public manifestations of consumerism, such as queues and riots, such activities never disappeared completely because the state could not reduce material desire, much less transform it into a socialist variety. The party admitted defeat, and in 1963 it banned Hong Kong feature films.[111] State consumerism only attempted to reorient material desires, rather than to eliminate their origins in self-expanding industrial capitalism. For those living in cities with access to the latest Hong Kong films and other new goods and services, the party's socialist rhetoric appeared to be less appealing compared to the compulsion to see the newest overseas films and to acquire the latest fashions.

Conclusion

During the Mao era, party policies surrounding economic propaganda did not shift the country along the spectrum of state-to-private industrial capitalism toward greater state capitalism in a monolithic, unilinear, or uniform way. The institutional arrangements of capitalism changed over time in response to economic circumstances and resistance from domestic critics. Although the party's stated goal was to build socialism en route to communism, which required eliminating market consumerism, it had to accumulate capital to pay for never-ending military costs, a growing bureaucracy, and industrialization. But as this and other chapters show, the party's need to prioritize immediate economic needs over long-term goals repeatedly stymied state efforts to replace consumerism. Furthermore, such compromises simply reproduced and expanded the very consumerism the state was targeting, thus undermining the espoused socialist values. Yet, anxious to retain control over capital, the party attempted to shift the institutional arrangements of the political economy back toward greater state consumerism and away from allowing advertising that stimulated "bourgeois" desires. In 1965, for instance, the Shanghai Film Bureau, which regulated film production, criticized film studios for producing movie advertisements that included too many images of stereotypical Western activities, household living environments, and clothing styles, arguing that they implicitly promoted Western capitalist lifestyles and undermined attempts to inculcate socialist values.[112]

CHAPTER 5

State Consumerism in the Service Sector

Writing in 1959, the influential economist Xue Muqiao claimed that, just ten years after the establishment of the People's Republic and three years after the conclusion of the Socialist Transformation, everything had changed. According to Xue, the party was indeed building socialism. Public ownership of the means of production meant that workers were no longer "alienated" from the fruits of their labor and the "surplus value" they had once generated for capitalists had been transformed into "socialist profit" (社会主义的赢利). The state had replaced exploitative wage labor with fixed salaries for state jobs and shares of the profits for collectives. As a result, labor had become "honorable" and profiting off the exploitation of others was considered "disgraceful." After the Socialist Transformation of the social relations of production, because workers rather than capitalists controlled the means of production, they tirelessly expanded the forces of production. As Marxists had long predicted, the negation of capitalism and succession to socialism with the introduction of new social relations of production had expanded the forces of production.[1]

But socialism promised more than material goods. If the transition to socialism described by Xue had occurred, ordinary citizens would have expected a similar transformation in their shopping experience away from the pre-1949 realities of luxury consumption for the few and deprivation for the rest. Party policies leading up to the Socialist Transformation "massified" consumption by providing more goods to laboring people (as did every variety of industrial capitalism across the state-to-private spectrum elsewhere in the world). Similar to the economic propaganda in Chapter 4, shopping and other service-sector industries created unintended consequences, depending on how customers interpreted their experiences. Unlike propaganda, however, shopping not only produced images, ideas, and desires but also immediate and tangible manifestations of inequality and social and class-based hierarchies. Whereas Shen Kuiyi, the rusticated student mentioned in Chapter 4, had to move from Shanghai to the

133

countryside to witness first hand the contradiction between propaganda and reality, people merely had to walk into a store to experience the consumption-based hierarchies and inequalities in their daily lives. Consumers, such as the former salesclerk Zhu Zhongyu, had expected that the Communist Revolution would provide a superior shopping experience for people on both sides of the sales counter. In theory, as owners of the means of production, clerks would no longer fear their capitalist bosses and shoppers would no longer fear being cheated by defective products and deceptive sales tactics in a capitalist mode of production designed to maximize profits.[2] The Ministry of Commerce's "socialist commerce" (社会主义商业) should have provided an anxiety-free socialist shopping experience. According to Zhu, the forced smiles of service workers under capitalism should have been replaced by "genuine socialist smiles" on both customers and clerks – and metaphorically on the state, which would benefit economically and politically from a satisfied population.[3]

Yet such "socialist smiles" failed to materialize. Neither service-sector workers nor their customers had much to smile about. Clerks experienced shortages of products to sell, irate customers, and long hours, and customers faced queues, shortages, and unhelpful, inexperienced clerks. As this chapter shows, the problems on both sides of the counter resulted from the central contradiction between the discourse of "liberation" – including the liberation of both service workers and their customers – and the policies of state capitalism. The party's prioritization of rapid industrialization at the expense of meeting the demand for more daily necessities underpinned its failures in the service sector. It was not the vague catch-all of socialism, but rather the state capitalist policies that explain the problems.

Even state media admitted that shopping under socialism could be grim. Nearly a decade after 1949, a *People's Daily* article wondered, "Why can capitalist commerce accomplish things that benefit consumers, while our socialist workers cannot? Shouldn't our service for consumers be better?"[4] As Xue Muqiao conceded in 1981, a moment when it became possible to openly criticize aspects of state control over the economy during the Mao era, the low quality of service at state-owned stores had political implications and had caused "harm to the prestige of socialist commerce."[5] Despite state efforts, the definition and practices of socialist commerce changed in response to the current economic and political contingencies, particularly the need to accumulate more rapidly. Although the party attempted to find ways to improve distribution and consumption, and adopted and aborted socialistic experiments, it never abandoned its overriding goal of using the country's limited resources to industrialize. The state wanted "socialist" experiments related to retailing and distribution to maximize control over labor, and to eliminate the siphoning of profits from the state rather than to "build socialism," and to create an ideal socialist marketplace. This chapter reinterprets state policies toward retail and distribution to show how party control over retailing may have fulfilled one goal of eliminating a class of people who profited through trade rather than through labor, but did so to better help the state control consumption.

Creating "Socialist Commerce," 1949–1958

In the People's Republic, state-controlled department stores became capital-intensive and technologically sophisticated means to generate, shape, and control demand. These were state versions of private retail institutions closely linked to industrial consumerism. During the Republican era, after they had encountered them abroad, Chinese had returned to establish the earliest department stores in Hong Kong and then in China.[6] Although the number of large retail stores had grown in the pre-1949 period, during the 1950s the state financed the creation of a national chain of smaller versions of the original department stores. Such state-owned chains represented a state-based, rather than a private capitalist-based, spread of a critical institution in industrial capitalism's capital-intensive retailing.[7] CCP efforts in the retail sector were part of a large, complex, and concerted effort to create what it described as "socialist commerce." First, long before the state took official control over commerce in 1956, it had set up organizations such as the China Department Store Company in April 1950 to distribute and manage the retailing of consumer products. The company was able to take on this immense task because within months after its establishment it had created a network of over one hundred stores across China, which by 1963 had grown to nearly 20,000 retail stores with some 2.4 million employees.[8] By 1951, for instance, the Zhejiang provincial government had established seventy-one new stores, including nineteen branches, a number that grew to 182 by 1954, by which time it had established stores in every county in the province.[9] Second, such stores affected sales and distribution beyond in-store customers by pioneering new retailing and distribution practices, including pre-order, mail-order, and purchases on credit, even for luxury items such as imported women's watches and cameras.[10] Party policies thus established the infrastructure for industrial consumerism, while state consumerist policies were attempting to suppress and channel consumer demand.[11]

The creation of a national network of department stores extended consumer products and practices of consumerism into the lives of millions who had never before experienced them.[12] The state's transformation of what had been high-end department stores into institutions serving a broader public attempted to convert the middle-class and the elite-focused consumerism of bourgeois department stores into something that reflected the needs and served the interests of a wider cross-section of society, or what the party called "the masses."[13] By massifying the retail experience through state-owned department stores, the party sought to begin marshaling the resources of this untapped, reserve army of consumers. The term that government officials used to describe this transformation of a bourgeois institution into a more "socialist" one is inelegant in both English and Chinese: "massification" (dazhonghua 大众化). Although dazhonghua is often translated into English as "popularizing," suggesting "popular" consumption and consumerism, the English term fails to communicate the party's goal. Whereas popularization seeks to make consumer goods widely available, massification intends to make consumer goods available specifically to "the masses" who labored rather than to the wealthy who lived off the labor of others.[14]

The highest-profile targets for massification were the large department stores in the major cities that served an elite clientele. As noted in Chapter 2, the party, following the doctrine of New Democracy, initially sanctioned bourgeois elements of Republican-era consumerism such as luxury products and department-store-based dance clubs, even as it began to restrict and criticize such consumerism. In terms of retailing, the post-1949 history of Shanghai's Nanjing Road area highlights the uneasy tension between tolerance and criticism. Nanjing Road was at the time the country's pre-eminent shopping street. The road and adjacent area were home to the established pillars of Republican-era consumerism, the Four Great Department Stores of Shanghai: Sincere (Xianshi, 先施), Yong'an (or Wing On, 永安), Sun (Xinxin, 新新), and Da Xin (or Da Sun, 大新).[15] These stores, which had helped solidify Shanghai's reputation as the foremost capitalist and consumerist city in the country, found it particularly difficult to navigate the party's simultaneous toleration of and attacks on consumerism.[16] Although all four struggled with supply shortages, blockades, factory closings, and difficulties covering payrolls at the end of the civil war and during the transitional period after 1949, during the 1950s the party's economic policies and promotion of the state consumerist ethos of hard work and frugal living made life even more complicated for these luxury chains.[17]

Take Yong'an Department Store as an example of the challenges facing private enterprises when competing against state capital. The store, which was managed by Guo Linshuang, a son of the department store's founder, provides a good example of the difficulties encountered by these formerly elite stores during the transition.[18] Initially, the policies of New Democracy allowed Guo to continue to build the store's image as a purveyor of bourgeois consumer goods through its strategy of high prices and profit margins, low product volume, and exclusivity. Its ever-changing stock of trendy products included fashionable clothing, imported watches, perfumes, and delicacies. Yong'an's other businesses, such as a dance hall and a Western-style restaurant, also began to recover from the chaos of war.[19] Soon, however, party policies pressured stores to cater to the "masses" with more affordable prices and an emphasis on availability rather than high quality. State media differentiated a socialist version of commerce from earlier capitalist practices by accusing bourgeois retailers such as Yong'an of generating "excessive profits," with reports depicting these profits as a hallmark of the compulsion of private capitalist enterprises to maximize returns on capital. Contrary to party charges, however, the lingering impact of the civil war forced more than 3,000 stores to close between August 1949 and March 1950, with stores selling high-end products hardest hit.[20]

The Yong'an business model faced new competition from within its own building. To combat speculation and suppress prices, in October 1949 the local Shanghai government established a state-owned company that rented out Yong'an's ground floor and sold some of the same state-supplied products as Yong'an sold upstairs.[21] Yong'an's state capitalist competitor priced its products more competitively because it had lower overheads and a lower tax rate. By 1953, this state-owned company had outgrown its initial location and taken over the newest and biggest of the original Four Great Department Stores, Da Xin, to become the Number One Department Store, a state-created mecca of consumerism that attracted visitors from around the country during the entire Mao era.[22]

As competition with state stores grew, Yong'an attempted to conform to the new hard work and frugal living political norms. But it did so only superficially. The store displayed less expensive mass products in its windows, though inside the store the business of selling luxury products continued as usual.[23] Guo Linshuang sought opportunities to profit from state initiatives, such as the promotion of designated children's spaces, by opening a Children's World section on the third floor. In the summer of 1950, Children's World used pre-1949-era marketing gimmicks to lure young consumers and their parents to the store, including raffles, free movies, and a small gift with each purchase. The store also tried to counter declining sales by expanding bourgeois forms of leisure and opening a new evening club. Even its sideline businesses – restaurants, dance halls, coffee shops, and bars – refused to undercut the store's luxury brand with services aimed at lower-income customers, such as selling takeout food or tea to go.[24] Despite the expansion of control over consumerism, private stores such as Yong'an continued to engage in the same bourgeois marketing and business practices that had brought them success before 1949.

After the state launched the Three/Five-Antis campaigns and the nationwide urban campaign against cadre corruption and business malfeasance in 1951 (discussed in Chapter 2), conspicuous consumption became much less conspicuous. Although Yong'an's evening rooftop club continued to do a brisk business for several months after the start of the campaign, members of Shanghai's economic elite ended or reduced their use of automobiles, stopped buying luxury items such as jewelry, and avoided displaying common markers of bourgeois status such as Western suits or evening gowns. Correspondingly, department stores saw a dramatic drop in business. In February 1952, shortly after the launch of the Five-Antis campaign, sales at Yong'an plummeted by two-thirds compared to the previous year. Forced to acknowledge that its customer base had changed, Yong'an, in a last-ditch effort to stay afloat, moved to "massify" its inventory with more affordable goods, such as washbasins, pans, and small coal stoves for heating and cooking. The party reinforced Yong'an's new commitment to mass-oriented consumerism by requiring that store managers attend dozens of political meetings in late 1953 and 1954.[25] Once a destination only for the very rich to buy imports, by the mid-1960s, as one reporter observed, the some 100,000 customers per day were "mostly government and factory workers, or peasants in for the day from the country" to select from the 36,000 products on offer, 95 percent of which were China-made.[26]

Similar to other privately owned companies during this period, however, the owners of Yong'an lost control from below as the store increasingly depended on state-run and joint state–private companies for merchandise. The supply of products, of both basic and luxury goods, became less reliable. Between 1953 and 1954, the store's product acquisitions fell by 61 percent, sales dropped by 53 percent, and inventory fell by 50 percent.[27] At this critical juncture, the state swooped in and offered joint public-private ownership. The party blamed Yong'an's demise on General Manager Guo Linshuang's "arrogance" in ignoring, or paying lip service to, state imperatives and not taking the advice of his working-class subordinates and claimed to be bailing out a business on the verge of bankruptcy. For Yong'an and countless other stores and private businesses, their conversion to joint public-private ownership, which was "joint" in name only, was the only way to survive. These businesses were now effectively state owned and state run, with the state paying the original owners a dividend (on an installment plan).[28] The state used its competitive and supply chain advantages to force out private enterprises, while generating positive political press due to its defeat of "capitalist exploiters" and the massification of a former bastion of elite consumption.

Although the state's coerced purchase of department stores ensured state control over the icons of nascent industrial consumerism, party efforts to transform them into an institution serving the goals of state consumerism proved much more difficult (Figure 5.1). Moreover, party efforts to transform these erstwhile bourgeois hotspots created a number of unintended (if predictable) consequences once the problems that shoppers encountered at stores became the sole responsibility and fault of the state. The shortages, queues, bad service, dated window displays, and other shortcomings of the shopping experience discussed below became not simply an economic problem but also a political problem. The party could no longer blame capitalism in general and the capitalist owners of the department stores in particular for the problems that shoppers encountered.

Socialistic Window Dressing

CCP attempts to transform longstanding capitalist retailing practices into "socialist commerce" affected every aspect of a store and the shopping experience, right down to the window displays. Directives from the national Ministry of Commerce, the organ responsible for creating and overseeing commerce, made clear that it viewed the quality of window displays and the interior design within the stores as basic elements of good service. Similar to the state-approved economic propaganda or the state-approved fashionable dress, proper window displays reflected well on socialism. According to a 1955 booklet on best practices, distributed to more than 8,000 stores across the country, maintaining window displays was a commercial and political act "requiring close attention" to make sure that, unlike capitalist displays and capitalist advertisements, the stores did not cheat consumers into buying products by making

上 海 市 第 一 百 貨 商 店

Figure 5.1. "Shanghai No. 1 Department Store" (1955). When the party expropriated the big department stores, it also "massified" these institutions of consumerism by spreading them (with much more modest versions) throughout the country and making the flagship stores in major cities welcoming to the entire population. These stores introduced a much broader cross-section of society to the latest practices in retailing, including the idea of window shopping, attractions such as the only escalator in operation in the country to whisk visitors to additional floors of products (in the center of the poster), and customer service (the help desk includes a suggestion box and several phones). Even those without the means to buy the products on display participated in consumerism by learning to desire new commodities. A ditty at the bottom of the poster goes: "The department store contains innumerable products. Cherished goods can be chosen to your heart's content. Buy whatever you need; your life gets better every year." Source: The International Institute of Social History (private collection).

exaggerated claims. Socialist window and product displays, the booklet declared, should only feature goods that stores had in stock and should help consumers locate what they were looking for rather than foster desires for new or fashionable items or inspire browsing. The instructions stated that stores should display products manufactured by state factories (rather than the remaining private factories) to help promote state capitalist manufacturers.[29] In line with the advertising, posters, and films discussed in Chapter 4, store window displays were to be easily comprehensible to the masses and were not to include too much or too abstruse text. The ministry's guidelines insisted that stores keep displays up to date – they were to change displays at least every three months, match them to the seasons, and feature goods appropriate to specific holidays. Displays around the October 1 National Day celebrations, for instance, were to celebrate the national accomplishments of the previous year. Simultaneously, the state wanted displays to exhibit the ethos of state consumerism by discouraging bourgeois tastes in favor of "simple living," which in turn meant exhibiting "national products" and goods priced "practically and realistically."[30] Although the state attempted to "build socialism" by modifying the existing infrastructure of capitalism such as window displays, its efforts backfired and expanded consumerism as a correlate of capitalism.

The window displays that had been a lively part of the pre-1949 urban visual culture declined in number as many stores closed, and those that survived were soon repurposed to reflect the new political order. The remaining displays were often political – as when the state required stores to use their displays to promote mass campaigns, such as the Resist America and Aid Korea campaign. Shortly after the start of the war in 1950, for example, members of the Department Store Labor Union redecorated major department stores to promote the campaign.[31] As the war progressed, to support Chinese accusations that the United States was using biological weapons, Yong'an posted nine photographs in its window display that supposedly showed American germ warfare in Korea and the north of China. Millions of people saw such window displays, including an estimated three million in the Yangzi river city of Wuhan over a period of four months and an estimated 180,000 window shoppers viewed the Beijing Xihongji Clothing display.[32]

Newspaper articles applauded the effort of these stores. But they also criticized stores that did not follow the guidelines established by the Ministry of Commerce. Within several years after 1949, critics began to note that stores did not regularly change their window displays. One article noted that at Beijing Dashilan, one of the busiest business districts in the city and right down the road from the Ministry of Commerce, seventy-six out of the eighty-eight store windows inspected had added propaganda displays in July. But by October, many stores still had their initial displays, which appeared to be dated. According to critics, such outdated window displays not only carried stale political messages but gave the impression that socialist commerce was frozen in time.[33] Although the state needed to use and subordinate capitalist infrastructure to promote its own purposes, it found it difficult to execute its mission.

In anticipation of the tenth anniversary of the founding of the People's Republic, in August 1959 the Ministry of Commerce held a National Window Advertisement and Product Display Conference. The conference tried to harness Shanghai's still-flourishing bourgeois visual culture to develop a socialist commercial visual culture similar to that found in the Soviet Union and to share it with the rest of the country.[34] The conference was attended by delegates from twenty-one of the top retailing cities in the country, including Beijing, Tianjin, Guangzhou, Wuhan, and Harbin, and by cadres responsible for commerce from fifteen other cities and from the Central Academy of Arts and Crafts. Delegates made field trips to representative stores throughout Shanghai, including the Number One Department Store, Number One Food Shop, Yong'an Department Store, the 10,000 Images Photo Studio, and other places. Despite the capitalist origins of the advertising practices they observed, the vice head of the Commercial Bureau's Artistic Office reminded participants that "our commercial advertising must be based on the nature and mission of socialist commerce . . . and implement the policies of the party and the state."[35] Likewise, in a report on "Several Issues on the Art of Window Display Design," Professor Wu Lao, head of the Department of Decoration at the Central Academy of Arts and Crafts, reminded the audience that store window displays should advertise "national economic achievements," that is, they were to transmit state economic messages.[36]

The presentations and discussions at the conference reveal the difficulties of reconciling socialist ideals with existing commercial practices. While the ideal display had to catch the attention of passers-by, it also had to avoid stimulating desires and sales by capitalist displays. Instead, socialist displays were simply to inform potential customers of the availability of products and to guide usage. These defenses were the same covers used to justify the continued use of advertisements. Commentators also stressed the utility of window displays by urging managers to view such displays not only as bland descriptions but also as unique pieces of socialist street art that beautified the city. One state-touted display, for example, featuring a girl surrounded by handkerchiefs arranged in the form of trees and flowers that revealed the different colors and patterns on the handkerchiefs on sale and suggested how one might use the handkerchiefs as hair bows, did not appear to be particularly "socialist."[37] In contrast, the Nanyang Sock and Shirt Company decorated its window with stacks of merchandise placed in geometric patterns that were eye-catching and that conveyed the idea of plenty, a popular propaganda trope. Number One Department Store on Nanjing Road featured a display with musical instruments in the foreground and the music and lyrics to the universally known song "Socialism is Good" in the background. Number One Store's other display combined merchandise with political propaganda by placing a television and radio in front of a poster of a huge peace dove carrying a banner reading "the voice of peace puts fear into American warmongers."[38]

The state consumerist ethos of frugal living was another key theme in the store window displays featured at the conference. The Nanjing Road Fashionable Clothing Store, for example, hung two posters, the first of which, by cartoonist Feng Zikai, suggested that in hardworking and thrifty households, "only the eldest child be given new clothing, then their clothing should be passed to the next child, and so on down the line." The other, part of a national campaign to promote diligence and thrift, featured a political slogan that urged people to consider their clothes "new for three years, used for another three, and carefully mended for another three."[39]

While this display, and others like it, presented frugality as a voluntary act of individual discipline, such admonitions to "save for a rainy day" represented yet another attempt by the state to lower consumer expectations and to suppress popular demand for products that would then require more state investment in the production of consumer goods (light industry) while state capitalism prioritized heavy industry. Furthermore, by valorizing frugality, these displays cast shortages of basic items such as clothing not as structural problems caused by the state's inadequate supplies or its accumulation priorities, but as problems caused by an individual's wastefulness. In this example, state consumerism, as with all consumerism, attempted to code the message one sent through individual acts of consumption. In both cases, consumerism became the means of creating and communicating identity.[40]

State capitalism's accumulation of the surplus relied on, as the state consumerist ethos emphasized, hard work and frugal living in the name of building toward a communist future. Gradually, however, "socialist commerce" gave socialism a bad name and undermined the legitimizing ideology of the party. Even at the beginning of the transition to a state-owned retailing environment in the mid-1950s, state emphasis on frugal living and avoiding waste reinforced the popular impression that socialist commerce, like the store windows themselves, was drab, unchanging, unresponsive, and unfashionable. In a news report from that period, for instance, reporter Shen Wenying noted that displays outside a privately owned store advertised products appropriate for the summer season, including t-shirts, mosquito nets, and hand-held fans, while the advertising

slides for a state-owned store shown at the Peaceful Movie Theater that the
audience derided were for winter clothing such as wool sweaters, thick socks,
and winter moisturizers. Shen saw this difference as a reflection of the neglect
of stores for the seasonal needs of their customers, an impression reinforced
by their dusty and poorly maintained interiors and bad service. Evoking
Mao's slogan that the purpose of the party was to "serve the people," she
argued that countless workers in state-run service industries had forgotten
their responsibility to "serve the consumer" (为消费者服务).[41] After the
Socialist Transformation, the tensions between political propaganda and
commercial appeal, and between bad "capitalist" and good "socialist"
displays, led stores to stick with displays that were drab and monotonous
but politically safe, thereby undermining party claims that they were creating
a superior "socialist commerce."[42] Correct "socialist" displays were ones that
facilitated the state's accumulation of capital, not displays that provided
people with the goods and services they needed or wanted.

Haggling

Inside the stores, the party tried to eliminate bargaining and haggling to
make commerce appear more socialist. Fixed prices were to capture more
profits by disempowering both merchants and consumers. Claiming that
socialist commerce served the interests of the people rather than profits, the
party argued that one way to ensure that the interests of the people
prevailed over profiteering, speculation, and inflation was to require fixed
prices (不二价, literally, "no second price"). In contrast, the party associated haggling with the chaos of capitalist markets, wherein everyone
sought to maximize self-interest.

Because haggling gave people a sense of control, changing this longstanding practice with a ban proved difficult. At the end of 1949, for
instance, Beijing's Dong'an Department Store no longer allowed salespeople to use the time-honored practice of beginning negotiations with an
inflated price, and it even announced over its loudspeakers: "We welcome
customers to report merchants in this store who inflate prices." The new
practice was a tough sell, especially among jewelry merchants who rented
space in the store and only reluctantly adhered to the new rule. At the start
of 1950, the Beijing city government imposed a wider ban on haggling,
declaring that all businesses that rented space in state-run stores were
required to post their prices. Although Dongdan People's Market implemented the new policy in mid-January, some stalls continued to expect
customers to haggle down from an inflated initial price, leading the

market's managers to try to shame merchants into compliance by posting signs on the stalls of the offending merchants reading, "This stall inflates prices. Buyer beware." When merchants or cadres posted fixed prices, however, merchants expected customers to haggle anyway, or they offered fixed prices to customers they suspected were state employees while haggling with others.[43]

The cadres responsible for setting prices blamed the problem partially on the difficulty of changing earlier "feudal" or "capitalist" consumer behavior into more "socialist" behavior. Customers believed that they needed to haggle to get a fair price, implying that they either did not know or did not trust the new state policy of having set prices. One letter to the *People's Daily* suggested that, to rectify this lack of trust, the entire country should follow Suzhou's example and hold an exhibition of deceptive traditional sales practices to teach consumers how merchants had used tricks such as haggling to capture "excessive profits."[44] Haggling, however, was an ingrained behavior. Salespeople at consignment shops complained that their customers rejected the notion that there was an objective price (or at least that the state had the capacity to enforce an objective price) and they expected to bargain. In response, some salesclerks began the transaction by quoting a higher price than the set price, which they could then lower to give the customers the impression that they were getting a special price. Rather than asking to pay less, a customer might instead suggest that a salesclerk "throw in a bit more" beyond the amount officially purchased. Expectations that prices were negotiable put clerks in an uncomfortable position between customers accustomed to receiving a discount and state-mandated rules that named haggling as a capitalist practice. Some clever salespeople adapted by splitting the difference, pretending to give customers more and using a sleight of hand to actually not provide anything extra.[45] After the Spring Festival of 1951, Beijing Chaoyang Gate Vegetable Market, the biggest in the city, allowed haggling within a narrow range, meaning that the final price still depended on the skill of the haggler.[46] Once again, state attempts to define and restrain consumerism encountered limits.

Although the state wanted the set-price policy to be a defining characteristic of socialist commerce, popular resistance meant the new policy did not take hold until after the Socialist Transformation, when the state virtually controlled urban retailing. Moreover, as with so many other reforms during the Mao era, whether or not people adhered to the new regulations varied over time and place. For instance, when the party lifted restrictions on individual plots, markets, and peddling after the Great Leap

Forward in the early 1960s, haggling re-emerged. The re-emergence of haggling and other forms of private enterprise throughout the Mao era illustrated Lenin's maxim that small-scale production produced capitalism "daily, hourly, spontaneously, and on a mass scale." Vociferous attacks on capitalist culture during the Cultural Revolution, the subject of Chapter 6, show how impossible it was for the party to reconcile its rhetoric with consumerism.[47] This underscored people's lack of confidence in the state's ability to ensure fair prices and people's attempts to exercise some control over their individual situations. These examples suggest that even when the party made efforts to eliminate market practices, its policies encountered limited success because it did not provide a compelling "socialist" alternative.

Greater "Socialism," Worsening Shopping, 1956–1960

Although the replacement of private markets with nearly complete state control of the economy by 1956 had helped stabilize prices, end runaway inflation, and decrease panic buying, the party's state capitalist policies also worsened the experience for many urban shoppers.[48] During the 1950s, party policies pushed retailers of all sizes into ever larger state-run organizations that restricted consumers' access to products by reducing the total number of shops and nearly eliminating street peddlers. By 1956, party policies herded shops into two ownership categories: those effectively owned and run by national, provincial, or local governments as joint public-private enterprises, such as Yong'an, and the very few small-scale mom-and-pop shops that sold state goods at set prices with set profits and tended to be more responsive to local needs than the large state-run stores. Scholarship on the Great Leap Forward has understandably focused on the party's emphasis on production at all costs, including the transfer of one-fifth of the agricultural workforce to factory work, which contributed to the Great Leap Famine.[49] Scholars have paid less attention to how party attempts to accrue capital restricted consumption in general, all the way down to the shopping experience for consumers in cities. Whereas the previous section examines how even party intentions to create a more "socialist" shopping experience yielded limited results, this section examines the inequalities that the party's state capitalist policies produced on a local level.

Policies expanding state control over sales and – at least as importantly – the labor force included reassigning peddlers to other work and merging small semi-private shops into state stores or herding them into large-scale cooperatives called people's communes. These cooperatives were the urban counterparts of the rural agricultural communes.[50] To better channel purchases to state rather than local products, the party prohibited rural communes from selling their non-agricultural sideline products (or "handicrafts") in the cities, reducing the supply of everyday products, from soap and brushes to blankets and spices. State desire to control the supply chain, however, meant products had to pass through multiple bureaucratic layers before making their way to the consumers, exacerbating shortages in some places and leading to overstocking in others. Moreover, the elimination of peddlers, who represented small-scale distribution networks and who had been licensed to buy products in the countryside and resell them in the city, meant the disappearance of countless sideline occupations facilitating consumer goods and services, such as selling foods like sesame seed oil, sweet potatoes, candies, and rice cakes; providing services like sharpening knives and scissors; and delivering household necessities such as cooking charcoal.[51] These everyday diminutions in the quality of life associated with Mao-era "socialism" were the consequences of state efforts to control labor and its surplus.

In stores, the few products on sale were frequently shoddy. The Socialist Transformation led not to the improvements in product quality predicted by Xue Muqiao but to the opposite, which the party privately admitted.[52] In part, this was due to policies that rewarded factory state-owned enterprise managers who met or exceeded state quotas, leading to an emphasis on quantity over quality. However, the widespread gray economy also incentivized factory workers to cheat customers by skimping on state-allocated raw materials or using inferior materials to meet state quotas and then using the remaining materials to produce or barter goods outside official avenues. The extreme decentralization of the economy during the Great Leap Forward, when the state encouraged communes and production brigades to set up small-scale factories only loosely controlled by the national government, further exacerbated these problems.[53]

Queues as Signs of Socialist Success

As the state's focus on capital accumulation became more pronounced over the course of the Great Leap Forward, shortages of consumer goods became more widespread, and by the height of the Great Leap in 1959 supplies of consumer products had become extremely limited. Whereas people once stood in line for only a few hard-to-get items (such as student-price movie tickets), now even everyday necessities, including vegetables, meat, and herbs, required queuing. Despite the party's use of three common ways to deal with shortages – prices, rationing, and queues – queues became an iconic image of shopping life, as they had in all other state capitalist economies.[54] Because long queues threatened to undermine faith in the party and its policies (and waste potential working hours), the party attempted to reduce them, though the party refused to allocate more capital to the production and distribution of consumer goods. Writer Hua Xinmin later recalled, for instance, that when the shortages and lines first began, state propaganda reassured students that these inconveniences were temporary and that communism was only a few short years away. Cadres at Hua's school warned students not to queue or hoard products, repeating the state line that queuing was a counterrevolutionary activity that suggested one did not believe official reassurances about supplies. People who queued for goods often cast a careful eye to avoid detection by people they knew, but these initial feelings of shame did not last. Queuing, which had been ordinary at the end of Nationalist rule but had largely disappeared during the first several years of the PRC, quickly became the norm again. The practice became so widespread that Hua noted that younger students, who had never experienced a queue-less China, no longer had reservations about being seen standing in queues.[55] The everyday experience of people waiting in line for daily necessities reflects again the party's prioritization of rapid industrial capital accumulation, despite the mounting and visible evidence that the consumer goods sector needed more resources.

Queues became a natural part of life in the late 1950s. A 1957 state report on the city of Taiyuan, south of Beijing, is typical. The report found people queuing everywhere, at grain stores and department stores to bathhouses and barbershops, some waiting in lines several hundred people long. Nor was there any guarantee that stock would still be available when one finally reached the front of the line.[56] Facing such a predicament, people adapted. Some left placeholders, such as an old basket; others brought stools to sit on while waiting; still others dispatched children to wait in line. People had to adjust their shopping habits. The custom of inviting friends and co-workers to dinner presented a logistical problem for the country's already stretched supplies and queue lines, especially during holidays when people hosted extended family and guests. Hua remembered that for Chinese New Year's Eve in the winter of 1959, additional demand and anxiety made lines longer and tenser than usual, leading local cadres to enlist him and his high-school classmates to maintain order at a local vegetable market and to ensure that nobody jumped the queue.[57]

As waiting in lines became familiar after the mid-1950s, articles in the *People's Daily* acknowledged widespread disappointment with the state's failure to deliver on its promise that "socialist commerce" would create better service. A report on a 1957 meeting of cadres and the approximately 400 households living in Nankai District of Tianjin voiced numerous complaints by local residents, mostly housewives, about poor service, limited stock, and long lines. Expressing her dissatisfaction about having to queue, one housewife observed: "Before Liberation, we had to queue and now after Liberation, we still have to wait in line. When *won't* we need to queue?" Another resident argued that shopping had become worse: whereas before Liberation, one could buy meat even "in the middle of the night," now meat was sold out by 10 o'clock in the morning. Others expressed anxieties about supplies and common practices such as joining queues out of panic and buying whatever was available regardless of need.[58]

State media coverage on queues attempted to reframe them as an individual problem to be managed by shoppers rather than a failing of current policies, much less of socialism. One *People's Daily* article quoted a housewife to remind readers of the pre-1949 hyperinflation that the party had ended and to reassure readers that now that prices had been stabilized, they no longer had to counter fears of inflation with panic buying. Another of the housewives cited in the article suggested that shoppers, rather than making queues even longer by joining them, should wait until there were fewer people in line. Housewives in the article also suggested that people could speed up store sales by buying entire packages of rice and wheat flour instead of buying small portions. Through the voices of ordinary consumers, state media urged shoppers to modify their own behavior by following the informal policy of "The Three Don't Queues": don't queue if there is already a long queue, if there is a shortage, or if you still have stock at home.[59] State media redirected blame for shortages and customers' inferior shopping experiences away from potential criticism of the state's (mis) allocation of resources and toward the individual behavior patterns of shoppers. In doing so, these articles again highlighted party priorities.

The *People's Daily* and other state media attempted to reframe complaints about queues by convincing people to interpret queuing as a positive sign. According to news reports, queues were not a consequence of shortages but rather they were a result of rising wages and improved living standards. People stood in line because they had more money to spend.[60] Articles attempted to counter negative reports by quoting satisfied customers. One middle-aged housewife, Zhao Lianhui, pointed out that shoppers were now queuing for better food: "Before we were poor people queuing for bad food; now we are prosperous people queuing for meat and rice. So there is a difference." Xu Shufen said that before 1949, his second son had once been beaten by a policeman while queuing in the middle of the night: "Before Liberation, queuing was a form of suffering. Now that my family earns more than RMB 200 every month, we are queuing for meat. This is a big difference."[61] In an even more elaborate defense, Sha Hang, writing in *Hangzhou Daily*, reported seeing a sign outside a store several days before Chinese New Year in 1958 that announced, "At 2 pm today, we will start selling. Sales will end when we sell out." Customers began to form an orderly queue outside the store six hours before the products went on sale. Sha Hang (and the editors who published the article) chose to interpret this as socialist culture in the making: "In one sense, this is a good phenomenon. First, forming a line without enforcement demonstrates the discipline and virtue of the masses. Second, this shows the increasing purchasing power of our people and the prospering economy." Despite its attempts at positive press, the state feared both the negative political implications of long lines and the wasted labor power they represented. As Sha Hang notes in the same article, "If we add up all the time wasted waiting in lines at small marketplaces and at public utilities, then it would be a huge number!"[62]

To reduce lines at stores, cadres restored some sales practices previously abolished as capitalist, including easing restrictions on peddlers and door-to-door salesmen. Some stores blamed queues on the inefficiencies shoppers encountered inside the stores and followed the Soviet example of having store clerks weigh and package predetermined quantities in advance and use platform scales rather than steelyard scales to accelerate the process and shorten wait times. Cadres mandated that service workers at grocery stores, and at train and bus stations, lengthen their operating hours to reduce lines. Other cadres required that clerks help throughout the entire store, rather than specializing in just one set of products. Cinemas expanded their sales offices, opened extra windows to sell tickets, permitted advance ticket sales, and reopened telephone ticket sales and delivery services that had been eliminated as capitalist practices catering to the bourgeoisie.[63] Despite the state's awareness of the problems that queuing represented, policies throughout the Great Leap Forward continued to favor rapid industrial accumulation over transforming the shopping experience, much less the underlying state capitalist political economy.

Unremunerated Labor During the Tianqiao Campaign, 1958–1960

The state, for all its flaws, attempted to address the problems outlined in the previous section. However, once again, the biggest state policy push toward "socialism" required a massive extraction of unremunerated labor. More "socialist commerce" translated into more extraction of people's labor, as examples from the previous section already suggest. The Great Leap Forward exacerbated the service-sector problems discussed above, when the state's accelerated rush toward industrialization transferred experienced store clerks to work in factories and on communal farms.[64] Following a policy to "replace men with women" and "replace the strong with the weak," more than one million men were transferred out of the commercial sector between 1958 and 1960.[65] To free up workers, Shanghai alone consolidated some 16,000 smaller businesses that served food to 500 central communal dining halls.[66] The replacements for the transferred workers included those who were older, sicker, weaker, and largely inexperienced, including more than half a million former housewives with no previous experience in the formal economy. Stores were now staffed by unmotivated and inexperienced clerks who were neither afraid of being fired nor incentivized by now outlawed bonuses or commissions to provide better services.[67]

Newspaper articles lambasted impatient shop clerks who rarely volunteered to assist customers, only grudgingly allowed customers to inspect products, and became angry if a customer opted not to buy anything. Such articles suggest that clerks were interested exclusively in transactions that required minimal effort, with one egregious offender even telling a customer that the store did not have in stock an item clearly visible on a shelf. According to such reports, clerks habitually argued with customers or insulted them, so much so that fights sometime broke out that landed both parties at the police station.[68] The low esteem in which store clerks were held led many of the new workers to avoid being spotted by friends and relatives while on the job. Workers arrived late, left early, and performed their work poorly while on the job. Problems such as pilfering and black marketeering grew. The situation got so bad that in 1961 the state launched a new campaign in cities to fight threats to state control over profits, for instance stealing, speculation, extravagance and waste, inattentiveness, and bureaucratism (that is, too many workers doing too little productive work). By the end of the 1950s, for many urban residents, state stores had become notoriously worse than the private stores that preceded them. In the words of a popular expression from 1960, "In a state store, the attitudes of the employees are really bad. One may make multiple requests without a single reply. When clerks open their mouths, their replies will irritate you."[69]

The state attempted to save capital for the industrial sectors by consolidating retailing into fewer but larger state shops staffed with fewer workers, thus reducing overhead costs. The state transferred hundreds of thousands of newer and inexperienced workers to other work and sent back tens of thousands of experienced commercial workers to retail sites. The number of commercial workers per capita, however, still did not return to earlier levels. In 1952, the national average was one retail salesperson for every eighty-one people, but by 1977 there was only one retail salesperson for every 214 people. Restaurants saw an even more precipitous decline in service people to customers ratios. In 1952, there was one restaurant for every 676 people, but only one per every 8,189 people by the end of the Mao era.[70] In other words, over the course of Mao's leadership, the average worker in the service industry served more than twice as many people as they did in the early 1950s. In northeast Liaoning province, which underwent dramatic industrial development, the number of stores and service shops in 1978 was one-fifth the number in 1957, and the number of restaurants only one-tenth. By 1978, Fuxin, a city in Liaoning with over 500,000 inhabitants, had 316 shops, down from more than 1,000 just twenty years earlier, when the city's population was only 140,000. The decline affected the countryside, where the number of cooperative shops and restaurants in the entire country totaled 580 by the end of 1979, down from 40,000 in 1957. Many communes – collections of villages that included thousands of households – did not have a single shop or restaurant.[71] The state thus addressed the problems in the retail sector by cutting labor overhead costs, despite the extra work and longer hours that these policies created for the remaining workers in the service sector. Little wonder then that service did not include a "socialist smile."

In response to growing public discontent, the party did what it routinely did to overcome a shortcoming resulting from its industrial goals: it launched a mass campaign. In this case, the party initiated the Commercial Leap Forward (商业跃进), a much less well-known service-sector mass campaign counterpart to the Great Leap Forward intended to improve "socialist commerce."[72] Just as Great Leap Forward policies demanded much more productivity out of farmers and factory workers, the Commercial Leap Forward attempted to simultaneously maximize productivity among service workers in retail stores and minimize state investments in the service sector – all while intensifying propaganda on worker-led initiatives to practice the ethos of hard work and frugal living.[73] Central to this effort was the Emulate Tianqiao, Catch Up with Tianqiao (学天桥, 赶天桥) campaign (hereafter Emulate Tianqiao), which was launched in 1958. The campaign encouraged stores throughout the country to adopt the practices of a model department store in Beijing's Tianqiao District to address the failings of service-sector policies, demonstrate the superiority of socialist commerce, and disseminate these ideas across the country.[74] But, above all, Emulate Tianqiao transferred the blame for the shortcomings of "socialist commerce" to individuals and processes rather than to the state and its priorities.

The Ministry of Commerce solicited examples of similar reforms from 60,000 commercial work units throughout the country to encourage stores to emulate them. This unprecedented organization of nationwide stores intended to both elicit and spread the best practices of socialist commerce from Harbin in the far northeast to Guangzhou in the far south to Wulumuqi in the far west.[75] From the submissions, the ministry selected some 200 national models and circulated the resulting materials in a multi-volume set of books, *The Red Flag of Commerce*. The Ministry of Commerce described the vast array of local modifications and experiments at Tianqiao and its emulators as unleashing the creativity of labor. As with so many of the policy experiments of the Mao era, including the broader Great Leap Forward itself, the ones associated with the Commercial Leap Forward relied on unremunerated labor, requiring little or no resources from the state besides state-led propaganda and worker coercion.[76]

The suggested practices in the multi-volume set and accompanying media blitz ranged from simple improvements to heavy demands on labor. Wuhan's Lifeng Department Store, for instance, improved its item display system by mandating that a set number of products should be on display in one location rather than scattered throughout the store. It also promoted a "customer is always right" motto: "Even if customers ask one hundred times, don't complain; even if customers are extremely picky, don't complain."[77] In the southwest corner of China, Kunming's own motto for its clerks was "Five Nos and Four Goods," referring to five things to avoid (mistakes, accidents, waste, embezzling, and products stocked past their sell-by dates) and four goods to embrace (service, study, cleanliness, and achievements).[78] Similarly, a store in Qingyang county in the northwest province of Gansu expanded its hours, without providing additional pay to its salaried staff. The store further claimed that its workers would open the shop even if "a customer came and knocked at the door in the middle of the night."[79]

Emulate Tianqiao rhetoric encouraged stores to demonstrate their commitment to building socialism by adopting the practices of the Tianqiao store. The top priority was to improve efficiency by reducing store staff by a target of 45 percent to transfer these "surplus" workers from unproductive service work to factories and farms. In one fell swoop, the campaign transformed workers deemed redundant by the state into participants in the Great Leap Forward and extracted the maximum amount of labor out of those left behind in the service sector by more than doubling their workloads.[80] Store employees now had to work longer shifts to cover the work of the transferred workers, working from 9.00 in the morning to 8.30 at night, and they were no longer allowed to go home to eat and rest in the middle of the day.[81] Ironically, these measures adopted pre-1949 practices, such as clerks who often lived in the stores where they worked. At meetings with workers' families, who were forced to find ways to deal with their absence, officials thanked them for supporting the Great Leap Forward, thereby folding the exploitative labor policies into the larger national political narrative and making it more difficult to express opposition. State media predictably reported that families expressed their support for the campaign and, by extension, the state.[82] In addition to shortages of products, such policies led to shortages of staff. Underpaid, overworked clerks meant customers almost never encountered "socialist smiles."

According to campaign propaganda, the mid-sized Tianqiao Department Store, which in 1958 had been open for five years, suffered from the same problems plaguing other state stores and offered the same bad service found throughout China.[83] The propaganda claimed, however, that by 1958 Tianqiao had mended its ways by making simple changes. Tianqiao employed model socialist clerks who pledged in customer service pacts to greet arriving customers with "Comrade! What do you need?"[84] Store clerks volunteered information about the best products, encouraged customers to inspect products without an obligation to buy, and suggested ways customers could save money, such as cutting cloth more efficiently to save fabric when making a garment. One reporter observed an instance when a saleswoman allowed a customer to buy a single pillowcase from a package of two, noting that "there must be someone who would like to buy the other one."[85] Visible even in a clerk's greetings was one of the ways a socialist veneer was combined with standard capitalist practices: the model greeting mixed the socialist "comrade" with the polite form of "you" (您), a respectful term of address later discouraged as "bourgeois" for putting the speaker in a subordinate position to the addressed.

The campaign highlighted a typical state attempt to improve the morale of service workers by attacking the popular view of service work as dead-end menial labor. Despite the widespread use of the slogan "to labor is most glorious" (劳动最光荣), specific programs to honor model workers such as Huang Baomei (discussed in Chapter 3) implied that physical labor was more respectable than service work.[86] To counteract this view, the Tianqiao campaign promoted the idea that clerks had been liberated by socialist commerce and should act and be treated accordingly. Staff with experience in capitalist stores, for instance, were called on to assure newer staff that their jobs were much more dignified than jobs working for capitalists, who had forced staff to wait on their bosses, light their cigarettes, serve them tea, and not go to bed before they did. Whereas shop owners in pre-1949 stores regularly scolded, beat, and bullied clerks with threats of termination, one veteran declared, "Who dares to insult us now?"[87]

According to party propaganda, socialism transformed Chinese society into "one big happy family," uniting workers and clerks. Signs on trams, for example, welcomed riders to "The Home of the Customers"; movie theaters posted signs that read "The Home of the Audience." "From morning till night, we treat the store as home" became a campaign slogan.[88] Managers told service workers that customers were guests in the homes of the clerks and should be treated accordingly. Likewise, customers were to think of clerks as their hosts rather than as their servants. Service workers who treated customers impolitely were compared to rude hosts, and customers who looked down on service workers, made unreasonable requests, or threatened to make formal complaints against them were accused of forgetting the concept of the Chinese nation as one big family. Describing what this attitudinal change looked like in practice, an article in *Hangzhou Daily* reported that a clerk at a Hangzhou silk store admitted that when the store had been under private ownership, he had treated rich people and poor farmers differently. After the store became state-owned, however, he was retrained to be patient and nice to everyone, regardless of their background. According to another Hangzhou clerk quoted in the article, "Before the Tianqiao campaign, salesclerks did not care about a customer's choice. Now we offer the customer advice."[89] The campaign attempted to create new social relations between customer and clerk. But it did so by focusing on the behavior of clerks and customers, while placing both sides in a social and material circumstance that rendered the realization of a socialist consumer experience impossible.

Although workers no longer worked for private capitalists, they did not control their workplaces, and state policies attempted to extract the

maximum amount of labor from workers without additional remuneration, such as bonuses or commissions, which were now disparaged as
capitalist practices. In addition to requiring service workers to serve more
customers and work longer hours, the Tianqiao campaign added even
more unpaid "political and ideological work" to their jobs, making them
responsible for spreading the idea that "serve the customer" was an occu-
pation-specific manifestation of the popular PLA slogan, "Serve the
People." Theoretically, service was an essential attribute of socialism
because it sought to serve the people and create an idealized shopping
experience in which all were welcome and all were equal, rather than
merely a tactic to maximize profits as it had been under capitalism. But,
as argued here, the driving force behind these variations of the directive to
serve the people ultimately was the central ideological demand of state
capitalism: individual self-sacrifice by adhering to the ethos of hard work
and frugal living for the collective good of the people and nation.[90] The
party's ready exploitation of the labor of service workers clarifies that
"Serve the People" was a façade that justified the increased extraction of
the surplus and its allocation to industrial production.[91]

Similar to other socialist rhetoric claiming that workers were the masters
of society, the new state discourse about shopping claimed that it was the
responsibility of salesclerks to represent the interests of their store, their
comrades who were consumers, and the country as a whole. This meant
that not only were the clerks working for little remuneration, but the
consumers had little to buy. Mass media such as the *People's Daily* pro-
mulgated this relationship with specific examples, such as the Hangzhou
fabric salesclerk Shen Baogen, who patiently explained to a customer that
although there was a dot on the edge of the cloth he wanted to buy, by
purchasing it anyway and salvaging the cloth, the customer would be
"saving money for the country."[92] Customers who nitpicked over products
favored their individual selfish interests over those of the country.[93] As part
of the state effort to convince consumers to embrace frugal living and
thereby advance the Great Leap Forward's goal of "increasing production
and saving resources," the state expected salesclerks to discourage unnecessary purchases. Another article in the multi-volume collection *The Red
Flag of Commerce*, which compiled the best practices of the Commercial
Leap Forward from stores around the country, praised a shop assistant at
a department store in Chengdu for telling a potential customer looking to
replace a shirt whose collar was worn out that he should instead go down to
the service department and have the worn collar replaced. The clerk then
told the customer that he could both save money for himself and "save

cloth for the country."[94] Another article in the compilation praised clerks at a major Chongqing department store for teaching frugality. In one example, a clerk informed a factory worker who had saved enough to buy a wristwatch that the store had none in stock because the country had only just begun to manufacture its own watches and imports were discouraged as a matter of national priority: "because our country is still poor, importing wristwatches will cost the country a huge amount of foreign currency." The clerk suggested that the worker instead save his money in the bank to help "accumulate construction capital," which would enable the nation to "build socialism even sooner, and then everyone will have a nice watch to wear." In both these cases, according to the accounts, the customers appreciated and followed the clerks' helpful and unsolicited advice.[95]

Tianqiao supposedly achieved this drastic transformation in employee attitude by not only reducing its total number of employees but also by increasing the responsibilities of managers. All managers waited on customers rather than simply overseeing clerks to show through their own example that service work was not degrading.[96] Recalling his process of learning to greet customers, one store manager's testimony inadvertently confirmed how entrenched the traditional disdain for service workers was:

> When the first customer arrived, I was too shy to greet him. But I was the union chair, so the other workers looked to me to take the lead. When a second customer showed up, I was about to greet him, but my throat felt stuck. Finally, when a third customer came, I greeted her in a low voice. My voice trembled, but it was a good start. Soon I didn't feel shy about greeting customers.[97]

In addition to expecting managers to do more, the Tianqiao campaign promoted the model store's pioneering use of new techniques to discipline workers and encourage harder work, all in the name of socialist worker empowerment. A blackboard posted in the store named the clerks with the highest sales, and shoppers were encouraged to offer comments in a special notebook on service lapses and any other aspect of service in the store.[98] In one month alone, the store received 685 comments regarding some forty salesclerks. Managers tallied the positive and negative comments, and stores held after-work meetings with workers to discuss improvements. The *People's Daily* claimed that these measures helped improve customer service, citing the case of Liang Cai who, after an investigation by outside observers, had identified weaknesses in his service work and markedly improved his record within six months. According to reports, Liang went so far as to use his spare time to make deliveries and repairs for customers during cold and inclement weather.[99] Another account told of a Tianqiao worker who helped a tractor operator stranded by a broken bicycle chain in the middle of the night by finding the store employee in charge of bicycles and having him make a difficult repair, thereby allowing the tractor operator to return to the front lines of production.[100]

Whether these stories are true or invented to promote the campaign, their underlying motive remains the same. Foremost, the stories promoted norms that valorized individual efforts and drew attention away from the larger structural problems created by state capitalist efforts to extract more unremunerated labor from employees and to equate that extraction with socialist behavior. Second, the stories disseminated the discourse of hard work and unselfishness by having workers happily sacrifice their health and well-being for the sake of production. Third, the stories reinforced the notion that service work remained inferior to productive, front-line industrial labor. These accounts imply that the time, energy, and health of service workers remained secondary to getting customers what they wanted or, in some cases, aiding labor that was more valuable to state capitalism (i.e., industrial workers).

Throughout the campaign, the state relentlessly promoted the idea that service workers laboring undue hours for no extra pay in harsh, customer-focused conditions was "socialist behavior." Tianqiao, like other state-designated model factories and communes throughout China, became a destination for public-inspection delegations. National leaders such as Beijing Mayor Peng Zhen and writer Guo Moruo (in whose calligraphy the store sign was written) made official visits, and on June 1, 1958, Premier Zhou Enlai conducted a two-hour inspection of the store and concluded that its business practices were, as advertised, "very advanced."[101] Visitors naturally included shop assistants from other locations – Hangzhou Liberation Street Department Store, for instance, sent dozens of sales clerks to intern there – but the Tianqiao model of selfless service was presented as a model of general socialist behavior, so the store welcomed factory workers, cadres, post-office workers, doctors and hospital staff, professors, and even teenage students. On the day one reporter visited Tianqiao's warehouse, he encountered 600 people on similar investigative missions (Figure 5.2).[102]

Open Shelves

Newspapers regularly reported on the successes of such improvements in "socialist commerce," which mirrored the best practices of private

Figure 5.2. Inspecting the Tianqiao Department Store. A caption accompanying the photo reads: "Xu Guixiang, a salesclerk at the Tianqiao Department Store, enthusiastically introduces its advanced experience to the Jilin Municipal Business Tour Group." In this idealized version of "socialist commerce," note the clean store with shelves visibly full of products and attentive clerks. The photograph also shows the use of glass displays to further grant access and amplify material desires, a retailing practice that first spread to major Chinese cities in the early twentieth century, and then, with the aid of the Ministry of Commerce, throughout the country in the Mao era. Source: 北京画册编辑委员会, ed., 北京 (Beijing) (Beijing: Beijing huace bianji weiyuanhui, 1959), 124. I am grateful to Alfreda Murck for sharing this photo.

capitalist enterprises abroad. In Beijing, according to one reporter, "No matter where you go – stores, restaurants and even bathhouses – customers are treated better than before." Provincial and local newspapers published stories and letters remarking on the improved quality of service in stores around the country.[103] A handful of stores began to experiment with even more cutting-edge retailing techniques, such as open shelves, which allowed customers to choose and inspect products rather than go through the extra hassle of asking a clerk. Despite the state billing this and other experiments as part of "socialist commerce," these techniques were the emerging best practices in industrial capitalism around the world that sought to lower labor costs and maximize inducements for customers to interact with commodities, learn about them, start to want them, and ultimately purchase them.[104] A foodstuffs store, for example, implemented the pre-1949 sales practice of dispatching a cart into neighborhoods so that people could buy products there rather than making a trip to the store. Other stores tried to help make cooking at home more efficient by doing more of the preparation work, including the grinding of meat. According to one report, in July 1958 alone Liberation Street Department Store in Hangzhou received over 4,000 handwritten notes praising the store.[105] One patron at the store even wrote a poem in the guest book testifying to the store's good service, describing the "warm smile" that greeted customers and the places provided to sit and drink a cup of tea and towel off sweat during hot weather: "Everyone praises the department store," it read, "and people all want to come and shop again."[106] The message was clear: the improvement of "socialist commerce" – including smiling clerks – depended on the expansion of labor exploitation to induce and deepen the customers' desire for commodities produced by the state.

Additional Experiments

During the Great Leap Forward, state capitalism removed a number of traditional restrictions that limited the state's ability to extract surplus labor. In particular, there was the introduction of women to the workforce outside of the household economy – a move that the state lauded as evidence of "liberation," but which often introduced the "double burden" on urban women of providing both waged and unremunerated household labor.[107] Although the party did help break gender barriers and advance greater gender equality in women's ability to commodify and profit from their labor – which was a goal during the Republican period as well – at this particular juncture the state enforced the entry of urban women into the labor force as a way to extract labor rather than primarily to serve a "socialist" goal of providing women with equal access to remunerated work.[108] State rhetoric, however, advertised the policies as "opportunities" for women to "display their potentialities" and, by working in the formal economy, "transform a consumer community into a producer community, drawing housewives into the ranks of workers."[109]

Meanwhile, the care work formerly performed by women outside the formal economy, which underpins capitalism, did not vanish and had to be replaced, whether by other family members or by women themselves after a full day of work. The collapse of the communal dining and children-rearing experiments of the Great Leap Forward further exacerbated the state's dependence on wage labor during the day and invisible household labor after working hours ended.[110] A large food store in Hangzhou established in May 1958 reported that by the end of that year, the number of women working there had increased from twenty-seven to sixty-two. Most were mothers; they had 120 children in total, and one woman had six children. When the Tianqiao campaign told the store to halve its work-force, workers initially assumed that these new women would be the ones to be let go. According to long-held stereotypes in the retail industry, women workers were not as good as their male counterparts because of the "Three Mores, Two Lesses, and Six Bad-Ats": women had more house-work responsibilities, more trivial interests, and were more finicky; they had less stamina and less occupational knowledge; and they were bad at deboning animal carcasses, selling meat, fish, vegetables, and watermelon, and making deliveries. Rather than sending the women employees back home, however, the party chose to make the store an experimental "shop run by women" by training the women to overcome their reluctance to do tasks conventionally done by men, particularly manual labor and making deliveries. Soon forty of the women had learned to ride a tricycle and transport heavy loads. Women also took over all the other positions monopolized by men, such as selling fish and meat, deboning meat, disemboweling chicken, and descaling fish. Claiming that it had con-quered service employees' shame about doing service work, the party shared the story of one young female clerk who had once staked out spots to hide whenever her friends came to the store but, due to coaxing from her co-workers, had overcome her embarrassment and quadrupled her sales.[111] Unremarked upon in the article, this woman, by overcoming her resistance to such work, enabled the state to extract more labor from her.

Nationwide efforts to promote better service in retail stores and encou-rage frugality among consumers provided socialistic cover for the shortages created by the state's industrial ambitions and encouraged the reserve army of consumers to minimize its demands. Under the banner of "Promoting Frugality," Shanghai's Number One Department Store responded to shortages by adding services rather than by adding products. The store increased its demands on clerks' labor rather than demanding more state resources. Salespeople taught customers how to maintain products, including how to wash wool clothing. Clerks offered to help customers mend or patch old clothes and even convert Western-style suits, now rendered unfashionable by state dictate, into outfits favored by young men. Efforts to conserve fabric by selling detachable collars rather than entire shirts became very popular, and the store created a large window display to promote what became known as a "frugality collar."[112] To satisfy demand in the absence of state-provided supplies, the store began to rent out products it had only sold, including cameras, alarm clocks, telescopes, and thermometers, and expanded its in-store repair services for everything from fountain pens and radios to clothing and children's toys. The store even dispatched staff to schools and military units to collect old or broken musical instruments, which the staff then repaired and resold. An extreme example of Number One's embrace of state consumerist frugality during this era of state capitalist-induced shortages was its offer to sell only one of a pair of shoes or socks if that was all that was needed.[113] Rather than acknowledging its shortfall of resources and demanding more from the state, Number One instead forced employees to work unpaid overtime, learn new sets of skills, and cope with the emotional work of handling irate customers. The store's focus on consumerist frugality thus relied on the unpaid extraction of excess labor from service workers.

The "socialist commerce" experiments during the Commercial Leap Forward illustrate how state capitalist policies attempted to maximize the extraction of labor and minimize the role of the consumer – promoted in private capitalism and consumerism – in driving accumulation through demand. These policies also attempted to minimize the state's allocation of resources into paying for workers' labor directly, through wages, or indirectly, through improved services. The Great Leap Forward saw the state's attempt to push its extraction of surplus labor to the absolute maximum, while cutting down on consumption to keep capital in state coffers.

The State Promoting and Discouraging Consumerism, 1960–1970

Once again, however, the state found consumer demand to be critical to accumulation. CCP attempts to force people to work endless hours to demonstrate their revolutionary enthusiasm had limited and diminishing results. The Great Leap Forward's extreme prioritization of production over consumption came at a massive cost, causing a devastating famine that killed millions of people and plunged the country into an economic recession. The party, with Mao's tacit support, set out to do what it could to repair the economy.[114] During the 1960s, the state returned to its initial post-1949 institutional arrangements of compromising with private capitalism and consumerism, as discussed in previous chapters, to generate the revenue necessary to restart the economy and continue industrialization.

The state sacrificed the self-described socialist goals of stable prices and egalitarian distribution by shifting its distribution policies for highly sought-after goods from a system based on rations and queues, which better hides the inequalities of distribution, to a system based on prices. Although it sustained fixed prices for eighteen categories of commodities that it considered necessities so as to avoid runaway prices with the reintroduction of markets, it also implemented a "high-priced commodities policy" for products such as watches and bicycles. Stores now sold these products openly, without ration coupons, to anyone who had the money to buy them.[115] One measure of the resurgent inequality that resulted from this policy was the increasing number of Beijing shops and restaurants that again featured expensive foods. On January 21, 1961, eleven food shops in the city began to sell expensive dishes. By the end of the year, the number had risen to sixty-two, and one year later to eighty-three. Prices for the best dishes reached RMB 10, during a period when the average worker earned under RMB 2 per day. In 1961, these high-end restaurants served 13,660,000 patrons; their sales reached RMB 33,850,000 and represented over a third of the total revenue of the food and beverage industry in Beijing. As planned, the state received its cut of this new consumer spending. In 1961, the high prices for state products, including the Three Great Things of wristwatches, bicycles, and sewing machines, redirected between ten and twelve million RMB back to state coffers.[116] In yet another policy area, despite its rhetoric about egalitarianism and frugal living, state capitalist policies took precedence over socialist ideals.

The state-sanctioned renewal of demand-driven supply influenced local economies. The government tolerated the re-establishment of countless mom-and-pop shops that the state had nearly eliminated during the consolidation of the Great Leap Forward period. In Beijing, for instance, the disappearance of snack shops forced all capable work units to sell breakfast and late-night snacks, leading to semi-authorized mom-and-pop shops springing up to fill the vacuum. The extreme scarcity of consumer goods during the Great Leap Forward had led to a resurgence of demand for private repair work because of the difficulties of replacing broken goods. Officials encouraged the reappearance of services that had disappeared in Beijing, such as repairing broken bowls and pots, with even some mandated price reductions for 500 types of repairs.[117] In all these cases, the state's deprioritization of consumer goods had unintentionally incentivized private economic activities and, in fact, had exacerbated people's need for them. In these examples, underinvestment in manufacturing consumer goods undermined state control over the economy and incentivized the further elaboration of gray markets.

Although some people welcomed this seeming thaw in state attempts to limit consumption and services, others protested. The latest conspicuous resurgence of consumerism and private capitalism caused concerns and a backlash that eventually, as noted in Chapter 3, led to the Socialist Education and Five-Antis campaign and reached extreme hostility during the Cultural Revolution. As the 1960s progressed, Mao and his supporters who witnessed the expansion of the inequalities associated with industrial capitalism, including their manifestations in consumerism, increasingly criticized the state's attempts to label capitalist practices as "socialist commerce." To dissenters, these practices signaled a capitalist restoration.

This growing radical interpretation of consumerism extended to the concept of good service. During the early days of the Cultural Revolution, past efforts to improve shopping by adopting any semblance of "bourgeois" practices were critiqued under the slogan, "Good service may cause revisionism." Cultural Revolution supporters reinterpreted the efforts by stores only a few years earlier to improve the shopping experience of socialist commerce by adding a wider variety of products or improving customer service – that is, practices at the heart of the Emulate Tianqiao campaign – as "preaching the bourgeois lifestyle and implementing a peaceful evolution" toward capitalist restoration, that is, following the Soviet path. According to this critique, colorful window displays spread "feudal superstitions" that "stank of corruption." Some Mao supporters, rejecting half-hearted party rhetoric that tried to put service work on a par with other forms of labor, attempted to ban service in restaurants, arguing that being served by others fostered "bourgeois forms of leisure" that "taught people to despise manual labor." Instead, they heralded self-service not as a form of capitalist labor-saving and inducing demand, but rather as a way to reduce conspicuous forms of subservience that created social hierarchies.[118] In Harbin's Laodaowai area, for instance, restaurant customers not only had to line up to order, pay for, and pick up their meals but they also had to wash their own dishes after they finished their meals and then arrange the bowls, plates, and chopsticks on the table for the next customer.[119] Attacks on service occurred at all levels of society. Hotels in Nanjing, for instance, eliminated single rooms because they were considered too bourgeois and began providing large communal beds capable of accommodating many guests. Even the mandate to repair rather than replace worn goods came under fire. Red Guards insisted that all freelance shoe-repair shops on streets and in alleys be immediately closed down and that a collective with lower set prices take over repair work.[120]

Red Guards in Shanghai attempted to implement even more extreme experiments. They proposed transforming the best-known commercial spaces for "socialist commerce" to socialist showplaces, three-dimensional areas to disseminate propaganda or, as they called them, "venues to promote Mao Zedong Thought." Their proposals included turning the Number One Department Store into a hall for reading the works of Chairman Mao, and converting Yong'an Department Store, which by this time had changed its name to The East is Red Department Store, into an exhibition hall to showcase the economic achievements of the Maoist line. Red Guards advocated turning the Red Guard Department Store into an exhibition hall to promote the achievements of the Dazhai commune's agricultural production. Through these changes, they argued, "the revolutionary masses who went to Nanjing Road would not only be able to shop but also could be educated profoundly in Mao Zedong Thought."[121]

These hostile attitudes toward consumerism varied across China. In 1966 and 1967, shopworkers whom the state had reassigned to the countryside during the Great Leap wanted to return to Shanghai and their original work units, and they demanded compensation for lost wages. When the Shanghai authorities agreed to pay back salaries and allow these workers to return to Shanghai, workers employed as casual and contract laborers demanded and received similar benefits.[122] Suddenly a large number of people in Shanghai had disposable currency, and many of them rushed to buy things with their new-found wealth. At Shanghai's Number One Department Store, many goods quickly sold out. In the morning of January 8, 1967, for instance, as soon as the store opened, some 300 people headed straight for the areas displaying the Three Great Things to buy whatever they could. Expensive watches sold out instantly and sales of high-quality clothing doubled. Customers during the shopping frenzy, as during normal times, rarely contemplated their actual needs or even the price of the offered goods. Rather, they worried about missing the opportunity to convert cash into commodities that would retain the best value. The panic was so widespread that workers left work to shop, leading to a shortage of stevedores at Shanghai port.[123] Local authorities, fearing that the panic purchasing would worsen in the lead-up to Chinese New Year in early February 1967, cancelled pay advances and eased the crisis by beseeching workers to slow down their purchases.[124]

The same service problems created by state capitalist policies persisted, and the state addressed them with the same ineffective socialistic solutions. In October 1970, after a radical wave of the Cultural Revolution had passed, Premier Zhou Enlai once again held up specific stores as models for retailers across the country and called for other stores to follow their lead by improving service (i.e., working harder), extending business hours (i.e., working longer), and adding new services (i.e., working more). Zhou later tried to address low morale among service workers by urging them to resist the idea that "service jobs have no future."[125]

Within a few years after the start of the Cultural Revolution, to facilitate greater accumulation Chinese society once again saw signs of a shift in the institutional arrangements of capitalism with a greater toleration of consumerism and private accumulation to improve commerce. From 1972 to 1976, for instance, Beijing restaurants added 2,046 tables and 12,100 seats by opening branches in non-commercial properties, and more than 300 food shops that offered breakfast and snacks were opened. The state began to reauthorize sideline businesses. Public bathrooms and repair shops that had long run at a deficit were allowed to make money by selling cold beverages and producing distilled water. Local governments allowed repair shops to sell commodities and make small machine parts. The administration helped open 427 "proxy restaurants" that received equipment, resources, and support from state-owned restaurants and food shops in exchange for a cut of the profits. Similar arrangements were reached to open 279 laundry stores, fifty-four small barbershops, and twenty-eight integrated repair shops and auto repair shops.[126] Although the launch of the Cultural Revolution saw the return of hostility toward open manifestations of capitalist practices, it also saw the revival of many of those same practices, often at the express behest of state directives. These examples again illustrate that even during the height of Mao-era iconoclasm, as long as the state accumulated sufficient amounts of capital to allocate to industrial development, implementing a socialist vision for the distribution of mass-produced products was secondary.

Conclusion

During the 1950s and 1960s, state intervention helped expand as well as channel consumerism. The infrastructure of consumerism – and therefore industrial capitalism – developed faster because the state created a network of stores more rapidly than could have been created by the country's private capitalists. The state contributed to a much faster concentration of control over retailing and a corresponding reduction of the total number of mom-and-pop stores, stalls, and peddler networks, as the party expanded a nationwide infrastructure for industrial consumerism out of the humble department store legacy of the Republican era. Through the establishment of thousands of department stores in cities and towns across the country (and tens of thousands of smaller shops in rural communes), the state introduced the training ground for new forms of behavior associated with mass consumption. It gave millions of people more places to shop and gave a wider range of social classes access to new categories of products, such as the Three Great Things and other mass-produced goods.

The impact of these stores extended beyond sales tallies. The stores introduced people to the experience of browsing, learning about, and desiring products – and even desiring specific brands – without expectation of purchasing (or even having the resources to buy). They also exposed visitors to new forms of display and interaction with products and new practices of customer service such as fixed prices. In this network of national stores, the party created institutions that valorized and celebrated consumerism at the expense of service workers, despite its simultaneous attempts to limit material desires based on an ethos of hard work and frugal living through propaganda campaigns.

As this chapter shows, many of the problems associated with the party's attempts to create a "socialist commerce" – indeed, many of the problems attributed to socialism in the popular imagination – were consequences not of the state efforts to "build socialism" but of the accumulation-at-all-costs priorities of state capitalism. State capital accumulation mattered more to the party than consumer goods production, the service industry, or customer satisfaction, and it papered over the cracks between its rhetoric and its policies with quick and inexpensive fixes that relied on the unremunerated labor of the workforce. Ultimately, the party's stated goal of shaping socialist commerce to "serve the consumer" was a state capitalist attempt to manage the reserve army of consumers and suppress its demands for the surplus. The state mobilized the army of consumers when it suited state goals and demobilized it, as was so often the case, when it did not. When people became restless and production slid, the state attempted to fix the problem through material incentives by shifting along the state-to-private spectrum of industrial capitalism once again toward more private capitalism and consumerism. In turn, this shift back toward consumerism increased concern among the party leaders, under the leadership of Mao, that the People's Republic was headed toward a restoration of capitalism and the negation of the Communist Revolution.

CHAPTER 6

Consumerism in the Cultural Revolution

Nearly two decades into "building socialism," the party had not yet rid China of what the party acknowledged as capitalist habits and practices. People, both inside and outside the party, noticed and challenged the persistence of practices at odds with the language and promises of the Communist Revolution and the state's tolerance and even dependence on them. In response, in early August 1966 the Central Committee called for yet another mass campaign, this one a cultural revolution that would advance the goals of the political and economic changes of the previous decades.[1] "Although the bourgeoisie has been overthrown," the party announced, "it is still trying to use the old ideas, culture, customs, and habits of the exploiting classes" – what it would term the "Four Olds" – "to corrupt the masses, capture their minds, and endeavor to stage a comeback."[2]

To thwart this attempted "capitalist restoration," the party turned to the masses, calling upon them "to meet head-on every challenge of the bourgeoisie in the ideological field and use the new ideas, culture, customs, and habits of the proletariat" – i.e., the Four News – "to change the mental outlook of the whole of society." According to the party, it was now up to the Chinese masses themselves to

> struggle against and overthrow those persons in authority who are taking the capitalist road, to criticize and repudiate the reactionary bourgeois academic "authorities" and the ideology of the bourgeoisie and all other exploiting classes and to transform education, literature, and art, and all other parts of the superstructure not in correspondence with the socialist economic base, so as to facilitate the consolidation and development of the socialist system.

Thus blaming "capitalist roaders, academics, and exploiting classes" for undermining the state's earlier attempts to build socialism, Mao and his allies now declared that attacking these four vague categories of "Olds" was the key to fulfilling the promise of the Communist Revolution and ridding

China of the capitalist elements that the party had tolerated and even facilitated through its own policies.[3]

The message found receptive audiences across China. As this chapter will argue, the violent nationwide mass movement that followed was not another top-down campaign waged by the state but evidence that tens of millions of people throughout the country had grave misgivings about the state capitalist policies and their inequitable outcomes. Animosity toward consumerism as a manifestation of industrial capitalist inequalities was not unique to the start of the Cultural Revolution but a reflection of a long-brewing undercurrent of popular dissatisfaction with the outcomes of the state capitalist priorities of the Mao era, heightened by the failure of party policies to fulfill the rhetorical aspirations of the Communist Revolution.

Although similar language attacking bourgeois culture had circulated in China for decades, Communist Party officials intensified the public rhetoric the summer preceding the official declaration of the Cultural Revolution. In June, an editorial in the *People's Daily* titled "Sweep Away all the Monsters" introduced the slogan "Destroy the Four Olds, Establish the Four News," which became synonymous with the early Cultural Revolution and legitimized much of the initial wave of destruction and violence that followed.[4] Unlike many other aspects of the Cultural Revolution, the activities associated with this call to destroy the Four Olds were not formally part of a state-orchestrated mass campaign, but, like the NPM in the early twentieth century, it was at least as much a bottom-up movement. These activities, as the first half of this chapter will show, constituted an attack on the material manifestations of the Four Olds that ranged from the destruction of churches and temples to the ransacking of the homes of "class enemies" in search of "incriminating evidence" and "bourgeois" possessions such as books, artwork, and jewelry. Across the country, participants in "destroy" activities made speeches, distributed pamphlets, and posted signs on the streets that criticized various fashions in hairstyles and dress as damning evidence of "bourgeois lifestyles." During the initial years of the Cultural Revolution (1966–8), this state-sanctioned attack on "capitalists" and bourgeois consumerism occurred at all bureaucratic levels and across broader society.

Popular and scholarly narratives of the Cultural Revolution focus on the extreme violence associated with political and student factionalism, justifiably so given its inestimable human and material tolls.[5] The nationwide political purges of 1967–8, known as the "cleansing of the class ranks," persecuted an estimated thirty-six million people, of whom an estimated 750,000 to 1.5 million were killed.[6] The widespread violence expanded beyond cities into the countryside and into ethnic minority regions in Tibet, Inner Mongolia, and Xinjiang.[7] Popular images of the "Great Proletarian Cultural Revolution" convey totalitarian conformity in appearance, socialist zealotry in thought, and wanton destruction of "feudal" and "bourgeois" material culture in deed. Yet, as the second half of this chapter will show, by highlighting the anti-capitalist rhetoric and seeming uniformity of the Red Guards, general histories of the era overlook the ways in which the activities of the Destroy movement ultimately did not build socialism but helped negate the Communist Revolution by introducing new and expanded forms of consumerism (Figure 6.1).[8]

The Destroy Movement's Attack on Expressions of Consumerism

Destroy activities targeted social institutions associated with consumerism, including retail stores, branding, advertising, and fashions. Building on the rural-focused Socialist Education Campaign and a second urban-based Five-Antis campaign of 1962–6, the Cultural Revolution's attempted solutions to the persistence of bourgeois practices depended on the activities of young participants called Red Guards. The Red Guards were informal associations of students that, in some cases, became paramilitary organizations. Their name, first adopted by Beijing middle-school students, encapsulated their goal: to guard or defend against decay of "the red": Mao Zedong Thought and the Communist Revolution. Attacking the Four Olds was their primary form of defending what they considered to be properly revolutionary.

Originally led by the children of cadres who blamed intellectuals and capitalists for social ills, as "On Khrushchev's Phony Communism" had done a few years earlier, the Cultural Revolution opened the door for much more direct critiques of the CCP by non-party members.[9] The beginning of the Destroy movement is usually associated with the start of a series of eight spectacular mass rallies that Mao presided over between August 18 and November 26, 1966.[10] From across the country, some ten million Red Guards and their teachers converged on the capital to attend these rallies in the largest public urban space in the socialist bloc – Tiananmen Square – outside the main entrance to the Forbidden City.[11] Signaling his support for the Red Guard organizations by donning an armband presented to him by one of the students, Mao and his allies used these rallies to endorse and further encourage Red Guard attacks on the vague categories of people and things classed as part of the "feudal-bourgeois-revisionist" elements that persisted even in what the party had declared was now a socialist country.

Figure 6.1. "Destroy the old world and build a new one" (1967). Signaling an endorsement at the highest levels of the party, an editorial from *People's Daily* on June 8, 1966, explained the rationale behind the Destroy movement: "To construct a new world, Chinese must first smash the old. To build a new ideology and new culture of socialism and communism, we must thoroughly criticize and eliminate the old ideology and the culture of capitalism and its influences." Source: The International Institute of Social History (Landsberger Collection).

In what became known as the Red Terror, Red Guards went to extreme lengths to attack any and all signs of the Four Olds.[12] The day following the first rally, Beijing's Red Guards took to the streets, smashing street signs with "old" names and replacing them with suitably "revolutionary" names, initiating a name-change trend that soon swept the country. The name of the Avenue of Eternal Peace running across the northern edge of Tiananmen Square, for example, was changed to the East is Red Avenue; a major road in the foreign embassy area became Oppose Imperialism Road; Yangwei Road in front of the Soviet Embassy became Oppose Revisionism Road; and the primary shopping street in the city, Wangfujing ("Prince's Palace Well"), became Revolutionary Road (see Figure 6.2). Prominent places associated with the "old society" fared no better: the Summer Palace built for emperors became Capital People's Park, and Tianqiao Theater, located near the

Figure 6.2. The road to revolution. This photo illustrates the Destroy movement's effort to replace bourgeois and feudal material culture with a socialistic alternative. Here pedestrians read an announcement by Red Guards explaining the changing of the name of a prominent shopping street in Beijing from Prince's Palace Well (Wangfujing) to Revolution Road. Source: *China Reconstructs*, vol. 16, no. 2 (1967), 7.

Tianqiao Department Store, was renamed the Red Guard Theater.[13] Similar renamings took place in other cities. On a single day of the destroy activities, September 16, 1966, Red Guards in Nanjing changed 1,082 street names and twenty-eight bridge names.[14]

With the blessing of national leaders and state media, Red Guard attacks on perceived manifestations of non-socialist culture, such as churches, temples, theaters, libraries, and historic sites, expanded in subsequent months. Across the country, countless old books were burned, including those in school libraries.[15] Red Guards even attacked sites officially designated as places of cultural or historical interest. In Beijing alone, of 6,843 such sites, 4,922 had been destroyed by the end of the Cultural Revolution.[16]

Retailing the Revolution

Along with changing street names, Red Guards also targeted stores. Although stores established after 1949 had usually chosen revolutionary-sounding or functional names, older ones had decided not to change their names or signs even after completion of the Socialist Transformation. In response to the Destroy movement, these pre-1949 visual holdovers were replaced with signs and names based on the new politically fashionable terms. Popular names included Worker-Peasant-Soldier, Revolution, Cultural Revolution, Red Flag, Red Guard, and the ever popular the East is Red. Even businesses without the "four old" names tried to make their names sound "new," such as the renowned Sichuan Restaurant which was renamed the Worker and Peasant Canteen. Wangfujing Department Store, named after the shopping street in Beijing, tried out various revolutionary alternatives before becoming Beijing City Department Store.[17] As these renamings suggest, even in the radically anti-capitalist phase of the Cultural Revolution, stores used their names to brand themselves as "socialist," despite their actual economic status or intended function.

Red Guards forcibly made some stores and restaurants change their names, while many others, echoing survival strategies adopted during earlier changes in policies and social attitudes toward consumerism, pre-emptively complied in the hope of continuing business as usual or expanding their customer base. The day after the first rally in Beijing, Red Guards from three local middle schools stormed the illustrious roast duck restaurant with the classical-Chinese-sounding name Quanjude and persuaded workers to destroy its seventy-year-old signboard. The business then chose the politically neutral name Beijing Roast Duck Restaurant and hoisted a banner encouraging workers-peasants-soldiers to dine there, adding five low-cost dishes to its menu.[18] Countless other stores followed suit as the destroy activities expanded.[19] In Hangzhou, Red Guards attacked the Four Olds on the streets of the city in late August by destroying some store and road signs and pasting handwritten big-character posters on storefronts. Fearing increased violence, Zhang Xiaoquan Scissors Factory, named after one of its founders during the Ming dynasty, became Hangzhou Scissors Factory; and Yunxiang Women's Clothing Store became Cherish the Military Women's Clothing Store.[20] Even state-owned enterprises faced increasing amounts of revolutionary fervor. In Shanghai, 3,000 of some 3,700 retail stores operated by eight Shanghai state companies changed their shop names and signs, with thirty-two renamed Red Guard. On Beijing's Wangfujing commercial thoroughfare, no fewer than six stores were renamed as the more socialist-sounding Red Flag.[21]

Attacking Additional Symbols of Consumer Culture

This extreme moment of anti-consumerism revived criticisms of window displays, advertising, and other aspects of the visual culture of consumerism for stimulating bourgeois material desires and consumerism while merely adding a socialistic veneer to capitalist practices. The wide-ranging attack on the visual culture traditionally associated with commerce extended to attacks on the doorway couplets adorning store entrances that expressed, in classical Chinese, the desire for good business and satisfied customers. Red Guards insisted, as one of their handbills testified, that stores remove window displays "full of perfumes and beauty products" and set up displays that emphasized Maoism in "frugal but tasteful ways."[22] Stores soon removed items for sale from their windows in favor of revolutionary decorations, such as red suns, copies of Mao's writings, banners with political slogans, and Little Red Books.[23]

Shanghai's Nanjing Road became ground zero in the fight against the "feudalism-capitalism-revisionism" represented by consumerism.[24] On August 23, 1966, tens of thousands of Red Guards converged in the commercial center, carrying placards with images of Chairman Mao and banners announcing "We are the critics of the old world" and "We are the creators of the new world."[25] Rejecting the party's earlier efforts to integrate socialism and consumerism in the form of "socialist commerce," Red Guards posted Mao's words everywhere inside the city's department stores. Even before the Red Guards appeared at their stores, many employees demonstrated an awareness of how seemingly innocuous things like store names could communicate social meanings by preemptively painting their doors red. The art deco Park Hotel, a symbol of the former Western imperialist presence in China, placed Mao's image and words in its more than 200 guest rooms and in its reception and lounge areas. Not all stores had such foresight, however, and Red Guards forced more than 2,000 of those that had not acted fast enough to replace their signs and change their names.[26] At Yong'an Department Store, Red Guards and complying staff members pasted big-character posters in the store's windows demanding that it change its anti-revolutionary name, which translates as "Forever Peaceful," to Forever Red, Fight Forever, or Red Guards. Newspapers circulated a photograph of Red Guards pulling down the massive sign at Shanghai's biggest amusement building, The Great World. Stores named after capitalists adopted revolutionary-sounding names, and the Bund, the former headquarters for many foreign companies, changed all of its foreign-language signage.[27]

Radical Red Guards, however, remained unmollified by such changes to conspicuous icons of consumerism and tried to transform stores into sites of political education. In November 1967, a big-character poster with the heading "Bombard Nanjing Road" that appeared in a window at the former Lihua Department Store, now renamed the Red Guard Department Store, proposed a more sweeping political transformation:

> Comrades! The Great Proletarian Cultural Revolution has been proceeding for over a year now. Are we to tolerate the current situation on Nanjing Road? We cannot. We cannot. We absolutely cannot. Smash the big stores, the famous stores, and the specialty shops. Turn them all into sites to promote Mao Zedong Thought. For example, Shanghai No.1 Department Store could be changed to a reading hall for the works of Chairman Mao; Yong'an Department Store, which has by now changed its name to The East is Red Department Store could be changed to an exhibition to showcase the economic achievements of the Maoist line; the Red Guard Department Store could be changed to an exhibition showcasing the achievements of Dazhai-style agriculture. These changes will allow the revolutionary masses who come to Nanjing Road not just to shop but more importantly also to be educated profoundly in Mao Zedong Thought.[28]

Although this proposal was never adopted, this poster and others like it reflect a rejection of the premise that consumer enterprises could be made socialist through the superficial changes encouraged by earlier party policies and the difficulty – perhaps even impossibility – of reconciling the goals of the Communist Revolution with the continued existence of capitalist commercial activity.

Red Guards similarly rejected the party's earlier attempts to create socialist advertising, attacking all forms of advertising as indoctrinating capitalism among the people.[29] Whether in response to pressure from Red Guards, fears of attack from those higher up the bureaucratic chain, or a genuine belief that consumerism was a manifestation of capitalism, the editors and managers of newspapers and periodicals soon eliminated almost all advertising, particularly for consumer goods. The state regulatory bodies charged with overseeing advertising in cities throughout China were disbanded, their members diverted to other work or sent to the countryside for "re-education." Although advertising did not disappear during the Cultural Revolution decade (1966–76), it consisted mainly of newspaper announcements about cultural performances, films, and the publication of political books and journals such as *Red Flag*.[30]

Indeed, during the Cultural Revolution, advertising was replaced in the visual culture of urban and commercial spaces with a dramatic increase in political propaganda, known as the sea of red. Red Guards plastered Mao's words and images everywhere: on buildings, on billboards, in homes and offices, on bicycles, three-wheeled carts, cars, and trains. A secretary who worked for Mao later said that cyclists riding on the streets without a small metal plate featuring a Mao quotation hanging from their bike could expect to be stopped by Red Guards.[31] The color red appeared on everything, from the armbands of the Red Guards to the Little Red Book to the ubiquitous Mao badges (discussed in Chapter 7), and on such unlikely locations as the walls of public toilets. Red Guards at the Beijing Institute of Aeronautics applied red paint to doors and walls along busy streets, government offices, schools, and even private residences. The sea of red extended to billboards displaying Mao slogans and images along roads, creating a socialistic urban aesthetic that would be associated with "Mao's China" for years to come.[32]

Red Guards did not merely attempt to destroy the Four Olds and commercialism but sometimes drafted both for their own Four New purposes. In their quest to eliminate social traditions that they labeled "old" and "feudal," Red Guards replaced customary forms of decoration, such as replacing traditional couplets, pasted on home doorways on the eve of the Lunar New Year, with quotations from Chairman Mao.[33] They demanded that theaters and movie houses begin their entertainment with quotations from Mao rather than scenic images or advertisements, and that theaters lower their ticket prices to better serve workers-peasants-soldiers. Attempts by Red Guards to transform bourgeois and traditional visual culture included suggesting that images of cats and dogs on envelopes or stamps – considered bourgeois pets – should be replaced with political themes.[34]

Problematic Products

Supporters of the Destroy the Four Olds movement influenced what could be sold by pressuring stores to remove or rebrand goods that the Red Guards labeled as "problematic products."[35] Luxury goods were obvious targets, including cosmetics (especially lipstick), gold and silver jewelry, high-heeled or embroidered shoes, expensive alcohol and cigarettes, Western-style suits and skirts, mechanical toys, playing cards used for gambling, and Chinese chess sets. Sometimes Red Guards targeted only product names and trademarks, particularly those that included religious or superstitious text or imagery, such as references to the god of longevity or the bodhisattva Guanyin and traditional greetings such as "I wish you long life and riches." On September 10, 1966, the Tianjin Industry and Commerce Administration Department issued an "Emergency Notice on Trademark Reform" that forbade the sale of products with trademarks that included traditional images or phrases, including "prosperity brought by the dragon and the phoenix," "the heavenly maidens and scattered blossoms," and the "talented scholars and beautiful ladies" that people considered to be role models for the upwardly mobile and that the state saw as the opposite of working-class heroes.[36]

Extreme interpretations of the Four Olds category during the Destroy movement politicized product names and trademarks, including those without obvious "feudal-capitalist-revisionist" implications. The movement, for instance, politicized names based on things as banal as birds, animals, insects, and flowers on the grounds that they "lacked a strong proletarian sense."[37] Not even customary food names escaped critique. The city of Wuhan, for instance, changed the name of eighty-one dishes sold in the food and drink industry for their Old associations. "Mapo doufu," which roughly translates as "pock-marked old lady bean curd," became the more benign-sounding "roumo mala doufu" or just "mala doufu," that is, "minced meat spicy bean curd."[38]

Moving beyond earlier efforts to purge foreign-language words from product names, the Destroy movement attempted to eradicate even Chinese words that sounded foreign, including words such as *qiaokeli* (chocolate), *jiake* (jacket), *kaqi* (khaki), and even *asipilin* (aspirin). Some Red Guards revived the efforts discussed earlier to disassociate Chairman Mao from generic product names, and thus from vulgar commerce, by removing the character of his surname, Mao, from product names. In addition to being a surname, *mao* could mean "hair," "wool," or "feather," so products targeted for name changes included *maoyi* (wool sweater), *maoxian* (knitting wool), and *maotan* (wool blanket). In Harbin, the Huili brand of gym shoes was the most fashionable and expensive brand on the market until a rumor spread that the pattern on the soles resembled the three Chinese characters for "Chairman Mao," and almost overnight no one wanted to be caught wearing them and treading on the Chairman's name. The writer Liang Xiaosheng later recalled walking down a street in Harbin with several of his classmates when another group confronted one of them for sporting a new pair of Huili shoes and forced the offending party to remove the shoes and burn them on the spot.[39] Demonstrating again how consumerism had permeated society and how it continued to expand, even such efforts to eradicate capitalist vestiges produced new branding hierarchies.[40]

During the Destroy movement, the combination of rumors, determined Red Guards, and vague definitions of what was an "old" led to purges of products and affected the range of available consumer goods. On August 24, 1966, for example, Red Guards from several Nanjing schools demanded that the Nanjing Central Department Market close for a day to check for Four Olds goods and to change its name to People's Market, and then watched as clerks removed several truckloads of items newly designated as contraband. Red Guards in Nanjing removed an estimated 20 percent of products from store shelves on the grounds they were "feudal, capitalist, or revisionist."[41] Likewise, students temporarily closed stores around Xinjiekou in Nanjing and spent four hours checking inventories and removing traditional markings such as auspicious symbols of dragons and phoenixes from the stores.[42]

These pressures and name changes hurt product availability and created product scarcity. Department stores instructed buyers to acquire only products considered revolutionary, suitable for the masses, and practical, and to avoid products tainted with feudal and capitalist associations.[43] Beijing City Department Store stopped selling over 6,800 products, or one-fifth of its products. Wuhan's top department store ceased sales of 4,200 items and reduced the number of items in the cosmetics section from some 200 to 15. Tianjin Department Store removed more than fifty cosmetic products, including moisturizers, powders, perfume, lipstick, rouge, eyebrow pencils, and nail polish, and stopped selling products with the word "fragrant" because it was a character long considered to be the epitome of a wasteful bourgeois lifestyle, the prime example being perfume, or "fragrant liquid." In total, the store removed RMB 15,000 worth of cosmetic products from its shelves, only resuming sales of such items in 1973 and even then, exclusively at specially designated counters.[44]

Shoppers, however, did not easily give up their favorite products and brands. Just as customers had only paid lip service to abandoning their preferences for imports right after 1949, stores and shoppers engaged in countless acts of minimal compliance. These acts of resistance suggest both a difference of opinion about what was offensively bourgeois and what was properly socialist, and a practical tactic that skirted the issue. Although some stores burned their stocks of contraband products, others found ways to sell them, such as wrapping "problematic products" in plain paper.[45] When Red Guard attacks on 4,354 feudal-bourgeois-revisionist products ended up driving many smaller retailers out of business, customers put new pressure on larger department stores to carry the offending products. One of these, Shanghai No.1 Department Store (formerly Da Sun/Daxin), found numerous ways to bypass new regulations, and it continued to carry more than 90 percent of the banned commodities, which comprised roughly 15 percent of its total inventory. Some stores opted to sell products without packaging or labels, and others asked factories to repackage products in plain packaging or to manufacture popular products such as thermoses in solid colors or without elaborate patterns. Ren Zheng, a eminent calligrapher, recalled asking a clerk at Shanghai No. 1 Department Store for a well-known brand of writing brush, a Zhouhuchen, which the clerk passed to him in a nondescript box, telling him in a low voice that it was in fact a Zhouhuchen brush that the store had held on to for longtime customers but was no longer allowed to sell under that name.[46] In another example, clerks at Tianjin Department Store tore off or defaced the packaging of some RMB 74,000 worth of products before selling them.[47] Despite the Red Guard's open hostility toward branding and toward some consumer products, many people and stores clearly valued branded products and attempted to evade the regulations.

Red Guard attacks on public-service industries further demonstrated the difficulty of eliminating entrenched "bourgeois" habits. Liang Xiaosheng, for instance, later recalled the effects of such destroy attacks in his Harbin neighborhood when he was a teenager. His barbershop, for instance, hung a notice on the window announcing that "Henceforth we will not cut any non-proletarian hairstyles. No hair will be longer than an inch. No hair oil, wax, or cream will be applied. For men: no sideburns or blow-drying. For women: no perms or curly hair." Elsewhere, barbershops and hair salons no longer providing hair washing, shaving, or pedicure services, and specific hairstyles deemed inspired by American subcultures such as the

Hong Kong style or "A-Fei style," which became associated with hooligans during the Mao era, were banned.[48] The restaurant across the street posted a sign that informed patrons: "Henceforth, the waiters and waitresses at our restaurant will not wipe tables or wash dishes. We are not the servants of the customers. Rather restaurants should be the homes of the customers. Customers should serve themselves and demonstrate the equality of all those living under advanced socialism."[49] Photo studios refused to take traditional family photos or photos with women and men standing too close to one another. Some studios implemented a "things we won't photograph" policy, including anyone wearing sunglasses (considered an A-Fei affectation), ethnic clothing, or Western-style wedding dresses. Some guesthouses stopped cleaning rooms and delivering hot water to guests, and massage and pedicure services were banned in public bathhouses.[50]

The enforcement of anti-bourgeois fashion trends continued for months by relying on Red Guard violence. During a visit to Beijing's leading commercial street in the winter of 1966–7, around the time of the Lunar New Year, Li Jingrong, a reporter with *Liberation Army News* (*Jiefangjun bao*), noticed that although many shops were closed due to the politicized environment, one barbershop remained open. Inside, however, Red Guards forced a line of women who had been waiting in the shop for perms to have their hair cut short or to even be shaved bald. When he stopped several young women rushing by without shoes on the cold winter street, one told him, just before being driven away by Red Guards wielding belts, "I should not have worn high-heeled shoes. They are part of the Four Olds, so the shoes were destroyed."[51]

Attacks by Red Guards in cities across China against people with "bourgeois" hairstyles and clothing were eerily similar to the politicization of personal appearance during the revolution of 1911. Anti-Manchu revolutionaries forced men to change the hairstyles imposed by the Manchu Qing dynasty (a shaved forehead and a long queue of hair); some defenders of the dynasty attacked men who wore Western-style suits and, by implication, who supported the revolution.[52] In the autumn of 1966, Red Guards in Guangzhou searched the streets for pedestrians wearing Four Olds clothing, using an ink bottle to test whether women's pants were too tight. After stopping a suspect on the streets, they would ask her to drop an ink bottle into the front of her pants. If her pant legs were wide enough to let the bottle drop to the ground, they allowed her to pass; otherwise the pants were deemed inappropriately tight and summarily shredded.[53] Such pant-shredding appears to have been a common occurrence.[54] Zheng

Guanglu recalled that Red Guards positioned at select street corners in Chengdu armed with large scissors would forcibly cut the hair of women wearing long braids or having wavy permed hair and slash flashy shirts or pants on the spot.[55]

Some fashions, as always, were seen as frivolous, and revolutionary credentials did not automatically protect a person's fashion choices. Twenty-one-year-old Hong Xia and her boyfriend, both of whom had been named ideologically reliable "advanced youth" in their work units, liked wearing trendy clothing. One day, however, as the couple went on a date to the Forbidden City, they were accosted by a group of Red Guards who shredded Hua's flowered dress and sliced open her boyfriend's pants and tossed them into the river. Not stopping there, they chopped off the couple's hairstyles, leaving Hua with a big cross cut into her hairdo.[56] In another case that made national news, the Red Guards of the Beijing No. 15 Girl's School, echoing Mao's anti-Soviet polemics of a few years earlier, declared that the uniforms worn by policemen were Soviet-inspired and thus were an example of "revisionist" culture. Reversing the party's earlier promotion of Soviet fashions, the students demanded that the uniforms be redesigned to be more politically correct, and powerful Mao supporter and Minister of Public Security Xie Fuzhi quickly agreed to purge the Soviet influences from the uniforms.[57]

The open-ended and changing interpretation of what constituted unacceptable clothing created anxiety and uncertainty among many ordinary people, especially in China's cities. Some people opted to preemptively stop wearing some of their favorite clothing to avoid rousing Red Guard ire. The two decades of "gender erasure" that followed 1949, when equality of the sexes largely meant that women were expected to look and act like men, had already influenced women's fashions. According to historian Antonia Finnane, 1965 was "the last year for some time that women would be licensed to 'dress up nicely.'"[58] As photographs from the period reveal, during the Cultural Revolution, nearly everyone, regardless of age or gender, changed their wardrobes to plain army-style fatigue green, dark blue, or gray outfits.[59] During the Destroy movement, Ding Shu's family went so far as to burn a photo of Ding's father wearing a suit and tie.[60]

The Destroy movement was a more radical and destructive version of earlier campaigns in which accusers cited possessions as proof positive that someone was a "class enemy." During the Cultural Revolution, one could literally wear class betrayal on one's sleeve. Just as fashionable women had been lambasted by critics during the NPM era for squandering national resources on frivolous fashions and buying imports from imperialist enemy countries, the Destroy movement attacked female transgressions of the dominant ideology reflected in their fashion choices.[61] In the early years of the PRC, the Republican-era stereotype of women as erotic objects transitioned to the glorification of the "productive female masses" – that is, women who sacrificed themselves for the good of the party and nation. Although attacks on ordinary women who did not project that image through their fashion choices could be swift and violent, Red Guards also attempted to force female members of the political elite to comply. They even dared to ask Song Qingling, widow of Sun Yat-sen, to change her hairstyle, but she refused, citing a promise to her mother that she would never cut her hair short.[62] They had more success, however, in making a national warning out of the personal style of Wang Guangmei, wife of Liu Shaoqi, vice-chairman of the CCP and formally the head of state. Before the Cultural Revolution, in a documentary shown across China, Wang had been celebrated as a fashion icon and symbol of China's growing power, particularly after a trip to Southeast Asia in 1963, when she wore a *qipao* and looked glamorous.[63] But after a *People's Daily* editorial attacked Liu in April 1967 as the "top party person in authority taking the capitalist road," Wang's fashion sense came to be seen as confirmation of her and her disgraced husband's "bourgeois tendencies."[64] Her accusers, charging her with corruption and being "captivated by luxury goods," cited numerous incidents when she had supposedly used state resources to improve her wardrobe.[65] On April 10, 1967, Red Guards at Tsinghua University, with support from the central government and a local PLA garrison, held a struggle session attended by 300,000 against some 300 enemies. The session created another iconic image of the Cultural Revolution's radicalism when Red Guards forced Wang Guangmei to wear high heels, a *qipao*, and a necklace made of ping-pong balls to mock the pearl necklace and outfit she had so memorably worn during her visit to Southeast Asia four years earlier.[66]

Beyond the extremism and violence that characterized the Destroy movement, its critique extended beyond the behavior of individuals to also attack the superficiality of state attempts to create socialist commerce. One Red Guard handbill, for instance, criticized earlier attempts to improve the socialist service economy in mass drives such as the Tianqiao campaign for "preaching the bourgeois lifestyle and implementing a peaceful evolution" toward capitalism, and denounced dazzling, colorful window displays as "ways to spread feudal superstitions."[67] In an apparent contribution to such criticisms, a *People's Daily* editorial in late August 1966 declared that going forward, "all products must be massified" and any store that previously served only wealthy customers had to reduce their prices and "abandon a view that sees itself as a famous store serving the bourgeoisie."[68] Lest the point be missed, in September 1968 the Revolutionary Committee of the Commerce Department altered Mao's slogan "Serve the People," which during the Commercial Leap Forward had been interpreted as "Serve the consumer," to indicate exactly which people were being referred to: "Serve the workers, peasants, and soldiers."[69] Despite this clarification, businesses encountered the same problem they had struggled with during all previous attempts to massify consumption: how to meet the goal of serving poorer people while also attracting paying customers and avoiding unemployment among service workers. That the Ministry of Commerce found it necessary to instruct service businesses that they would not be allowed to close down suggests how difficult many businesses found navigating this dilemma.[70]

Although these attempts to smash consumerism reflect an underlying awareness that it remained rampant, the task of identifying class enemies and stamping out insidious practices also relied on communication through branding and consumption. As we shall see in the next section, the attacks during the Cultural Revolution did not attempt to negate capitalism by transforming social relations but instead by inculcating a new series of brand hierarchies and social expressions of personal value, and thereby continuing to facilitate the expansion of consumerism.

The Reproduction and Spread of Consumerism in House Ransackings

According to the original destroy slogan, China had to "destroy the Four Olds" in order to "establish the Four News." On one level, destroy activities reveal a frenzied attempt to build socialism from the ground up by eliminating the perceived remnants of "feudalism" and capitalism that were inhibiting the building of socialism (Marx's "birthmarks"). But once again, the socialist rhetoric of the Cultural Revolution was accompanied by policies that were socialistic. Despite the Red Guards' vociferous rhetoric and wanton violence, they left largely untouched the institutions of industrial capitalism that continued to produce social inequalities. As the remainder of this chapter will show, the destroy activities so closely associated with the Cultural Revolution ultimately did more to negate socialism than destroy capitalism. Because Red Guards attacked only surface-level manifestations of capitalism and consumerism while ignoring the underlying institutional arrangements that prioritized capital accumulation over equalizing social relations, their extreme efforts during the Cultural Revolution not only failed to achieve their stated goal but also backfired and further fueled the development and spread of consumer patterns.

Among the disturbing images of the Cultural Revolution are the rampant house ransackings by violent teenage ideologues searching the homes of "class enemies," beating the occupants, and confiscating or destroying possessions matching the Four Olds in the name of safeguarding the Communist Revolution.[71] During the initial months of the destroy activities, the homes of targeted elites were raided multiple times by different groups, including neighborhood committees, local schools, and even the victims' own work units. Movement participants in Shanghai searched at least 84,222 homes of the "bourgeoisie." In late August and September of 1966, Red Guards in Beijing raided the homes of 33,695 families, searching for possessions newly designated as contraband, including specific types of furniture, clothing, shoes, bedding, as well as makeup, televisions, pianos, and even accordions.[72] Ransackers, applying the broad and open-ended definitions of the Four Olds however they understood them (or however it suited them), impounded, stole, or destroyed artifacts considered old, currency, gold and silver bars, and other valuables. Throughout China, Red Guards confiscated at least sixty-five tons of gold, tens of millions in RMB, millions in US dollars and other foreign currencies, and untold amounts of jewelry and other valuables.[73]

House ransackings remain a notorious aspect of the Cultural Revolution in part because the targets included venerated intellectuals and artists, including the novelists Lao She, Ba Jin, and Ding Ling (whose house was searched more than ten times).[74] Between August 23 and September 8, 1966, Red Guards in Shanghai searched the homes of some 1,231 "elite intellectuals" and teachers.[75] On August 24, 1966, for example, Red Guards raided the house of Liang Shuming, the prominent educator and organizer of an earlier rural rejuvenation movement, and burned all of his books, except those by Mao or those on Marxism-Leninism, and all the paintings collected by his great-grandfather, grandfather, and father. As Red Guards tossed his copy of the *Cihai*, the comprehensive dictionary of classical Chinese, into the bonfire, they told him that "the *New China Dictionary* (first published in 1957) suffices for the use of our revolutionary Red Guards; these feudal relics are useless."[76] Two months later, on October 22, 1966, Red Guards from the Film Academy broke into the home of distinguished historian Hou Wailu, which had already been searched and sealed by another group of Red Guards, and smashed or confiscated all of his remaining possessions, including cash and priceless antiques, leaving him penniless and hungry.[77] Those conducting the ransackings pushed the definition of the Four Olds to the limit, such as when Red Guards instructed one of China's pre-eminent writers, Shen Dehong (better known by his pen name Mao Dun), to discontinue using a table lamp, a gift from a Polish friend, because it featured naked Venus figures that they deemed indicative of "bourgeois decay."[78]

Red Guards targeted all manner of signs of consumerism and capitalism to accomplish several political ends. "Bourgeois" artifacts supplied Red Guards with incriminating evidence to use against their political enemies, in the same way that the possession of nice things had evinced corruption among cadres and capitalists during the Three/Five-Antis campaign. In one notable example, on September 4, 1966, Li Fanwu, governor of Heilongjiang province, was subjected to a mass struggle session attended by more than 100,000 spectators, during which Red Guards accused him of "attempting to hide precious objects," in this case, three wristwatches, two pins, and two artificial-leather handbags that the Red Guards had discovered while ransacking the home of his niece and had seized as evidence of his corruption. Li Zhensheng, who covered the session as a photographer for the provincial newspaper, was close enough to this supposed evidence to see that one of the watches had a worn-out leather band, another had a band of plain metal, and the third had no band at all.[79]

In addition, ransacking houses led countless others to attempt to comply with the latest definitions of unacceptable consumption in the hope of avoiding similar scrutiny. Peking University literature professor Yue Daiyun recalled that she and all of her colleagues anxiously disposed of any newly demonized possessions before their homes were inspected.[80] In Harbin, Li Zhensheng likewise purged his possessions in anticipation of a house ransacking that, in his case, never came:

> Like everyone else at the time, I rid myself of 'suspect' belongings, such as an edition of love poems by Pushkin and a book of paintings by Xu Beihong, who had studied in France and was criticized during the Cultural Revolution for his nudes. I also hid under my bed three stamps that displayed works by Goya, including his painting *Naked Maya*, and some old silver coins with likenesses of Chiang Kai-shek and the self-proclaimed emperor Yuan Shikai.[81]

A retired cadre blogging under the name Jiangshanqiangu recalled that although Red Guards repeatedly ransacked his family's home in Shenyang, an intensely painful loss for him had been the pre-emptive selling of his bicycle, a high-quality East German import for which he received far less than he had paid, suggesting that local markets were flooded with other high-end bicycles from families similarly purged of their possessions.[82] Such possessions apparently flooded local markets, and others, who were less liable to be subject to political suspicion, perhaps, took advantage by making purchases. Ownership of consumer goods continued to distinguish types of people, albeit in new ways.

Despite the extreme hostility toward consumerism that the ransackings of the early years of the Cultural Revolution represented, they also produced new forms of consumerism based on the confiscated items. An unanticipated consequence of the house ransackings was the increased exposure they provided to Red Guards and millions of other people to bourgeois things and bourgeois lifestyles. House searches provided Red Guards from various social and economic classes with an opportunity to see how their economic betters lived. Even during the height of the Destroy movement's anti-consumerism activities, the Old things continued to maintain their appeal, now extended even to those attacking them. Older Red Guards assigned Liang Xiaosheng and his friends to safeguard a makeshift warehouse full of confiscated bourgeois possessions until the state assumed possession of them. Liang and his friends took the opportunity to rummage through expensive traditional furniture, clothes, thousands of books, artwork, clocks, and other items that until then they "had only seen in movies." What attracted their attention was a drawer full of every conceivable type of watch: wristwatches, pocket watches, gold and silver watches, watches displaying the date, watches with diamonds. Liang recalled that everyone grabbed a favorite and "pretended to be wealthy." They even tried on confiscated clothing, including Western-style suits, and "dressed like gentlemen."[83]

But the Red Guards who participated in the ransacking of houses were not the only ones to be exposed to the bourgeois products they appropriated. Throughout, Red Guards set up public exhibitions of impounded products that they presented as evidence of the "bourgeois" or "rich landlord" statuses of their "class enemies." Many of these displays were used to shame and intimidate those known to possess the same products, such as intellectuals with suspect class backgrounds. Yue Daiyun recalled that the university required faculty in every department to visit an exhibition of materials confiscated by the Red Guards. The exhibition included a "collection of photographs, paintings, books, artifacts, stamps, and identification papers of former [Nationalist] officials," though what Yue found "most eye-catching was a string of high-heeled shoes confiscated from various homes around campus." According to a student guide, the exhibition had a threefold purpose: to reveal the significance of the class struggle at Peking University; to illustrate the sufferings of the workers, peasants, and soldiers; and to expose the bourgeois lifestyles of faculty and cadres.[84]

Although these so-called class-education exhibition centers may have accomplished their goals, they also let non-elites see for themselves items that at the time were only available to the wealthy customers of the leading bourgeois department stores.[85] In 1966, Yang Yaojian, then a thirteen-year-old sixth-grader at Chongqing's Lianglukou Primary School and a member of a Little Red Guards organization, attended a Red Guards Rebellion Achievement Exhibition, held at the city museum to educate people about class struggle. The museum grouped visitors by work unit, with factory workers, farmers, and soldiers granted special access. The contraband on display included pianos, mahogany furniture, elaborate bathtubs and folding screens, jewelry, antiques, guns, drugs, opium pipes, and even certificates and letters with Chiang Kai-shek's signature. Newly confiscated items arrived daily. One day, Yang recalled, a Red Guard leader showed up wearing three watches on his arm, which he turned over to the exhibition. Yang used this opportunity to read confiscated books that had been deemed "poisonous weeds," especially detective stories and adventures of swordsmen that were otherwise unavailable. According to Yang, visitors did get the intended message: at a time when most were living hand-to-mouth, the displayed items "showed how big the gap was between the rich and poor" and reinforced the need for continued class struggle against the bourgeoisie.[86] Equally critically, however, the items on display stirred up a desire for many of the products that people had little hope of otherwise encountering, much less acquiring. Moreover, the displays facilitated consumerism by allowing people to interact and learn to desire things, under the guise of educating themselves about proper socialist practices.

Once having been awakened to consumerist desires, many participants in destroy activities found opportunities to satisfy a new compulsion to acquire material goods. At least one such opportunity was predictable. As confirmed by an exchange of documents between the Cultural Revolution committee of the small city of Wuzhou in southwestern Guangxi province and regional and national Cultural Revolution committees regarding local officials' plans to deal with confiscated goods, theft ran rampant. Moreover, as the documents reveal, the state did little to prevent the theft, damage, or destruction of the seized goods, agreeing that the local committee should hold on to confiscated gold, silver, foreign currency, large amounts of cash (one family in Wuzhou had thousands of RMB in cash), and luxury consumer goods such as expensive leather coats and watches. Although the party did set limits on what could be confiscated, declaring that ordinary items such as clothing fabric should be returned to their owners, Red Guards and government officials faced few penalties for overstepping their authority, nor were they held responsible for stolen or damaged property or required to pay for anything they had taken. State directives simply instructed the ran- sackers to turn over the valuables or "otherwise face consequences."[87] The vagueness of this warning left open to interpretation what a valuable item was, and the stipulation that a reasonable use of property and expenditure of confiscated money could be exempt with "an appropriate explanation" tacitly fueled the Red Guards' consumerist tendencies to use these items and to spend money as they saw fit.

Between 1966 and 1968, as Red Guard organizations toppled the established political authorities and claimed authority, innumerable organizations and individuals seized confiscated possessions. According to Zhao Yuan, a Red Guard then in his final year at Chengdu's No. 1 Middle School, Red Guards claimed to be "borrowing" watches and bicycles from the homes they searched. And they did not always limit themselves to one item per person. He reported that some of his classmates competed to acquire things such as watches and they "often wore two watches on both their left and right arms, and some even wore a range of watches," transforming these material manifestations of bour- geois status to trophies for the Red Guards. According to his account, female students used the ransackings as an opportunity to enhance their wardrobes.[88] Among the general public, Red Guards became so asso- ciated with stealing private possessions that at one point rumors circu- lated that they were hoarding gold.[89] Some Red Guard organizations in power by 1967 misused state resources by using public cars and taking trips on planes. In one Shanghai Red Guard organization, for instance, leaders seized trucks, jeeps, motorcycles, six Soviet cars, and seventeen bicycles.[90] These and numerous other examples demonstrate how the destroy activities had the contradictory effect of turning would-be anti- capitalists into the equivalent of corrupt cadres or non-law-abiding citizens and awoke the consumerist tendencies of even the revolutionary vanguard.

As destroy activities proceeded unchecked, petty criminality and appropriation of state resources grew. Even workers who were not directly involved in the ransackings took advantage of the distrust of political authority cultivated by the Cultural Revolution to take things from their workplaces or to repurpose factory supplies to meet their own desires for consumer items. Guan Shengli recalled that in the factory where he worked, one worker stole glass and iron to make his own fish tank; another worker confiscated copper wire to make a birdcage, though raising birds had been denounced as bourgeois; and a third worker took home potted flowers.[91] Others pinched tools or stole fabric to make their own mops. Still other workers used working hours to make plastic cigarette boxes, bicycles and bicycle accessories, desk lamps, knives, furniture, and windows and doors to use or to trade. Although the evidence suggests that at the beginning of the Cultural Revolution workers were doing these things discreetly, eventually many workers conducted such activities brazenly, with groups of people working together to seize, transport, and sell public property.[92]

At the highest echelons of the political and social hierarchies, destroy activities provided opportunities for leaders to steal national cultural relics and assemble private collections. For instance, Guan Weixun, who worked as a tutor to Ye Qun, the wife of Lin Biao (a primary promoter of the Mao cult), reported that when Ye heard that other officials were taking valuable confiscated antiques for their own use, she wanted a share of the loot for herself. Lacking a connoisseur's eye, she asked Guan and other staff members to go to the warehouses and take valuables for her.[93] Between 1967 to 1970, Lin Biao and Ye Qun dispatched their secretaries to the Cultural Relics Management Office to "buy" antiques, paying a pittance of what they were worth.[94]

Corruption ran so rampant that a better name for the movement might have been Confiscate and Re-circulate the Four Olds. Items classified as worthy of destruction often ended up in the hands of different owners. Gold and silver goods, pianos, furniture, difficult-to-find books, and valuable collections of ancient Chinese art, including paintings and calligraphy, found their way into the possession of local Red Guards. Beyond those items that were retained as trophies or personal possessions, many confiscated items later appeared in state-owned stores and in gray markets throughout the country, which were filled with rare or otherwise unattainable products. In Chengdu of Sichuan province, for instance, such goods showed up both in flea markets and specialty markets for books confiscated during the ransackings or stolen from libraries.[95]

Circulation Central: The Huaihai Road State Used Goods Market

In Shanghai, seized and stolen products recirculated across all levels of society. The best antiques not appropriated by officials often ended up in the Shanghai Museum, while ordinary goods sometimes recirculated through second-hand stores, such as the city's well-known state-owned Huaihai Road State Used Goods Market, known as the Huaiguojiu (淮国旧). Huaiguojiu opened on September 29, 1954, on the Shanghai shopping street, Huaihai Road, in the former French concession.[96] The market's initial mandate was to sell off goods left behind or confiscated by the state from the fleeing Nationalist officials, including Chiang Kai-shek and his supporters, two million of whom fled from mainland China to Taiwan in the final years of the civil war in 1948–9. In 1956, the store, which occupied 10,000 square feet of property between Huaihai and Changle Roads, expanded its services and replenished its stocks by selling on consignment things that were previously owned by individuals. Products on offer included everything from antiques, used clothing, watches, clocks, leather coats, shoes, radios, and high-end branded goods such as Rolex and Omega watches and Leica cameras.

In addition to functioning as a marketplace, Huaiguojiu also served as an exhibition of the material culture underlying the bourgeois lifestyles that many of the people who visited it had few opportunities to encounter. The unavailability and array of merchandise attracted far more window shoppers than customers who could afford a second-hand Rolex watch. Although two other stores, the Friendship Store and the Overseas Chinese Store, carried the most desirable of these bourgeois products, they catered to foreigners and overseas Chinese. By contrast, Huaiguojiu allowed ordinary people to buy goods in RMB and without ration coupons, providing a way for those with cash to circumvent the restrictions and to enjoy bourgeois niceties.

Although the products on offer at the store were specific to Shanghai – where the supply of such goods and the memory of the bourgeois lifestyles of pre-1949 China were stronger – the store was also a popular destination for out-of-town visitors. Shanghai remained China's consumer capital despite the anti-consumerist rhetoric of the Cultural Revolution because state policy reproduced the city's primacy as a consumer destination. In addition to showing people luxury goods, Huaiguojiu also gave less wealthy people access to nicer things by selling factory seconds of much-desired products. Although the quality of factory seconds may have been lower, their lower prices allowed more people access. Zhu Haiping, for example, recalled once going there to buy a pair of heavily discounted Huili brand gym shoes. The shop assistant let him inspect the shoes and informed him that the Huili line was so high quality that they were manufactured for export, but because a pair had a minor discoloration, it cost only RMB 1.80, half its original price. He immediately purchased the shoes and was ecstatic to "show off my new pair of shoes in front of my classmates."[97] The store played a specific role in the ecology of shopping in Shanghai by providing shoppers and visitors with a reference point for learning, identifying, and ranking global brands – that is, for developing the language of consumerism – as such brands still circulated in China, though they were mostly second-hand.

Huaiguojiu's function as a reference point for foreign brands expanded as a consequence of the house ransackings during the Cultural Revolution when people took their own or stolen things to sell there. As Shanghai resident Shen Jialu recalled, the store "opened a window for Chinese to see Western material culture firsthand." Moreover, people practiced the culture of consumerism, and even connoisseurship of luxury products, in plain view on the doorsteps of Huaihai Store. Huaihai Store also spawned collectors and devotees of the products on offer, particularly watches. Hu Mingbao who, after retiring from the military in 1968, spent forty years fixing countless watches, later reported that he had first learned about the differences among watches and how to repair them at the store, where he and other devotees congregated: "I remember I spent half a day at Huaihai Store every Sunday. We gathered around the back door where a group of people always assembled to discuss and debate watches, clocks, and antiques. We could inspect these goods while experts, including store clerks, discussed them . . . . I still wear the first watch I bought there."[98]

During the Cultural Revolution, the store embodied the central contradiction between the anti-bourgeois rhetoric of the Mao era and the actual practice of consumerism. On the one hand, banners over Huaihai Store (as over other stores at the time) proclaimed its mission to fulfill Mao's mandate to "Develop the economy and ensure supplies."[99] But as one frequent patron observed, another of the slogans it displayed stated, "Practice thrift and support the household," using the notion of "thrift" to refer to its sale of used items, giving the store political cover to continue selling what the patron acknowledged were "many items symbolic of a bourgeois lifestyle."[100] As elsewhere in China, such politically correct slogans, marketing, and branding were critical to the store's continued success during the Cultural Revolution and supported the myth that the extreme "anti-capitalist" activities of the Cultural Revolution destroyed the vestiges of capitalism.

The store also undermined the socialist pretense of the ration system by allowing wealthier people to sell off products and maintain their bourgeois lifestyles. A widow of one Shanghai capitalist began selling her valuable possessions at the beginning of the Cultural Revolution. Although Red Guards had ransacked her house, she still had jewelry and valuable mahogany furniture that she sold to avoid possible confiscation by Red Guards. The state had stopped paying interest on private businesses expropriated in the Socialist Transformation and she needed the money.[101] Her transactions – like countless others – hence recirculated the bourgeois material culture that was repeatedly and explicitly targeted for destruction.

During the Destroy movement, the social value or meaning of such products varied depending on who owned them, facilitating a brisk second-hand business for the Four Olds.[102] Before 1949, the party assigned class origins to all families based on their economic situation, which was then passed down patrilineally during the Mao era. The "best" classes (known as the "five red classes" or categories) were the working class, poor and lower-middle peasants, revolutionary cadres, soldiers, and martyr families, while the "bad" classes (known as the "five black classes" or categories) included landlords, rich farmers, counterrevolutionaries, bad-influencers, and rightists. The division of classes reflected the "bloodline theory," which held that political lineage, or class origin, determined a person's class nature, a theory popularized in the expression, "A hero's child is a brave man; a reactionary's child is a bastard."[103] While the wrong products in the hands of members of the five black classes confirmed their status as enemies of the revolution, the same items in the hands of the five red classes were deemed harmless. For that reason, many owners of banned objects they feared would be confiscated or destroyed by Red Guards sold them cheaply to purchasers who could often use or display them with limited negative ideological associations.[104] Red Guard activities thus reproduced the sorts of gray market activities and market capitalist activities they supposedly deplored. The bloodline theory and its manifestation in the consumer markets created a loophole that made it easy for some members of the red classes to justify not destroying the Four Olds belonging to one's family or for stealing them during raids. This ambiguity in the social meanings of a given object meant that there were very few absolutes when it came to interpreting what was a Four Old, and it contributed to the difficulty of identifying exactly what was an offending item.

A quintessential example of how context defined a product's political value was the watches worn by Red Guards. Even as competitive consumerism led Red Guards to emulate the better-offs they so ruthlessly attacked, once in their possession, these established markers of status became revolutionary status symbols, proud tokens that commemorated one's participation and success in a raid. Consequently, watches did not carry the negative associations one might expect a luxury product would have had during the Cultural Revolution. Rather, they served as symbols that their wearers had the right revolutionary family background to allow them to ransack homes, and they demonstrated their successful engagement in revolutionary activities. As Xu Youyu, then a middle-school student, recalled, in his circles, those who were qualified to be Red Guards and search homes soon changed their appearance. Many of the males aimed to acquire enough watches to wear them on both their right and left wrists, or even on their entire arms. Likewise, female Red Guard classmates started wearing elegant embroidered handkerchiefs that they had confiscated during the raids, an unthinkable fashion choice for those with bad class backgrounds. Far from feeling that they were adopting the Four Olds, these Red Guards, according to Xu, took pride in their new possessions. One classmate known for being adept at searching homes enjoyed showing off the hidden treasures of the bourgeoisie that he had unearthed, including a gold pocket watch.[105]

People with the appropriate lineage and political background might influence the social meaning of a Four Old object and thus preserve ownership in the name of the state. According to Shen Jialu, Huaiguojiu sold some bourgeois products, such as luxury furniture, to factories that repurposed them: "I once saw many mahogany tables in various designs disassembled and put on a truck. They were sold and sent to a musical instrument factory to make traditional instruments such as the *jinghu*. Those luxury furniture items that symbolized bourgeois lifestyles were turned into musical instruments to serve the revolution and government policy."[106] Similarly, musical instruments used in traditional Peking opera were modified for use in Peking model operas and their uses extended.[107] That the party was aware that this practice possibly contradicted the goals of the Destroy movement is suggested by its ordering the shops that repaired these instruments to remove their brand-name insignias, usually the names of the celebrated craftsmen who made them.[108] This kind of repurposing or rebranding also took place at the national level, where Zhou Enlai and others redefined and even protected some churches and Buddhist temples as "cultural treasures."[109] Zhou reportedly stopped the

Red Guards from looting the Forbidden City by renaming the city of Beijing "East is Red" and replacing the lions in front of the Tiananmen entrance to the Forbidden City with statues of Mao, much as department stores added socialistic window dressings to downplay the capitalist activities inside.[110] Clearly, the Cultural Revolution soon came to include tactics for avoiding the destruction of all Four Olds.

Fashioning a Revolution

In yet another contradiction of the Cultural Revolution, despite the high-profile anti-fashion violence of the Destroy movement, the movement helped create – and even compel – new socialistic fashions and therefore expanded people's desire for material goods. Chairman Mao himself inadvertently promoted perhaps the biggest fashion trend of the Cultural Revolution: the wearing of military uniforms (accessorized with a Red Guard armband). Beginning with the first rally in August 1966, Mao chose to appear before the millions assembled (and tens of millions of others who saw photographs) wearing a military uniform and, as noted, accepted an armband from the Red Guard Song Binbin (Figure 6.3). His choice was deliberate and, given that he had not worn such a uniform in decades, forced his staff to scramble to find a military officer with a similar physique.[111] Mao intended the uniform to symbolize his support for the Cultural Revolution and his tacit support for the violent activities of its most fervent participants who would "make revolution" and destroy the remnants of capitalism and feudalism. At the same time, by wearing a uniform Mao wanted to endorse the favored garb of the Red Guards, who made up the vast majority of the assembled millions. The widely circulated image that showed Mao as "commander-in-chief" wearing a military uniform endorsed and spread a burgeoning fashion for wearing PLA uniforms beyond the children of military families.[112] Thus, at the same time as state media were trying to halt the spread of consumerism through economic propaganda, the media were also reinforcing the desire for uniforms. An anti-fashion became fashionable.

During the Cultural Revolution, the fashion of citizens wearing PLA uniforms was unintentionally fueled by an increase in the supply and variety of uniforms. But access was unequally distributed. With the termination of the military rank system on the eve of the Cultural Revolution in June 1965, the old PLA uniforms, which had marked differences in rank by differences in the quality of their fabric, were replaced with new, undifferentiated uniforms.[113] The army changed its uniforms to a bright "national

Figure 6.3. Mao-endorsed fashions. In this iconic image from a Red Guard rally in Tiananmen Square, Song Binbin puts a Red Guard armband on Chairman Mao. The widely disseminated photograph was interpreted as Mao endorsing the Red Guard movement by agreeing to don an armband. Youngsters across the country, however, found it easier to emulate his "revolutionary" anti-fashion fashion choices – the PLA uniform and Red Guard armband – than enact his ideas of class struggle. Source: *China Reconstructs*, vol. 15, no. 10 (1966), 16.

defense green"; the air force switched to green tops and blue pants; and the navy modified its uniforms to what was called "mouse gray." As the military retired the old uniforms from active use, the availability of a larger supply and variety of uniforms allowed youngsters from non-military families to wear military uniforms. The different fabrics of each rank in the older uniforms also provided the variation that is central to any fashion trend. The older uniforms, for instance, were made of superior fabrics and included richer colors, more sizes, and a more fitted style. Anyone who had access to the old wool uniforms tended to consider anyone wearing the new national defense green uniform an unfashionable arriviste. There were even differences among the new uniforms, as a cadre's uniform sported four pockets while a soldier's uniform only had two pockets. These small distinctions meant that different fashions sprung up among those from elite military families and those in the general population who only had access to the national defense green options, which became popular during the Cultural Revolution. Old Red Guards (that is, those who were first to form Red Guard organizations at the start of the Cultural Revolution) who came from elite family backgrounds and had access to the older ranked uniforms looked down on the newer Red Guards who wore the newer military uniforms, once again demonstrating how fashion functions to communicate identity and to structure hierarchies.[114]

Although technically civilians were not allowed to wear military uniforms, the state did not enforce this regulation, and even before the Cultural Revolution, children in military families wore their parents' old uniforms. This practice not only saved money and cloth rations, thus demonstrating one's commitment to living frugally, but also signaled the high status of a family as a member of the military and the red classes. As the Cultural Revolution took hold, signaling one's family class background through what one wore could become a life-or-death matter. Such personal branding was significant enough that even on cold winter days, teenagers from military families would often leave open the top button of their coats to allow their officer uniforms to be seen. Among children of the military, the variety of uniform styles meant that they could use stylistic differences to communicate status. According to editor and writer Liu Yangdong, who was a primary school student in Beijing at the start of the Cultural Revolution,

> Teenagers started wearing their parents' military uniforms at the start of the Cultural Revolution. They had different uniforms to choose from. Winter uniforms, for instance, were made of nice wool, and higher ranks had nicer uniforms. The uniform of a lieutenant-colonel was made of thick yellow wool with a tufted collar, while a general's uniform had a genuine leather collar.[115]

The spreading fashion of PLA uniforms extended from head to toe. At its height, Beijing youngsters would occasionally snatch the military-style hats of others. The most fashion-conscious aimed to have military boots to match their uniforms, especially in winter, and ideally captains' boots, which were difficult to obtain. Some people had shoe-repair shops make them a pair. The uniform fashion even impacted teens' desire for Huili gym shoes, which, despite the rumors that had led to their unpopularity in Harbin, retained their cachet across the rest of the country. Although the shoes were popular because they could be worn for different sports as well as for everyday activities, customers rejected those offered in blue because they did not match the most available military uniform color.[116]

As the desire for military uniforms spread beyond those with family connections to them, the supply of discarded PLA uniforms could not meet demand, creating shortages that further fueled people's compulsion to own them. The desire for PLA uniforms was so great that many, perhaps even most, of the non-soldiers were wearing homemade versions. As one young man from Guangdong province recalled, he was so eager to participate in the fashion that he bought a counterfeit army uniform after someone had stolen the real one that he had obtained from a colleague married to a soldier. As he pointed out, the PLA did not sell its surplus clothing and therefore any civilian who wore a fashionable army uniform, cap, or shoes was likely wearing a fake.[117] This rampant imitation furthered the compulsion people felt to acquire new fashions and products, thus displaying the nature and operation of consumerism even at the height of the Cultural Revolution. No longer reflecting military background or rank, military uniforms and their imitations became valuable because they communicated one's political up-to-date-ness, much like the Soviet fashions popular in China during the 1950s. The increased availability of sewing machines now made it easier for ordinary people to copy the coveted PLA uniforms. Not everyone, however, dared to wear PLA uniforms, real or fake; although there was no formal prohibition against members of the five black classes wearing such gear, doing so risked Red Guard criticism. That the Red Guards often confiscated or destroyed such clothing, however, also suggests that for at least some members of the five black classes, the risk was worth it.[118]

Conclusion

In the end, the Destroy movement, much like earlier intersections of politics and consumerist activities, such as the NPM during the Republican era, reproduced and reinforced the very consumerist impulses it tried to control or eradicate. The Cultural Revolution inspired a new generation to engage in the impulse to distinguish itself via the acquisition and display of very specific products in its supposed quest for a more egalitarian socialist society. While promoting new forms of social hierarchy through the possession of material manifestations of inequality, the Cultural Revolution also broadened the reach of consumerism to tens of millions of new participants across the country.

Even at its violent apex, the Cultural Revolution rarely targeted the underlying economic, political, and institutional arrangements that created the social inequalities that the Red Guards claimed to despise. The failure of the Cultural Revolution to destroy the "feudal" and "capitalist" culture should thus be seen not as a failure of politics but as a problem inherent in the Communist Revolution. The participants in destroy activities were not ending the consumerist manifestations of industrial capitalist inequality but building on them, albeit with the differences in access to products arising from the institutional arrangements on the state capitalist side of the spectrum of industrial capitalism. From this perspective, such notorious activities associated with the Cultural Revolution represent not the Mao era's greatest effort to build a socialist alternative and save the Communist Revolution, but a next step in the expansion of capitalism and consumerism.

CHAPTER 7

The Mao Badge Phenomenon as Consumer Fad

Beyond purging the bourgeois and feudal elements from Chinese society, a primary goal of the Cultural Revolution was to inculcate Chinese youth with revolutionary socialist cultural values. The movement's leading proponent, Mao Zedong, saw youth as a critical tool to combat what he saw as the growing rise of a capitalist-style bureaucracy within the Chinese state. More specifically, Mao worried that members of the bureaucracy, with their power to appropriate and distribute the surplus, were becoming invested in preserving the higher status and better lifestyles that came with such power. In short, the institutional arrangements of state capitalism were creating the equivalent of the bourgeoisie class in a market capitalist country. To counteract this growing internal threat to the party's revolutionary goals, Mao turned to the younger generation. In 1965 Mao told American reporter Edgar Snow that he envisioned that these young people, who had not been schooled in revolutionary principles as part of the earlier revolutionary struggles, had the potential either to advance the "continued development of the revolution toward communism" or to "negate the revolution and do bad things."[1] Based on his endorsement and encouragement, Mao endeavored to enlist the Red Guards by inculcating in them the values necessary to fulfill the promise of the Communist Revolution.

During the early years of the Cultural Revolution decade, Mao and the other leaders of the party set out to inspire and reinforce these ideals among the young through activities such as those described in the Chapter 6, including attending huge rallies, engaging in revolutionary activities, and displaying their revolutionary ardor by wearing military-style clothing or owning copies of Mao's writings. Although less well known outside of China than the *Quotations from Chairman Mao*, one of the powerful totems of revolutionary identity during the early years of the Cultural Revolution decade was the Mao badge. These badges, which sported images of Mao and sometimes revolutionary slogans attributed to him,

200

rose to prominence after the first of the mass rallies in Tiananmen Square on August 18, 1966.[2] Soon, tens of millions of Red Guards nationwide aspired to attend such a rally, catch a glimpse of Mao, declare their commitment to Mao and the Revolution, and bring home a Mao badge as proof of their visit.

As this chapter will show, the symbolic and social value these badges created for their owners soon provoked a wave of material desire that propelled the production, distribution, and accumulation of billions of badges across the country and the globe.[3] Although this Mao badge fad, like the larger Cultural Revolution of which it was a particularly visible part, was initiated by the state to achieve what it perceived to be an urgent political goal, it also provides a prime example of the self-expanding and compulsive nature of consumerism.[4] The mania for Mao badges reflected the three central attributes of industrial consumerism – being largely mass produced, endlessly exchanged and discussed, and worn to communicate identities and social standing. But the badge fad also shared features with consumer fads everywhere. Fads are an intensified form of fashion: they emerge suddenly, are embraced with great passion, quickly move from a small subsection of society to broad participation, and then end almost as suddenly as they begin.[5] Fads are usually inexpensive and easy to join, encouraging participation and emulation, and producing an initial burst of public enthusiasm in which demand outstrips supply, often leading people to resort to extreme actions in order to participate. As such fads develop, they tend to induce a desire that becomes completely abstract from the initial use or social value of that product, creating new hierarchies of belonging and difference.

As Mao surveyed the throngs of adoring teenagers who swarmed Beijing in the late summer of 1966, little could he have imagined that the mobilization of these young protagonists during the Cultural Revolution would help spread the exact values it was intended to counteract. Although the sentiments shouted by the Red Guards in Tiananmen Square and throughout the country appeared to manifest Mao's fondest hopes for their generation, the mania for Mao badges provides further and compelling evidence of how everyday actions served to further the practices of consumerism and the negation of the Communist Revolution.

State Origins of the Badge Fad

As is typical of fads, the vast majority of Mao badges were produced within a very short period of time, beginning in the opening months of the

Cultural Revolution in 1966–7, reaching a peak around the Ninth National Congress of the party in April 1969, and promptly declining after June 1969. Although the fad sprang up in various places across the country, its first movers were high-ranking cadres who obtained Mao badges through state production and distribution channels that were activated to create and spread the fashion. By mid-October 1966, only two months after the first Red Guard rally in Beijing, high-ranking cadres, including Marshal Lin Biao and Premier Zhou Enlai, appeared in public, and in newspaper images circulated across China, wearing Mao badges on their jackets. The fashion spread further as government officials began giving Mao badges as gifts to visitors to the capital, as when Zhou presented a delegation of students from Xinjiang with 10,000 badges to take back home to use as gifts.[6] Within months, the fad was well underway, and cadres at all levels of government proudly put on their Mao badges.[7]

The fad's spread and diversification over such a short period of time was due in part to the state's prior history of developing and promoting badges. The party had created the first badges with images of Mao in the 1930s, decades before the Tiananmen rallies, and they had become part of the original Mao cult in the 1940s.[8] These badges served as medals awarded for meritorious service or to commemorate important events, such as completion of public works or construction projects. These initial badges were produced in small quantities and presented to and worn by select and distinguished groups of people. Rather than featuring images of only Mao, they sometimes portrayed Mao alongside other national heroes, including the writer Lu Xun, General Zhu De, and Marshal Lin Biao. Following the establishment of the People's Republic, private companies began commercializing the image of Mao and sometimes complemented state-sponsored and individual badge production and distribution with high-quality luxury items commercially produced for special occasions. In 1950, for instance, the Shanghai stationery store Lao Feng Xiang produced a small number of 22 karat gold Mao badges to commemorate the new government, providing another example of an upper-class store attempting to reinvent itself by embracing the new order, while commercializing socialistic fashions. At the time, however, the vast majority of badges were still produced by the state for official purposes. In 1951, delegates to the National Committee of the Chinese People's Political Consultative Conference, for instance, received bronze badges as part of the government's Resist America and Aid Korea campaign.[9]

Before long, other segments of the population also desired Mao badges. Some started to create their own badges, such as Chinese soldiers fighting in the Vietnam War in the early 1960s who fashioned badges from scrap metal from downed US planes.[10] According to a 1967 article in the *People's Daily*, a Beijing factory worker, Tian Zhihai, created the Mao badges that sparked the fad in August 1966. Tian made molds for products such as the good-luck charms worn by newborn babies, and spent eight arduous months using images of Mao printed in the *People's Daily* to produce an acceptable Mao badge. The new product was an immediate hit with the factory's customers, and as the fad took hold, the factory shared its molds with other producers around the country, helping accelerate nationwide production. Due to the rapid capital accumulation and industrial investment of the 1950s, the state already had in place machinery to promote the fad, to expand production, to meet consumer demand, and, in the process, to earn money for a state factory.[11]

A primary early sponsor of the badge fad was the mobilization of an actual army of consumers. When Marshal Lin Biao took charge of the PLA in the aftermath of the Great Leap Forward, he promoted Mao badges as an expression of loyalty within the larger Mao cult.[12] In May 1967, front-page articles in national newspapers celebrated Lin's decision to issue all PLA personnel with a set of two badges – one in the shape of a star with Mao's image at its center and a rectangular one, beneath which was printed the socialist slogan "Serve the People," rendered in Mao's calligraphy.[13] "Serve the People" was the title of a speech Mao had given in honor of a fallen soldier and it encapsulated the premise upon which Chinese state capitalism was based – the self-sacrifice of diligent workers and frugal consumers for the collective good of the people and the nation.[14] In a political economy that continued to spread capitalism, it is a predictable contradiction that this original badge, with its slogan implicitly valorizing consumer frugality, became a valuable and widely desired badge.[15]

Officials used the resources of state capitalism and state consumerism to further mobilize the reserve army of consumers through direct efforts to stimulate and fulfill popular demand, notably by lowering badge prices and increasing production. The Ministry of Finance awarded special Cultural Revolution tax breaks to factories that produced revolutionary products, including badges. On August 27, 1966, less than two weeks after the first mass rally, the National Price Committee of the State Council issued a directive that required stores across the country to maintain low prices on all Mao-related products, including posters, sculptures, Mao's poems and calligraphy, picture frames, and, of course, badges. These price cuts applied to ink blocks and calligraphy brushes, presumably to encourage the making of big-character posters.[16] The committee also warned against price-gouging and urged local officials to "ensure prices are not inflated" and are reduced to "a price near production costs." The state mandated increases in the supply of badges, such as ordering Shaanxi province, with a population of twenty-two million, to produce thirty million badges.[17] State control over the economy therefore supplied both the initial demand and the initial supply that launched the badge fad, thus representing the state's attempt to generate more revenue by using consumer culture and capitalist market-setting techniques to pursue capital accumulation.

Although countless people acquired Mao memorabilia to demonstrate their genuine loyalty to Mao, the Communist Revolution, and China, the badge fad also benefited immeasurably from the climate of extreme pressure to participate, a fact attested to in countless memoirs of the era.[18] Pressure from the Red Guards and the broader environment promoting a sea of red helped fuel the desire for, or at least the political necessity of, professing one's loyalty by possessing Mao-themed objects.[19] Some state-run venues made wearing a Mao badge mandatory; in Shanghai, for example, movie theater staff checked patrons for badges as well as tickets.[20] Some schools went so far as to require students to bring three items to school each day: the Selected Works, Quotations from Chairman Mao, and a Mao badge. Red Guards inspected students as they arrived. They turned away students who did not have all three items, leading many students to seek to obtain fashionable versions of each item.[21]

The state's mobilizing popular participation in the Mao badge fad soon produced insatiable demand. As production ramped up during the initial year of the Cultural Revolution, more people began to own and wear Mao badges. By the end of 1967, as the scope of the Cultural Revolution expanded and new revolutionary committees gained more political and social power, each committee wanted its own custom badge and thus increased production. At that point, according to estimates, more than half of the population owned badges (59 percent), a number that climbed to 89 percent in 1968 and to nearly the entire population (94 percent) one year later.[22] In cities such as Guangzhou, some residents tried to help ensure that everyone had a badge by taking up collections of badges to send to poorer parts of the country.[23] Although claims that everyone in the country had a badge are extremely unlikely, no other object aside from the Quotations from Chairman Mao was so ubiquitous at the time, transcending age and gender and, to a lesser extent, ethnicity. The total number of Mao badges produced between 1966 and 1971 has been estimated at between 2.5 and 5 billion.[24] Despite the great range of

Figure 7.1. Mao badge diversity. Note the diversity of badge sizes, images, and materials (plastic, aluminum, and porcelain). This assortment includes a glow-in-the-dark badge in the lower right as well as, above it, Mao looking right, a potentially risky image for the maker for suggesting Mao was endorsing right-wing politics. The badge in the shape of the star in the far lower right was half of the pair given to PLA soldiers but later worn by others.

these estimates, even the lowest estimate is spectacularly large and many times China's population of some 700 million (Figure 7.1).

A Self-Expanding Badge Fad

Soon, however, the demand for badges grew beyond the state's ability to meet or control it, making it difficult to estimate the actual total of authorized and unauthorized badges that had been produced. As the fad gained momentum, state-sanctioned badge manufacturers had incentives to underreport their badge production to keep more badges to distribute among their respective work units or to trade for other things.[25] In any case, evidence points to enormous quantities of both authorized and unauthorized badges produced by state work units. At the fad's height in 1969, over 20,000 "factories," most of them unauthorized, were producing Mao badges, illustrating the ability of state consumerism to mobilize enormous material desire and not exclusively promote hard work and frugal living.[26] Across China, work units, both large and small, were redirecting state-allocated resources to the making of Mao badges. In the northeast city of Dalian, for instance, even Rising Sun Store, the smallest commercial work unit in the city, made its own badges, as did workers at Route 5 Bus Station, the smallest public transport work unit in Beijing, and at the party branch of Shenyang Glass Measurement Device Factory, the smallest work unit in that city.[27]

The unauthorized production and distribution of Mao badges meant that the state was unable to maintain a monopoly over the allocation of capital or profits reaped from the sale of badges. Unauthorized producers exchanged their Mao badges on gray markets and even in the open, bartering them with other work units or distributing them within their own work units without official permission. Authorized producers, too, often engaged in unauthorized distribution. A blogger using the pseudonym Mo Ren, for example, recalled that as a young student in 1967 his father's friend took him to visit one of the best badge factories in Wuhan, where he received samples of all the badges that the factory had made as well as samples of those it had exchanged with other manufacturers.[28] Numerous anecdotes from across the country reveal how such activities undermined state capitalist control over the economy, and even seemingly minor misallocations of state resources came at the expense of other state goals.

The individual production and personalization of badges further undermined state capitalism by reallocating labor and material resources away from their intended destinations. As the Cultural Revolution led to the suspension of classes and high unemployment among young people, many had plenty of time for other activities, including do-it-yourself badge production. A youngster in Wuhan, for instance, accompanied his uncle to his work unit, a local engineering school, where they used school equipment to churn out bare metal badges that the young boy then hand-painted at home, creating what he claimed were "the best badges in town."[29] Some reports describe people obtaining semi-finished badges on the gray market and then finishing them with oil paint and adhesive in their spare time or during their state-run training classes.[30]

Although cadres may have encouraged DIY production by young people or having work unit members make badges together, the badge fad redirected state resources and labor into private badge production far beyond any official authorization. People making badges in the Sanming region of Fujian province, for instance, repurposed hospital syringes to customize badges because the syringes were sharp enough to inject paint onto the delicate badge surfaces. Individuals making their own badges found that they could create badges with higher exchange and social values by stealing unfinished badges from their workplaces and then applying unique colors. Many work units and factories that wanted their own badges obtained unpainted ones from manufacturers and painted them themselves during work hours. Such practices also extended to the state bureaucracy. Some revolutionary committee members considered badge production and distribution so compelling that they used their own work time to paint, dry, and distribute badges, donning the badges they had made as soon as they had finished drying.[31]

On the demand side, the badge fad began to expand at an uncontrollable rate. Whatever one's personal reason for wearing a badge, it indirectly added peer pressure for others to do the same, thereby expanding the use of consumption both to communicate an identity and to compete. Obtaining and wearing a Mao badge served as protection from the Red Guards, who used badges to signal their inclusion in the privileged class of the revolutionary vanguard. Even non-diehards realized the social and exchange values of the badges. As the compulsion to acquire badges increased, it led to intense competition to acquire new badges, with sometimes drastic real-world consequences. Politically, beyond insulating oneself from possible Red Guard attacks, wearing a badge could be a useful way to advance one's social standing. Prior to the badge fad, demonstrating loyalty to the party had already become a critical and competitive criterion for membership in party youth organizations that could lead to full party membership and all its social and economic benefits. The competitive nature of upward mobility in New China indirectly contributed to young people's endless demand for badges.

Collecting and displaying the latest, best, and biggest Mao badges was both a political strategy and a small but visible strategy for social and economic advancement. As sociologist Joel Andreas notes, after the elimination of private ownership over the means of production during the Socialist Transformation, a new ruling class gradually appeared, based on the remaining two forms of capital – cultural capital derived from education and political capital based on one's relationship to the party and state. Social advancement largely depended on these cultural and political forms of capital. Moreover, the educational path to gaining cultural capital was more difficult so that many more Chinese youth sought to acquire political capital by joining the party. For the politically mobile, the easiest way to attain party membership was to advance through the various levels of party-run organizations. Given that the rewards of party membership were great and the alternatives for class advancement limited, the process was highly competitive. Nearly all children between the ages of six and fourteen were members of the Young Pioneers (often called Red Scarves, as they used the wearing of such a scarf to signal membership), but only 20 percent of teenagers and young adults advanced from the Young Pioneers to membership in the Communist Youth League. Of these 20 percent, only 5 percent of the adult population reached the brass ring of party membership, along with the positive job prospects and status that accompanied such membership.[32] In the highly competitive world of political maneuvering, prospective cadres seized every means available to distinguish themselves from their peers.

The Expanding Meanings and Uses of Badges

But beyond one's particular social standing, Mao badges became a way to differentiate oneself through the connoisseurship and possession of material goods – quite the opposite of the goals of the Cultural Revolution – and to signal one's relative wealth and connections. Just as the acquisition of the Three Great Things discussed in Chapter 1 demonstrated one's competence in acquiring difficult-to-obtain items under an economy of planned consumer shortages, displaying a rare badge showed that one could thrive in an environment in which distribution relied on more than money. Displaying a sophisticated knowledge of both badges and the Three Great Things became markers of class and social standing. For example, showing (and showing off) one's collection and the relative value of badges became popular topics of conversation and social activity. Badges possessed varying local values. People sent badges to friends and relatives in other parts of the country knowing that their badges would be more valuable in other places.[33] Qing Cha, the pseudonym of a blogger, recalls his parents collecting Mao badges when he was a child, a very popular pastime that provided an opportunity for people to "compare and brag about the quality and number in their collections." When guests came over, his parents would display their badges and occasionally make trades.[34] These everyday acts of sociability – displaying, handling, and exchanging badges with friends or relatives – further increased people's awareness of and desire for badges.

As the fad progressed, people further instrumentalized badges as bribes and gifts, highlighting the gray economy that operated alongside the formal state economy. People collected, traded, and gave badges away to curry favor across all levels of society. Arguably, badges became more useful than cash for everyday bribes, as one still needed the appropriate ration coupons to buy things with cash and in places short on goods and cash that relied on barter economies. In the hierarchy of items used to bribe someone or to build connections, badges were sometimes more effective and desirable than cigarettes or alcohol. Red Guard memoirs recount incidents when badges facilitated bribes or favors. While demanding cash was considered politically unacceptable behavior, requesting a badge for a favor minimized the risks of such behavior, particularly in the charged political environment that attacked anything and everything that smacked of "capitalism." Former Red Guard Ken Ling recalls accepting badges rather than cash in exchange for giving strangers bicycle rides during one of the Red Guard marches, then trading one of those badges for a truck ride: "The drivers did not dare openly ask money from us, for fear that we would take down their license numbers and report them .... Instead, they asked for Mao badges, which they could trade on the black market."[35]

At times, people substituted badges for cash. Someone going to a park, for instance, might give the sales booth a low-end Mao badge rather than buy an admission ticket. If caught on a train without a ticket, a person might try to give the conductor a Mao badge as a substitute.[36] Some students and factory workers used badges to gamble when playing cards or chess.[37] In short, badge transactions became ordinary occurrences, their utility further sustaining the fad and the consumerism it generated. People speculated on the increasing value of badges by collecting dozens, hundreds, and perhaps thousands, hoarding them like the proverbial miser hoards gold. The ubiquity of trade in badges again highlights how even the vitriolic attacks on capitalist tendencies during this period masked the underlying capitalist institutional arrangements of the economic and political structures of the PRC. Labor did not cease to be commodified but was paid for in an alternate currency.

If every Mao badge had been identical, the fad may well have faded sooner – or not taken on the qualities of a fad in the first place. Instead, the ever-expanding range of place brands, styles, and quality of badges led to a "badge inflation," similar to that seen with other desirable consumer goods, such as the compulsion to replace still-working watches with more fashionable watches. Millions of people similarly felt compelled to upgrade to more fashionable badges as the ones they owned fell from favor or to expand their collections to demonstrate their sophisticated and discriminating knowledge of available options. In the badge economy, as in all similar consumer fads, a small or ordinary badge might have been desirable when the fad began, but over time one sought more unusual or bigger badges to communicate the same level of status. As badge possession became more widespread, the complex, fluid hierarchy of badge values further fueled competitive and conspicuous consumption as badge owners tried to distinguish themselves from their peers by having more fashionable badges. The explosion of these fad-driven consumption patterns continually undermined state capitalism and state consumerism and contributed to the shift along the state-to-private spectrum toward a more market-based variety of capitalism and consumerism.

The endless variety of badges that was eventually produced – tens of thousands of different badges – can still be seen in the numerous books and websites produced by the vast community of badge collectors that re-emerged after Mao's death.[38] Then, as now, subtle differences among badges led to different valuations, and some badges were trendier or more valuable than others.[39] Although the state ostensibly created Mao badges to increase ideological fervor, the badge fad, which replicated the consumerist effect of branding, demonstrates the self-expanding nature of consumerism. As the fad took on a life of its own, both the social value and the exchange value of badges came to be determined along four main axes: political meaning, relative rarity, material differences, and size.

Among these, badges first varied in their social value of communicating their loyalty to Mao and the Revolution (and therefore also their potential exchange value) based on their political messages and implications. Badges often included a revolutionary slogan other than "Serve the People," such as "It is right to rebel" and "May Chairman Mao Live Forever." The backs of badges typically included the name of a work unit, a commemorative reason for the badge's production, and a date and place of manufacture, all of which created a branding-like effect and in turn made a badge more exclusive and therefore more valuable to collectors.[40] According to the memoirs of Red Guards, badges from places associated with Mao, especially his birthplace, were among the particularly desirable. Likewise, people valued some visual symbols more than others, such as the character for "loyalty," which could appear on the front or the back; the image of a sunflower, a symbol of devotion; or a mango, a symbol of Mao's benevolence.[41] In Beijing, the most popular Mao badge was the original two-piece badge set made specifically for the General Political Department of the PLA, which people valued so highly that, according to one source, a few dozen could be traded for a high-end brand of bicycle such as a Flying Pigeon.[42]

A second axis of value was availability, and like any limited-edition product, badges made in very small quantities became extremely valuable and desired. The coveted Shaoshan Mao badge, featuring an illustration of Mao's former house in the village of Shaoshanchong in its background, was so rare that only four could be swapped for a Flying Pigeon bicycle.[43] Besides a genuine desire to pay respect to Mao at his birthplace – that is, the ostensible purpose of the badge – the exchange value of the badges obtained from Shaoshan helped entice more Red Guards to visit. Yao Xiaoping and his classmates, for instance, were so delighted to discover during their pilgrimage that each visitor to Mao's natal village house received a set of four souvenir badges that they visited the house multiple times, enduring six-hour queues each time.[44] The seeming motivation behind their repeated trips was not to pay their respect or to study the central message of anti-bourgeois consumerism and anti-capitalism underlying Mao's Cultural Revolution, but to convert their labor (waiting in line) into more useful badge capital.

Private and local uses of a wide variety of materials constituted a third axis of differentiation among badges and badge values. Although plated aluminum was the most used, Mao badges were also made from gold, silver, bronze, stainless steel, tin, and practically every other metal, including lead, aluminum foil, and even artillery shell casings.[45] Work units with access to other materials, such as iron, enamel, and plastic, often reallocated such materials to unauthorized badge production or adopted other local materials, including bamboo, ceramic, wood, bone, marble, glass, and cardboard. By 1968, porcelain badges created in Jingdezhen, the producer of imperial porcelain, began to appear. Although people considered badges made from more expensive materials more desirable, both for their prestige and their rarity, collectors sought to include badges made of a variety of materials in their collections.[46]

But the most visible (or at least most symbolic) sign of badge inflation was the growing size of the badges themselves, which soon grew from under a half-inch to as large as a dinner plate. As Jicai Feng recalls, in part "the larger they were, the more loyal the wearer supposedly was – and certainly the more startlingly visible they were." But, as he admits, much of their allure was that "all in all, these badges were the newest, largest, and most fashionable of their kind at the time."[47] Size became so valuable that

Figure 7.2. A self-expanding badge fad. Mao badges not only grew in size but also, similar to the production of other consumer goods, in complexity. The size expanded from the modest badge on the left, through the medium-sized one in the middle (with the character for "loyalty" 忠 written at the bottom), to the final image with Mao hovering above the entrance to the Forbidden City, the traditional seat of power.

smaller badges were recycled to make larger and more visible badges. Despite numerous accounts of people fearing that inappropriately handling an object with Mao's image would be considered a sign of disrespect or, worse, dissent during the Cultural Revolution, smaller images of Mao were willingly destroyed to make larger, more fashionable, and more valuable ones (Figure 7.2).[48]

The Great (Badge) Exchange

A further example of the unintended consequences of the state-directed attempt to inculcate revolutionary values in the younger generation is another contradictory but largely unstudied event during the Cultural Revolution: the Great Exchange of Revolutionary Experiences. The Great Exchange program, initiated shortly after the first rally in Tiananmen Square, authorized free travel for millions of students to and from Beijing and other revolutionary sites across the country to attend political rallies to raise their revolutionary consciousness.[49] In what in effect was a major state reallocation of resources away from a strict focus on industrialization to the political goal of inculcating socialist values, the state ordered that the national transportation network of trains, trucks, and ships provide free transportation and local governments offer free room and board for tens of millions of teenagers. Predictably, the costs to the economy were enormous. In 1966, the massive increase in passenger transport displaced an estimated ten million tons of goods and materials, such as coal, timber, steel, and building products, negatively affecting factory production and capital construction.[50] As a result, it did not take long for the industrialization priorities of the state to reassert themselves over the secondary goal of spreading socialist culture. The program was terminated after only a few months. During its existence, however, the program profoundly affected the spread of the badge fad and of consumerism more broadly.[51]

The stated goal of the Great Exchange was to provide the post-revolutionary generation of students – those same students Mao worried would gradually negate the revolution – with a firsthand appreciation of the results of the Communist Revolution and the sacrifices of its participants. The Great Exchange was also intended to motivate Red Guards to spread the Cultural Revolution to communities throughout the country where local cadres may have been blocking its implementation. Students, few of whom had traveled beyond their hometowns, found the offer of free travel and political engagement an irresistible opportunity, and in the following months, Red Guards and other youngsters from across China flocked to Beijing hoping to glimpse Mao in person, prompting the Chairman to hold an additional seven rallies. By November 20, 1966, when the state finally suspended the free travel opportunity, some ten million students, and also sometimes their teachers, had visited Beijing – so many that the capital had to erect a tent city on the grounds of the Temple of Heaven to house 400,000 visitors at a time. But Beijing was only one destination in this massive field trip: in total, the central government organized 4,000 reception points at and along the way to places with special significance to the history of the Communist Revolution and the lives of its major figures.

The Great Exchange met many of its political goals. As one historian of the Mao cult notes, the Great Exchange "more than any other factor contributed to the spreading of the Mao cult and the nation-wide attacks against old culture."[52] At the same time, however, the program undermined state capitalism by diverting resources from the state's industrial priorities and by unleashing millions of Red Guards across the county, thereby also expanding the reach of the Mao badge fad and the demand for additional reallocations of capital into badge production and accumulation. Although the rallies in Tiananmen Square were the most popular destination for acquiring authorized badges, students also flocked to spots along the more than 5,000-mile Long March and other "sacred places of the revolution," many in rural locations, collecting badges at each stop on their pilgrimage. Tens of thousands visited the significant sites daily, such as Mao's birthplace at Shaoshan in rural Hunan province, where so many students arrived that the local badge factory could not meet demand and the state had to set up a special resupply network to meet the extra demand, as badges were flown in daily from Shanghai to Changsha and then trucked to Shaoshan.[53]

Whatever success the program may have had in spreading revolutionary values or destroying the "old culture," the student participants also embraced the Great Exchange program as an opportunity to engage in some of the very activities under attack during the Cultural Revolution, including shopping and tourism. The Great Exchange consequently introduced forms of consumerism and associated behavior already popular in Shanghai and other big cities to millions of rural teenagers who otherwise would not have had the resources or opportunities to travel to such places.[54] In addition to providing the traveling students with a chance to collect badges at various revolutionary sites, the program exposed them to a wider range of badges worn by other students as informal markets and badge exchanges sprang up in gathering spots, such as train stations and even at the revolutionary sites the state encouraged them to visit.

Red Guards from smaller cities and towns soon learned to emulate their big-city counterparts not only by wearing Mao badges but also by trading them illicitly. A typical story is that of Gao Yuan, who acquired his first two badges while on a Great Exchange pilgrimage to Beijing. Among the trees in a pine grove on the south side of Tiananmen Square, he reported, "we discovered a brisk trade in Chairman Mao badges. [. . .] I inquired whether anyone would sell me a badge. 'We are not speculators,' said one boy. 'We only trade. Two small ones for a big one.'" Gao did not have any badges to trade, but the boys had a work-around, agreeing to trade ten photos of Mao for one badge. Gao quickly bought two packets of Mao photos and swapped them for the badges: "I pinned one on my chest and the other inside my pocket. I was sure I could feel Chairman Mao's radiance burning into me."[55] The contradiction of using a market to satisfy desires at the height of the Cultural Revolution was lost on both Gao and the badge barterers, whose complex motivations and political ardor became instrumentalized or converted into material desires.

According to dozens of accounts by Great Exchange participants, the badges distributed at significant revolutionary places further incentivized students to travel, creating a feedback loop in which more travel generated a desire for more badges. In his memoirs of his days as a Red Guard from Changsha, for instance, Liang Heng recounts admiring a beautiful badge, larger than any he had seen, worn by a cousin. When the cousin informed him that he had been given the badge during a school trip to Shaoshan, Liang Heng "resolved that someday I would go too, even if I had to walk there."[56] The difficulty of collecting badges from distant or hard-to-reach places also increased the social value of such badges and made students more eager to travel to such places or to obtain them from other collectors.[57]

Through the Great Exchange, the state provided the most inexpensive and readily available way to learn to desire the right badges and, perhaps, to build a diverse and valuable collection of badges. In October 1966, Yao Xiaoping and his classmates, like millions of students from across China, took advantage of the program to visit places such as Wuhan, Guangzhou, and Changsha, where, judging from their accounts, they learned more about the tremendous diversity of badges than about revolutionary history. In Guangzhou, they visited the twentieth annual Chinese Export Trade Fair (also known as the Canton Fair), which was underway despite Cultural Revolution denunciations of capitalism (Figure 7.3). Reflecting earlier forms of socialist propaganda, the main hall was filled with images of Mao and banners containing Mao slogans, and Yao recalled that a top attraction at the fair was a grand glass case displaying a beautiful collection of Mao badges.[58] They could look but could not buy. According to another account, although visitors needed a ticket to gain admission to the fair and the products on display were sold only to foreigners, locals used personal contacts with businesspeople from Hong Kong and Macau to buy badges on their behalf.[59]

The lure of the badges was powerful enough that local officials eventually used them to encourage student tourists to leave the cities. In Shanghai, when a large number of Great Exchange visitors who had flooded into the city lingered after the state suspended the program and ordered the visitors to return home, local officials enticed students to depart by issuing them with highly prized special Mao badges as they checked out of their campus accommodations or produced train tickets proving their impending departure.[60] The practice was so effective that

Figure 7.3. Trading in revolution. Although wary of trade with market capitalist countries, the party needed to export products to pay for technology and food imports. Even during the height of the Cultural Revolution, the Canton Trade Fair continued, albeit with socialistic cover in the form of banners covering the exterior that included, on either side of the Mao portrait, "Long Live the Great Leader Chairman Mao" and "Long Live the Great Chinese Communist Party." The poster on the right (behind the bus) reads: "Following Mao Zedong, the whole world turns red." Meanwhile, inside this same fair in 1968, organizers sold over 230,000 badges. Source: 中国出口商品交易会 (Chinese Export Commodities Fair) published as a supplement to *Jingji daobao*, April 15, 1968: 38.

when local Shanghai factories began to run out of raw materials for badge production in December 1966, the Shanghai office responsible for distributing badges gave first priority to providing badges to visiting students who were voluntarily departing.[61]

The Great Exchange thus unwittingly negated its own goals by turning students into collectors and tourists, promoting consumerism along with the socialist values that Mao had hoped to inculcate. For millions of Chinese youth, the Great Exchange provided, as officials had hoped, an opportunity to swap "revolutionary experiences" and engage in mass politics. It also gave them an opportunity to tour the country and participate in consumer fads, along the way learning about new dimensions of the fad from fellow exchange students. Just as many memoirs of Mao-era China provide vivid tales of learning about and eventually acquiring the Three Great Things discussed in Chapter 1, many memoirists writing about the start of the Cultural Revolution include stories of badge acquisition and trading. As Chinese youth and others supposedly were building socialism, they were also building their badge collections (Figure 7.4).

State Crackdown

Whereas many Chinese wanted badges for their stated and obvious purpose – to communicate a personal loyalty to Mao and the party and fervor for the revolution – the fact that they did so through consumption (rather than, say, through quiet reflection) again demonstrates the persistence and expansion of consumer culture throughout the Mao era. Badges, unlike the omnipresent posters and other representations of Mao, gave wearers an individual connection to Mao and an opportunity for personal expression, especially when the wearers made their own badges, or what Red Guard Liang Heng describes as "national symbols of fervor and sincerity."[62] Nonetheless, even at the very height of the Cultural Revolution, these expressions of patriotic fervor and party loyalty undermined the stated purpose of the Cultural Revolution and, indeed, the larger Communist Revolution that the Red Guards claimed to be advancing.

Eventually, government officials, including Mao himself, realized that the Mao cult in general and the badge fad in particular had grown out of hand and had become the opposite of the ethos of hard work and frugal living. Whatever political power they had provided was eventually offset by the costs in terms of material and labor and the growing evidence that the fad was reproducing the exact "feudal" and "capitalist" cultural manifestations

海内存知己,天涯若比邻。1970.6.14.

Figure 7.4. Class photo. In the Beijing Middle School #101 graduation photo (the Chinese at the top is a line from a poem frequently used on such occasions), most students wear badges, and some also wear Red Guard armbands. By 1970, most urban households would have had a collection of badges to choose from for these formal occasions. Many, including Hu Yafei (third from the right in the middle row), chose a porcelain badge. Source: Yafei Hu and L. James Hammond, "My Youth in China" (2017). Used with permission.

that the Cultural Revolution intended to eliminate. Mao's own personal misgivings, as well as the depth and breadth of the desire to own and display badges, are demonstrated by an incident recalled by Xie Jingyi, one of Mao's confidential secretaries. According to Xie, she and other staff around Mao had joined in the mania for collecting badges, and in late 1967, she decided to show her collection to Mao. When Xie explained that everyone had badges and that many had much larger collections than hers, "Mao's face immediately turned serious. I knew he was unhappy; I never saw this expression. I became nervous and closed the badge album." Mao, likening collecting badges to the now banned-as-bourgeois hobby of collecting stamps, proclaimed, "Good grief, this is extremely wasteful!" When Mao asked her to hand over her album, however, she refused: "What if you throw them away? I have been collecting them for a long time and take good care of them." Xie's collection had become so meaningful to her that she was willing to defy Mao in an act that clearly did not demonstrate loyalty to him or to his vision for China. Nonetheless, Xie saw Mao's reaction as the beginning of the end of the fad.[63]

The growing recognition of the counterrevolutionary effects of the badge fad was further fueled by the increasing visibility of and complaints about the gray and black markets that developed to trade badges. These illicit markets, much like those that developed to provide wider access to the Three Greats, demonstrate the difficulty of reining in the forces of consumerism once they had been set in motion. Despite government attempts to keep Mao badges outside of the marketplace, as the fad grew, numerous and increasingly brazen illicit gray and black markets trading in badges developed across China. Because markets and engaging in trade were labeled capitalist and hence were disrespectful, people referred to the places where one could buy or swap badges by the euphemism "exchanges." These exchanges were a consequence of both the growing supply and the insistent consumer demand. As billions of badges circulated across China, many people had superfluous badges that they wanted to sell or to trade for other badges to fill out their collections. Furthermore, the failure of state capitalism to control production had led to unregulated, decentralized badge production and countless poor-quality products with awkward patterns and shapes or poor likenesses of Mao (or, worse, likenesses that looked more like the primary Cultural Revolution target Liu Shaoqi). The low quality of badges available through state-sanctioned channels led many people to look outside the state distribution system to acquire more desirable badges, much like they looked for other consumer products in the early 1960s. As the desire for badges grew more intense, people began to look beyond their natural informal exchange circles of friends, relatives, and colleagues, resorting to trading with complete strangers if need be. The badge trade thus exemplifies the limits of state capitalism and consumerism in the 1960s – the more the state attempted to restrict badge supply through formal state channels, the more it incentivized people to engage in the illicit buying and selling of goods and services.

Badge markets sprang up in the very center of the capital. Two of Beijing's three main commercial areas, Wangfujing and Xidan, featured markets where badge exchanges took place each morning.[64] The largest black market was located just outside Tiananmen Square, the site of the massive Red Guard rallies that had launched the Cultural Revolution. There some traders operated openly, while others were more discreet, pinning badges to the inside of their jackets or coats and revealing only a few badges at a time to potential customers. Rumor had it that Ye Qun (wife of Marshal Lin Biao, Mao's presumptive successor) was a keen collector not only of the antiques and other banned goods noted in the Chapter 6, but also of badges, and she frequently disguised herself and went to the market in search of the latest variations.[65]

In a further demonstration of the self-expanding nature of capitalism in the Mao era, innumerable people participated in such markets by exchanging badges and trading them for cash, banned books, and ordinary items such as light bulbs and eggs.[66] According to newspaper reports, one teenager who wanted pocket money sold more than 2,000 badges within three days and had another 969 badges in his possession when he was apprehended.[67] Writer Chang Jung recalled that her thirteen-year-old brother collected Mao badges to fund his purchase of banned books on the gray market.[68] At these markets, enterprising students looking for a source of income sold newsletters originally intended for restricted cadre audiences and traded them for badges.[69] Although the best-known gray and black markets were in cities such as Shanghai and Beijing, other cities had less conspicuous markets. Peter Zhou, who was twelve in 1966, later remembered that such markets had formed in various districts of Wuhan and that "people found lots of pleasure in swapping the badges and bragging about their collections."[70]

Eventually, however, the conspicuousness of these exchanges caught the attention of officials, who declared that turning Mao's image in the form of badges into a commercial product rather than a devotional object, as was the original intention, was disrespectful to Mao. The market was chaotic and egregious in Shanghai, the first place to have badge exchanges, where the number of illegal badge exchanges grew from twelve to thirty-five in only a few months in the spring of 1967.[71] Officials in Shanghai consequently ordered undercover police, Red Guards, and workers to patrol the area and search for speculators. As early as January 1967, some members of the Shanghai workers revolutionary rebel corps and of the Red Guards formed a group to attack the growing number of badge exchanges, although they lacked the strength and authority to suppress them on their own. Soon, however, a public campaign claiming that these markets were evidence of capitalism and its participants were class enemies for engaging in capitalist behavior was launched.[72] A letter from the rebel corps of the Shanghai Industrial and Commercial Administrative Bureau published in *Liberation Daily* on February 12, 1967, waved away participants' claims that market-goers were merely promoting the noble goals of "building friendships" and "expressing devotion" to Chairman Mao by "exchanging" badges as excuses for buying and selling badges. The article charged that the exchanges were forms of capitalism where "counterrevolutionary activities are conducted in the name of the revolution" and they were clear evidence that "an intensive, complicated class struggle exists."[73] After publication of the rebel corps' letter, the local political leadership united under the Shanghai Revolutionary Committee (SRC), which included representatives of the PLA, and took a series of countermeasures against the illegal production, distribution, sales, and purchase of Mao badges, targeting the exchanges as egregious attempts at "capitalist restoration."[74] On March 11, 1967, a "Notice on Banning Places of Exchange of Commemorative Badges, Strictly Managing the Production of Commemorative Badges" was jointly issued by the SRC's Grasp Revolution Promote Production Front Line Headquarters, the Shanghai Municipal Public Security Bureau, and the Shanghai Industry and Commerce Administrative Bureau. The notice was a cease-and-desist warning to all "illegal producers" who were illegally buying, reselling, and stealing badges. Henceforth, it declared, only the Shanghai Light Industry Bureau and the Handicraft Industry Bureau would have the authority to produce badges, and all others producing badges were ordered to surrender them. Ten days later, the SRC circulated a notice that forbade non-specialist producers – meaning unauthorized factories – from making badges and demanded that state-designated badge producers make badges only as authorized.[75]

Despite the concerted effort to stop or regulate the production and trade of badges, at the height of the fad the self-expanding and compulsive nature of consumerism appeared to prevail over the efforts by the Red Guards and the police. At least in Shanghai, the badge business – production and consumption – continued to flourish. During a crackdown on unauthorized producers within work units in the spring of 1967, policing forces seized some 416 badge molds, 466,000 unfinished badges, and more than 300 kilos of materials. Local governments cracked down on badge exchanges, with the police dealing with 14,769 people, including repeat offenders, and confiscating sixty-three molds and 91,301 badges.[76] Unfortunately for the policing forces, the problem of commercialized badges extended far beyond the existence of these markets or a few teenagers making or stealing badges in their spare time. Some powerful work units in cities such as Shanghai manufactured badges without authorization, making a crackdown much more complicated. The multifaceted approach that officials in Shanghai were forced to take to eliminate the entire chain linking badge producers, sellers, and consumers highlights both the difficulty of preventing the expansion of badge markets and their deep roots in Chinese society.

Policing forces could not fully suppress the markets – and the consumerism and private capitalism they represented – because the power and will to crack down on these activities varied across the country, and even within the state itself. Unauthorized badge production and circulation continued outside of Shanghai long after the crackdown had completed its work in the city.[77] This included within the military itself, which produced some of the best-quality badges, and the SRC lacked the authority to stop the practice. Although on paper it was easy to enlist the military's cooperation, in practice it proved much more difficult to stamp out this valuable source of side income. On May 5, 1967, the SRC invited the top officers stationed in Shanghai to a meeting with representatives from the Shanghai government offices overseeing the industry. Participants at the meeting agreed that military stationed within the city could manage production as it saw fit, but that military personnel from outside the city had to have the appropriate letters of authorization and production would be managed by the Shanghai Light Industry Bureau and the Handicraft Industry Bureau. This agreement, however, was unenforceable across the innumerable unauthorized work units making badges for the military, which continued to find ways to meet consumer demand. The Shanghai branch of the People's Bank of China reported, for instance, that in November 1967 an air force unit made 276 gold-plated badges without permission and, when it ran out of gold, it attempted to requisition more from the bank by claiming it was needed to manufacture plane components. Later investigations discovered that some of the original gold supplied by the PLA came from robbing graves.[78]

To meet demand, the state continued to set up large badge factories even as officials in Beijing began to question the scope of badge production. In early 1968, the Red Rebel Revolutionary Committee of Heilongjiang Province in Harbin, a major industrial city in northeast China, established a dedicated Mao badge factory, the Heilongjiang Badge Factory. The committee allocated impressive amounts of resources to the factory and production began apace. By April, the factory had eighty employees, including skilled craftsmen, a 32,000 square-foot factory floor, and advanced equipment transferred from other factories in the city. In a major improvement over smaller local badge factories, the new factory had strict quality control and destroyed any badges with scratches, bubbles in the paint, or unclear lettering. Once finished, workers placed the badges in specially made handmade boxes. The badges made by this factory supplied the special needs of the Provincial Revolutionary Committee, which in January 1969, three months before the start of the Ninth National Congress of the CCP in April, ordered tribute badges from the factory to commemorate the congress. The factory made 30,000 badges and reserved 10,000 as gifts, although there were only some 1,500 delegates. The plan to present others with the best badges worked. Compared to other badges brought to the congress, which were deemed too numerous or too large, the Heilongjiang badges were a hit.[79] By investing time, labor, and resources into badge production, provincial leaders turned the desire of delegates for the nicest badges into symbolic capital that they could use down the road.

Even two months later, after the CCP Central Committee finally forbade further production and other factories stopped manufacturing badges, the Heilongjiang Badge Factory continued to make badges for another six months to meet the demand from officers and technicians working overseas who continued to order badges to give as gifts, including one final badge, inscribed with "The magnificent 1970s." Although the factory, which had grown to 130 workers, closed by the end of the year, it continued to produce badges until the overseas and domestic markets dried up, demonstrating that the pursuit of profits enabled by the fad operated at an institutional as well as an individual level.[80]

While officials in places such as Heilongjiang continued to use the means of production to fuel a consumer fad, some contemporary observers were becoming uncomfortable with it. Ordinary individuals to the Chairman himself had already begun to note the contradiction that the Great Proletarian Cultural Revolution was reproducing extreme versions of "feudal" and "bourgeois" culture. Some outraged opponents of the fad dared to express their doubts publicly. In April 1968, Jiang Mingliang, then a teenage student in Xi'an, wrote a letter to Mao and the CCP Central Committee complaining that the Cultural Revolution was turning China into a "society that promoted blind devotion" and comparing Mao-related "loyalty" activities and goods to those of a feudal cult.[81] Arguing that the badge fad and other aspects of the cult of personality around Mao were wasting, or at least misallocating, millions of RMB and materials that could have been used to build factories or planes, Jiang concluded that the current situation did not represent implementation of the slogan "Serve the People," but rather reflected the opposite values. Jiang was so enraged that he sent his letter to Mao and wrote it out on a thirty-five-page big-character poster that he pasted up on his campus. For pointing out these contradictions between the party's rhetoric of socialism and its actual policies, Jiang was jailed and beaten.[82]

Jiang was not alone. After graduating from a small-town high school in Mao's home province of Hunan, Xiao Ruiyi (b. 1948) became another letter writer who denounced the practices of the Cultural Revolution as negating its stated goals. Xiao wrote a 12,000-character-long letter to Chairman Mao in the late spring of 1968 expressing his disbelief at the manifestations of the Mao cult. According to Xiao, "Now everyone in the entire country, except the Chairman himself, has a Mao badge or Mao quotation plate, even top national leaders who work closely with the Chairman. But the Chairman does not put a stop to it. We honestly have a difficult time understanding why not." Citing many of the same kinds of evidence also noted by Jiang, Xiao thought the spread of the Mao cult had become excessive. "Mao posters are hung everywhere; in one restaurant, I even saw more than 70 posters hanging"; bookstores offered few options other than *Mao's Selected Works* and *Quotations from Chairman Mao*, which were published in a variety of shapes and colors.[83] Given how dangerous criticism could be in the political atmosphere of the Cultural Revolution, such testimonies from disillusioned people reflect a contemporaneous awareness of how deep-rooted the consumerist fad for Mao badges had become and how far it had strayed from its original purpose of instilling revolutionary values.

Criticism of the tremendous waste of resources that might otherwise go to industrialization and national defense was not lost on the leadership of the party. Indeed, around the time of the Ninth Congress in April 1969, the allotment of aluminum for the production of badges had culminated in metal shortages so acute that they caught the attention of Mao, who is reputed to have declared, "Give me back the planes," a quote that highlights the trade-offs between consumer goods and military priorities.[84] As work units were churning out badges to commemorate the Ninth Congress, members of the leadership started to call for an end to the excesses of a consumer fad that increasingly appeared to be negating the goals of the Cultural Revolution. Zhou Enlai, for instance, criticized the fad and the larger Mao cult as directly contravening the objectives of the Cultural Revolution. In a long speech at the National Planning Symposium on March 24, 1969, Zhou denounced the squandering of resources on Mao memorabilia from badges to books. Expressing serious doubts that this excessive production was actually disseminating Mao Zedong Thought, he pointed to ironies of the mania such as how the quest for more and cheaper production had led to a lack of quality control and wasteful excess. Zhou also lamented that the production of new and improved versions of the *Quotations from*

Chairman Mao and of badges reflected and reinforced the "three major inequalities," noting that "people in the cities have many more copies than those living outside the cities; cadres in high positions have more copies than the generals," and some families in the countryside have none (Figure 7.5).[85] Reporting that hoarding had become a problem, with some cadres possessing more than the hundred Mao badges and

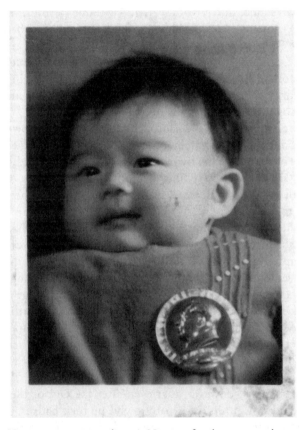

Figure 7.5. Heartwarming inequality. A Nanjing family *c.* 1970 photographed their healthy infant with the latest Mao badge obtained from the father's factory. As was customary, this Mao badge was pinned above the wearer's heart (thereby allowing Mao to be held dear). The father was a work leader in a good factory who usually received more badges than ordinary workers. Although China produced billions of badges, enough to provide for every man, woman, and child, not everyone had the same access. Source: The private collection of Xi Chen.

dozens of copies of the *Quotations from Chairman Mao*, Zhou wondered aloud, "How is this not wasteful?"[86]

Under such pressure from the leadership, the fad seemed to end almost as quickly as it began, and the reserve army of consumers demobilized. Just as state intervention had quickened badge consumption, it also moved to end it. A nationwide crackdown on badges began on June 12, 1969, when the CCP Central Committee issued a document titled "Several Issues Worthy of Attention Concerning the Promotion of Chairman Mao Images" that stated unequivocally that "without permission from the central government, it is forbidden to make more Mao badges." The national government also banned other aspects of the Mao cult that had helped drive demand for badges. By 1970, only a few dedicated factories, such as Shaoshan Chairman Mao Badge Factory and Beijing Red Flag Badge Factory, were still producing badges, and nearly all unauthorized production by work units and the military had ceased.

Given the sheer scale of unauthorized production, however, other reasons besides the government order appear to have played a role in the collapse of the badge fad by 1970.[87] American journalist Edgar Snow, who spent six months in China beginning in late 1970, noted that although all officials still wore badges in early 1971, the badge fad continued to fade, particularly following the death of Lin Biao, who had been the biggest promoter of the Mao cult and the badge fad, in a plane crash in 1971, reportedly while fleeing to Moscow after a failed coup attempt. Following his death, the party leadership moved away from endorsements of the "cult of the individual" and expunged Lin and his closeness to Mao from all party propaganda.[88] The badge cult, which had always been connected with Lin, faded fast. According to one estimate, by 1972, the year after Lin Biao's death, only 10 percent of Chinese were wearing Mao badges. By 1974, two years before Mao's death, ordinary Chinese and leaders other than Zhou Enlai seldom wore Mao badges.[89]

Evidence suggests, however, that even after the end of the fad, some individuals and work units were loath to give up their badges, even if they had stopped wearing them. As late as the end of the 1970s, work units felt it necessary to ask their employees to hand in their Mao badges, roadside recycling centers collected badges as scrap metal, and the Central Propaganda Department mandated that the political departments in every work unit dispose of all "loyalty items," including destroying all "substandard, damaged, and bad quality items as well as any having Lin Biao quotations."[90] Yet it was impossible to dispose of the billions of pieces of Mao memorabilia, as there were too many pieces in too many places. According to a July 19, 1978, report received by the Central Propaganda Department, for example, soldiers cleaning military warehouses discovered that many still held a vast array of "loyalty items" that had been collected from military units as well as from the civilian population. Likewise, Kunming Military Region in the southeast discovered more than 2,300 kg (5,070 pounds) of aluminum Mao badges, ten sets of steel badge molds, 720 plastic sculptures, one hundred plaster and porcelain sculptures, 250 iron sheets imprinted with Mao's image, 550 plywood boards with similar images, and 6,000 Plexiglas badges with Mao slogans.

Even four years after Mao's death and the arrest of the "Gang of Four" in 1976, the Central Committee was still finding it necessary to chastise collectors and to instruct officials to discourage the continued interest in saving and displaying "individual cultural relics," that is, Mao memorabilia. Furthermore, an increasing number of local organizations devoted to collecting and exchanging such items began to emerge across the country. The committee attempted to discourage such consumption by labeling such collections as "extravagance and waste," the opposite of the ethos of hard work and frugal living. On that pretext, it ordered that any remaining Mao badges be seized and recycled "to avoid the extreme waste of metal."[91]

Ultimately, however, this attempt to reassert state priorities was as ineffective as earlier policies had been in stamping out the desire for badges. Countless people ignored or resisted the order by holding on to their badges and collections, and some salvaged badges from waste and recycling stations. Although the state employed its powers to reduce the production, circulation, and consumption of Mao badges and quashed the fad, judging from the large number of Mao badges that survived, it remained difficult to convince many people to part with their prized material possessions. One group of workers disobeyed orders and saved what may have been the biggest badge ever from the heap of scrap. According to Chen Huabin, a worker at Hainan Island Machine Factory, the entire factory – some 700 workers – conspired to ignore the order and save the massive 6.5-foot-tall Mao badge that they had made in 1969. Chen himself, a foreman at the warehouse where the badge was kept, vowed to protect the badge and even contemplated moving it to his hometown to keep it safe, though he abandoned the plan out of fear it might be discovered. Nevertheless, he managed to keep the badge hidden behind the shelves in the warehouse for fifteen years, until it was discovered when the warehouse was relocated.[92]

Conclusion

Viewed through the lens of the badge fad, the Cultural Revolution did not end capitalism, even momentarily, but rather served as the apotheosis of self-expanding and compulsory consumerism during the Mao era. Under state direction but without state authorization, the intense demand for badges shifted the allocation of surplus capital from state capitalist priorities, such as industrialization and military defense, to the ultimate consumerist activity – billions of articles of communist consumer kitsch fueling a consumer fad that mirrored and enhanced economic, geographical, and status hierarchies. Even at its most overt anti-capitalist turn, far from leveling social inequalities as the party promised, the Mao era witnessed not only the survival but the growth of consumer culture through people's compulsive participation in the largest consumer fad in history. Moreover, the chief agent of the "capitalist restoration" and negation of the revolution, as Mao feared, was the "revolutionary generation" itself. Young people born into New China, supposedly free from the stains of earlier imperialist, capitalist, and feudal domination, became the primary conduits of recreating and expanding capitalism, consumerism, and the accompanying social inequalities.

Afterword

A little over a decade following Mao's death, markets for Mao badges reappeared in both China and abroad, and by the end of the 1980s Mao badges had become one of the top ten collectables in China.[1] In 1990, Wang Anting entered the *Guinness Book of World Records* for his collection of more than 50,000 badges.[2] By 2010, some 15 million Chinese had become collectors, some having amassed more than 100,000 badges and, like Wang Anting, they had opened their own public display rooms.[3] Today, every local Chinese flea market has some badges for sale, and Taobao.com, the online Chinese equivalent of eBay, hosts thousands of sellers and more than a hundred pages of badge listings. Production of new badges resumed, particularly in 1993, on the centennial of Mao's birth, along with the sale of badges as tourist trinkets and good-luck charms in Mao's hometown of Shaoshan.[4] This more recent history of badges is not a crass antithesis (or, negation) of the history of the Mao era but rather a logical extension: from their inception, badges fueled the compulsory and self-expanding consumerism and capitalism that underpinned the entire Mao era.

I suggest that we need to reframe the policies and practices of the Mao era as manifestations of different institutional arrangements along a state-to-private spectrum of industrial capitalism. Such a reinterpretation challenges established views both inside and outside China, including the party claim that ever since the Communist Revolution it has been continuously "building socialism" en route to communism. The party, in its efforts to avoid identification with the "mistakes" of Mao-era attempts to "build socialism" that contributed to the Great Leap and Cultural Revolution disasters, has declared that China has now entered the period of "reform and opening" to "build socialism."[5] Mao's successor, Deng Xiaoping, famously stated that the newest incarnation of that longstanding national goal is to "build socialism with Chinese characteristics."[6] In the same way that the party earlier invoked Marx's concept of capitalist "birthmarks" that would persist after the revolution, the qualification "with Chinese characteristics" provides theoretical cover for the ever-expanding evidence of the contradiction between socialist words and party practices. In fact, the policies of this new stage of building socialism are nearly the opposite of those of the Mao era. They have included "opening" China to international capitalist investment and "reforming" domestic life by downplaying much of the earlier Communist revolutionary rhetoric of class struggle and egalitarian goals.[7] Now, much more boldly than then, the party's framing of its policies interprets even the hallmarks of capitalism manifest in the inequality of consumerism as part of the process of "building socialism."[8]

The picture emerging on the role of self-expanding and compulsory consumerism in shaping the Mao era is one of negating not capitalism but rather the goals of the Communist Revolution. This new perspective demonstrates continuity between the Mao era and the eras that both preceded and followed it, showing that the industrial consumerism first introduced on the eve of the Republican era in the late nineteenth century expanded in the Mao era to provide the groundwork for the rapid acceleration of consumerism since the late 1970s. Consequently, this perspective challenges the scholarly view that the Mao era constituted a socialist revolutionary detour from the introduction of consumerism during the Republican era to its re-emergence following the liberalization of the Chinese economy in the late 1970s. The findings here show that throughout the entire twentieth century, the Chinese state attempted to harness expanding consumerism and manage its reserve army of consumers to serve rapid state-led industrialization – in other words, to serve state capitalism.

Another historical continuity revealed in this history of consumerism is how deeply Chinese state policies were shaped by international rivalries, domestic exigencies, and fear of falling farther behind in global capitalist competition. We have seen that during the Republican period, the NPM – to promote China-made products and to boycott imports – attempted to manage the reserve army of consumers in response to international competition from European, Japanese, and US companies. During the Mao era, Cold War military and economic pressures continually and profoundly shaped state efforts to harness capital and consumerism. Beginning in the 1970s, state policies of accumulation shifted the institutional arrangements in the direction of encouraging greater private consumerism so as to absorb the growing output of China's domestic industrial capitalism, including incentivizing the rural labor force with material rewards. In response to the visible hand of the Chinese state,

China's rivals abroad have continued to criticize Chinese policies as exceptional, unfair, and even "state capitalist," thereby representing China as a unique threat.[9] But whatever fears the rest of the world might have about China's emergence as a military and economic power, China's state capitalist and consumerist policies have been inexorably motivated by Chinese perceptions of threats to its security and of China's comparative backwardness vis-à-vis its global industrial capitalist rivals.

Ultimately, evidence of growing state-supported industrial consumerism calls into question the utility of continuing to think of China during this period as socialist. Even if nearly everyone accepted the prevailing political rhetoric and assumed that their experiences were indeed socialist, a closer look shows that many had serious doubts about the accuracy of the official claims that China was negating capitalism and building socialism. We have seen that ordinary citizens publicly expressed their doubts in direct forms, such as in letters and posters, and in indirect forms, ranging from outright strikes to unseen slowdowns. More frequently, they expressed their doubts by ignoring the state consumerist ethos of hard work and frugal living and cultivated their own material desires, desires that expanded and became increasingly compulsory throughout the era. Such doubts were shared by many within the party, including Mao himself. But even as party elites debated whether or to what extent a "socialist" country should use markets and materialism to aid accumulation, nothing in the Mao era consistently put a priority on building democratic worker control over production and distribution or consumption based on communal needs. Accordingly, "building socialism" fails to describe the Mao era even by the party's basic definition of socialism. Despite promises by party leaders to end the exploitation and inequality they identified with industrial capitalism, the party continues to use state power to build capitalism, thereby exacerbating the inequalities and negating its own Communist Revolution.

This analysis of the continual expansion of consumerism suggests an ongoing need to move past Cold War-era binaries, such as planned economy vs. free markets, dictatorship vs. democracy, interests of the collective vs. freedom of the individual, public vs. private enterprise, or stability vs. competition. Although dividing states along these lines has served useful analytical and political purposes for scholars and commentators on both sides of the divide, the findings here, and those by other scholars as well, suggest that these dichotomies may have become so politicized and inaccurate that they hide more than they reveal. Instead of falling neatly into such categories, state capitalism during the Mao era shifted back and forth along various points on a state-to-private spectrum of industrial capitalism, each permutation affecting consumerism in a different way. During the late 1950s and late 1960s, the political economy moved in the direction of state-controlled accumulation, whereas during the early 1950s, early 1960s, and 1970s the political economy shifted toward market-mediated accumulation and "bourgeois" consumerism. Although in every case these shifts were justified as a necessary part of party efforts to "build socialism" in order to reach communism, the existence of such shifts reveals that neither the state's vision of socialism nor its practice of state capitalism and consumerism were static. Demonstrating that the terms *state capitalism* and *state consumerism* refer not to a fixed but rather to a fluctuating point on the state-to-private spectrum of industrial capitalism provides a reminder that all economies mix elements of institutional arrangements associated with both ends of the spectrum, and that all forms of industrial capitalism involve attempts to manage consumer desires.

Viewed from the perspective of this history of consumerism during the Mao era, the post-Mao policy changes promoting greater consumerism in China appear to be less of a break with Maoist ideology and policy and more as yet another shift in the institutional arrangements developed by the Chinese state to facilitate capital accumulation. Such shifts also suggest that, aside from state capitalism and private capitalism, there are other varieties of capitalism in between these poles, and certainly there is a greater range of institutional arrangements than is usually acknowledged.[10] Expanding the study of the varieties of capitalism to include "socialist" countries such as China presents an opportunity to render the history of capitalism and consumerism as more truly global, and to think of the Mao era as part of an integrated world history rather than an isolated "socialist" interlude.

Notes

Introduction

1. Although the terms *consumerism* and *consumer culture* are synonymous, I use *consumerism* to emphasize that it is a correlate of *capitalism*. Similarly, I use the term *industrial consumerism* as a correlate of *industrial capitalism*, both of which were present in China since the end of the nineteenth century. Unless otherwise stated, consumerism refers to *industrial* consumerism. Although this book documents the ascendance of capitalism and consumerism, it does not suggest their complete dominance. To avoid implying a much greater development of consumerism (and capitalism) than appropriate for China during the Mao era, I do not use the term *consumer society*, used by historians of America in works such as Lawrence B. Glickman, *A Living Wage: American Workers and the Making of Consumer Society* (Ithaca, NY: Cornell University Press, 1997). In contrast to writings on consumerism by authors such as Klein and Schor who use the term *consumerism* pejoratively, I use both the terms consumerism and capitalism as neutral descriptors of social relations. Naomi Klein, *No Logo: Taking Aim at the Brand Bullies* (New York: Picador, 1999); Juliet B. Schor, *The Overspent American: Why We Want What We Don't Need* (New York: HarperPerennial, 1999).
2. I use "Mao era" as a neutral shorthand to refer to nearly the first three decades of the PRC, from its founding in 1949 until the death of Mao in 1976. While using the "Mao era" as shorthand, I avoid using the common terms "Maoist China" and "Mao's China" because they tend to overemphasize the role of one person in determining the era. For reasons that will become clear, I also do not use the terms "socialist China" or "Communist China." When applied to the entire post-1949 period, socialist/Communist China is misleading in many ways. Even the CCP identifies the political economy of the first six years preceding the official Socialist Transformation ending in 1956 as "state capitalist" and not "socialist," much less "communist." Third and finally, I also break with convention and avoid using the CCP construct of 1978 as the major turning point from one era to another; instead I end what I refer to as

233

the Mao era in 1976, the year Mao died. This rejection of 1978 as a singular turning point is consistent with recent literature stressing continuity. In addition to my conclusion, for a discussion of the continuity across 1978, see Frederick C. Teiwes and Warren Sun, "China's New Economic Policy under Hua Guofeng: Party Consensus and Party Myths," *China Journal*, no. 66 (July 2011), 1–23. I also discuss the myth of 1978 in "Make Some Get Rich First: State Consumerism and Private Enterprise in the Creation of Postsocialist China," in Juliane Fürst, Silvio Pons, and Mark Selden, eds., *Cambridge History of Communism. Vol. III, Endgames. Late Communism in Global Perspective, 1968 to the Present* (Cambridge: Cambridge University Press, 2017), 3.449–73. Note that I no longer use the term "postsocialist."

3. My understanding of the Mao-era political economy relies on and contributes to the explanations provided in standard reference works, such as Carl Riskin, *China's Political Economy: The Quest for Development Since 1949* (Oxford: Oxford University Press, 1987); Chris Bramall, *Chinese Economic Development* (London: Routledge, 2009); and Muqiao Xue, *China's Socialist Economy* (Beijing: Foreign Languages Press, 1981). Even these books specializing in the political economy of the Mao era, however, make only passing reference to consumption and no mention of consumerism or consumer culture.

4. The CCP's stated goal was "building socialism" (建设社会主义) or "socialist construction" (社会主义建设), terms it used interchangeably. For the sake of consistency, I generally translate both of these terms as "building socialism" and seldom use "socialist construction." "Building" emphasizes, as the party did (and still does), that its version of "socialism" was an ongoing transformation, a process of becoming, with many stages leading to communism. Although the terms appeared earlier, after 1953 the national party newspaper *Renmin ribao* (*People's Daily*, hereafter *RMRB*) includes innumerable articles with "building socialism" and "socialist construction" in their titles. On the importance of translating these "formulations" (提法) correctly, see Michael Schoenhals, *Doing Things with Words in Chinese Politics: Five Studies* (Berkeley: Institute of East Asian Studies, University of California, 1992). On the role of the *RMRB* in communicating state policy, see Guoguang Wu, "Command Communication: The Politics of Editorial Formulation in the *People's Daily*," *The China Quarterly*, no. 137 (March 1994), 194–211. Building on George Lakoff's observations of how the repetition of slogans and phrases frames issues, sets political agendas, and becomes part of the hardwiring of an individual's brain, I also try to avoid using party framings such as "before/since Liberation," "building socialism," and "reform era" without qualification. *The Political Mind: A Cognitive Scientist's Guide to Your Brain and Its Politics* (New York: Penguin, 2009), 83–4.

5. I use "CCP," "the party," and "the state" interchangeably and as the equivalent of the common academic practice of labeling the fusion of the party and the state apparatus as the "party-state." As I try to make clear in the book, the CCP and the Chinese state, as with any other party or state, were neither the same institution nor monolithic. Although I periodically address differences between individuals and factions and attempt to specify people within the party or specific institutions within the state, the focus of this study is on the larger social origins and outcomes of policies rather than on the intentions of various individuals or divisions within and between the party and the state, topics studied by other scholars, as observed in the notes.

6. Many forms of capitalism predated *industrial* capitalism. On the range of forms of capitalism across time and place, see Jürgen Kocka, *Capitalism: A Short History*, tr. Jeremiah M. Riemer (Princeton, NJ: Princeton University Press, 2016). This book only addresses industrial capitalism. Therefore, throughout, I use "capitalism" as shorthand for "state-to-private spectrum of industrial capitalism."

7. Both sides of the Cold War popularized the concepts of "capitalism" and "socialism" (or "communism") as frameworks to describe the battles between diametrically opposed ways of life, or what two scholars of state capitalism call an "inter-capitalist rivalry" (Adam Buick and John Crump, *State Capitalism: The Wages System under New Management* [Basingstoke: Macmillan, 1986], front matter). The terms *capitalism* and *socialism/communism* became – and remain – politically useful on both sides for building domestic cohesion and discipline, as well as in the battle for the hearts and minds of the opposing populations. See, for instance, Mary Kaldor, *The Imaginary War: Understanding the East–West Conflict* (Oxford: Blackwell, 1990); Oscar Sanchez-Sibony, *Red Globalization: The Political Economy of the Soviet Cold War from Stalin to Khrushchev* (Cambridge: Cambridge University Press, 2014).

8. *State capitalism* refers to political economies where production and consumption are more heavily organized and managed by the state rather than by private markets, private enterprises, and private individuals. Although in this sense state capitalism is the opposite of private capitalism, I use the term to refer not to a static set of institutional arrangements but to a spectrum of industrial capitalism, which may range from totally state controlled to completely market mediated within a political economy dominated by the reinvestment of capital to create and accumulate more capital. On the concept of state capitalism and its application to "socialist" countries, see Stephen A. Resnick and Richard D. Wolff, *Class Theory and History: Capitalism and Communism in the U.S.S.R.* (New York: Routledge, 2002), 85–129. Critiques of "socialist" countries as actually "state capitalist"

have been around longer than such countries themselves. For an early critique of the PRC as state capitalist, see Ygael Gluckstein, *Mao's China: Economic and Political Survey* (Boston: Beacon Press, 1957). Others came to similar conclusions. In the mid-twentieth century, the state capitalism critique also had American proponents such as C.R.L. James and Grace Lee Boggs. Likewise, the similarities in political economies across national and ideological cases were so great that writers of the Frankfurt School in the late 1930s and early 1940s saw state capitalism as a shared attribute of otherwise politically diverse countries, from "totalitarian" to democratic, including both Nazi Germany and the Soviet Union, and pondered whether state capitalism was the future of capitalism that all countries inevitably would share. See Eike Gebhardt and Andrew Arato, eds., *The Essential Frankfurt School Reader* (New York: Continuum, 2007), 71–94. For a chart of different degrees of state capitalist countries in the contemporary world, see Joshua Kurlantzick, *State Capitalism: How the Return of Statism Is Transforming the World* (New York: Oxford University Press, 2016), ch. 2. None of these varieties of industrial capitalism, however, include worker control over production and distribution, which a basic tenet of socialism – and party propaganda – would appear to have required. Despite the non-working-class origins of the party leadership, state media often included, for instance, the slogan, "the working class must exercise leadership over everything" (工人阶级必须领导一切). For an example of the application of the term *state capitalism* to contemporary China, see Barry Naughton and Kellee S. Tsai, eds., *State Capitalism, Institutional Adaptation, and the Chinese Miracle* (Cambridge: Cambridge University Press, 2015).

9. The CCP told itself and the world that the manifestations of capitalism that continued in China during this period were remnants of the "old society" that the building of socialism would eliminate. With this interpretation, the CCP was following the political lead of Lenin, Stalin, and the Soviet Union by quoting a minor passage written by Marx and claiming that socialism was a distinct stage of development from communism. Socialism and communism are actually terms Marx uses interchangeably. The CCP then used this "two-stage" reinterpretation to explain the apparent contradictions between its claims to be "building socialism" and the on-the-ground policy outcomes that included the existence of a state, labor markets, distribution based on "work" rather than "need," worker strikes, commodity production, gender hierarchies, and other attributes of industrial capitalism. The "two-stage" interpretation of Marx relies on his "Critique of the Gotha Programme" (1875), originally written not as a major work but as marginal notes. In Gotha, Marx famously writes that post-revolutionary societies would be "stamped with the birthmarks of the old society from whose womb it

emerges." https://www.marxists.org/archive/marx/works/1875/gotha/cho1.htm. Consulted July 9, 2018. For Lenin's interpretation, see Lenin, Vladimir, "The Economic Basis of the Withering Away of the State," *The State and Revolution.* (1918). https://www.marxists.org/archive/lenin/works/1917/staterev/ch05.htm. Consulted May 20, 2018. For an overview of Gotha and these reinterpretations, see Michael A. Lebowitz, *The Socialist Alternative: Real Human Development* (New York: Monthly Review Press, 2010), 42–75; and Michael A. Lebowitz, *The Socialist Imperative: From Gotha to Now* (New York: Monthly Review Press, 2015), 85-124. Paresh Chattopadhyay labels these reinterpretations "totally anti-emancipatory, based on their complete misreading if not utter deformation of Marx's (and Engels') own texts" in *Marx's Associated Mode of Production: A Critique of Marxism* (New York: Palgrave Macmillan, 2016), 8.

10. While these party debates reveal the difficulties of "building socialism," they also provide evidence of fundamental doubts that what the party was constructing could not be wished away with theoretical elaborations relying on one or another Marxist political economy concept. Moreover, as examples in later chapters will show, both political elites as well as people from all walks of life pondered the apparent contradiction, demonstrating Marx's observation that "the desire to convince oneself of the non-existence of contradictions is at the same time the expression of a pious wish that the contradictions which are really present should not exist." Karl Marx, *Theories of Surplus Value* (Moscow: Progress Publishers, 1968), 2.519. As later chapters show, the party papered over the contradiction by simply adding the word "socialist" to their policies, including "primitive socialist accumulation," "socialist advertising," and a "socialist commerce" replete with "socialist window displays." But, in the final analysis, the meaning of an open-ended and indeterminate "socialism" and subordinate terms such as "socialist commodities" was either adjusted to suit policies prioritizing accumulation or else the contradiction was simply ignored. All sides of the debate within the party claimed to adhere to an interpretation of Marxist notions, such as the "law of value," "commodities," "wage labor," "primitive accumulation," and "capital." Party shifts in the institutional arrangements of capitalism toward greater use of markets, material incentives, and other attributes of private capitalism and consumerism had political supporters who justified these policies in "socialist" terms; see, for instance, Yün Ch'en et al., *Ch'en Yün's Strategy for China's Development: A Non-Maoist Alternative* (Armonk, NY: M.E. Sharpe, 1983). For an example of the adjustment of the meaning of terms rather than of policies, see the discussion of prices as they relate to the labor theory of value in the volume by economist Audrey Donnithorne, *China's Economic System* (New York: Praeger, 1967), 439.

11. Mao regularly and informally used the concept of negation (and I do the same) to label policies and their outcomes as warnings of threats to the

fulfillment of the Communist Revolution. These warning signs included phenomena as ordinary as the consumerism among urban youth and as specific as the policies in Yugoslavia and the USSR that Mao criticized. For instance, in 1957 Mao criticized Stalin by claiming, "The October Revolution negated capitalism but it refused to admit that socialism may be negated too." "Interjections at Conference of Provincial and Municipal Committee Secretaries (Collected) (January 1957)," in Mao Zedong, *Miscellany of Mao Tse-Tung Thought (1949–1968)* (Springfield, VA: Joint Publications Research Service; distributed by the National Technical Information Service, US Department of Commerce, 1974), pt.1, 50. For an introduction to Mao's writing on historical materialism and his use of the concept of negation, see Nick Knight, "Introduction: Soviet Marxism and the Development of Mao Zedong's Philosophical Thought," in Nick Knight, ed., *Mao Zedong on Dialectical Materialism: Writings on Philosophy, 1937* (Armonk, NY: M.E. Sharpe, 1990), 3–83, esp. 20–4.

12. In 1960, while writing marginalia on Soviet economics texts, for instance, Mao said that workers possessed personal property and also many other goods that they enjoyed as part of society, which he labeled "social consumption" or "public property." See Mao Zedong, *A Critique of Soviet Economics*, tr. Moss Roberts (New York: Monthly Review, 1977), sec. 31: "Individual Property." Similar terms one might use to describe the opposite of "bourgeois" consumption include "public consumption" and "collective consumption." Manuel Castells discusses the concept of collective consumption in reference to the state reproduction of the urban capitalist labor force by providing housing and health care through non-market means; see his "Collective Consumption and Urban Contradictions in Advanced Capitalism," in Ida Susser, ed., *The Castells Reader on Cities and Social Theory* (Oxford: Blackwell, 2002), 107–29.

13. See Xiaobo Lü and Elizabeth J. Perry, eds., *Danwei: The Changing Chinese Workplace in Historical and Comparative Perspective* (Armonk, NY: M.E. Sharpe, 1997).

14. As scholarship during the last several decades has shown, capitalism always varies and always includes non-private capitalist institutional arrangements of extraction. For an introduction to the more expansive definitions and analyses of capitalism adopted here that include the continual use of expropriation to facilitate capitalist expansion, see Nancy Fraser and Rahel Jaeggi, *Capitalism: A Conversation in Critical Theory* (Cambridge: Polity, 2018). Because industrial capitalism as a global system is characterized by its flexibility and adaptation to local circumstances, the countless noncapitalist aspects of the Mao era do not serve as proof that China was not a capitalist economy or was in the process of becoming

Communist. For more on such noncapitalist attributes, see Tiejun Cheng and Mark Selden, "The Construction of Spatial Hierarchies: China's *Hukou* and *Danwei* Systems," in Timothy Cheek and Tony Saich, eds., *New Perspectives on State Socialism in China* (Armonk, NY: M.E. Sharpe, 1997), 23–50; Andrew G. Walder, "Property Rights and Stratification in Socialist Redistributive Economies," *American Sociological Review*, vol. 57 (1992), 524–39. For inequalities of distribution within individual industrial workplaces, see Walder's *Communist Neo-Traditionalism: Work and Authority in Chinese Industry* (Berkeley: University of California Press, 1986), 76–81. As for international comparisons, in his *China under Mao: A Revolution Derailed* (Cambridge, MA: Harvard University Press, 2015), 330, Walder concludes that China was "the world's most unequal socialist economy."

15. On the burgeoning scholarship on the persistence of capitalist activities, see, for example, Xu Bin, "'地下经济'的顽强生存与民营企业的先发优势 (The tenacious survival of the "underground economy" and the first-mover advantages of private-owned corporations), *Shangye jingji yu guanli*, no. 1 (2010), 51–60, 68; and the work by Feng Xiaocai, especially, "社会主义的边缘人: 1956年前后的小商小贩改造问题" (The marginalized people of socialism: The transformation of small business hawkers circa 1956), *Zhongguo dangdai shi yanjiu*, no. 3 (August 2011), 3–45; "一九五八年至一九六三年中共自由市场政策研究" (A study of the free market policy of the CPC from 1958 to 1963), *Zhonggong dangshi yanjiu*, no. 2 (2015), 38–53. See also Zhang Xuebing, "中国计划经济时期的'地下经济'探析" (An analysis of the 'underground economy' during the period of China's planned economy), *Zhonggong dangshi yanjiu*, no. 4 (2012), 39–48. A new English-language account of private economic activity in the Mao era and thereafter is Zhang Qi and Mingxing Liu, *Revolutionary Legacy, Power Structure, and Grassroots Capitalism under the Red Flag in China* (Cambridge: Cambridge University Press, 2019), esp. 130–203; for the Chinese version: Zhang Qi and Liu Mingxing, 权力结构、政治激励和经济增长 基于浙江民营经济发展经验的政治经济学分析 (Power structure, political incentives, and economic growth: A political economy analysis based on the experiences of Zhejiang's private economic development) (Shanghai: Gezhi chubanshe, 2016), 101–59; Gao Wangling, 中国农民反行为研究 (1950–1980) (Research on the counter-strategies of Chinese peasants [1950–1980]) (Hong Kong: Zhongwen daxue chubanshe, 2013), 187–94, 201–34. As noted in the footnotes in Chapter 7, of particular value is: Jin Dalu, 非常与正常-上海 "文革"时期的社会生活 (The extraordinary and the ordinary: Social life in Shanghai during the "Cultural Revolution"), 2 vols. (Shanghai: Shanghai cishu chubanshe, 2011), vol. 2.

16. With the term "three major inequalities" (三大差别), rather than follow convention and translate *chabie* (差别) as "difference," I translate the term by another one of its meanings, that is, "inequality." Party leaders invoked the term to propose, legitimize, and critique policies based on the impact of inequalities. For an example related to the establishment of people's communes in the late 1950s, see Xu Lin, "从我国社会主义建设实践看消灭城乡差别, 工农差别和体力劳动与脑力劳动差别的问题" (Seeing the inequalities between urban and rural areas, workers and peasants, and manual and mental labor in the practice of socialist construction in China), *Jiaoxue yu yanjiu* (1959), 23–40.

17. In addition to these three forms of inequalities, the party attempted to address other forms of inequalities created by industrial capitalism, such as those related to gender, region, ethnicity, and especially the cadre class. On women, see, for instance, Delia Davin, *Woman-Work: Women and the Party in Revolutionary China* (Oxford: Clarendon Press, 1976); Zheng Wang, *Finding Women in the State: A Socialist Feminist Revolution in the People's Republic of China, 1949–1964* (Berkeley: University of California Press, 2017).

18. For Lenin's quote in its original context, see Vladimir Lenin, "An Essential Condition of the Bolsheviks' Success," in *"Left-Wing" Communism: An Infantile Disorder* (1920), www.marxists.org/archive/lenin/works/1920/lwc/c ho2.htm. Consulted March 28, 2018.

Self-Expanding and Compulsory Consumerism

1. For an introduction to the concepts of self-expanding capital in Marx from which I draw this self-expanding and compulsory consumerism correlate, see Geoffrey Pilling, *Marx's Capital: Philosophy and Political Economy* (London: Routledge & Kegan Paul, 1980), ch. 3; Karl Marx, *Capital: A Critique of Political Economy*, 3 vols., tr. Ben Fowkes (London: Penguin Books, 1990–2), 247–57 and 1056; and Michael Heinrich, *An Introduction to the Three Volumes of Karl Marx's Capital* (New York: Monthly Review Press, 2012), 221. In discussing consumerism, I borrow the notion of "compulsion" from Marx, who writes that capital compels capitalists to accumulate capital and compels the proletariat to sell their labor power in return for wages so as to enable their survival. See, for instance, Karl Marx, *Grundrisse: Foundations of the Critique of Political Economy*, tr. Martin Nicolaus (New York: Vintage Books, 1973), 248. On the compulsion of industrial capitalism to create the "false needs" that fuel consumerism, see Wolfgang Fritz Haug, *Critique of Commodity Aesthetics: Appearance, Sexuality, and Advertising in Capitalist Society* (Minneapolis: University of Minnesota Press, 1986).

2. A radio was sometimes substituted for a sewing machine or was added to the Three Greats. For an example of the early use of the term by the state, see Lin Ping, Song Qiong, and Wang Yu, "'少校政委'的原形" (The real nature of "Major Commissar"), *Jiefangjun bao*, April 9, 1958.

3. 山东省日用机械工业制 *1915–1985* (Records of the Shandong everyday goods machinery industry, 1915–1985) (Shandong: Shandongsheng riyong jixie gongye gongsi, 1988), 190, 119, 253.

4. By 1968, the state was promoting the Three Greats as part of the Three Greats campaign (三大件会战). For the campaign in Shandong, see Qingdaoshi shizhi bangongshi, ed., 青岛市志: 轻工业志建材工业志 (Qingdao annals: Light industry/building materials industry) (Beijing: Xinhua chubanshe, 2000), 54–5. In Wuhan, the campaign began in 1970; see Zhao Dexin, ed., 湖北省志工业志稿: 轻工业) (Hubei province annals: Light industry) (Beijing: Zhongguo qinggongye chubanshe, 1994), 16–17.

5. By the mid-1980s, the Three Greats had also spread throughout the countryside, where nearly half of the families owned sewing machines. Shangyebu baihuo ju, ed., 中国百货商业 (Chinese general commerce) (Beijing: Beijing daxue chubanshe, 1989), 159.

6. In the 1990s, a stereo, a refrigerator, and a computer constituted the Three Great Things; and in the 2000s, they included even more expensive, technologically complex items, such as an automobile, a condo, and a vacation abroad. As Chapter 2 makes clear, I emphasize how self-expanding demand was compulsory rather than, as suggested by others, simple emulation, which implies more individual agency. Although I do not address international competition here, such competition was part of the compulsory aspect of the expanding consumerism. "Socialist" countries were forced to compete not only in terms of weapon technologies but also in terms of consumer goods. The best-known such competition, between a "socialist" country and a market capitalist country, occurred during the 1959 "kitchen debate" between Khrushchev and Vice President Richard Nixon, when Muscovites were enthralled by an exhibition of US consumer appliances. See Susan E. Reid, "Cold War in the Kitchen: Gender and the De-Stalinization of Consumer Taste in the Soviet Union under Khrushchev," *Slavic Review*, vol. 61, no. 2 (2002), 211–52. The confrontation with rapid Soviet-style industrialization and consumerism was acute in cases where the two met head-to-head. See Mark Landsman, *Dictatorship and Demand: The Politics of Consumerism in East Germany* (Cambridge, MA: Harvard University Press, 2005). Landsman mentions "Western-style consumerism" (p. 3), "Western consumerism" (p. 210), and "capitalist consumerism" (p. 217) without specifying his meaning or use of the term "consumerism."

7. "Record of Conversation between Polish Delegation and PRC Leader Mao Zedong, Wuhan," April 2, 1958, History and Public Policy Program Digital Archive, AAN, KC PZPR, sygnatura XI A 130, Dept. V China 074/19/58. Obtained by Douglas Selvage and translated by Malgorzata Gnoinska, at https://digitalarchive.wilsoncenter.org/document/117780. Archived February 5, 2018. Because blogs are fleeting, to ensure future access to these critical sources, "archived" refers to the date on which I archived the post at the Internet Wayback Machine: https://archive.org/web/. If the original link no longer works, one can find an "archived" post there.

8. See Francesca Bray, *Technology and Gender: Fabrics of Power in Late Imperial China* (Berkeley: University of California Press, 1997). Bray writes: "In this sense the most important work that technologies do is to produce people: the makers are shaped by the making, and the users shaped by the using" (p. 16).

9. Sheila Fitzpatrick, *Everyday Stalinism: Ordinary Life in Extraordinary Times, Soviet Russia in the 1930s* (New York: Oxford University Press, 1999), 266–7.

10. Martin K. Whyte and William L. Parish, *Urban Life in Contemporary China* (Chicago: University of Chicago Press, 1984), 85–100.

11. For examples of the introduction of new marketing techniques, see Sherman Cochran, *Big Business in China: Sino-Foreign Rivalry in the Cigarette Industry, 1890–1930* (Cambridge, MA: Harvard University Press, 1980). The relationship between industrial capitalism and consumerism in the original industrializing countries has been extensive. See, for instance, classic studies, such as those by Neil McKendrick, John Brewer, and J. H. Plumb, *The Birth of a Consumer Society: The Commercialization of Eighteenth-Century England* (Bloomington: Indiana University Press, 1982); John Brewer and Roy Porter, eds., *Consumption and the World of Goods* (London: Routledge, 1994). For an overview of the concept and historiography of consumer culture, see Frank Trentmann, "Introduction," in Trentmann, ed., *Oxford Handbook of the History of Consumption* (Oxford: Oxford University Press, 2012: 1–19), and his *Empire of Things: How We Became a World of Consumers, from the Fifteenth Century to the Twenty-First* (New York: HarperCollins Publishers, 2016).

12. Andrew Godley, "Selling the Sewing Machine Around the World: Singer's International Marketing Strategies, 1850–1920," *Enterprise and Society*, vol. 7, no. 2 (2006), 266–313; Andrew Gordon, "Selling the American Way: The Singer Sales System in Japan, 1900–1938," *Business History Review*, vol. 82, no. 4 (2008), 671–99.

13. Vanessa Ogle, *The Global Transformation of Time: 1870–1950* (Cambridge, MA: Harvard University Press, 2015). On the centuries-long creation of homogenous "abstract time" as the measure of an activity and its links to the history of industrial capitalism, see Moishe Postone, *Time, Labor, and*

Social Domination: A Reinterpretation of Marx's Critical Theory (Cambridge: Cambridge University Press, 1993), 202–11.

14. Peter Oakley, "Ticking Boxes: (Re)Constructing the Wristwatch as a Luxury Object," *Luxury*, vol. 2. no. 1 (2015), 41–60 (at pp. 46–9). Indeed, demand for watches in the military was so high that in the late 1950s soldiers participated in watch smuggling. Wen Gongfeng, "一场 '走私手表' 引发的风波" (A crisis sparked by watch smuggling), *Dongguan ribao*, April 12, 2011, A11.

15. On the implementation of standardized time and the corresponding need for watches and clocks among railway workers, see Elisabeth Köll, *Railroads and the Transformation of China* (Cambridge, MA: Harvard University Press, 2019), 248–53.

16. The classic treatment of the links between "time discipline" and capitalism is E. P. Thompson, "Time, Work-Discipline, and Industrial Capitalism," *Past & Present*, no. 38 (December 1967), 56–97. See also Chuck Koeber, "The Social Reorganization of Time: The 'Great Speedup' and the Transformation of Time and Work Discipline," *Humanity & Society*, vol. 41, no. 2 (2017). 143–57.

17. For a list of top manufacturers, their locations, primary brands, and a table of annual production and exports, see Shangyebu baihuo ju, ed., 中国百货商业 (Chinese general commerce), 165, 173.

18. Shanghai difangzhi bangongshi, "钟表, 自行车及缝纫机价格" (The price of clocks and watches, bicycles, and sewing machines), February 21, 2003, at www.shtong.gov.cn/Newsite/node2/node2245/node4487/node56918/node56920/userobject1ai45655.html. Archived March 18, 2018.

19. Shangyebu baihuo ju, ed., 中国百货商业 (Chinese general commerce), 169, 175.

20. On the ways political leaders, intellectuals, businesspeople, and others stressed the importance not only of assimilating industrial processes and the skills required to use everyday technologies – such as how to ride a bicycle – but also the necessity of mass-producing the technologies as a measure of national well-being, see Karl Gerth, *China Made: Consumer Culture and the Creation of the Nation* (Cambridge, MA: Harvard University Asia Center, 2003), ch. 2.

21. "我国开始自制手表" (Our country begins to make watches), *Wenhui bao*, April 2, 1955; Zhang Di, 中国第一块手表诞生记 (The birth of China's first watch). 河东区文史资料选辑第17辑 (Collection of cultural and historical materials on Hedong District, vol.17) (Tianjin: Tianjinshi Hedongqu weiyuanhui xuexi wenshi ziliao weiyuanhui, 2005), 150–4. Other cities began to produce watches between 1955 and 1960, such as Shanghai's the East is Red (东方红) brand, Beijing's Model No. 1 (北京1型) brand, Guangzhou's Yangcheng (羊城) brand, Dandong's Andong (安东) brand, Qingdao's New Qingdao (新青岛) brand, Chongqing's Satellite (卫星) brand, and Nanjing's

July First (七一) brand. Lu Xiangbo, "图说早期国产表的发展轨迹和时代 烙印" (The picture shows the development of early domestic watches and the brands at that time), *Zui shijian* (May 2016), 26–35 (see pp. 26–7, for photos).

22. Shen Jialu, "A581: 中国手表的始祖" (A581: The progenitor of China-made watches), at http://blog.sina.com.cn/s/blog_4be1d27f0100d7p0.html. Archived November 12, 2017. The first model was the A581, with "58" representing the first year of its manufacture and "1" signifying that it was the first model. For a brief documentary on the factory, see Shanghai watch segment tour of the factory. *China Today 1959 No. 17.* Available from the database produced by Adam Matthew: "Socialism on Film: The Cold War and International Propaganda," www.socialismonfilm.amdigital.co.uk .ezproxy.princeton.edu/Documents/Details/N_507739_China_Today_ No_49. Consulted June 14, 2019.

23. Shanghai difangzhi bangongshi, "钟表, 自行车及缝纫机价格" (The price of clocks and watches, bicycles, and sewing machines). On comparable priority consumption in the Soviet Union, see Fitzpatrick, *Everyday Stalinism*, 55–6. In contrast to the frequent attacks on cadre privileges in China, the Soviet Union appears to have had an easier time accepting such mental/manual inequalities as expressed in privileged access, though not always outright ownership. See Chapter 3.

24. Shangyebu baihuo ju, ed., 中国百货商业 (Chinese general commerce), 175-6.

25. Edward J. M. Rhoads, "Cycles of Cathay: A History of the Bicycle in China," *Transfers*, vol. 2, no. 2 (Summer 2012), 95–120.

26. On urban material and leisure markers of industrial capitalist modernity in Shanghai, see Leo Ou-fan Lee, *Shanghai Modern: The Flowering of a New Urban Culture in China, 1930–1945* (Cambridge, MA: Harvard University Press, 1999).

27. Liu Shanling, 西洋风: 西洋发明在中国 (Wind from the West: Western inventions in China) (Shanghai: Shanghai guji chubanshe, 1999), 27.

28. David Arnold, *Everyday Technology: Machines and the Making of India's Modernity* (Chicago: University of Chicago Press, 2013), 51–6. See also Wiebe E. Bijker, *Of Bicycles, Bakelites, and Bulbs: Toward a Theory of Sociotechnical Change* (Cambridge, MA: MIT Press, 2002); David V. Herlihy, *Bicycle: The History* (New Haven: Yale University Press, 2006).

29. Marx, *Capital: A Critique of Political Economy*, 165.

30. Marx, *Capital: A Critique of Political Economy*, ch. 1: The Commodity (p. 163).

31. Huangji zahuo pu, "中国手表往事" (The past of Chinese watches), June 20, 2009, at http://blog.sina.com.cn/s/blog_609dafof0100eeft.html. Archived November 12, 2017.

32. Xu Tao, 自行车与近代中国 (Bicycles and modern China) (Shanghai: Shanghai renmin chubanshe, 2015), 219–20.

33. Xu Tao, 自行车与近代中国 (Bicycles and modern China), 217–20.

34. The industrialist Kojima Kazusaburô, for instance, founded three factories – in Shenyang, Tianjin, and Shanghai – all of them named Changhe, and all of which produced the Tiemao (Iron Anchor) bicycle brand.

35. Rhoads, "Cycles of Cathay," 105–6.

36. Wang Haibo, comp., 中华人民共和国工业经济史 (A history of the industrial economy of the People's Republic of China) (Taiyuan: Shanxi jingji chubanshe, 1998), 857–9.

37. For an overview of the development of bicycle manufacturing during the Mao era, see "Dangdai Zhongguo" congshu bianjibu, ed., 当代中国的轻工业 (Light industry in contemporary China) (Beijing: Zhongguo shehui kexue chubanshe, 1986), 2.176–97.

38. Zhonggong Shanghaishi diyi shangye ju weiyuanhui sanfan zhengfeng lingdao xiaozu bangongshi, "局党委扩大会议有关党委官僚主义方面的综合材料" (Comprehensive materials on the bureaucratic aspects of party committees for the expanded meeting of party committees), Shanghai Municipal Archives (hereafter SMA) B123-4-568 (July 31, 1960), 7.

39. For an example of the futility of the state's efforts to suppress local markets in Zhejiang for ration coupons and other items in the early 1960s, see Qi Zhang and Mingxing Liu, *Revolutionary Legacy, Power Structure, and Grassroots Capitalism under the Red Flag in China* (Cambridge: Cambridge University Press, 2019), 151–3.

40. Xinxin Zhang and Ye Sang, *Chinese Profiles* (Beijing: Chinese Literature, 1986), 9.

41. Su Feng, "改革开放初期北京安置待业青年与多种经济形式的起步" (The arrangements for youth waiting for employment in Beijing and the beginning of various economic forms during the early reform and opening-up), *Dangdai Zhongguo shi yanjiu*, vol. 24, no. 4 (2017), 50–62.

42. Rhoads, "Cycles of Cathay," 108.

43. For additional examples of market research conducted by urban-based factories on product preferences – including brand preferences based on styles – in the countryside, see Hsia Kung, "Producing Goods for the Peasants," *China Reconstructs*, vol. 13, no. 11 (1964), 18–20.

44. For a description of the uses of sewing machines in one rural county in the mid-1920s, see Mao Zedong, *Report from Xunwu*, tr. Roger R. Thompson (Stanford: Stanford University Press, 1990), 92–5. Mao notes that only four machines in the county of 120,000 helped introduce Shanghai- and Guangzhou-inspired fashions.

45. See Tim Putnam, "The Sewing Machine Comes Home," in Barbara Burman, ed., *The Culture of Sewing: Gender, Consumption and Home Dressmaking* (New York: Berg, 1999), 269–83. On the ways new technologies such as sewing machines led to social changes, for example, the end of footbinding, see Laurel Bossen and Hill Gates, *Bound Feet, Young Hands: Tracking the Demise of Footbinding in Village China* (Stanford: Stanford University Press, 2017).

46. Arnold, *Everyday Technology*, 42–51. For examples of the impact beyond ownership, see Andrew Godley, "Global Diffusion of the Sewing Machine, 1850–1914," *Research in Economic History*, vol. 20 (2001), 1–46. For a general history of Singer's domination of global markets, see Robert Bruce Davies, *Peacefully Working to Conquer the World: Singer Sewing Machines in Foreign Markets, 1854–1920* (New York: Arno Press, 1976); Godley, "Selling the Sewing Machine Around the World."

47. Shanghai qinggongye zhi bianzuan weiyuanhui, ed., 上海轻工业志 (Shanghai light industry annals) (Shanghai: Shanghai shehui kexue chubanshe, 1996), 22.

48. "Dangdai Zhongguo" congshu bianjibu, ed., 当代中国的轻工业 (Light industry in contemporary China), 2.227.

49. For a list of the twenty-eight cities manufacturing sewing machines, see Wang Qianli, ed., 缝纫机 (Sewing machines) (Beijing: Zhongguo caizheng jingji chubanshe, 1964), 9–10.

50. "Dangdai Zhongguo" congshu bianjibu, ed., 当代中国的轻工业 (Light industry in contemporary China), 2.229-30.

51. Women who used their sewing machines to earn additional income did not advertise their work. Rather, the household economy was part of the extensive informal, or gray, economy, to be discussed below, that existed alongside the dominant state economy.

52. Unstructured interview with Mrs. Wang Yushi (b. 1955 in Ji'nan; married to Feng Guoqing, b. 1953), conducted and recorded by her daughter, Feng Ying, August 8, 2014, on topics suggested by this author. Follow-up questions and answers, August 18, 2014. Wang Yushi originally worked at the Ji'nan Railway Bedding and Clothing Factory (济南铁路被服厂) making uniforms for railway workers.

53. For one such story, see Xie Chenjian, "'三转一响': 我们那个年代的时尚故事" ("The three things that go round and the one that makes a sound": Stories about fashion from our times), *Minjian wenhua luntan*, no. Z1 (May/June 2000), 28–31.

54. Neil Jeffrey Diamant, *Revolutionizing the Family: Politics, Love, and Divorce in Urban and Rural China, 1949–1968* (Berkeley: University of California Press, 2000), 115.

55. On the history of watches and their connection to larger social and economic changes, see Stephen Kern, *The Culture of Time and Space 1880–1918* (Cambridge, MA: Harvard University Press, 1983); Alexis McCrossen, *Marking Modern Times: A History of Clocks, Watches, and Other Timekeepers in American Life* (Chicago: University of Chicago Press, 2013).

56. Zhu Zhanliang, "上海轻工业名牌产品初探" (A brief analysis of Shanghai light industry brand products), *Shanghai jingji yanjiu*, no. 9 (September 1981), 7–11. On the ways products, specifically watches, that are luxuries for some become necessities for others as part of a "system of needs," see Pierre Bourdieu, *Distinction: A Social Critique of the Judgement of Taste*, tr. Richard Nice (Cambridge, MA: Harvard University Press, 1984), 375.

57. Midwives studied by Gail Hershatter, for instance, marked events outside "campaign time" in terms of births, marriages, and other family and emotional events. See her *The Gender of Memory: Rural Women and China's Collective Past* (Berkeley: University of California Press, 2011).

58. Huangji zahuo pu, "中国手表往事" (The past of Chinese watches).

59. Huangji zahuo pu, "中国手表往事" (The past of Chinese watches).

60. In Republican cities, "A man who could afford it would also maintain a concubine in addition to his wife. Like wearing imported clothes and wearing a watch, maintaining a concubine was a marker of high status in Chinese society." Lin Qihong, *Social Life of the Chinese* (*in Peking*) (Peking: China Booksellers, 1928), 112, 119, 127.

61. Diamant, *Revolutionizing the Family*, 81.

62. Diamant, *Revolutionizing the Family*, 123.

63. Elisabeth Croll, "Marriage Choice and Status Groups in Contemporary China," in James L. Watson, ed., *Class and Social Stratification in Post-Revolution China* (Cambridge: Cambridge University Press, 1984), 175–97.

64. Diamant, *Revolutionizing the Family*, 115.

65. Li Dong, "永远的歼6" (The eternal J-6), in Shanghai difangzhi bangongshi, ed., 人民军队中的上海兵 (Shanghai soldiers in the People's Army) (Shanghai: Shanghai renmin chubanshe, 2013), 349.

66. Xiang Xiaomi, 记忆洪荒 (A flood of memories) (Beijing: Beijing chubanshe, 2013), 101–2.

67. Unstructured interview with Mrs. Wang Yushi, August 8, 2014. Follow-up questions and answers, August 18, 2014.

68. Ni Ping, "上海牌手表" (Shanghai wristwatches), in Wang Xiaozhen, ed., 商品的故事 (Stories about merchandise) (Guangzhou: *Nanfang ribao* chubanshe, 2000).

69. On bribing children with watches to perform better on school examinations, see Guang Jun, "杭六中召开家长会议" (A parents' meeting at Hangzhou No. 6 Middle School), *Hangzhou ribao*, March 27, 1957.

70. Unstructured interview with Cao Dongmei, conducted by the author, July 11, 2015.

71. Rhoads, "Cycles of Cathay," 105. Along with women riding bicycles, the rural soldiers who conquered Hangzhou saw other activities as problematic, including taking a rickshaw was considered exploitative and wearing Western suits was seen as bourgeois.

72. According to Amir Moghaddass Esfehani, "it was considered absolutely disgraceful to be seen pedaling through the streets, mounted on a machine, always in a delicate situation leading to a state of exhaustion." Amir Moghaddass Esfehani, "The Bicycle's Long Way to China: The Appropriation of Cycling as a Foreign Cultural Technique (1860–1940)," in *Cycle History 13, Proceedings of the 13th International Cycling History Conference*, ed. Nicholas Clayton and Andrew Ritchie (San Francisco: Van der Plas Publications, 2003), 94–102, and posted as "Bicycle," at http://imperialtours.net /blog/bicycle. Archived November 12, 2017.

73. I term this type of illicit economic activity a "gray economy," in contrast to economic activities that are hidden from the state, as implied by the term "underground economy," or conducted in opposition to the state in a "black market." All three of these alternative economies were present in China throughout the entire Mao era, though not much is known about them and the amount of gray- and black-market activity varied widely. See Anita Chan and Jonathan Unger, "Grey and Black: The Hidden Economy of Rural China," *Pacific Affairs*, vol. 55, no. 3 (Fall 1982), 452–71. Further investigations will likely continue to reveal extensive economic activity beyond the state economy. For an introduction to smuggling, see Philip Thai, *China's War on Smuggling: Law, Economic Life, and the Making of the Modern State, 1842–1965* (New York: Columbia University Press, 2018).

74. On Zhejiang province, see Xu Bin, "'地下经济'的顽强生存与民营企业的先发优势" (The tenacious survival of the "underground economy" and the first-mover advantages of privately owned enterprises), *Shangye jingji yu guanli*, no. 1 (2010), 51–60, 68. Even after the Socialist Transformation was completed in 1956, state media continued to present regular accounts of the "spontaneous" emergence of private businesses. For one such account in the *People's Daily*, see "反击资本主义自发势力 进一步加强市场管理 上海全面清查处理自发工业户" (Fight back against spontaneous capitalist forces, reinforce the regulation of markets, and launch a comprehensive investigation of Shanghai's spontaneous businesses), *RMRB*, October 13, 1957, 4.

75. Ren Yuanhang, "蔬菜地区部分农民滋长浪费现象" (The phenomenon of overspending among vegetable farmers), *Hangzhou ribao*, July 25, 1957; "钱要用在刀口上" (Money ought to be spent on the blade [which is a play on the

Chinese expression "钱要用在刀口上," that is, money ought to be saved for important matters]), *Hangzhou ribao*, August 22, 1957.

76. Wen Gongfeng, "一场 '走私手表' 引发的风波" (A crisis sparked by watch smuggling), *Dongguan ribao*, April 12, 2011. For details about one smuggler, see Li Ke and Yao Changgan, "不法商人向人民赎罪的道路" (Law-breaking merchant atones for his crime), *Zhejiang ribao*, February 8, 1952.

77. Jiang Yigao, "'倒卖'粮票换手表" ("Speculating" on grain ration coupons for a wristwatch), *Longmeizhen*, no. 10 (2009), 39–43.

78. Unstructured interview with Grace Cheng, conducted by the author, August 14, 2014.

79. Unstructured interview with Mrs. Wang Yushi, August 8, 2014.

80. Transmitted by the Central Committee, "广东省清理 '小钱柜', '小仓库' 的情况汇报" (Report on the cleaning up the "small cashboxes" and "small warehouses" in Guangdong province), January 16, 1964, in Yongyi Song, ed., 中国文化大革命文库 (Chinese Cultural Revolution database) (Hong Kong: Xianggang Zhongwen daxue, Zhongguo yanjiu fuwu zhongxin, 2002) (cited hereafter as *WDGW*). The rationale would later be enshrined in the post-Mao era, when sacrificing the environment and discarding the goal of economic equality were upheld as "temporary steps," that is, the necessary means to support the goal of "building socialism with Chinese characteristics."

81. This entire account comes from: Taiyuan shichang wujia guanli weiyuanhui, "太原市市场物价管理委员会关于河北省定县定州人民公社所属笔表厂 皮麻厂在本市以自行车手表非法换取国家器材一案的处理决定" (Ruling on factories owned by Dingzhou People's Commune due to its illegal activities of exchanging bicycles and watches for state equipment and material), September 1, 1961, East China Normal University collection.

82. Indeed, the responses of cadre-in-chief, Mao Zedong, to such market realities varied from attempts at times to stamp them out in the later 1950s and at the start of the Cultural Revolution to tacit and policy approvals at other times. For an example of the latter in the very same year that the Socialist Transformation was completed, see Mao Zedong, "同民建和工商联负责人的谈话" (Conversation with the principals of the China Democratic National Construction Association and the Federation of Industry and Commerce), February 7, 1956, *Dang de wenxian*, no. 6 (1998), 8–10.

83. "东北铁路公安局发给哈尔滨人民法院的公函" (Official correspondence from the Northeast Railway Police Station to the People's Court of Harbin), December 25, 1951 (contained in the Stanford University, Collection of Contemporary Chinese Political Archives 1949–80, Box 49: 东北铁路公安局文书档案: 案件调查, 处理, 批示, 判决书, 事故报告等, 1951–53).

84. Liu Shaoqi, "刘少奇关于 '四清' '五反'蹲点问题的报告" (Liu Shaoqi's report on the issue of the "four clean-ups" and the "five antis"), September 16, 1964, in 批判资料: 中国赫鲁晓夫刘少奇反革命修正主义言论集 (1958.6–1967.7) (Beijing: Renmin chubanshe ziliaoshi, September 1967).

85. Issued with instructions by the Central Committee, "中国人民银行关于整顿信用社, 打击高利贷的报告" (Report by the People's Bank of China regarding rectifying credit cooperatives and opposing usury), October 24, 1963, in *WDGW*.

86. Transmitted by the Chinese People's Political Consultative Conference, "广东省清理 '小钱柜', '小仓库'的情况汇报" (Report on cleaning up the "small cashboxes" and "small warehouses" in Guangdong province), January 16, 1964, in *WDGW*.

87. Zhang Huihu, "戴六块表的坏人" (The bad guy with six watches on his wrists), in Wang Xiaozhen, ed., 商品的故事 (Stories about merchandise), 40–1.

88. Shen Jialu, "A581: 中国手表的始祖" (A581: The progenitor of China-made watches).

89. For an example of the state reassuring workers that inequality of distribution – wages based on work rather than based on need – was a necessary part of a socialist society and implied that both cadres and ordinary citizens had doubts, see Jackie Sheehan, *Chinese Workers: A New History* (London: Routledge, 1998), 60–1. On policies that contributed to deepening income inequality among urban factory workers, see Nara Dillon, *Radical Inequalities: China's Revolutionary Welfare State in Comparative Perspective* (Cambridge, MA: Harvard University Asia Center, 2015).

90. Chen Yilin, "三块手表" (Three watches). *Wenshi yuekan*, no. 12 (December 2008), 68.

Building State Capitalism Across 1949

1. In Heilongjiang in the northeast, for instance, party land reforms of 1947 included a "chopping and excavating campaign." Cadres exhorted farmers to descend on the nearby cities and towns and expropriate the (often hidden) possessions of absentee landlords. The term "chopping and excavating" (砍挖) refers to the expression, "砍大树, 挖浮财." The first half, "chopping big trees" (砍大树), metaphorically refers to destroying the "big" forces of rural "feudalism," particularly "big landlords" (大地主). The second half, "挖浮财," refers to "uncovering the assets possessed by landlords and rich peasants," including cash, grain, and clothing. Luo Hanping, "东北解放区1947年土改中的'砍挖运动'" (The chopping and digging campaign during Land Reform in the liberated districts of Northeast China in 1947), *Shiji qiao*, no. 4 (2004), 31–3.

2. For a summary of party policy toward the cities, see Frederic Wakeman, Jr., "'Cleanup': The New Order in Shanghai," in Jeremy Brown and Paul G. Pickowicz, eds., *Dilemmas of Victory* (Cambridge, MA: Harvard University Press, 2007), 21–58. On attempts by labor to capitalize on the revolution by taking revolutionary socialist rhetoric regarding workers at face value and Mao's subsequent backpedaling on his promises, see Elizabeth J. Perry, "Masters of the Country? Shanghai Workers in the Early People's Republic," in Brown and Pickowicz, eds., *Dilemmas of Victory*, 59–79. On Stalin's influence on restraining CCP policies and preference for a long transitional period of socialism in China, see Hua-Yu Li, *Mao and the Economic Stalinization of China, 1948–1953* (Lanham, MD: Rowman & Littlefield, 2006). On the pre-1949 history of inflation and an overview of the other reasons the party chose immediate economic stability over a more radical agenda, see the summary in Alexander Eckstein, *China's Economic Revolution* (New York: Cambridge University Press, 1977), 159–71.

3. For a description and photo, see Xiong Yuezhi, ed., 上海通史, 第II卷: 当代政治 (General history of Shanghai: Volume II, Contemporary politics) (Shanghai: Shanghai renmin chubanshe, 1999), 4–7. For photos and an account of the soldiers sleeping on the streets of Shanghai, see www.shtzb.org.cn/node2124/node2132/node2134/u1a1779764.html. Archived April 19, 2018.

4. For more on the party's attempts to lure capitalists back to China, see Sherman Cochran, ed., *The Capitalist Dilemma in China's Communist Revolution* (Ithaca, NY: Cornell East Asia Program, 2015).

5. Thomas N. Thompson, *China's Nationalization of Foreign Firms: The Politics of Hostage Capitalism, 1949–57* (Baltimore: School of Law, Occasional Papers/Reprint Series in Contemporary Asian Studies, University of Maryland, 1979), 14; Jonathan J. Howlett, "'The British Boss Is Gone and Will Never Return': Communist Takeovers of British Companies in Shanghai (1949–1954)." *Modern Asian Studies*, vol. 47, no. 6 (2013), 1941–76 (see pp. 1952–7). On its attempts to prevent the flight of foreign capital, see Shao Wenguang, *China, Britain and Businessmen: Political and Commercial Relations, 1949–57* (Basingstoke: Macmillan, 1991).

6. Karl Marx, *Capital: A Critique of Political Economy*, 3 vols., tr. Ben Fowkes (London: Penguin Books, 1990–92), 873.

7. Eckstein, *China's Economic Revolution*, 26. On the PRC's ecological inheritance, see Micah S. Muscolino, *Ecology of War in China: Henan Province, the Yellow River, and Beyond, 1938–1950* (Cambridge: Cambridge University Press, 2015). On the economic impacts, see William C. Kirby, "The Chinese War Economy," in James C. Hsiung and Steven I. Levine, eds., *China's Bitter Victory: The War with Japan, 1937–1945* (Armonk, NY: M.

E. Sharpe, 1992), 185–212. On the social and economic impacts of warfare in mid-twentieth century China, see Rana Mitter, *Forgotten Ally: China's World War II, 1937–1945* (Boston: Houghton Mifflin Harcourt, 2013); Diana Lary, *China's Civil War: A Social History, 1945–1949* (New York: Cambridge University Press, 2015).

8. In his study of global warfare, historian William MacNeill blames trade restrictions as the reason China fell behind militarily. William H. McNeill, *The Pursuit of Power: Technology, Armed Force, and Society since AD 1000* (Oxford: Basil Blackwell, 1982), 147. For an example of the importance of foreign weaponry in twentieth-century Chinese warfare, see Steven I. Levine, *Anvil of Victory: The Communist Revolution in Manchuria, 1945–1948* (New York: Columbia University Press, 1987). On the relationship between state finance, war, and inflation in mid-century China, see Gregg Huff, "Finance for War in Asia and its Aftermath," in Michael Geyer and J. Adam Tooze, eds., *The Cambridge History of the Second World War: Volume 3, Total War: Economy, Society and Culture* (Cambridge: Cambridge University Press, 2015), 56–93.

9. See Kuisong Yang and Sheng Mao, "Unafraid of the Ghost: The Victim Mentality of Mao Zedong and the Two Taiwan Strait Crises in the 1950s," *China Review*, vol. 16, no. 1 (Spring 2016), 1–34. Political and even personal survival was at stake. Mao had learned the hard way the importance of competing for military supremacy two decades earlier, when the Nationalists purged Communist Party members from their ranks, nearly eliminating them. He famously concluded that "political power grows out of the barrel of a gun," and thought it better that the CCP control its own army and one day control the production of guns rather than rely on imports. On the difficulties that the party faced conquering all of China after 1949, see Jeremy Brown and Paul G. Pickowicz, eds., *Dilemmas of Victory: The Early Years of the People's Republic of China* (Cambridge, MA: Harvard University Press, 2010), especially the chapters by Chen Jian and James Z. Gao on the conquests of Tibet and Xinjiang, respectively.

10. For a summary of China's involvement in the Korean war, see Lanxin Xiang, *Recasting the Imperial Far East: Britain and America in China, 1945–1950* (Armonk, NY: M.E. Sharpe, 1995); Kathryn Weathersby, "Stalin, Mao, and the End of the Korean War," in Odd Arne Westad, ed., *Brothers in Arms: The Rise and Fall of the Sino–Soviet Alliance, 1945–1963* (Washington, DC: Woodrow Wilson Center Press and Stanford: Stanford University Press, 1998), 90–116; Chen Jian, *China's Road to the Korean War: The Making of the Sino–American Confrontation* (New York: Columbia University Press, 1994); Shu Guang Zhang, *Mao's Military Romanticism: China and the Korean War, 1950–1953* (Lawrence: University Press of Kansas, 1995);

David Clayton, *Imperialism Revisited: Political and Economic Relations between Britain and China, 1950–54* (New York: St. Martin's Press, 1997).

11. As defense analyst Tai Ming Cheung concludes about the Mao era, "virtually all of the country's most advanced industrial sectors were either directly or indirectly associated with the defense economy." Tai Ming Cheung, *Fortifying China: The Struggle to Build a Modern Defense Economy* (Ithaca, NY: Cornell University Press, 2009), 25. On the ways the quest to build a bomb shaped the Chinese economy, see John Wilson Lewis and Litai Xue, *China Builds the Bomb* (Stanford: Stanford University Press, 1988). According to their estimates, the total cost for developing a nuclear bomb was RMB 10.7 billion, or US \$4.1 billion in 1957 prices, the equivalent of the entire Chinese defense budgets for 1957 and 1958 (p. 108). The tradeoffs between spending on the military and consumption are more thoroughly discussed in histories of the Soviet Union, which had faced foreign threats much earlier, including the Nazi invasion. See, for instance, John Barber and Mark Harrison, eds., *The Soviet Defence-Industry Complex from Stalin to Khrushchev* (Basingstoke: Macmillan, 2000); David R. Stone, *Hammer and Rifle: The Militarization of the Soviet Union, 1926–1933* (Lawrence: University Press of Kansas, 2000); and, in particular, for the competitive technological pressures in the military industry leading the Soviet Union to use forms of market competition, see Mark Harrison, ed., *Guns and Rubles: The Defense Industry in the Stalinist State* (New Haven: Yale University Press, 2008).

12. A large literature has revived earlier interpretations that capitalism depends on noncapitalist expropriations elsewhere, whether between nation-states or within a single nation-state. The *loci classici* on the relationship between imperialism and capitalism are the writings by Rosa Luxemburg and Lenin. Luxemburg defines imperialism as "the political expression of the accumulation of capital in its competitive struggle for what remains still open of the non-capitalist environment." Rosa Luxemburg, *The Accumulation of Capital*, tr. Agnes Schwarzschild (London: Routledge, 2003), 426. These original insights underwent periodic revivals in historical writings, including writings by Immanuel Wallerstein, such as *The Capitalist World-Economy: Essays* (Cambridge: Cambridge University Press, 1979). Scholarship on dependency and world-systems theory further examines how military competition structured global markets. See Christopher K. Chase-Dunn, ed., *Socialist States in the World-System* (Beverly Hills: Sage Publications, 1982). For a more recent argument on how the Global North expands capitalism through the Global South, see John Smith, *Imperialism in the Twenty-First Century: Globalization, Super-Exploitation, and Capitalism's Final Crisis* (New York: Monthly Review Press, 2016). For an illustration of the transnational origins of American capitalism that revives scholarly

attention to these links for a new generation of scholars, see Sven Beckert, *Empire of Cotton: A Global History* (New York: Alfred A. Knopf, 2014). On the links between the interrelated spread of the institutions of capitalism and consumerism more generally, see Victoria de Grazia, *Irresistible Empire: America's Advance through Twentieth-Century Europe* (Cambridge, MA: Belknap Press of Harvard University Press, 2005).

13. The classic analysis of such "latecomers" to industrial capitalism is Alexander Gershenkron, *Economic Backwardness in Historical Perspective* (Cambridge, MA: Belknap Press of Harvard University, 1962). Although not framed as a form of capitalist competition, the civil war forced the party to innovate militarily to gain military and market dominance over the Nationalists. In *Anvil of Victory*, Levine argues that the CCP acquisition of weapons in Manchuria from the Japanese and the Soviets, not the "Yan'an way," won the civil war.

14. Mao Zedong, "On Coalition Government" (April 24, 1945), in *Selected Works of Mao Tse-tung* (Peking: Foreign Languages Press, 1965), 3.255–320, at p. 3.302. Every aspiring leader, whether regional or Nationalist, in Republican-era China would have learned the same lesson. See Edward A. McCord, *The Power of the Gun: The Emergence of Modern Chinese Warlordism* (Berkeley: University of California Press, 1993). There is a vast literature on the connections among warfare, state-making, and economics in the industrial capitalist era. See Geoffrey Parker, *The Military Revolution: Military Innovation and the Rise of the West, 1500–1800*, 2nd ed. (Cambridge: Cambridge University Press, 2016).

15. For a representative example of a discussion on balancing accumulation vs. consumption and the need to discourage excessive consumption, see Mao Zedong, "Talks at the Hangzhou Conference (Draft Transcript)" (January 3–4, 1958), in Roderick MacFarquhar, Timothy Cheek, and Eugene Wu, eds., *The Secret Speeches of Chairman Mao: From the Hundred Flowers to the Great Leap Forward* (Cambridge, MA: Council on East Asian Studies, Harvard University, 1989), 380–1, 383, and 385.

16. For a specific example of the linking of frugality and household management, see the speech by Zhang Yun, vice president of the All-China Women's Federation at the Third National Congress of Chinese Women, "勤俭建国勤俭持家为建设社会主义而奋斗" (Strive to build socialism with hard work and frugality, manage the household with industry and thrift), *RMRB*, September 10, 1957, 4.

17. State-sponsored frugality campaigns to direct scarce capital into state hands were not unique to China or "socialist" countries. On national policies promoting high savings rates, see, for instance, Sheldon Garon, "Luxury Is the Enemy: Mobilizing Savings and Popularizing Thrift in Wartime

Japan," *Journal of Japanese Studies*, vol. 26, no. 1 (Winter 2000), 41–78. One can find similar state policies in any book on rationing and savings bond campaigns during the world wars. Scholars of the PRC have long recognized the general similarities between the Mao era and the wartime economies, wherein the state demanded that individuals work hard and live frugally for the common good. Examples include: Barry M. Richman, *Industrial Society in Communist China: A Firsthand Study of Chinese Economic Development and Management, with Significant Comparisons with Industry in India, the U.S.S.R., Japan, and the United States* (New York: Random House, 1969), 223–364; Andrew G. Walder, *Communist Neo-Traditionalism: Work and Authority in Chinese Industry* (Berkeley: University of California Press, 1986), 113–22.

18. William Kirby succinctly describes the continuities between the Nationalists and Communists: "What distinguished the Communist party-state, and indeed ultimately set it apart from its predecessor, was its attempt to take these trends – political, economic, and military – to the most extreme conclusions." William C. Kirby, "The Nationalist Regime and the Chinese Party-State, 1928–1958," in Merle Goldman and Andrew Gordon, eds., *Historical Perspectives on Contemporary East Asia* (Cambridge, MA: Harvard University Press, 2000), 230.

19. See Karl Gerth, *China Made: Consumer Culture and the Creation of the Nation* (Cambridge, MA: Harvard University Asia Center, 2003), where I discuss the National Products Movement in Republican-era China and (in the Conclusion) its implications for the political economy during the Mao era. This discourse of good/bad consumption linked to morality and good governance had earlier manifestations. See, for instance, Craig Clunas, *Superfluous Things: Material Culture and Social Status in Early Modern China* (Honolulu: University of Hawai'i Press, 2004); Wu Renshu,品味奢华: 晚明的消费社会与士大夫 (A taste of luxury: Consumer culture in the late Ming dynasty and scholar-officials) (Beijing: Zhonghua shuju, 2008).

20. Popular hostility toward private capitalism began well before the Second Sino-Japanese War (1937–45), but it increased during the war, especially toward those businesspeople who had collaborated with the Japanese during their occupation of eastern China. See Parks M. Coble, *The Shanghai Capitalists and the Nationalist Government, 1927–1937*, 2nd ed. (Cambridge, MA: Council on East Asian Studies, Harvard University, 1986); Parks M. Coble, *Chinese Capitalists in Japan's New Order: The Occupied Lower Yangzi, 1937–1945* (Berkeley: University of California Press, 2003). On the renewal of an NPM-style anti-US product boycott on the eve of 1949, see Chou Ping-kun, "The 1947 Boycott of U.S. Goods," *China Reconstructs*, vol. 14, no. 1 (1965), 40–2.

21. On the meaning and development of this concept, see Roman Rosdolsky, *The Making of Marx's "Capital,"* tr. Pete Burgess (London: Pluto, 2004), ch. 18.

22. See Hans van de Ven, "The Military in the Republic," *The China Quarterly*, no. 150 (June 1997), 352–74; Rana Mitter, *Forgotten Ally: China's World War II, 1937–1945* (Boston: Houghton Mifflin Harcourt, 2013); and, for the Mao era specifically, see Covell Meyskens, *Mao's Third Front: The Militarization of Cold War China* (Cambridge: Cambridge University Press, 2020).

23. Mao Zedong, "Talks at the Hangzhou Conference (Draft Transcript) (January 3–4, 1958), 377–91, at p. 378. Moreover, Stalin had endorsed the CCP's policies. Andrei Ledovsky, "Two Cables from Correspondence between Mao Zedong and Joseph Stalin," *Far Eastern Affairs*, no. 6 (2000): 89–96, at p. 95.

24. Party officials instructed soldiers and cadres entering the cities not to interfere with private enterprise. For this and other regulations regarding the capitalists, see Chen Boda, "不要打乱原来的企业机构" (Don't throw into disarray the existing structure of capitalist enterprises), in 中国人民解放军入城政策 (Policies regarding the People's Liberation Army's takeover of cities by the People's Liberation Army) (Hankou: Xinhua shudian, 1949). Chen Boda's notice was also printed in *RMRB*, February 5, 1949, 1. Here "expropriate" refers to when public institutions – national, regional, or local – confiscate private capital: land, businesses, machines, and other forms. This is sometimes called "nationalization." But even though the "nation" enacted the policies, it was not the only recipient of the expropriated capital. Expropriated land and businesses (capital) were placed under the immediate control of communes, urban governments, and other subnational public entities. In China, this general policy was called the Socialist Transformation (社会主义改造), referring to the specific expropriation from capitalists and landlords during 1953–6.

25. In 1967, for instance, Mao acknowledged the compromise as such when he met with a delegation from Albania and expressed regret about the need in 1949 to give capitalists a place in New China. "Stenographic Note held during the Conversation between Chairman Mao Zedong and Vangjel Moisiu and Myfit Mushi in Shanghai" (August 16, 1967), History and Public Policy Program Digital Archive, AQSH, F. 14/AP, M-PKK, V. 1967, Dos. 47, Fl. 1–8. Obtained and translated by Elidor Mëhilli. At https://digitalarchive .wilsoncenter.org/document/117304. Consulted December 28, 2018.

26. The three most important articles by Mao that justify this strategy of a "united front" with the capitalists are: "Analysis of the Classes in Chinese Society" (March 1926), "The Chinese Revolution and the Chinese Communist Party" (December 1939), and "On New Democracy" (January 1940). *Selected Works*

of Mao Tse-tung (Peking: Foreign Languages Press, 1965), 1.13–19; 2:305–31; and 2: 339–82.

27. Datong Guan, *The Socialist Transformation of Capitalist Industry and Commerce in China* (Peking: Foreign Languages Press, 1960), 46. Mao's "The Present Situation and Our Tasks" (December 25, 1947), at www .marxists.org/reference/archive/mao/selected-works/volume-4/mswv4_24 .htm. Archived May 21, 2018, outlines the goals of the new-democratic revolution, which include protecting the assets of the national bourgeoisie.

28. "From the Journal of Pavel F. Yudin: Record of Conversation with Mao Zedong on 21 December 1955," History and Public Policy Program Digital Archive, AVPRF fond 0100, opis' 49, papka 410, delo 9, listy 11–19. Translated by Gary Goldberg, at https://digitalarchive.wilsoncenter.org/do cument/117834. Consulted December 28, 2018.

29. *The Common Program and Other Documents of the First Plenary Session of the Chinese People's Political Consultative Congress* (Peking: Foreign Languages Press, 1950), 1–20. Of course, the pressures that state policies exerted on private capital, especially large industrial capital that the state had already coveted, were sufficient to motivate many leading capitalists to leave. See the case studies of such deliberations in Cochran, ed., *The Capitalist Dilemma in China's Communist Revolution.*

30. Carl Riskin, *China's Political Economy: The Quest for Development since 1949* (Oxford: Oxford University Press, 1988), 95.

31. Feng Chen, *Economic Transition and Political Legitimacy in Post-Mao China: Ideology and Reform* (Albany: State University of New York Press, 1995), 23–34.

32. *The Common Program and Other Documents*, Art. 28.

33. For an analysis of the class implications of this concept of the surplus, see Stephen A. Resnick and Richard D. Wolff, *Knowledge and Class: A Marxian Critique of Political Economy* (Chicago: University of Chicago Press, 1987). For a discussion of labor relations compatible with my analysis, see Jake Werner, "Global Fordism in 1950s Urban China," *Frontiers of History in China*, vol. 7, no. 3 (September 2012), 415–41.

34. For illustrations of how one might apply the central the concepts of Marx – including value, capital, commodities, and exploitation – to capitalism in China and the Soviet Union, see Adam Buick and John Crump, *State Capitalism: The Wages System under New Management* (Basingstoke: Macmillan, 1986) and Stephen A. Resnick and Richard D. Wolff, *Class Theory and History: Capitalism and Communism in the USSR* (Abingdon: Routledge, 2013).

35. The CCP inherited the industries and also the bureaucracy to manage them. See William C. Kirby, "Continuity and Change in Modern China: Economic Planning on the Mainland and on Taiwan, 1943–1958," *The Australian Journal of Chinese Affairs*, no. 24 (July 1990), 121–41. See also Liu Suinian and Wu Qungan, eds., *China's Socialist Economy: An Outline History (1949–1984)* (Beijing: Beijing Review, 1986), 9.

36. Xue Muqiao, *China's Socialist Economy* (Beijing: Foreign Languages Press, 1981), 19.

37. *The Common Program and Other Documents*, Art. 29. For an overview history of this category, see Jianzhong Tang and Laurence J. C. Mao, "Evolution of Urban Collective Enterprises in China," *China Quarterly*, no. 104 (1985), 614–40.

38. Odd Arne Westad, *Decisive Encounters: The Chinese Civil War, 1946–1950* (Stanford: Stanford University Press, 2003), 94–5.

39. Thomas D. Lutze, *China's Inevitable Revolution: Rethinking America's Loss to the Communists* (New York: Palgrave Macmillan, 2007). Their rhetoric heightened the popular (and academic) equation of "communism" with the state takeover of private capital. In the United States, the "loss of China" to "communism" and the rise of right-wing politics in the postwar era were closely connected. For an introduction to the China Lobby in the United States, that is, supporters of Chiang Kai-shek and the Nationalists and later anti-Communists, see Larry Ceplair, *Anti-Communism in Twentieth-Century America: A Critical History* (Santa Barbara: Praeger, 2011), ch. 7, which discusses the virulently pro-private capitalist John Birch Society, named after an American Baptist missionary killed by the CCP army in 1945.

40. Thompson, *China's Nationalization of Foreign Firms*. Foreign companies trying to stay in business were "hostages" because they could not withdraw their fixed and immovable capital (such as machinery) and had difficulties securing exit visas for their human capital (employees). In addition, like their Chinese counterparts, they were "hostage" to the state expectation that they continue operating – and employing individuals in a bad economy – despite mounting losses. Bankruptcy or closure required state permission. Businesspeople from market capitalist countries concluded they were being systematically targeted. In any case, their businesses became untenable. Aron Shai, *The Fate of British and French Firms in China, 1949–54: Imperialism Imprisoned* (Basingstoke: Macmillan, 1996), 23.

41. Quoted in Thompson, *China's Nationalization of Foreign Firms*, 31.

42. Shai, *The Fate of British and French Firms in China*, 20, which provides a list of names of these companies.

43. *The Common Program and Other Documents*, Art. 30.

44. For case studies of the impacts of what he labels as "bureaucratic capitalist state-making" with the Nationalist Party (Kuomintang, or KMT) of Chiang Kai-shek and rural society, see Ralph A. Thaxton, *Salt of the Earth: The Political Origins of Peasant Protest and Communist Revolution* (Berkeley: University of California Press, 1997).

45. The state identified 123,000 national capitalist industrial enterprises that employed 1.64 million people and 130,000 national capitalist commercial enterprises employing 990,000 people. Liu Suinian and Wu Qungan, eds., *China's Socialist Economy*, 9.

46. Xue Muqiao, *China's Socialist Economy*, 21.

47. Gu Hua, *A Small Town Called Hibiscus*, tr. Gladys Yang (Beijing: Foreign Languages Press, 2015).

48. I discuss one such case of workers resenting the continued bourgeois perks of the owners (in this case, the use of a private elevator and an apartment atop the factory) in Karl Gerth, "Wu Yunchu and the Fate of the Bourgeoisie and Bourgeois Lifestyles under Communism," in Cochran, ed., *The Capitalist Dilemma in China's Communist Revolution* (Ithaca, NY: East Asia Program, Cornell University, 2015), 175–202.

49. According to Lu Hanchao's study of the lifestyles of "national capitalists" in Shanghai during the decades before 1966, "as far as material comfort was concerned, the old rich still lived an infinitely better life than most Chinese at the time, despite the constant political campaigns against them" (p. 74). "Bourgeois Comfort under Proletarian Dictatorship: Home Life of Chinese Capitalists before the Cultural Revolution," *Journal of Social History*, vol. 52, no. 1 (2018), 74–100.

50. In 1956, some 800,000 private capitalists whose capital was acquired by the state received interest paid at a rate of between 3.5 and 5 percent, depending on their assets, for ten years or longer. Lu Hanchao, "Bourgeois Comfort under Proletarian Dictatorship," 75. By some estimates, 300,000 of these former capitalists survived in 1966 (including over 90,000 in Shanghai alone). Audrey Donnithorne, *China's Economic System* (London: Allen & Unwin, 1967), 146–7. These payments continued until the termination of fixed-interest payments to capitalists in 1967, as reported by Xue Muqiao, *China's Socialist Economy*, 30.

51. Sylvia Chan, "The Image of a 'Capitalist Roader' – Some Dissident Short Stories in the Hundred Flowers Period," *The Australian Journal of Chinese Affairs*, no. 2 (July 1979), 77–102.

52. On the connection between the costs of war and other domestic impacts, see Chen, *China's Road to the Korean War*, 220–1. Westad, *Decisive Encounters*, 399, notes that the connection between Chinese domestic policies and the Korean War has not yet been treated in full detail.

53. For instance, Daniel H. Bays, *A New History of Christianity in China* (Malden, MA: Wiley-Blackwell, 2012), 158–82; Philip L. Wickeri. *Seeking the Common Ground: Protestant Christianity, the Three-Self Movement, and China's United Front* (Maryknoll, NY: Orbis Books, 1988); Philip West, *Yenching University and Sino-Western Relations, 1916–1952* (Cambridge, MA: Harvard University Press, 1976), ch. 7.

54. On activities in other cities, see Que Wen et al., 抗美援朝畫冊: 第二冊 (Resist America and Aid Korea album: Volume 2) (Beijing: Renmin meishu chubanshe, 1951).

55. See Qi Kang, "对期刊界抗美援朝宣传的一些意见" (Some opinions on propaganda in periodicals related to Resist America and Aid Korea), *RMRB*, December 27, 1950, 5.

56. For reports on different locations, see "上海工商界记忆犹新 美货泛滥成灾的故事" (Shanghai business and industrial communities still remember U.S. goods running rampant), *RMRB*, November 18, 1950, 2; "京市工商界各行业分别集会, 控诉美帝摧残民族工商业, 决心实践工商界五项爱国公约" (Business circles and industry in Beijing meet and denounce American imperialism for destroying national industry and commerce, determined to practice the five patriotic conventions of the business community), *RMRB*, November 18, 1950, 2; "津工商界控诉美帝经济侵略, 美货倾销时扼杀了我民族工商业" (Tianjin's business and industry circles denounce American imperialism for its economic invasion, and killing our national industry and businesses by dumping goods in China), *RMRB*, November 29, 1950, 2; "美帝国主义势力被驱逐后 福州民族工业获生 机" (After expelling the American imperialist forces, people's industry and business in Fuzhou are revived), *RMRB*, December 18, 1950, 2. Collections of similar articles in pamphlet form include: Qin Benli, 美帝经济侵华史 (A history of the American imperialist economic invasion of China) (Beijing: Shijie zhishi chubanshe, 1950); Deng Pu, 美帝侵略上海的罪证 (Evidence of the US imperialist invasion of Shanghai) (Beijing: Shijie zhishi chubanshe, 1950); 美帝怎样摧残我工商业 (How US imperialism destroyed our country's industry and commerce) (Beijing: Shiyue chubanshe, 1950); 美帝摧残下的中国民族工商业 (US imperialism destroyed Chinese national industry and commerce) (Shanghai: Xinhua shudian huadong fendian, 1951); Wei Zichu, 美帝在华经济侵略 (The US imperialist economic invasion of China) (Beijing: Renmin chubanshe, 1951).

57. These headlines come from the Shanghai-based *Wenhuibao*, November 4, 1950, and *Jiefang ribao* (cited hereafter as *JFRB*), November 30, 1950. Similar headlines appeared in regional and national newspapers throughout the country.

58. In November and December, the *People's Daily* published many articles about US economic imperialism during the early postwar era. See Chong Ye, "北京工商界向美国侵略者示威" (Demonstration by Beijing industrial and commercial circles against the American invaders), *RMRB*, December 10, 1950. 1.

59. "重庆工商界纷纷控诉，美帝摧残我民族工商业" (Chongqing's business and industry denounce the American imperialist destruction of our people's industry and commerce), *RMRB*, November 27, 1950, 2; "美帝控制中国海关时的罪恶" (Crimes committed by the American imperialists when they controlled Chinese customs), *RMRB*, November 27, 1950, 2. On the US trade embargo, which lasted until 1972 and was even more serious than the one imposed on the Soviet Union, see Xin-zhu J. Chen, "China and the US Trade Embargo, 1950–1972," *American Journal of Chinese Studies*, vol. 13, no. 2 (2006), 169–86.

60. Although it is unclear whether the Three/Five-Antis were intended to be two discreet campaigns, I treat them here as one because they provide evidence of the same state attempt to crack down on the misuse of capital, whether by "corrupt" state officials or by "greedy" private capitalists.

61. In the CCP's own words, the Three/Five-Antis campaign was waged in the service of the transition toward greater state capitalism. Article 10 of the 1954 Constitution speaks of "using" the good aspects of the capitalists, "restricting" their potential damage, and gradually "transforming" their enterprises to state ownership. *The Constitution of the People's Republic of China* (Peking: Foreign Languages Press, 1954): 76. For a clear, contemporaneous articulation of the place of "state capitalism" in the transition to socialism, see Zhou Enlai, "社会主义改造与国家资本主义" (Socialist Transformation and state capitalism) (September 11, 1953), in Zhonggong zhongyang wenxian yanjiushi, ed., 周恩来统一战线文选 (Selected writings by Zhou Enlai on the United Front) (Beijing: Renmin chubanshe, 1984), 253–7.

62. The campaign began on August 31, 1951: Peter S. H. Tang. *Communist China Today*, 2 vols. (New York: Praeger, 1957–58), 339. Note that "anti-bureaucratism" (反官僚主义) was a common party term of criticism that referred to too many people doing unproductive, even redundant, administrative work to avoid engaging in manual labor in factories or on farms. For an overview, see Michael M. Sheng, "Mao Zedong and the Three-Anti Campaign (November 1951 to April 1952): A Revisionist Interpretation," *Twentieth-Century China*, vol. 32, no. 1 (2006), 56–80. For example, one report criticizes a state-run food factory that had 700 workers but only 300 of them were engaged in actual food production. "华东工业部直属厂矿浪费现象严重，初步估计约值四百多亿" (Waste in factories and mines directly under the Ministry of Industry in East China is serious,

with preliminary estimates of a cost of more than forty billion yuan), *Neibu cankao* (Internal reference) (cited hereafter as *NBCK*), December 8, 1951.

63. "北京市反贪污反浪费反官僚主义运动现已进入号召贪污, 行贿分子自动坦白阶段" (The anti-corruption, anti-waste, and anti-bureaucracy campaign in Beijing has now entered the stage of calling on the embezzlers and those involved in bribery to voluntarily confess), *NBCK*, December 31, 1951. For a report on corruption in the Guiyang tax office, see "贵阳发现干部订立集体贪污合同" (Guiyang discovers cadres who collude to sign a collective corruption pact), *NBCK*, December 1, 1951.

64. For instance, "南充市政建设浪费国家财产巨大" (Extreme wastes of state assets by Nanchong municipal construction), *NBCK*, January 8, 1952; "中国银行天津分行修建房屋有严重铺张浪费现象" (Extreme extravagance and waste in the rebuilding of the Bank of China, Tianjin Branch, office), *NBCK*, January 14, 1952.

65. Theodore H. E. Chen and Wen-hui C. Chen, "The 'Three Anti' and 'Five Anti' Movements in Communist China," *Pacific Affairs*, vol. 26, no. 1 (1953), 4–5; Feng Xiaocai, "Rushing toward Socialism: The Transformation and Death of Private Business Enterprises in Shanghai, 1949–1956," in William C. Kirby, ed., *The People's Republic of China at 60: An International Assessment* (Cambridge, MA: Harvard University Asia Center, 2011), 240–58.

66. *NBCK*, March 10, 1952.

67. Foreign Office 371/99233 (December 12, 1951), 2.

68. This type of material compensation seems similar to the sort of welfare demanded by workers depicted in Mark W. Frazier, *The Making of the Chinese Industrial Workplace: State, Revolution, and Labor Management* (New York: Cambridge University Press, 2002), 109, 115, and leads one to wonder if the party was implying that similar worker demands were "bourgeois." Frazier provides examples of how the better material conditions (e.g., hot plates and lamps in offices) cast suspicion on the supervisors.

69. On this shift in focus, see Zhang Ming, "执政的道德困境与突围之道: 三反五反运动解析" (The moral dilemma of being in power and the ways out: The "Three-Antis" and "Five-Antis" campaigns), *Ershiyi shiji*, no. 92 (2005), 46–58. See also "Kang Kao Summarizes 3-Anti and 5-Anti Movements in Northeast," Xinhua, June 25, 1952, translated in *Current Background*, no. 201 (August 12, 1952), 16–20.

70. "中央转发北京市委关于三反斗争的报告的批语" (January 5, 1952) (Comments and instructions of the Central Committee on transmitting the report by the Beijing Municipal Committee on the struggle against the Three-Antis), in 建国以来毛泽东文稿 (Mao Zedong's manuscripts since the founding of the state) (Beijing: Zhongyang wenxian chubanshe, 1989),

3.21–2. The report is signed by the Central Committee, but it is based on a draft written by Mao.

71. Yu Guangyuan, "反对资产阶级的进攻，坚持工人阶级的领导权" (Resist the attacks by the bourgeois class, determinedly uphold the leadership of the working class), *Xuexi zazhi* (January 1952), 13–18.

72. A. Doak Barnett, *Communist China: The Early Years, 1949–55* (New York: Praeger, 1964), 150, quoting a businessman from Shanghai who had recently fled to Hong Kong.

73. Gu Weijin, "上海私营企业中的六十多万工人店员在'五反'运动中发挥了巨大的力量" (Over 600,000 workers and shop assistants in Shanghai's private enterprises play a tremendous role in "Five-Antis" movement), *RMRB*, May 10, 1952, 2; Song Cheng, "工会组织'三反''五反'运动中更加壮大了" (Trade union organizations grow stronger in the Three/Five-Antis movement), *RMRB*, May 13, 1952, 2. On CCP attempts to transfer worker loyalties to the state, see Walder, *Communist Neo-Traditionalism*, 85–113; Yang Kuisong 杨奎松, "1952 年上海'五反'运动始末" (The whole story of the Shanghai "Five-Anti" campaign in 1952), *Shehui kexue*, no. 4 (2006), 5–30.

74. "上海解放日报举办反盗窃斗争座谈会，高级店员揭发资产阶级的丑恶本质,详述打破顾虑检举不法资本家的经过" (Shanghai's *Liberation Daily* holds symposium on anti-theft; senior shop assistants expose the ugly nature of the bourgeoisie and elaborate on the process of crushing fears and prosecuting illegal capitalists), *RMRB*, March 7, 1952, 3.

75. Feng Xiaocai, "Between Class Struggle and Family Loyalty: The Mobilization of Businessmen's Wives and Children during the Five-Antis Movement," *European Journal of East Asian Studies*, vol. 13, no. 2 (2014), 284–304.

76. Barnett, *Communist China*, 145.

77. "广州'五反'第二期工作已进入最后阶段，迅速彻底处理了九十个行业中的前三类户五千多户" (The second phase of Guangzhou's 'Five-Antis' has entered its final stage, and over 5,000 households in the first three categories of 90 industries have been dealt with quickly and thoroughly), *RMRB*, April 29, 1952, 2.

78. "NCNA Correspondent's Review of Victory of 5-Anti Campaign in Shanghai," *Xinhua*, June 7, 1952, translated in *Current Background*, no. 201 (August 12, 1952), 23–4.

79. For example, Gerth, "Wu Yunchu and the Fate of the Bourgeoisie."

80. Cited in Frazier, *The Making of the Chinese Industrial Workplace*, 116.

81. According to historian Yang Kuisong, during the month prior to mid-February, there were forty-nine suicides among Chinese businesspeople in Shanghai (and another sixteen attempted suicides). In only four days, from February 12 to February 15, there were twenty-two suicides and another seventy-three for the entire month. Until late February, those who

committed suicide were mainly petty capitalists. But thereafter, more medium-sized and large capitalists took their own lives: Yang Kuisong 杨奎松, "1952 年上海 '五反' 运动始末" (The whole story of the Shanghai "Five-Anti" campaign in 1952), 5–30.

82. Gordon A. Bennett, *Yundong: Mass Campaigns in Chinese Communist Leadership* (Berkeley: Center for Chinese Studies, University of California, 1976).

83. "GAC Directive to Conclude 5-Anti Campaign," Xinhua, June 14, 1952; translated in *Current Background*, no. 201 (August 12, 1952), 4–5. For a description of the classification of law-breaking capitalists, see "Provisions Laid Down by the Economy Practice Investigation Committee of the Central People's Government for the Disposal of Cases of Corruption and Waste, and for the Conquest of Bureaucratic Deviations," Xinhua, March 11, 1952, translated in *Current Background*, no. 168 (March 26, 1952), 4–9.

84. "Five-Anti Movement Victoriously Concluded in Canton," translated in *Current Background*, no. 201 (August 12, 1952), 28–9. For a description of the campaign in Shanghai, see "[NCNA] Correspondent's Review of Victory of 5-Anti Campaign in Shanghai," Xinhua, June 7, 1952, translated in *Current Background*, no. 201 (August 12, 1952), 23–4; John Gardner, "The *Wu-Fan* Campaign in Shanghai: A Study in the Consolidation of Urban Control," in A. Doak Barnett, ed., *Chinese Communist Politics in Action* (Seattle: University of Washington Press, 1969), 477–539.

85. Yang Kuisong, "1952年上海 '五反'运动始末" (The entire story of Shanghai's Five-Anti campaign in 1952), 5–30 (at p. 8). On the economic impact more generally, see Bennis Wai-yip So, "The Policy-Making and Political Economy of the Abolition of Private Ownership in the Early 1950s: Findings from New Materials," *China Quarterly*, no. 171 (2002), 682–703.

86. Wu Xiaobo, 历代经济变革得失 (The successes and failures of the economic reforms in history) (Hangzhou: Zhejiang daxue chubanshe, 2016), 181. Other estimates of the total amount confiscated vary from US$500 million to upwards of US$1.25 billion. Barnett, *Communist China*, 160; *Weekly Bulletin*, Chinese News Service, New York, June 3, 1952 (Republic of China Publication); Chen and Chen, "The 'Three Anti' and 'Five Anti' Movements in Communist China," 3–23, 18. In the short run, these resources provided the state with sorely needed capital to wage the war in Korea and, according to Mao, would "see [China] through another eighteen months of war." Mao Zedong, "Let Us Unite and Clearly Distinguish Ourselves and the Enemy" (August 4, 1952), *Selected Works of Mao Tsetung* (Beijing: Foreign Languages Press, 1977), 5.80.

87. Gerth, "Wu Yunchu and the Fate of the Bourgeoisie"; Chen Zhengqing, "Socialist Transformation and the Demise of Private Entrepreneurs: Wu

Yunchu's Tragedy," *European Journal of East Asian Studies*, vol. 13, no. 2 (2014), 240–61.

88. For more information on these policies, see "GAC Directive to Conclude 5-Anti Campaign," 4–5; and "3-Anti, 5-Anti Movements Victoriously Concluded in Tientsin," Xinhua, June 14, 1952, translated in *Current Background*, no. 201 (August 12, 1952), 14–15. See also Yang Kuisong "1952 年上海 "五反"运动始末" (The entire story of Shanghai's Five-Anti campaign in 1952), 5–30.

89. In 1960, for instance, a party office in Shanghai wrote a sixty-five-page report on the persistence of Three-Antis activities. It detailed a long list of waste, including a medical supply company ordering tens of thousands of pieces of equipment only to have them languish in storage, tape recorders uninspected for quality control breaking down during the interrogation of a "counter-revolutionary," and a state pen factory having to recall hundreds of thousands of poor-quality fountain pens. Zhonggong Shanghaishi diyi shangyeju weiyuanhui sanfan zhengfeng lingdao xiaozu bangongshi, "局党委扩大会议有关党委官僚主义方面的综合材料" (Comprehensive materials on the bureaucratic aspects of party committees for the expanded meeting of party committees), SMA B123-4-568 (July 31, 1960), 3–6.

90. Satyananda J. Gabriel finds rural institutions of control so extreme as to label them "state feudalism" in *Chinese Capitalism and the Modernist Vision* (London: Routledge, 2006), 18–44.

91. Xiong Yuezhi, ed., 上海通史, 第11卷, 当代政治 (General history of Shanghai: Volume 11, Contemporary politics), 24.

92. Richard Day, "Preobrazhensky and the Theory of the Transition Period," *Soviet Studies*, vol. 27, no. 2 (1975), 196–219; E. A. Preobrazhenskiĭ and Donald A. Filtzer, *The Crisis of Soviet Industrialization: Selected Essays* (White Plains, NY: M.E. Sharpe, 1979), xi–liii. Even before 1949, virtually the entire CCP elite had read Stalin's canonical text, *The History of the All-Union Communist Party (Bolshevik) Short Course*, to which Mao referred in order to justify similarly extractive policies and emphases on industrialization. Hua-Yu Li, "Instilling Stalinism in Chinese Party Members: Absorbing Stalin's *Short Course* in the 1950s," in Thomas P. Bernstein and Hua-Yu Li, *China Learns from the Soviet Union, 1949–Present* (Lanham, MD: Lexington Books, 2011), 107–30.

93. Felix Wemheuer, *Famine Politics in Maoist China and the Soviet Union* (New Haven: Yale University Press, 2014), 40–6. For this section, I rely heavily on this book, which provides a comparison of the policies of extraction and their devastating consequences in "socialist" countries. For an interpretation of Chinese capitalism based on the concept of primitive accumulation lasting from 1850 to 1980, including the "state socialist" extraction of the rural

surplus, see Ho-fung Hung, *The China Boom: Why China Will Not Rule the World* (New York: Columbia University Press, 2016), 34–51.

94. J. V. Stalin, *Problems of Leninism* (Moscow: Foreign Languages Publishing House, 1953), 454–8.

95. The pressing need for capital and the ongoing experience of imperialist aggression made the CCP and Mao unable or unwilling either to import capital or to slowly accumulate it through more gradual industrialization and initial allocations of scarce capital to improve agricultural yields.

96. For introductions to the battle between the state and farmers over the division of the harvest, see Jean C. Oi, *State and Peasant in Contemporary China: The Political Economy of Village Government* (Berkeley: University of California Press, 1991); Mark Selden, *The Political Economy of Chinese Socialism* (Armonk, NY: M.E. Sharpe, 1988), ch. 3.

97. See, for instance, Premier Zhou Enlai's description of the commune's success in eliminating these inequalities, in Mao Yisheng, "知识分子要跟上祖国跃进的脚步: 茅以升代表的发言 (Intellectuals should follow the Leap Forward of the motherland, Speech by Mao Yisheng), *RMRB*, April 28, 1959, 9. The CCP justified other policies for addressing the "three major inequalities," including rusticating urban youth. See "坚持知识青年上山下乡的正确方向" (Persist down the correct path in the Down to the Countryside Movement), *RMRB,* July 9, 1967.

98. Gregory Rohlf, "The Soviet Model and China's State Farms," in Bernstein and Li, *China Learns from the Soviet Union*, 197–228.

99. Relying on the work of scholars such as Kate Zhou, historian Frank Dikötter has repopularized the interpretation that in the late 1970s there was a bottom-up, non-state initiated "reform" era of decollectivization and resumption of private accumulation in the countryside. See his *The Cultural Revolution: A People's History, 1962–1976* (New York: Bloomsbury Press, 2017). See Kate Xiao Zhou. *How the Farmers Changed China: Power of the People* (Boulder, CO: Westview Press, 1998).

100. While the average state ration of cloth during nearly the entire Mao era in rural China was some 5.5 meters, in his research on the history of cloth in twentieth-century China, Jacob Eyferth has calculated that the average rural person required a minimum of nine meters of cotton cloth each year. With less than that, one would have to remain indoors during bad weather. The figure for a social minimum was higher, requiring eleven meters to dress according to basic standards. To avoid gradually having to go naked, the average person living in the countryside had to engage in illicit economic activities, such as stealing cotton and redirecting labor to making homespun textiles. Jacob Eyferth, "Beyond the Maoist Commodity: Material Life in Rural China, 1950–1980." Paper presented at the workshop, "Material

Culture in Maoist China," King's College, London, May 18, 2019, 13–14. Cited with permission.

101. In *China under Mao: A Revolution Derailed* (Cambridge, MA: Harvard University Press, 2015), sociologist Andrew Walder traces many of the tragedies of the Mao era to the CCP's internal self-governance, particularly how it managed and incentivized cadres.

102. For an overview of the changing techniques used by the state to capture a larger share of the harvest, see Oi, *State and Peasant in Contemporary China.*

103. Leon Trotsky coined the term "price scissors" and originally applied it to the Soviet economy during the New Economic Policy (NEP) of the early 1920s. Robert Service, *Trotsky: A Biography* (Cambridge, MA: Belknap Press of Harvard University Press, 2009), 304.

104. On the motivations for this strategy, and its strengths and weaknesses, see Chris Bramall, *Chinese Economic Development* (London: Routledge, 2009), 87–8.

105. For an example of the need to make compromises across class lines to find literate local cadres, that is, those already with more human capital, see Anita Chan, Richard Madsen, and Jonathan Unger, *Chen Village: Revolution to Globalization*, 3rd ed. (Berkeley: University of California Press, 2009). Very few of the classes that the CCP wanted to empower had the basic skills necessary to conduct state business and to facilitate state extractions.

106. For details on the "Communist Wind," see David Zweig, *Agrarian Radicalism in China, 1968–1981* (Cambridge, MA: Harvard University Press, 1989), 161–2; William A. Joseph, *The Critique of Ultra-Leftism in China, 1958–1981* (Stanford: Stanford University Press, 1984), 118.

107. Thomas P. Bernstein, "Mao Zedong and the Famine of 1959–1960," *China Quarterly*, no. 186 (2006), 421–45.

108. In Lin Ping, Song Qiong, and Wang Yu, "'少校政委'的原形" (The real nature of the "Major Commissar"), *Jiefangjun bao*, April 9, 1958, the authors label Wang a "rightist" and claim he is disgruntled because his salary is insufficient to fulfill his dream of acquiring the Three Great Things.

109. These terms come from the work of James C. Scott. See his *Weapons of the Weak: Everyday Forms of Peasant Resistance* (New Haven: Yale University Press, 1985) and his "Everyday Forms of Resistance," in Forrest D. Colburn, ed., *Everyday Forms of Peasant Resistance* (Armonk, NY: M.E. Sharpe, 1989), 3–33.

110. On rural strategies to counter state extractions, state responses, and rural counter-responses, see Ralph A. Thaxton, *Catastrophe and Contention in Rural China: Mao's Great Leap Forward: Famine and the Origins of Righteous*

Resistance in Da Fo Village (Cambridge: Cambridge University Press, 2008), especially chs. 5 and 6, which document each of the strategies.

111. On how the party prioritized feeding Tianjin, for instance, see Jeremy Brown, *City versus Countryside in Mao's China: Negotiating the Divide* (New York: Cambridge University Press, 2012), 65–9.

112. Books documenting examples of these extreme measures include Xun Zhou, *The Great Famine in China, 1958–1962: A Documentary History* (New Haven: Yale University Press, 2012); Xun Zhou, *Forgotten Voices of Mao's Great Famine, 1958–1962: An Oral History* (New Haven: Yale University Press, 2014); Jisheng Yang, *Tombstone: The Untold Story of Mao's Great Famine* (London: Penguin Books, 2013).

113. Zhongguo guowyuyuan, Zhishi qingnan shangshan xia xiang lingdao xiaozu bangongshi, ed., 全国城镇知识青年上山下乡统计资料, 1962–1979 (Beijing, 1981).

114. Selden, *The Political Economy of Chinese Socialism*, 19–23.

115. See Brown, *City Versus Countryside in Mao's China*, 141–59.

116. Xue Muqiao, *China's Socialist Economy*, 45.

Soviet Influences on State Consumerism

1. Mao Zedong. "论人民民主专政" (On the People's Democratic Dictatorship), June 30, 1949. See www.marxists.org/chinese/maozedong/marxist.org-chinese-mao-19490630.htm. Archived July 15, 2018. This was also translated and published in pamphlet form. *On the People's Democratic Dictatorship* (Peking: Foreign Languages Press, 1967), 20.

2. Propaganda posters from the 1950s informed viewers what the PRC received from the Soviet Union: industrial, military, and agricultural technology; know-how from its experts; and cultural exchanges. For examples, see http://chineseposters .net:80/themes/sino-soviet-cooperation.php. Archived June 29, 2017.

3. For an overview of the geopolitical turning points in the Sino-Soviet Alliance, see Sergey Radchenko, "The Rise and the Fall of the Sino-Soviet Alliance 1949–1989," in N. Naimark, S. Pons, and S. Quinn-Judge, eds., *The Cambridge History of Communism* (Cambridge: Cambridge University Press, 2017), 243–68.

4. Shu Guang Zhang, *Beijing's Economic Statecraft during the Cold War, 1949–1991* (Washington, DC: Woodrow Wilson Center Press and Baltimore: Johns Hopkins University Press, 2014), 21–95.

5. Li Ruojian, 虚实之间: 20世纪50年代中国大陆谣言研究 (Between fact and fiction: An analysis of rumors in China during the 1950s) (Beijing: Shehui kexue wenxian chubanshe, 2011), 101, 109.

6. Mao Dechuan, "国民党军修建利用岱山机场的前前后后" (The complete story of the KMT army's building of and using the Daishan airport for military

purposes), in Zhongguo renmin zhengzhi xieshang huiyi, Zhejiangsheng Daishanxian weiyuanhui wenshi ziliao weiyuanhui (中国人民政治协商会议．浙江省岱山县委员会文史资料委员会), eds. 岱山文史资料 (Daishan historical materials) (1991), 3.17–19; "上海解放初期警备工作的日日夜夜" (Days and nights of garrison work during the early days of Shanghai's liberation) and "把上海的天空保护起来" (Protect the Shanghai sky), in Zhongguo renmin jiefangjun Shanghai jingbeiqu zhengzhibu, Zhonggong Shanghai shiwei dangshi yanjiushi, eds., 警备大上海 (Guard great Shanghai) (Shanghai: Shanghai yuandong chubanshe, 1994), 25–6, 132–40.

7. For the Soviet explanation of how economic practices associated with capitalism, such as commodity production, remained compatible with Marxism, see Stalin's classic text, translated and published in China shortly after the original was released: Sidalin [Joseph Stalin], 苏联社会主义经济问题 (Economic problems of socialism in the USSR) (Beijing: Renmin chubanshe, 1952). Also published in *Xuexi*, no. 8 (November 1952), 3–27. China also released an English edition: Joseph Stalin, *Economic Problems of Socialism in the U.S.S.R.* (Peking: Foreign Languages Press, 1972). On China's following of the Soviet example of labeling commodity production as "socialist," see Laurence Coderre, "A Necessary Evil: Conceptualizing the Socialist Commodity under Mao," *Comparative Studies in Society and History*, vol. 61, no. 1 (2019), 23–49.

8. The CCP directed the Propaganda Department to instruct all local propaganda organizations to promote a positive awareness of the Soviet relationship; see Yan Li, *China's Soviet Dream: Propaganda, Culture, and Popular Imagination* (London: Routledge, 2018), 28–32. On the difficulty of overcoming existing animosity toward the Soviets, see Miin-ling Yu, "Learning from the Soviet Union: CPC Publicity and Its Effects – A Study Centered on the Sino-Soviet Friendship Association," *Social Sciences in China*, vol. 26, no. 2 (2005), 100–11. On mass mobilization to support the relationship, see K. E. Priestley, "The Sino-Soviet Friendship Association," *Pacific Affairs*, vol. 25, no. 3 (1952), 287–92. On institutional imports such as management techniques, see Deborah A. Kaple, *Dream of a Red Factory: The Legacy of High Stalinism in China* (New York: Oxford University Press, 1994).

9. These same values were communicated in literature, such as in the Soviet socialist realist novel *How the Steel Was Tempered*, in which bourgeois love takes a backseat to revolutionary commitment. Donghui He, "Coming of Age in the Brave New World: The Changing Reception of the Soviet Novel, *How the Steel Was Tempered*, in the People's Republic of China," in Bernstein and Li, *China Learns from the Soviet Union, 1949–Present* (Lanham, MD: Lexington Books, 2010), 393–420. On Soviet influences more generally, see Krista Van

Fleit Hang, *Literature the People Love: Reading Chinese Texts from the Early Maoist Period (1949–1966)* (New York: Palgrave Macmillan, 2013); Nicolai Volland, *Socialist Cosmopolitanism: The Chinese Literary Universe, 1945–1965* (New York: Columbia University Press, 2017), esp. ch. 4.

10. 伊 奥库涅夫, "苏联妇女穿什么衣服" (What do Soviet women wear?), *Sulian funü*, no. 4 (April 1956), 46–7. Chinese articles also supported nicer clothing to both reflect improved living conditions and even frugality, as the amount of cloth required to make a *qipao* was less than that required to make a cadre uniform. See, for instance, "穿花衣服是不是资产阶级思想?" (Is dressing in flowery clothes bourgeois thinking?), *Zhongguo qingnian*, no. 22 (1954), 32; Xiao Ling, "一件花旗袍引起的风波" (Controversy over a flowered *qipao*), *Zhongguo funü*, no. 4 (April 1956), 18–19.

11. In addition to the works cited below, introductions include: Lorenz M. Luthi, *The Sino-Soviet Split: Cold War in the Communist World* (Princeton, NJ: Princeton University Press, 2008); Mingjiang Li, *Mao's China and the Sino-Soviet Split: Ideological Dilemma* (London: Routledge, 2012); Danhui Li and Yafeng Xia, *Mao and the Sino-Soviet Split, 1959–1973: A New History* (Lanham, MD: Lexington Books, 2018).

12. For an overview of the three distinct models on offer, see Thomas P. Bernstein, "Introduction: The Complexities of Learning from the Soviet Union," in Bernstein and Li, eds., *China Learns from the Soviet Union*, 1–23 (at pp. 7–8).

13. For an overview of the Soviet policies and a comparison with corresponding PRC policies, see Stephen A. Smith, "Introduction: Towards a Global History of Communism," in S. A. Smith, ed., *The Oxford Handbook of the History of Communism* (Oxford: Oxford University Press, 2013), 1–34. After China broke with the Soviet economic model and criticized its Elder Brother in the early 1960s, Khrushchev may have responded by cracking down on artistic genres deemed bourgeois. See Sergey Radchenko, *Two Suns in the Heavens: The Sino-Soviet Struggle for Supremacy, 1962–1967* (Washington, DC: Woodrow Wilson Press and Stanford: Stanford University Press, 2009), 52–6. For an introduction to late Soviet consumerism, see Natalya Chernyshova, *Soviet Consumer Culture in the Brezhnev Era* (London: Routledge, 2013); James R. Millar, "The Little Deal: Brezhnev's Contribution to Acquisitive Socialism," *Slavic Review*, vol. 44, no. 4 (1985), 694–706.

14. On the Chinese equation of the Soviet model with socialism, see Hanbing Kong, "The Transplantation and Entrenchment of the Soviet Economic Model in China," in Bernstein and Li, eds., *China Learns from the Soviet Union*, 153–66 (at p. 162).

15. Histories of the NEP provide a good example of how the imperatives for accumulation led to policy reversals and a shift toward greater private

capitalism, including the relegalization of private trade and small-scale manufacturing. See Alec Nove, *An Economic History of the U.S.S.R., 1917–1991*, 3rd ed. (Harmondsworth: Penguin, 1992), 78–114; Alan M. Ball, *Russia's Last Capitalists: The Nepmen, 1921–1929* (Berkeley: University of California Press, 1987).

16. The term "Big Deal" comes from Vera S. Dunham, *In Stalin's Time: Middleclass Values in Soviet Fiction*, enlarged and updated ed. (Durham, NC: Duke University Press, 1990). Dunham originally applied the interpretation to the post–World War II era. However, the idea of a compromise between the Soviet leadership and a privileged segment of society both predates her work and her periodization. By the late 1930s, Soviet state consumerism condemned asceticism and egalitarianism. Aspiring for higher incomes and nicer lifestyles became the goals of the new Soviet middle class. See Jukka Gronow, *The Sociology of Taste* (London: Routledge, 1997), 55–61. Before Dunham, the most famous of such critiques of the CPSU came from Trotsky. But others had also identified the end of the Soviet Union's equation of building socialism with self-sacrifice and the state toleration of hedonism in the 1930s as pivotal. See Nicholas S. Timasheff, *The Great Retreat: The Growth and Decline of Communism in Russia* (New York: E.P. Dutton, 1946); Milovan Djilas makes a similarly well-known argument in *The New Class: An Analysis of the Communist System* (New York: Praeger, 1957). In contrast to Trotsky's bureaucracy, Djilas' new class, or Durham's middle class, Sheila Fitzpatrick, *The Cultural Front: Power and Culture in Revolutionary Russia* (Ithaca, NY: Cornell University Press, 1992), 216–37, argues for a new class that is striving to "become cultured" rather than bourgeois. This concept has been further developed by others, such as Vadim Vokov, "The Concept of *kul'turnost*': Notes on the Stalinist Civilizing Process," in Sheila Fitzpatrick, ed., *Stalinism: New Directions* (London: Routledge, 2000), 210–30; and Catriona Kelly, *Refining Russia: Advice Literature, Polite Culture, and Gender from Catherine to Yeltsin* (Oxford: Oxford University Press, 2001), 230–393.

17. David Crowley and Susan E. Reid, "Style and Socialism: Modernity and Material Culture in Post-War Eastern Europe," in Susan Emily Reid and D. J. Crowley, *Style and Socialism: Modernity and Material Culture in Post-War Eastern Europe* (Oxford: Berg, 2000), 1–17 (at pp. 10–11).

18. Denis Kozlov and Eleonary Gilbourd, *The Thaw: Soviet Society and Culture during the 1950s and 1960s* (Toronto: University of Toronto Press, 2013). On the economic experiments in the 1950s and early 1960s, before and after Stalin's death in 1953, see Nove, *An Economic History of the U.S.S.R.*, 331–77. See, for instance, the example of state efforts to shift from coercion

to incentive in popular participation in state lotteries in Kristy Ironside, "Khrushchev's Cash-and-Goods Lotteries and the Turn Toward Positive Incentives," *The Soviet and Post-Soviet Review*, vol. 41, no. 3 (2014), 296–323. Emblematic of expanding consumerism – both in numbers of participants and capital-intensiveness of material desires – was perhaps the decision in the 1960s to mass produce private automobiles. Lewis H. Siegelbaum, *Cars for Comrades: The Life of the Soviet Automobile* (Ithaca, NY: Cornell University Press, 2008), 84–7.

19. Kate Brown, *Plutopia: Nuclear Families, Atomic Cities, and the Great Soviet and American Plutonium Disasters* (Oxford: Oxford University Press, 2013), 255–67 (at p. 260).

20. Both quotes from Brown, *Plutopia*, 260. The author uses the city to illustrate national policies and trends contributing to consumerism. See pp. 255–67. Note that the author has an entire chapter devoted to "a socialist consumers' republic" (ch. 29) and makes a reference to the Soviet Union as "state capitalism" (p. 267).

21. Lipstick's newfound acceptability was ironic because the Communist Youth League had been founded to counter the bourgeois values spreading during the Soviet Union's initial compromise with capitalism during the pro-market NEP era. Elena Osokina, *Our Daily Bread: Socialist Distribution and the Art of Survival in Stalin's Russia, 1927–1941*, ed. Kate Transchel, tr. Kate Transchel and Greta Bucher (Armonk, NY: M.E. Sharpe, 2001), 133; Peter Gooderham, "The Komsomol and Worker Youth: The Inculcation of 'Communist Values' in Leningrad during NEP." *Soviet Studies*, vol. 34, no. 4 (1982), 506–28.

22. See Dunham, *In Stalin's Time*, 43.

23. Shen Zhihua estimates that 5,000 advisors arrived between 1949 and 1953, with 11,000 more coming to China by 1958, and another 2,000 by 1960: Shen Zhihua, 苏联专家在中国 *(1948–1960)* (Soviet Experts in China, 1948–1960) (Beijing: Zhongguo guoji guangbo chubanshe, 2003), 408–10. See also Shen Zhihua and Guy Alitto, "A Historical Examination of the Issue of Soviet Experts in China: Basic Situation and Policy Changes," *Russian History*, vol. 29, no. 2/4 (2002), 377–400 (at p. 380); and Deborah Kaple, "Agents of Change: Soviet Advisers and High Stalinist Management in China, 1949–1960," *Journal of Cold War Studies*, vol. 18, no. 1 (2016), 5–30.

24. Mikhail A. Klochko, *Soviet Scientist in Red China*, tr. Andrew MacAndrew (New York: Praeger, 1964), 53–4.

25. Shaw-tong Liu, *Out of Red China*, tr. Jack Chia and Henry Walter (New York: Duell, Sloan, and Pearce, 1953), 164–5.

26. G. Ganshin and T. Zazerskaya, "Pitfalls Along the Path of 'Brotherly Friendship' (A Look at the History of Soviet-Chinese Relations)," *Far Eastern Affairs*, no. 6 (1994), 63–70 (at pp. 68–9). As one scholar of the

Sino-Soviet relationship has concluded, "The many advisers and cultural figures who traveled to China generally assumed the Chinese should be grateful to be exposed to the world of socialism and its culture and believed they had more to teach than to learn. Socialist publics throughout the bloc felt the same way." Austin Jersild, "Socialist Exhibits and Sino-Soviet Relations, 1950–60," *Cold War History*, vol. 18, no. 3 (2018), 275–89 (at p. 281).

27. Yang Kuisong, 毛泽东与莫斯科的恩恩怨怨 (Gratitude and resentment between Mao Zedong and Moscow), 4th ed. (Nanchang: Jiangxi renmin chubanshe, 1999), 326–7.

28. Klochko, *Soviet Scientist in Red China*, 63.

29. For a photo of Wang, with permed hair, and further details of her encounters with Soviet experts, see Yang Jun, "82岁的王明荣忆当年: 在苏联专家科的日子" (Wang Mingrong, 82, recalls her time at the Soviet Expert Department), http://zaozhuang.sdnews.com.cn/shys/201511/t201511 29_2006884.htm. Archived June 26, 2019.

30. Li, *China's Soviet Dream*, 93, 114n13.

31. Jersild, "Socialist Exhibits and Sino-Soviet Relations, 1950–60," 285.

32. For example, the CCP introduced Soviet popular music to instill belief in the party and its goal of creating a new Socialist Person but it could not control the reception of those songs that were used to express individualism and to introduce Soviet ideas of romantic love. See Yu Miin-ling, "從高歌到低唱: 蘇聯群眾歌曲在中國" (From singing loud to singing low: Soviet mass songs in China), *Zhongyang yanjiuyuan jindaishi yanjiusuo jikan*, Academia Sinica, no. 53 (September 2006), 149–91.

33. Jian Zang, "The Soviet Impact on 'Gender Equality' in China in the 1950s," in Bernstein and Li, eds., *China Learns from the Soviet Union*, 259–74.

34. See, for instance, Judd Stitziel, *Fashioning Socialism: Clothing, Politics, and Consumer Culture in East Germany* (Oxford: Berg, 2005).

35. In 1956, for instance, Beijing hosted a fashion exhibition featuring 500 articles of clothing "suitable for different gender, age, career, body shape, and seasons." Dian Yi, "记首都的服装展览会" (Fashion exhibition in the capital), *RMRB*, April 1, 1956, 2.

36. A. Doak Barnett, *Communist China: The Early Years, 1949–55* (New York: F. A. Praeger, 1964), 16. In the Mao era, individual Chinese citizens' choice in dress advertised one's utility for productive work and, by extension, communicated one's commitment to proletarian values. Choosing the correct outfit signaled one's affinity to the ideals of the Communist Revolution. Thorstein Veblen, "The Economic Theory of Woman's Dress," *The Popular Science Monthly*, vol. 46 (1894), 198–205.

37. Using clothing styles to make political statements has a long history in China, including among the male revolutionaries overthrowing the Qing dynasty in

1911–12, who separated themselves from the non-revolutionaries through their clothing by wearing Western-style suits rather than long gowns and vests, a style that early participants in the NPM insisted be made from "national product" fabrics. Karl Gerth, *China Made: Consumer Culture and the Creation of the Nation* (Cambridge, MA: Harvard University Asia Center, 2003), ch. 2.

38. For an overview of Mao-era fashions that ends the once common assumption that everyone dressed nearly the same, see Antonia Finnane and Peidong Sun, "Textiles and Apparel in the Mao Years: Uniformity, Variety, and the Limits of Autarchy," in Wessie Ling and Simona Segre-Reinach, eds., *Making Fashion in Multiple Chinas: Chinese Styles in the Transglobal Landscape* (London: I.B. Tauris, 2018), 16–43. On pre-1966 trends and the state role in them, see Tina Mai Chen, "Dressing for the Party: Clothing, Citizenship, and Gender-Formation in Mao's China," *Fashion Theory*, vol. 5, no. 2 (2001), 143–71.

39. Finnane and Sun, "Textiles and Apparel in the Mao Years," 38.

40. Chen Yu, 中国生活记忆: 建国60年民生往事 (Recollections of life in China: 60 years of everyday happenings since the establishment of the state) (Beijing: Zhongguo qinggongye chubanshe, 2009), 22–3.

41. Tina Mai Chen, "Proletarian White and Working Bodies in Mao's China," *positions: east asia, cultures critiques*, vol. 11, no. 2 (2003), 378.

42. Su Xiu, 我的配音生涯 (My career doing voiceovers) (Shanghai: Wenhui chubanshe, 2005), 325–6.

43. James Z. Gao, *The Communist Takeover of Hangzhou: The Transformation of City and Cadre, 1949–1954* (Honolulu: University of Hawai'i Press, 2004), 74, 79. However, at the height of demand for red fabric, acquisition required political connections. Elizabeth J. Perry and Li Xun, *Proletarian Power: Shanghai in the Cultural Revolution* (Boulder, CO: Westview Press, 1997), 77. For an overview of Red Guard fashions, see Verity Wilson, "Dress and the Cultural Revolution," in Valerie Steele and John S. Major, eds., *China Chic: East Meets West* (New Haven: Yale University Press, 1999), 167–86; Antonia Finnane, *Changing Clothes in China: Fashion, History, Nation* (New York: Columbia University Press, 2008), 227–55.

44. "一位劳模的美丽记忆" (Beautiful memories of a model worker), in Shanghai yingxiang gongzuo shi 上海影像工作室著, ed., 百姓生活记忆:上海故事 (Memories of people's life experiences: Shanghai stories) (Shanghai: Xuelin chubanshe, 2012), 130.

45. On the successful replacement of imported pens such as Parker with China-made pens, see Chu Chan-liang, "Fountain Pens for Everyone," *China Reconstructs*, vol. 13, no. 4 (1964), 26–7. On state production of fountain pen fashions, see movies such as *A Nurse's Diary* (护士日记) (1957). In the film, the character Gao Changpin, a cadre from a spartan and remote

construction site, visits Shanghai to recruit medical staff. Gao, along with other characters in positions of authority and respect, wears a cadre suit, replete with a fountain pen in the top left pocket. To view the film, see http://v.youku.com /v_show/id_XNDciOTEwNDQ=.html. Consulted July 7, 2016.

46. Xu Hualong, 上海服装文化史 (A history of Shanghai clothing culture) (Shanghai: Dongfang chuban zhongxin, 2010), 270.

47. Finnane, *Changing Clothes in China*, 205.

48. Chen Yu, 中国生活记忆: 建国60年民生往事 (Recollections of life in China: 60 years of everyday happenings since the establishment of the state), 22. For photographs of railway workers in these uniforms, see https://baijiahao .baidu.com/s?id=1558818607754058&wfr=spider&for=pc. Archived December 27, 2018.

49. Xu Hualong, 上海服装文化史 (A history of Shanghai clothing culture), 271. For a photograph of Liang Jun on the 1 RMB note, see www.chinanews.com/sh/ 2013/10–30/5442425.shtml. Archived December 27, 2018. For Tian Guiying, see http://cimg2.163.com/catchimg/20100119/10408290_0.jpg. Archived December 27, 2018.

50. The history of the Soviet fashion industry is extensively covered in Jukka Gronow and Sergey Zhuravlev, *Fashion Meets Socialism: Fashion Industry in the Soviet Union After the Second World War* (Helsinki: Finnish Literature Society, 2014). See also Juliane Fürst, "The Importance of Being Stylish: Youth, Culture and Identity in Late Stalinism," in Juliane Fürst, ed., *Late Stalinist Russia: Society Between Reconstruction and Reinvention* (London: Routledge, 2006), 209–30. There is no comparable study of the Chinese fashion industry in the Mao era.

51. Xu Hualong, 上海服装文化史 (A history of Shanghai clothing culture), 270.

52. For a description of the early adoption and abandonment of the dress as a summer uniform for women in the PLA, see Xu Ping, "军版'布拉吉'" (The military version of the "bulaji"), *Junying wenhua tiandi* (January 2018), 37–8.

53. Li, *China's Soviet Dream*, 39.

54. Shi Shenglin, "苏联大花布和手表" (Soviet patterned fabric and watches), http://blog.sina.com.cn/s/blog_65d891800102e53r.html. Archived November 7, 2017.

55. Quoted in Shi Shenglin, "苏联大花布和手表" (Soviet patterned fabric and watches).

56. "支持姑娘们穿花衣服" (Encourage young women to wear flowered clothing), *Zhongguo qingnian bao*, May 17, 1955. For an overview of fashions in the 1950s, see Finnane, *Changing Clothes in China*, ch. 8.

57. Tian Fanghua (pseudonym), "谈'浪费美学'" (Let's talk about the aesthetics of wastefulness), *Zhongguo dianying*, no. 3 (1958), 68. Zhang Jian, "卓娅头 和布拉吉" (The Zoya hairstyle and *bulaji*), *Jinwan bao*, December 31, 2018.

58. "一位劳模的美丽记忆" (Beautiful memories of a model worker), 132.
59. "支持姑娘们穿花衣服" (Encourage young women to wear flower-patterned clothing), *Qingnian bao*, May 17, 1955.
60. Li Pao-kuang (Head of the Service Department, All-China Democratic Women's Federation), "Speaking of Women's Clothing," *Women of China*, no. 1 (Spring 1956), 22–3.
61. Li, *China's Soviet Dream*, 129–30.
62. Quoted in Wang Chenlong, "男青年们的花衬衫" (Young men's colorful shirts), *Jiari 100 tian*, no. 9 (September 18, 2009).
63. Guo Yuyi, "苏联花布" (Soviet printed cloth), *Taiyuan ribao*, January 12, 2010.
64. Guo Yuyi, "苏联花布" (Soviet printed cloth).
65. Shen Kun, "老县城记" (Mcmorics of my county), in 沈琨文集: 散文卷4 (The collected works of Shen Kun: Prose, Volume 4) (Beijing: Zuojia chubanshe, 2012), 10.
66. Zhang Quanqing, "建国初期的苏联大花布" (Soviet big-flower-patterned cloth in the early days of the founding of the PRC), Sina blog, posted June 9, 2012, http://blog.sina.com.cn/s/blog_5d6e47e601014t8x.html. Archived June 27, 2019.
67. Liu Yajuan, "国家与都市之间: 上海劳模形象建构与流变的个案研究 (1949–1963)" (Between the state and the metropolis: A case study of the construction and change in the image of Shanghai model laborers, 1949–1963), *Zhonggong dangshi yanjiu*, no. 5 (2016), 70.
68. "一位劳模的美丽记忆" (Beautiful memories of a model worker), 129. The article quotes material from the documentary by the same name: "一位劳模的美丽记忆" (Beautiful memories of a model worker), www.sava.sh.cn/visual/video/2014-05-22/4216.html. Consulted December 28, 2018. All references are to the text.
69. Huang Baomei, "我决心带头穿起漂亮的服装" (I took the lead in wearing beautiful clothing), *Xinmin wanbao*, March 5, 1956.
70. "一位劳模的美丽记忆" (Beautiful memories of a model worker), 132. Elsewhere she noted that young women were especially conscious of their looks. Sun Shizheng, "黄宝妹谈苏联" (Huang Baomei talks about the Soviet Union), *Xinmin wanbao*, November 7, 1954.
71. Fang Zhuangchao and Wang Yongnian, "接受黄宝妹等意见, 杨浦区一家理发店扩充" (Taking the advice of Huang Baomei and others, a barber in Yangpu District expands his business), *Xinmin wanbao*, December 28, 1956.
72. According to a newspaper account, Huang received letters from workers throughout the country who wanted to date her, implying that women who wore similar clothing would attract many suitors. So many letters reportedly arrived that the labor union at the cotton mill assigned a worker to write

replies. At some point, perhaps to dampen romantic interest in her, the *People's Daily* published an article that referred to her husband and son, implying that she was off the market. Liu Yajuan, "国家与都市之间: 上海劳模形象建构与流变的个案研究 (1949–1963)" (Between the state and the metropolis: A case study of the construction and change in the image of Shanghai model laborers, 1949–1963), 7–71.

73. Zhu Ye, "新服装送到了国棉十七厂" (Newly designed clothes are delivered to state Number 17 Cotton Factory), *Xinmin wanbao*, March 21, 1956.

74. Tian Peijie, "追忆苏联大花布" (Chasing Soviet printed cloth), www.zhengshangci.com/newsx.asp?id=664. Archived September 3, 2018; Finanne, *Changing Clothes in China*, 205–6.

75. Liu Yajuan, "国家与都市之间: 上海劳模形象建构与流变的个案研究 (1949–1963)" (Between the state and the metropolis: A case study of the construction and change in the image of Shanghai model laborers, 1949–1963), 68–78. For example, Huang performed on stage with Xu Yulan (徐玉兰), a famous actress. Chen Ying, "黄宝妹初唱 '盘夫', 徐玉兰合作演曾荣" (Huang Baomei sings traditional Shaoxing opera with Xu Yulan), *Xinmin wanbao*, March 20, 1958.

76. Li, *Mao's China and the Sino-Soviet Split*, 21–2.

77. The CCP long had reasons to doubt the commitment of the CPSU to build international socialism, much less support the CCP. In 1959, Mao summarized the Soviet lack of support for the CCP-led revolution: "In 1945, they did not permit [us to make] revolution, but afterwards they consented. From 1949 to 1951, they doubted that [ours was] a real revolution and they began to be unwilling to conclude a mutual-aid alliance treaty but then they changed their mind. During the last ten years, they have helped us build many factories." "Mao Zedong, Outline for a Speech on the International Situation," December 1959, History and Public Policy Program Digital Archive, tr. David Wolff; Zhonggong zhongyang wenxian yanjiushi, ed., 建国以来毛泽东文稿 (Mao Zedong's manuscripts since the founding of the state) (Beijing: Zhongyang wenxian chubanshe, 1993), 8.599–603, https://digitalarchive.wilsoncenter.org/document/11889. Consulted December 28, 2018.

78. Odd A. Westad, *The Global Cold War: Third World Interventions and the Making of Our Times* (Cambridge: Cambridge University Press, 2005), 65.

79. Li, *China's Soviet Dream*, 32–5.

80. Sergey Radchenko, "The Rise and the Fall of the Sino-Soviet Alliance 1949–1989," 244–8.

81. Roxane Witke, *Comrade Ch'iang Ching* (Boston: Little, Brown, 1977), 258–9.

82. Lowell Dittmer, *Liu Shao-ch'i and the Chinese Cultural Revolution: The Politics of Mass Criticism* (Berkeley: University of California Press, 1974), 27.

83. Liu Shaoqi, as quoted in Elizabeth McGuire, *Red at Heart: How Chinese Communists Fell in Love with the Russian Revolution* (New York: Oxford University Press, 2018), 286. Chinese complaints about their exposure to poorly behaved Soviet students and bad food resulted in the Chinese side being segregated at Lumumba University in 1960 (at p. 289). McGuire estimates that China sent more than 8,000 students to Lumumba University in the 1950s and early 1960s, as well as an additional 8,500 for short-term training. In addition to Liu Shaoqi, future President Jiang Zemin and Premier Li Peng also sent their children (at p. 284).

84. For an overview of the policy, see Po I-po [Bo Yibo] (薄一波), "Industry's Tasks in 1959," *Peking Review*, no. 1 (1959), 9–11.

85. Ygael Gluckstein, *Mao's China: Economic and Political Survey* (Boston: Beacon Press, 1957), 75. This summary of the Great Leap policies and outcomes – but not my own state capitalist interpretation – relies on Chris Bramall, *Chinese Economic Development* (London: Routledge, 2009), 118–41.

86. Bramall, *Chinese Economic Development*, 130–1.

87. The CCP continued to experiment with its rural industrialization strategy through its Third Front policies beginning in 1964. See Barry Naughton, "The Third Front: Defence Industrialization in the Chinese Interior," *The China Quarterly*, no. 115 (1988), 351–86. On broader social consequences, including the ways Third Front industrialization introduced or greatly expanded local inequalities even as it sought to bridge urban–rural and coastal-interior inequalities, see Covell Meyskens, *Mao's Third Front: The Militarization of Cold War China* (Cambridge: Cambridge University Press, 2020).

88. For an interpretation of the Mao-era disasters as outcomes of a political party that overly disincentivized feedback from lower levels of the party hierarchy, see Andrew G. Walder, *China Under Mao: A Revolution Derailed* (Cambridge, MA: Harvard University Press, 2015).

89. The nine commentaries are available in many places. They were printed in *RMRB* on September 6, September 13, September 26, October 22, November 19, and December 12, 1963, and February 4, March 31, and July 14, 1964, and also reprinted in Zhonggong zhongyang wenxian yanjiushi, ed., 建国以来重要文献选编 (A selection of major documents since the founding of the state) (Beijing: Zhongyang wenxian chubanshe, 1997–8), 17. 1–45, 56–76, 92–133, 314–44, 450–84, 529–70; 18. 81–135, 363–415; and 19. 16–78.

90. *The Polemic on the General Line of the International Communist Movement* (Peking: Foreign Languages Press, 1965).

91. Xi Ping, "上海市地下工厂不断发展" (Underground factories in Shanghai continue to develop), *NBCK*, November 23, 1956.

92. Xu Wen, "苏州市工商业公私合营后 出现地下工厂七千二百四十户" (After the formation of joint state-private enterprises, Suzhou discovers 7,240 underground factories), *NBCK*, November 11, 1957.

93. "四川等地发现不少'地下工厂'和黑市交易" (Many "underground factories" and black market transactions have been discovered in Sichuan), *NBCK*, February 1, 1960; "一批投机倒把牟取暴利的地下工厂" (A batch of profiteering underground factories), *NBCK*, May 18, 1963.

94. Tong Xiwen, "旅大出现一批地下工厂" (Some "underground factories" discovered in LüDa [Lüshun and Dalian]), *NBCK*, December 27, 1962.

95. "临朐县多次发现奸商出卖假冒化肥" (Profiteers sell counterfeit fertilizer in Linqu county), *NBCK*, December 27, 1962.

96. Luthi, *The Sino-Soviet Split*, 274–85.

97. This calculation comes from research by Sun Peidong, "视听暴力: '九评' 的生产传播及红卫兵一代的记忆" (Audio-visual violence: The production and transmission of the nine commentaries and memories of the Red Guard generation), *Sixiang*, no. 35 (2018), 57.

98. Pang Xianzhi and Jin Chongji, 毛泽东传, 1949–1976 (The life of Mao Zedong, 1949–1976) (Beijing: Zhongyang wenxian chubanshe, 2003), 1.723–61; Radchenko, *Two Suns in the Heavens*, 23–70; Roderick MacFarquhar, *The Origins of the Cultural Revolution*, 3 vols. (New York: Columbia University Press, 1974, 1983, 1997). For the context of the commentaries, see MacFarquhar, *The Origins*, 3.362–64. As noted in the Introduction, the CCP was not the first nor the only source of criticism of the "socialist" credentials of the Soviet model.

99. As Kim Il Sung, leader of North Korea, told Liu Shaoqi, "These [commentaries] are not what Khrushchev needs; they are what the people of the world need. . . . In order to protect the purity of Marxism and oppose revisionism, this is a necessary path [and we must] participate in this struggle. Albania and China are leading the charge, and we [North Korea] are behind [Albania and China]." "Minutes of Conversation between Liu Shaoqi and Kim Il Sung," September 15, 1963, History and Public Policy Program Digital Archive, PRC FMA 203-00566-05, 91–100. Obtained by Shen Zhihua and translated by Jeffrey Wang and Charles Kraus, https://digitalarchive .wilsoncenter.org/document/116542. Consulted December 28, 2018.

100. Roderick MacFarquhar and Michael Schoenhals, *Mao's Last Revolution* (Cambridge, MA: Belknap Press of Harvard University Press, 2008), 485.

101. On mass campaigns as the prelude to the Cultural Revolution, see MacFarquhar and Schoenhals, *Mao's Last Revolution*; Richard Baum and Frederick C. Teiwes, *Ssu-Ch'ing: The Socialist Education Movement of 1962–1966* (Berkeley: Center for Chinese Studies, University of California,

1968); Cyril Chihren Lin, "The Reinstatement of Economics in China Today," *The China Quarterly*, no. 85 (1981), 1–48.

102. Yang Kuisong, 毛泽东与莫斯科的恩恩怨怨 (Gratitude and resentment between Mao Zedong and Moscow), 490–1.

103. Yan Mingfu, 亲历中苏关系: 中央办公厅翻译组的十年 (1957–1966) (A personal account of Sino-Soviet relations: A decade in the Translation Group of the General Office of the CCP Central Committee [1957–1966]) (Beijing: Zhongguo renmin daxue chubanshe, 2015), 321. The team even attempted to distribute the commentaries within the Soviet Union. The Chinese embassy in Moscow, for instance, distributed Russian translations through the mail and among Chinese students studying abroad. Radchenko, *Two Suns in the Heavens*, 58–64. For a discussion of the wide range of techniques used by the state to disseminate similar sorts of knowledge, see Jennifer E. Altehenger, *Legal Lessons: Popularizing Laws in the People's Republic of China, 1949–1989* (Cambridge, MA: Harvard University Asia Center, 2018).

104. "关于赫鲁晓夫的假共产主义及其在世界历史上的教训 (九评苏共中央的公开信)" (On Khrushchev's phony communism and its historical lessons for the world), *RMRB*, July 14, 1964, 1. On Mao's involvement in revising it, see Wu Lengxi, 十年论战: 1956–1966 中苏关系回忆录 (A decade of polemics: A memoir of Sino-Soviet relations, 1956–1966) (Beijing: Zhongyang wenxian chubanshe, 1999), 506–16.

105. On the concept and its popularization of permanent revolution in China after 1958, see Nick Knight, "Mao Zedong on the Chinese Road to Socialism, 1949–1969," in Nick Knight, *Rethinking Mao: Explorations in Mao Zedong's Thought* (Lanham, MD: Lexington Books, 2007), 217–47; John Bryan Starr, "Conceptual Foundations of Mao Tse-Tung's Theory of Continuous Revolution," *Asian Survey*, vol. 11, no. 6 (1971), 610–28; Stuart Schram, "Mao Tse-tung and the Theory of the Permanent Revolution, 1958–1969," *The China Quarterly*, no. 46 (1971), 221–44. Note that during the Cultural Revolution Mao's modified version of the concept became the "continuous revolution" (继续革命) of class warfare.

106. "Phony Communism" reminded people that the tactics employed by "capitalist restorationists" would be both "open and hidden" in the economic and cultural spheres. Capitalist restorationists would attempt to "corrupt the proletariat and other working people with bourgeois ideology." In addition, "Phony Communism" flagged rural sources of capitalist restoration, with evidence of the general (rural) population choosing practices resembling market capitalism and its manifestations in consumerism. As noted in Chapter 2, the CCP was wary of collective ownership fomenting market capitalist practices and remained anxious to

gain state "ownership by the whole people." Until then, the private capitalist economy would not "disappear completely" and "spontaneous capitalist tendencies" would be "inevitable."

107. "Phony Communism" indirectly labels the Soviet Union as "state capitalist" by claiming that it followed the negative example of Yugoslavia, which had become a proxy for CCP criticism of the Soviet Union since 1958. See "Yugoslavia Becomes the 'Mirror' of Revisionism, 1958," in John Gittings, *Survey of the Sino-Soviet Dispute: A Commentary and Extracts from the Recent Polemics, 1963–1967* (Oxford: Oxford University Press, 1968), 85-8.

108. Stuart Schram, ed., *Mao Zedong Unrehearsed: Talks and Letters, 1956–71* (Harmondsworth: Penguin, 1974), 217. However, the ninth commentary – and Mao – held off concluding whether these "bad elements" represented the entire party, forming what Djilas called a "new class," or simply included corrupt individuals, in which case the party needed yet another rectification campaign and more training. Stuart R. Schram, "Mao Tse-tung's Thought from 1949 to 1976," in John King Fairbank, and Roderick MacFarquhar, eds., *The Cambridge History of China*, vol. 14: *The People's Republic of China*, part 2: *Revolutions Within the Chinese Revolution, 1966–1982* (Cambridge: Cambridge University Press, 1991) 15.73–4.

State Consumerism in Advertising, Posters, and Films

1. Published at a time when the state pressed for ever greater investment – and a corresponding decrease in consumption – a representative discussion of the state's view of social consumption and how the entire social product was allocated to "the working people" (劳动人民) is Yang Bo, "我国国民收入中积累和消费的关系" (The relationship between accumulation and consumption in the national income of our country), *RMRB*, October 13, 1958, 7. Articles from this time provided primers for cadres on how to explain the shortages of consumer goods and the need for frugality. See, for instance, the detailed case study on Henan county where women demanded more sewing machines and youngsters wanted more bicycles, in "教育群众正确认识消费和积累的关系" (Educating the masses to correctly understand the relationship between consumption and accumulation), *RMRB*, July 7, 1958, 2. After learning the party's position, one commune member reportedly concluded, echoing the sacrifice-now-enjoy-later party line: "When production is not managed well, we cannot even have a bicycle; but when production is developed, then we can even buy a car."

2. Economic propaganda is a subset of the array of attempts by the CCP to shape public opinion. Other categories where one would likely find examples of

economic propaganda – and contradictory receptions to it – include, to borrow the categories of one academic survey, newspaper articles (not only advertising), radio programming, big-character posters, film, art, and literature. Frederick T. C. Yu, *Mass Persuasion in Communist China* (New York: Praeger, 1964). See also Alan P. L. Liu, *Communications and National Integration in Communist China* (Berkeley: University of California Press, 1975).

3. On the persistence of advertising utilizing bourgeois images after 1949, see Karl Gerth, "Compromising with Consumerism in Socialist China: Transnational Flows and Internal Tensions in 'Socialist Advertising'," *Past & Present*, no. 218 (Spring 2013), 203–32. For a version that includes different examples, see 葛凯 [Karl Gerth], "社会主义中国与消费主义的妥协" (The contradictions between socialist China and consumerism), *Huadong shifan daxue xuebao*, no. 4 (Winter 2013), 59–60. The first third of this chapter reframes and expands these two articles.

4. In addition to state propaganda in mass media, in the 1950s people encountered and participated in state-sponsored "socialist" spectacles. See Chang-tai Hung, *Mao's New World: Political Culture in the Early People's Republic* (Ithaca, NY: Cornell University Press, 2011).

5. On the centrality of advertising in industrial capitalism, see William Leiss et al., *Social Communication in Advertising: Persons, Products, and Images of Well-Being* (Toronto: Methuen, 1986), 49–90. On the omnipresence of the term "liberation" in the Mao era, see Harriet Evans, "The Language of Liberation: Gender and *Jiefang* in Early Chinese Communist Discourse," in Jeffrey N. Wasserstrom, ed., *Twentieth-Century China: New Approaches* (London: Routledge, 2003), 193–220.

6. Philip M. Taylor, *Munitions of the Mind: A History of Propaganda from the Ancient World to the Present Age*, 3rd ed. (Manchester: Manchester University Press, 2003), 211.

7. Liu Jialin, 新编中外广告通史 (A general history of Chinese and world advertising) (Guangzhou: Ji'nan daxue chubanshe, 2004), 146. Liu is contradicted by a list and an imprint of the business seals of sixty advertising agencies still in existence in 1956; see SMA B98-1-23 (January 16, 1956). In Tianjin, the CCP combined thirty-nine advertising agencies into one; see Su Shimei, 中国近现代商业广告史 (A history of modern and contemporary advertising in China) (Kaifeng: Henan daxue chubanshe, 2006), 102–3.

8. I address the implications of the resanctioning advertising for revenue and staffing in Karl Gerth, "Compromising with Consumerism in Socialist China." *Liberation Daily* was hardly alone among state organs that relied on capitalist practices to generate revenue. For an example of extensive smuggling by various government offices, including in their import–export businesses, see "全国各机关团体在穗采购物资自办进口货, 武装走私现象严重" (Agencies and

organizations purchase goods and foreign products in Guangzhou without permission, armed smuggling becomes rampant), *NBCK,* March 8, 1952.

9. "关于广告的健康性与严肃性: 答杨宏諴建议" (Response to Yang Hongxian about the healthiness and seriousness of advertisements), *RMRB,* April 29, 1950, 6. On the importance of *Liberation Daily,* which along with *People's Daily, Jiefangjun bao,* and *Xuexi,* was the primary avenue that the CCP used to disseminate official policy, see Patricia Stranahan, *Molding the Medium: The Chinese Communist Party and Liberation Daily* (London: Routledge, 2015). Stranahan summarizes *Liberation Daily's* importance in this way: "It propagandized the official line in a general way while simultaneously providing concrete guidelines for cadres implementing that line. Truth mattered less than ideological correctness as articles became the horns through which the Party sounded its message" (p. 165).

10. For example, Guo Min, "谈广告" (About advertisements), *RMRB,* July 16, 1956, 7.

11. See the illustrations featuring Klansmen and US oppression of blacks in *Xuanchuan hua ziliao,* no. 3 (January 1951), 15; Xu Muzhi, 这就是美國 (This is America) (Shanghai: Dadong shuju, 1951), n.p.

12. On the history of the company, which later moved to Hong Kong, then Taiwan, and finally back to China in 1991, see Li Xiaojun, 牙医史话: 中国口腔卫生文史概览 (A narrative history of dentistry: An overview of Chinese dental hygiene) (Hangzhou: Zhejiang daxue chubanshe, 2014), 331. On its later history, see Wu Hanren and Bai Zhongqi, 双城故事 从上海到台北的一次文化平移 (Stories of two cities: A cultural shift from Shanghai to Taipei) (Shanghai: Shanghai wenhua chubanshe, 2014), 161–62.

13. David Ciarlo, *Advertising Empire: Race and Visual Culture in Imperial Germany* (Cambridge, MA: Harvard University Press, 2011), 228–30. On the spread of capitalist advertising practices to China during the Republican era through multinationals, see the work by Sherman Cochran, especially "Marketing Medicine and Advertising Dreams in China, 1900–1950," in Wen-hsin Yeh, ed., *Becoming Chinese: Passages to Modernity and Beyond* (Berkeley: University of California Press, 2000), 62–97. To those familiar with the history of late nineteenth-century America, the logo evoked a minstrel show, wherein performers (often white) put on blackface makeup and lampooned recently freed blacks. Neil Herndon, "Effective Ethical Response: A New Approach to Channel Stakeholder Needs for Ethical Behavior and Socially Responsible Conduct," *Journal of Marketing Channels,* vol. 13, no. 1 (2006), 1, 63–78.

14. On the links between consumerism and raising awareness of personal deficiencies through advertising, see James B. Twitchell, *Adcult USA: The*

Triumph of Advertising in American Culture (New York: Columbia University Press, 1996), 16–32.

15. Li Xiaojun, 牙医史话: 中国口腔卫生文史概览 (A narrative history of dentistry: An overview of Chinese dental hygiene), 269. The book reprints several different Heiren advertisements, including a billboard (at pp. 327–31).

16. Banzhimendi de sixiang, "半殖民地的思想应予肃清, 国货商标不要用洋文, 黑人牙膏商标没有一个中国字, 应该改正过来" (Semi-colonial thinking should be eradicated, no more foreign language on trademarks of national products. The Heiren toothpaste trademark does not have Chinese characters and should be corrected), *Xinmin wanbao*, August 1, 1950. For another example of outraged readers complaining about trademarks using foreign languages, see Wu Yanheng and Cheng Shen, "某些货物商标广告缺乏爱国主义精神" (The trademarks and advertisements for some products lack patriotism), *RMRB*, July 19, 1951, 2; and Wang Zhengmin, "科学技术刊物不应用外文登广告" (Science journals should not publish advertisements in foreign languages), *RMRB*, February 6, 1952, 6.

17. Wen Hu, "国货商标不用洋文, 百昌行虚心接受" (No foreign language on national product trademarks, Baichanghang is receptive), *Xinmin wanbao*, August 27, 1950.

18. These advertising techniques were holdovers from a common Republican-era commercial practice. Those claiming to manufacture national products attempted to have it both ways by emphasizing, on the one hand, their "Chineseness" during surges of patriotic sentiment and NPM activities such as boycotts and, on the other, the international standards and prestige of imports by using foreign words and images. Karl Gerth, *China Made: Consumer Culture and the Creation of the Nation* (Cambridge, MA: Harvard University Asia Center, 2003), 189–90.

19. The same advertisement can also be seen in other newspapers of the time, such as *Ningbo dazhong*, September 21, 1951.

20. Ding Hao (poster designer), "我们为参加国家工业化建设而自豪" (We are proud of participating in the founding of our country's industrialization) (1954), http://chineseposters.net/posters/e16-17.php. Archived July 1, 2017. The larger website, maintained by poster collector Stefan R. Landsberger, includes an annotated collection of such women. See especially the section on "Iron Women, Foxy Ladies," https://chineseposters.net/themes/women.php. Archived April 9, 2018.

21. *JFRB*, October 2, 1949 (presumably approved for publication and put into final copy on National Day). There were many similar advertisements featuring elegantly dressed, shapely bourgeois women in *qipaos* with permed hair or men in Western suits with slicked-back hair. *Dagongbao* Shanghai (cited hereafter as *DGB* SH), April 10, 1951.

22. For an introduction to commercial advertising, specifically cigarettes, in *Shenbao*, see Weipin Tsai, *Reading Shenbao: Nationalism, Consumerism and Individuality in China, 1919–37* (London: Palgrave Macmillan, 2010). On the steady expansion of tobacco consumption among the new social classes, especially after the creation of domestic cigarette companies, see Carol Benedict, *Golden-Silk Smoke: A History of Tobacco in China, 1550–2010* (Berkeley: University of California Press, 2011), 149–77.

23. *JFRB*, October 26, 1949.

24. *JFRB*, March 20, 1951.

25. *DGB* SH, February 4, 1951.

26. Nine leading newspapers had vowed to adhere to such a ban by the end of 1950. "广州各影院拒映美国影片 沪各报停刊美国电影广告" (All cinemas in Guangzhou refuse to show American films; all newspapers in Shanghai stop publishing advertisements for American films), *RMRB*, November 14, 1950, 3. For a lengthy critique by one reader of the "unhealthy content" of advertising and how it contradicted socialism, see Chen Mo 陈默, "电影广告中的不健康成分" (Unhealthy content in film advertisements), *RMRB*, December 6, 1950, 5.

27. Companies often requested extra time to adhere to the new regulations based on current stocks, so the following memory is possibly true: a blogger (He Yu Laoda 赫玉老大), who worked in the aviation industry as a young man in Beijing in the 1960s, claimed to have encountered the original brand name during the Cultural Revolution and to have helped change it. While brushing his teeth one day, he had pondered the discrepancy between the name of the best-selling toothpaste his family used, Heiren, and Mao's writings about the struggles of blacks in America and the liberation movements in Africa. He wondered: "Why use a black person as a logo? Isn't this discriminatory toward black people?" So he composed a letter complaining to the authorities and claimed the name change to Heibai (black/white) began only shortly thereafter. "文革中黑人牙膏品牌改黑白牙膏是我惹的祸" (I am to blame for the name change of Heiren to Heibai Toothpaste during the Cultural Revolution), http://blog.sina.com.cn/s/blog_572822c70100qxh9.html. Archived December 13, 2018.

28. For an illustration of the new Heibai logo, see Zuo Xuchu, ed., 民国商标图典 (An illustrated book of trademarks in modern China) (Shanghai: Shanghai jinxiu wenzhang chubanshe, 2013), 495.

29. Chao Qi, "反对资产阶级的广告术" (Oppose bourgeois advertising techniques), *RMRB*, December 31, 1954, 2.

30. Wei Baoxian, "吉林省日用化学工厂应纠正制作商品广告中的浪费" (The waste in advertising of the toiletry industry in Jilin should be corrected), *RMRB*, April 10, 1955, 6.

31. On the history of toothpaste company mergers into state ownership, see Li Xiaojun, 牙医史话: 中国口腔卫生文史概览 (A narrative history of dentistry: An overview of Chinese dental hygiene), 269. The controversy over the name of Heiren did not end there. Whereas the name of the toothpaste in China during the 1960s and 1970s remains unclear, internationally the English name Darkie remained in place into the mid-1980s. When the American multinational Colgate acquired Hawley and Hazel in 1985, the company received complaints (perhaps thanks to the clandestine activities of its rival Proctor & Gamble) from civil rights groups in the United States about the logo. In addition, the African American comedian Eddie Murphy expressed outrage on a nationally televised talk show. Colgate eventually responded by changing the name of the product to Darlie and made the character of indeterminate race, though the Chinese name, Heiren, remained. Herndon, "Effective Ethical Response," 1, 63–78.

32. On this critique, see Christopher Lasch, *The Culture of Narcissism: American Life in an Age of Diminishing Expectations* (New York: Warner Books, 1980), 71–7. There is a large literature on the links among advertising, the expansion of needs, and the advent of industrial capitalism. See, for instance, Stuart Ewen, *Captains of Consciousness: Advertising and the Social Roots of the Consumer Culture* (New York: McGraw-Hill, 1976); Roland Marchand, *Advertising the American Dream: Making Way for Modernity, 1920–1940* (Berkeley: University of California Press, 1985); Stuart Ewen, *All Consuming Images: The Politics of Style in Contemporary Culture* (New York: Basic Books, 1988).

33. See János Kornai, *The Socialist System: The Political Economy of Communism* (Oxford: Clarendon Press, 1992).

34. Ilya Ilf and Eugenii Petrov, *Little Golden America: Two Famous Soviet Humorists Survey These United States*, tr. Charles Malamuth (New York: Farrar & Rinehart, Inc., 1937), 87. The authors criticize American advertising practices in dozens of places in the book.

35. Philip Hanson, *Advertising and Socialism: The Nature and Extent of Consumer Advertising in the Soviet Union, Poland, Hungary, and Yugoslavia* (London: Macmillan, 1974), 1–2.

36. For criticism of newspapers in cities throughout China using national holidays as an excuse to publish advertising supplements and generate more revenue, see Bao Quan, "反对刊登广告中的铺张浪费现象" (Oppose the extravagance and waste in advertising), *RMRB*, June 18, 1955, 2. The state responded to such criticism by again promising to enforce regulations on advertising. See "对本报批评的反应" (Response to criticism of our newspaper), *RMRB*, August 4, 1955, 3.

37. For a comprehensive study of the case of Yugoslavia, see Patrick Hyder Patterson, *Bought and Sold: Living and Losing the Good Life in Socialist Yugoslavia* (Ithaca, NY: Cornell University Press, 2011).

38. Despite such efforts to create a "socialist" advertising culture, historian Patrick Patterson concludes in his study of the same in Yugoslavia: "Yet beyond the verbiage, no sustained attempt to construct a consistently socialist practice of consumer persuasion can be found in these texts." Patrick Hyder Patterson, "Truth Half Told: Finding the Perfect Pitch for Advertising and Marketing in Socialist Yugoslavia, 1950–1991," *Enterprise & Society: The International Journal of Business History*, vol. 4, no. 2 (2003), 179–225 (at p. 221); Hanson, *Advertising and Socialism*, 29–31. Although advertisements in "socialist" countries shared some of these basic features, attempts to create a standard justification for the inherent contradiction of "socialist advertising" yielded heterogeneous results. There was never a unified socialist bloc of countries with a single, unified "socialist" policy toward advertising. Some countries, for instance, allowed advertisements for bourgeois products, such as perfume, that others, including China, did not. Despite these superficial differences, justifications for continuing to harness advertising on behalf of socialism appeared across the state capitalist countries at different times and in different ways. On the Soviet embrace of bourgeois advertising, see Randi Cox, "All This Can Be Yours! Soviet Commercial Advertising and the Social Construction of Space, 1928–1956," in Evgeny Dobrenko and Eric Naiman, eds., *The Landscape of Stalinism: The Art and Ideology of Soviet Space* (Seattle: University of Washington Press, 2003), 125–62.

39. "商业广告" (Commercial advertising), SMA B135-1-551 (1957).

40. Anastas Mikoyan was an appropriate person to cite as he was respected in China after having been sent to China by Stalin on the eve of the establishment of the PRC to mend relations. Chen Jian, *Mao's China and the Cold War* (Chapel Hill: University of North Carolina Press, 2001), 44–5.

41. As the report concludes, "commercial advertisements are a part of socialist commerce that cannot be eliminated." "商业广告" (Commercial advertising).

42. The new name of the product retained part of its old name to maintain some brand recognition, but it dropped the "5 minute" claim.

43. All these examples come from "商业广告" (Commercial advertising).

44. "为大批生产的药品不能宣传广告的通知" (A notice stating that pharmaceutical products that have not yet been massively manufactured should not be promoted through advertisements), SMA B123-4-556 (April 17, 1959).

45. See "提高商业广告思想艺术水平，更好地为生产和消费者服务" (Raising the ideological and artistic standards of commercial advertising to better serve production and consumers) and "提高商业广告水平" (Raising the standards of commercial advertisements), both in *JFRB*, August 4, 1959.

46. See, for instance, suggestions on making book advertising more appealing: Jin Mei, "'书刊广告' 这品种 (Advertisements about books and magazines), *RMRB*, January 13, 1962, 6. For a defense of trademarks as potentially noncapitalistic, see Chen Huaxin, "商标广告杂话" (A chat on trademark advertisements), *RMRB*, November 18, 1961, 6, who argues that trademarks are a form of information rather than an advertisement designed to deceive consumers.

47. Propaganda posters from the early 1960s included many examples featuring attractive women without any political messages. Stefan R. Landsberger, "'Life as It Ought to Be': Propaganda Art of the PRC," *IIAS Newsletter*, no. 48 (Summer 2008), 27.

48. On the importance of this slogan, see Qi Weiping and Wang Jun, "关于毛泽东'超英赶美'思想演变阶段的历史考察" (Historical research on the formation and development of Mao Zedong's Thought of "surpassing Great Britain and catching up with the United States"), *Shixue yuekan*, no. 2 (2002), 66–71.

49. Shanghai shi guanggao gongsi (Inspection Group of the Shanghai Advertising Agency), "关于服务质量与设计质量问题的调查报告" (Inspection report on issues of service and design quality in the advertising industry), SMA B123-5-78 (September 11, 1961).

50. Shanghai shi guanggao gongsi (Inspection Group of the Shanghai Advertising Agency, "关于服务质量与设计质量问题的调查报告" (Inspection report of issues of service and design quality in the advertising industry), SMA B123-5-78 (September 11, 1961). The report explains that in line with the other policy changes of the early 1960s, designers should be given higher salaries and bonuses based on work. Unincentivized designers had evaded work by plugging any and all products into a few preset designs. The results included medical product advertisements with completely unrelated clichéd images of factories, trucks, or the countryside, and products that were randomly placed against landscape backgrounds. Unincentivized designers missed deadlines. In the second quarter of 1961, two-fifths of all customers experienced delayed deliveries of one to three months, meaning they missed promotional windows. Summer advertisements for T-shirts and mosquito coils, for instance, were not ready until the fall. Clients complained of the terrible take-it-or-leave-it design service, short working hours, and frequent holidays, and some opted to give up on advertising altogether to avoid the hassles.

51. "中央宣传部关于禁止用毛主席字拼凑商标的通知" (Notice of the Central Propaganda Department on prohibiting using Chairman Mao's calligraphy in the creation of trademarks) (April 4, 1964), in Zhongyang xuanchuanbu bangongting, ed., 党的宣传工作文件选编 (1949–1966) (Selected documents of party propaganda work [1949–1966]) (Beijing: Zhonggong zhongyang dangxiao chubanshe, 1994), 1.491 (internally circulated to county-level cadres and above). This was a longstanding criticism but, apparently, it was frequently ignored. For a reader's complaint about the inappropriate but routine use of Mao's signature and inscriptions on advertising copy, see Wei Huamin, "读者来信" (Letters from readers), *RMRB*, September 29, 1951, 2. Wei complains that a fire extinguisher company used Mao's signature and his memorable line (in a 1930 letter) that "a single spark can start a prairie fire" (星星之火, 可以 燎原). Intended as a call to arms for the demoralized CCP, the saying was used by the company to teach people to be worried about the possibility of fires and the need to be prepared by buying its product.

52. "商标工作座谈会纪要" (An outline of the trademark meeting), SMA, Document 2 B170-1-1079 (February 6, 1964).

53. For a brief introduction to Mao-era propaganda posters, visit chineseposters .net, which provides a thorough introduction to posters and includes an extensive, multilingual bibliography. In China, as well as other industrial capitalist countries, there was a fluid relationship between advertising and politics. Witness the mobilization of advertising and industrial graphics for military and political campaigns in market capitalist countries throughout the twentieth century. For instance, see Elizabeth E. Guffey, *Posters: A Global History* (London: Reaktion Books, 2015).

54. CCP promotion of social consumption continued in the post-Mao era, including in what is known as "GDP worship." Since the 1980s, China's impressive GDP growth rates are used, both inside and outside China, to demonstrate the success of Chinese policies and its economic model. There are countless other examples. As a student in China in the mid-1980s, I regularly encountered *China Daily* headlines on national production accomplishments – e.g., "Fertilizer production up 3.7%!" – that people at home and abroad were meant to consume as evidence of policy success and shared abundance.

55. To complement the emphasis on advertising as a form of economic propaganda, this section focuses on economic propaganda posters rather than posters promoting political, military, or social political themes, such as the figure of Mao, the importance of sport and physical fitness, the worthiness of emulating revolutionary role models (e.g., Lei Feng), and political unity with ethnic minorities. Of course, the same poster could deliver more than one

message. Military parades and other symbols of military power, such as a mushroom cloud, were also forms of economic propaganda that reminded viewers that the surplus went to fill national, collective needs. For an introduction to Chinese propaganda posters during the Mao era, see the essays in Harriet Evans and Stephanie Donald, eds., *Picturing Power in the People's Republic: Posters of the Cultural Revolution* (Lanham, MD: Rowman & Littlefield, 1999). In addition to easy access on the web by searching "Chinese propaganda posters," there are many published collections. Two that include commentary are: Stefan Landsberger, *Chinese Propaganda Posters: From Revolution to Modernization* (Armonk, NY: M.E. Sharpe, 1995); Anchee Min, Jie Zhang, and Duoduo, *Chinese Propaganda Posters* (Cologne: Taschen, 2008). Landsberger has compiled an extensive online collection organized by categories: www.iisg.nl/landsberger/. Consulted December 11, 2018.

56. Social realism stands in sharp contrast to what one scholar of American advertising has labeled "capitalist realism," which emphasizes consumption, individualism, and private ownership. Michael Schudson, *Advertising, the Uneasy Persuasion: Its Dubious Impact on American Society* (New York: Basic Books, 1986).

57. "Advertising in the Communist Press: And What It Reveals About Living," *East Europe*, vol. 8 (September 1959), 31–8.

58. Elizabeth Swayne, "Soviet Advertising: Communism Imitates Capitalism," in C. H. Sandage and Vernon Fryburger, eds., *The Role of Advertising* (Homewood, IL: R. D. Irwin, 1960), 96.

59. On the ways advertising uses images to persuade people through emotional appeals, see Paul Messaris, *Visual Persuasion: The Role of Images in Advertising* (Thousand Oaks, CA: Sage Publications, 1997).

60. On the Soviet inspiration, see Victoria E. Bonnell, *Iconography of Power: Soviet Political Posters under Lenin and Stalin* (Berkeley: University of California Press, 1997).

61. For these and other others mentioned, see the collection 十年宣传画选集 (A selection of propaganda posters during the ten years) (Shanghai: Shanghai renmin meishu chubanshe, 1960). For a longer list of poster categories and examples, including these, see Shen Kuiyi, "Publishing Posters Before the Cultural Revolution," *Modern Chinese Literature and Culture*, vol. 12, no. 2 (Fall 2000), 184–5.

62. Stefan R. Landsberger and Marien van der Heijden, *Chinese Propaganda Posters: The IISH-Landsberger Collections* (Munich: Prestel, 2009), 2.

63. According to the editor of a 1960 anthology of posters, the mission of propaganda posters (宣传画) was "publicizing and agitating for political movements and economic production" conducted through "high volume printing and circulation throughout the whole nation"; 十年宣传画选集

(A selection of propaganda posters during the ten years), quoted in Shen, "Publishing Posters Before the Cultural Revolution," 177. "Propaganda poster" is a general category that includes subcategories such as reproductions of paintings.

64. Landsberger, "'Life as It Ought to Be,'" 26.

65. Taylor, *Munitions of the Mind*, 202; See one such example of primary students looking at such a display in Huang Shengmin, Ding Junjie, and Liu Yinghua, eds., 中国广告图史 (An illustrated history of Chinese advertisements) (Guangzhou: *Nanfang ribao* chubanshe, 2006), 239.

66. There he met an elderly farmer who told him that two neighboring villages had to be abandoned when their residents starved to death during the Great Leap famine. This ended his belief in socialist propaganda. Shen, "Publishing Posters Before the Cultural Revolution," 196. For an overview of the policy, see Thomas P. Bernstein, *Up to the Mountains and Down to the Villages: The Transfer of Youth from Urban to Rural China* (New Haven: Yale University Press, 1977).

67. For example, see the reactions of the students rusticated from Guangzhou, in Anita Chan, Richard Madsen, and Jonathan Unger, *Chen Village: Revolution to Globalization*, 3rd ed. (Berkeley: University of California Press, 2009).

68. On pre-1949 attempts to limit the economic and cultural impact of Hollywood, see Zhiwei Xiao, "Anti-Imperialism and Film Censorship During the Nanjing Decade, 1927–1937," in Sheldon Hsiao-peng Lu, *Transnational Chinese Cinemas: Identity, Nationhood, Gender* (Honolulu: University of Hawai'i Press, 1997), 35–58.

69. See Tina Mai Chen, "Propagating the Propaganda Film: The Meaning of Film in Chinese Communist Party Writings, 1949–1965," *Modern Chinese Literature and Culture*, vol. 15, no. 2 (Fall 2003), 154–93; Zhao Qian, "成都解放后看电影实行 '一票一座'" (After Liberation, Chengdu introduces a "ticketed seat" system for films). See http://news.sina.com.cn/c/2009-09-28/055116369525s.shtml. Archived August 26, 2018. For statistics on audiences, see Yingjin Zhang, *Chinese National Cinema* (New York: Routledge, 2004), 192, 201.

70. See Bonnie S. McDougall, *Mao Zedong's "Talks at the Yan'an Conference on Literature and Art": A Translation of the 1943 Text with Commentary* (Ann Arbor: Center for Chinese Studies, University of Michigan, 1980). Mao based his position on earlier Chinese and foreign ideas of the role of the arts to advance politics. See Paul G. Pickowicz, *Marxist Literary Thought in China: The Influence of Ch'ü Ch'iu-pai* (Berkeley: University of California Press, 1981).

71. For an overview of Chinese exports, see Tina Mai Chen, "International Film Circuits and Global Imaginaries in the People's Republic of China, 1949–57," *Journal of Chinese Cinemas*, vol. 3, no. 2 (2009), 149–61.

72. See Paul Clark, *Chinese Cinema: Culture and Politics Since 1949* (Cambridge: Cambridge University Press, 1987), 30–4.

73. Odd Arne Westad, *Decisive Encounters: The Chinese Civil War, 1946–1950* (Stanford: Stanford University Press, 2003), 278–9.

74. The culture industry, in other words, had people with their own vested interests in banning films from market capitalist countries that had something to do with their own personal gain and not necessarily the larger state capitalist goals. Zhiwei Xiao, "The Expulsion of American Films from China, 1949–1950," *Twentieth Century China*, vol. 30, no. 1 (November 2004), 65–6. An article published in the November 18, 1950, *Dagongbao* argued that the cost of imported Hollywood films between 1945 and 1950 could have paid for the production of 2,800 Chinese films (see Xiao, "The Expulsion of American Films," 72n34).

75. Xiao, "The Expulsion of American Films," 69.

76. Chen Mo, "电影广告中的不健康成分" (Unhealthy content in film advertisements). For a reader's complaint that film advertising opted to make money rather than promote socialist values, see Dong Juxian, "电影广告应当严肃" (Film advertising should be serious), *RMRB*, March 11, 1951, 5.

77. "读者来信: 翻译影片的片名应该改进" (Letters from readers: The translations of film names should be improved), *RMRB*, August 26, 1951, 2; Liu Dishan, "苏联电影在中国: 五十年代的考察" (Soviet movies in China: An examination of the 1950s), *Dianying yishu*, no. 4 (2008), 55–60.

78. Qian Xuezhao, "来信摘要" (Abstracts of letters), *RMRB*, March 21, 1951, 6; see also Chen Bingkun, "应注意电影 注广告" 和 "说明" 的思想内容" (The need to pay attention to ideological aspects of film "advertisements" and "introductions"), *RMRB*, September 11, 1951, 2.

79. Mi Ruo, "'上影画报' 的方向是什么?" (What is the direction of *Shanghai Film Pictorial*?), *Zhongguo dianying zazhi*, no. 10 (1958), 71–2. The magazine *Dazhong dianying* (*Mass Films*) was criticized for disseminating bourgeois consumerism. See Gao Hongtao, "我们对 '大众电影' 方向的看法" (Our view of the direction of *Mass Films*), *Zhongguo dianying zazhi*, no. 12 (1958), 52; Han Jianwen, "'大众电影' 的封面和封底" (The cover page and back page of *Mass Films*), *Zhongguo dianying zazhi*, no. 12 (1958), 52–3.

80. Clark, *Chinese Cinema*, 39.

81. Zhang Shuoguo, "解放初期上海电影发行放映初探 (1949–1952)" (A preliminary study on the distribution of movies in Shanghai during the early years of Liberation [1949–1952]), *Dianying yishu*, no. 1 (2008), 96. See also Huang Zongjiang, ed.,美国电影: 帝国主义的侵略工具 (American films: Tools of imperialist invasion) (Nanjing: Jiangnan chubanshe, 1951); Bo Fen, 好莱坞: 电影帝国 (Hollywood: Cinematic imperialism) (Shanghai: Hufeng chubanshe, 1951).

82. "中国人民电影事业一年来的光辉成就" (The glorious achievements of the Chinese people's film industry during the past year), *Wenhuibao*, January 6, 1951.

83. Huang Zongjiang, "美国电影毒在那里" (Where is the poison in American films), in Nanjing wenlian dianying bu, ed., 美国电影: 帝国主义的侵略工具 (American films: Tools of the imperialist invasion), 1–19. Earlier articles expressing similar sentiments include: "本报座谈会记录妇女界对美国电影的看法" (Our newspaper symposium records women's views on American films), *Wenhuibao*, September 19, 1949; Wang Jing'an, "要发动广大群众了解美片的毒素" (The need to mobilize the masses to understand the toxins in American films), *Wenhuibao*, September 19, 1949.

84. "西片发行职工发表声明, 坚决拥护停映美片, 抛开个人利益为抗美而奋斗" (Western film distributors issue statements that strongly advocate a stop to showing American films, to leave aside their personal interests and strive for resistance to the United States), *Wenhuibao*, November 17, 1950. See also Ji Zhifeng, "制毒大本营, 好莱坞的剖视" (The basecamp of poison: An analysis and observation of Hollywood), in Huang Zongjiang, 美国电影: 帝国主义的侵略工具 (American films: Tools of the imperialist invasion), 27–8.

85. Chen Cangye, "我对美国电影的看法" (My view of American imperialist movies), *Wenhuibao*, September 16, 1950.

86. Chen Haorong, "我同意陈苍叶的看法" (I agree with Chen Cangye's points), *Wenhuibao*, October 7, 1950.

87. "对症下药" (Find the right medicine), *Wenhuibao*, October 7, 1950.

88. Zhang Shuoguo, "解放初期上海电影发行放映初探 (1949–1952)" (A preliminary study on the distribution of movies in Shanghai during the early years of Liberation [1949–1952]), 95–6. China was not the only postwar country anxious about the spread of Hollywood and the "irresistible empire" of America. On European anxieties, see Victoria De Grazia, *Irresistible Empire: America's Advance Through Twentieth-Century Europe* (Cambridge, MA: The Belknap Press of Harvard University Press, 2005).

89. Xiao, "The Expulsion of American Films," 68.

90. Tina Mai Chen, "Film and Gender in Sino-Soviet Cultural Exchange, 1949–1969," in Thomas P. Bernstein and Hua-Yu Li, eds., *China Learns from the Soviet Union, 1949–Present* (Lanham, MD: Lexington Books, 2010), 443n13.

91. Zhang Shuoguo, "解放初期上海电影发行放映初探 (1949–1952)" (A preliminary study on the distribution of movies in Shanghai during the early years of Liberation [1949–1952]), 97–100.

92. Chen Chi-hua, "Films for the People," *People's China*, vol. 24, no. 10 (December 16, 1953), 10–13.

93. "电影院， 电影放映队应重视影片内容的解说工作" (Cinema and traveling film production teams should pay attention to the interpretation of film content), *RMRB*, August 5, 1952, 2; "帮助工农兵看电影" (Help workers, peasants, and soldiers watch films), *RMRB*, June 15, 1952, 3; "电影放映前后应多作宣传工作" (The need to do more promotion work before and after playing a film), *RMRB*, June 30, 1952, 2; "中国影片经理公司总公司　注意关于翻译片的宣传解释工作" (China Film Management Corporation: Pay attention to the publicity and interpretation of translated films), *RMRB*, July 3, 1952, 3.

94. Liu Dishan, "苏联电影在中国：五十年代的考察" (Soviet movies in China: An examination of the 1950s).

95. Matthew D. Johnson, "International and Wartime Origins of the Propaganda State: The Motion Picture in China, 1897–1955," PhD dissertation, University of California, San Diego, 2008, ch. 5; Zhang Jishun, "Cultural Consumption and Popular Reception of the West in Shanghai, 1950–1966," *The Chinese Historical Review*, vol. 12, no. 1 (Spring 2005), 97–126.

96. Zhang, *Chinese National Cinema*.

97. See Chen, "Propagating the Propaganda Film," 154–93.

98. For an analysis of the themes in mass-produced "people's literature" (人民文学), see Krista Van Fleit Hang, *Literature the People Love: Reading Chinese Texts from the Early Maoist Period (1949–1966)* (New York: Palgrave Macmillan, 2013). Hang demonstrates that pre–Cultural Revolution literary production was not merely didactic but also intended to entertain and attract large audiences. As a result, writers had leeway to experiment. For a contrasting emphasis on the CCP's successful use of cultural production (the visual and performance arts) to advance its political agenda, see Hung, *Mao's New World*.

99. See Gerth, *China Made*, ch. 7.

100. I thank Bian He for pointing out the Mao-era function of diaries as a way for people to police themselves, using the CCP's definitions of "bourgeois" and "socialist" thought and action.

101. Zhou Wenlin, "资产阶级思想无孔不入" (Bourgeois thoughts are pervasive), *Hangzhou ribao*, January 26, 1964. As noted, it is impossible to know whether such letters are from real people or are editorial fabrications. For my purposes, the question of veracity is secondary to my point that these letters propagated state consumerist norms to newspaper readers rather than reflecting the "real thoughts" of "average" Chinese.

102. Li Arong, "要把无产阶级家谱续好" (We need to continue the proletarian family line), *Hangzhou ribao*, February 22, 1964.

103. These four films show the "socialist" values that the state propagandized. In *Bumper Harvest* (丰收, 1953), a local party secretary visits Beijing, where an audience with Chairman Mao and a visit to a state farm inspires him to launch a "patriotic production campaign" (爱国增产运动) in his village. The name of the film gives away its ending. In *A Wave of Unrest* (一场风波, 1954), a daughter uses the 1950 Marriage Law to fight the head of the village clan so that both she and her mother (a widow who customarily would not remarry) can marry the men they love and happily continue farming on behalf of the country. In *Summer Story* (夏天的故事, 1955), an educated youth returns to his home village to help with production. He uses the knowledge learned in school to voluntarily investigate the long-term accounting problems caused by two farmers who use their control of the accounts to embezzle grain. In the end, he decides to forego returning to school and assumes control of the accounts and manages a village plan to establish a tractor station. In *Spring in the Marshes* (水乡的春天, 1955), a village overcomes adversity by transforming marshland into productive paddy fields, resulting in a bumper harvest.

104. Meng Liye, "从农村来的一封信" (A letter from the countryside), *Dianying yishu*, no. A2 (1956), 73.

105. Zhang Jishun, 远去的都市: 1950年代的上海 (A city displaced: Shanghai in the 1950s) (Beijing: Shehui kexue wenxian chubanshe, 2015), 283.

106. Due to these films, comfortable lifestyles became so associated with market capitalist countries that "Western" (洋) became a shorthand for the comfortable, Westernized lifestyle on display in Hong Kong films. Zhang Jishun, "Cultural Consumption and Popular Reception of the West in Shanghai, 1950–1966," 109–11.

107. Zhang Jishun, 远去的都市 (A city displaced: Shanghai in the 1950s), 300.

108. Zhang Jishun, 远去的都市 (A city displaced: Shanghai in the 1950s), 309.

109. Zhang Jishun, "Cultural Consumption and Popular Reception of the West in Shanghai, 1950–1966," 116–17.

110. Zhang Jishun, 远去的都市 (A city displaced: Shanghai in the 1950s), 295–6.

111. Zhang Jishun, 远去的都市 (A city displaced: Shanghai in the 1950s), 284–5.

112. "上海市电影局" (Shanghai municipal movie office), SMA, B170-1-1149 (March 22, 1965).

State Consumerism in the Service Sector

1. Xue Muqiao and his co-authors explain the theoretical basis of the Socialist Transformation of the capitalist sector and its "socialist" outcomes in Xue Muqiao, Su Xing, and Lin Zili, 中国国民经济的社会主义改造 (The Socialist Transformation of the national economy in China) (Beijing:

Renmin chubanshe, 1959). For the quoted words and terms, see pp. 24, 50, 141, 147, and 154.

2. Robert C. Friend, "What Is It Like to Go Shopping in China?" *China Reconstructs*, vol. 13, no. 4 (1964), 31–3.

3. Zhu Zhongyu, "为社会主义而笑" (Smiling for socialism), *RMRB*, March 26, 1958, 8. His conclusion anticipates sociological work on how capitalism commodifies expression, emotion, and "the presentation of the self" as part of emotional labor. See, for instance, the work by Erving Goffman, including *The Presentation of Self in Everyday Life* (Woodstock, NY: Overlook Press, 1973) and Arlie Russell Hochschild, particularly *The Managed Heart: Commercialization of Human Feeling* (Berkeley: University of California Press, 1983).

4. "商业工作　定能跃进" (Commercial work definitely can make a leap forward), *RMRB*, February 14, 1958, 1.

5. Muqiao Xue, *China's Socialist Economy* (Beijing: Foreign Languages Press, 1981), 120–1. The CCP did have successes that they trumpeted as victories for consumers. For instance, as the CCP told the population and the world, it defeated hyperinflation and the associated mass anxieties. In 1976, the CCP contrasted Chinese price stability with the "turmoil" in capitalist countries, where "ordinary people and their families are haunted daily by inflation." Kuang-hsi Peng, *Why China Has No Inflation* (Peking: Foreign Languages Press, 1976), front matter.

6. Lian Lingling (Lien Ling-ling), 打造消费天堂: 百货公司与近代上海城市文化 (Creating a paradise for consumption: Department stores and modern urban culture in Shanghai) (Beijing: Shehui kexue wenxian chubanshe, 2018), 10–11; Shanghai baihuo gongsi, Shanghai shehui kexueyuan jingji yanjiusuo, Gongshang xingzheng guanliju, eds., 上海近代百货商业史 (A history of modern department store commerce in Shanghai) (Shanghai: Shanghai shehui kexue chubanshe, 1988), 101–8; Ching-hwang Yen, "Wing-on and the Kwok Brothers: A Case of Pre-war Chinese Entrepreneurs," in Kerrie L. MacPherson, ed., *Asian Department Stores* (Surrey: Curzon, 1998), 47–65.

7. On the links between the shift from small shops to department stores that accompanied the expansion of industrial capitalism and the need for larger, more capital-intensive retailing and marketing, see Geoffrey Crossick, and Serge Jaumain, eds., *Cathedrals of Consumption: The European Department Store, 1850–1939* (Aldershot: Ashgate, 1999).

8. On the expansion of this chain of stores, see Wang Xiaotian and Liu Zhixin, "中国百货公司在京成立 领导组成全国工业品推销网 增设省市分支公司一百余处" (China Department Store Company established in Beijing, forming a national industrial sales network and adding more than a hundred provincial and municipal branches), *RMRB*. April 4, 1950, 4. On the growth of

its network over the following years, see Shangyebu baihuoju, ed., 中国百货商业 (Chinese general commerce) (Beijing: Beijing daxue chubanshe, 1989), 17–31.

9. Zhejiang baihuo gongsi, ed., 浙江百货商业志 (Annals of Zhejiang department store commerce) (Hangzhou: Zhejiang renmin chubanshe, 1990), 7–9, which includes the names of the cities and counties in the province that set up stores. Note that "department store" describes any store selling many different types of items, in contrast to specialty stores. Their size varied from massive stores in major cities to more modest one-story operations in provincial towns.

10. Zheijiang baihuo gongsi, ed., 浙江百货商业志 (Annals of Zhejiang department store commerce), 56.

11. On the way pre-1949 department stores – and other forms of commodity displays such as advertising and exhibitions – began to industrialize consumption and facilitate expanding consumerism, see Karl Gerth, *China Made: Consumer Culture and the Creation of the Nation* (Cambridge, MA: Harvard University Asia Center, 2003), chs. 5 and 6. On department stores more generally, see Rudi Laermans, "Learning to Consume: Early Department Stores and the Shaping of the Modern Consumer Culture (1860–1914)," *Theory, Culture & Society*, vol. 10, no. 4 (November 1993), 79–102.

12. The network of the Zhejiang branch stores helped spread products such as thermoses to rural residents; see Zhejiang baihuo gongsi, ed., 浙江百货商业志 (Annals of Zhejiang department store commerce), 97–8. The policies of provincial and local self-reliance helped industrialize the country faster but they limited the economies of scale and duplicated production occurring elsewhere. Zhejiang, for instance, raised provincial self-sufficiency for everyday manufactured goods from 50 percent in 1957 to 80 percent by 1963 (p. 32). On the costs/benefits of the policies of self-sufficiency and their contribution to inter-provincial inequality, see Carl Riskin, *China's Political Economy: The Quest for Development since 1949* (Oxford: Oxford University Press, 1987), 201–22.

13. The CCP preferred "the masses" rather than "the proletariat," which implied an urban workforce rather than, as intended at the time, a workforce that included other working classes such as peasants and soldiers.

14. "私营工商业应当力求改造" (Private industry and commerce should strive for transformation), *RMRB* June 17, 1950, 1.

15. On the pre-1949 history of Nanjing Road and the department stores catering to elites, see Wellington K. K. Chan, "Selling Goods and Promoting a New Commercial Culture: The Four Premier Department Stores on Nanjing Road, 1917–1937," in Sherman Cochran, ed., *Inventing Nanjing Road:*

Commercial Culture in Shanghai, 1900–1945 (Ithaca, NY: East Asia Program, Cornell University, 1999), 19–36; Yang Tianliang, "上海四大百货公司" (Shanghai's four great department stores), in Xin Ping, Hu Zhenghao, and Li Xuechang, eds., 民国社会大观 (A comprehensive view of society in the Republic of China) (Fuzhou: Fujian renmin chubanshe, 1991), 353–8.

16. On the early history of Yong'an Department Store, see Wellington K. K. Chan, "Personal Styles, Cultural Values and Management: The Sincere and Wing on Companies in Shanghai and Hong Kong, 1900–1941," *Business History Review*, vol. 70, no. 2 (1996), 141–66. On this culture more generally, see Leo Ou-fan Lee, *Shanghai Modern: The Flowering of a New Urban Culture in China, 1930–1945* (Cambridge, MA: Harvard University Press, 1999).

17. Shanghai shehui kexueyuan jingji yanjiusuo, ed., 上海永安公司的产生, 发展和改造 (The birth, development, and transformation of Shanghai's Yong'an Company) (Shanghai: Shanghai renmin chubanshe, 1981), 236; Lien Ling-ling, "上海百货公司的社会主义改造, 1949–1956 (The socialist transformation of Shanghai Department Store, 1949–1956), in Hsieh Kuo-hsing, ed., 改革与改造, 冷战初期两岸的粮食, 土地与工商业变革 (Reform and reconstruction: The transformation of rice supplies, land reform, and industry and commerce in early Cold War Mainland China and Taiwan) (Taipei: Institute of Modern History, Academia Sinica, 2010), 340–1.

18. Guo was known as Leon Kwak, Lam Shuen Kwok, or L. S. Kwok. On his pre-1949 activities, see Wen-hsin Yeh, *Shanghai Splendor: Economic Sentiments and the Making of Modern China, 1843–1949* (Berkeley: University of California Press, 2007), 162–83.

19. Shanghai shehui kexueyuan jingji yanjiusuo, ed., 上海永安公司的产生, 发展和改造 (The birth, development, and transformation of Shanghai's Yong'an Company), 262–3.

20. Shanghai shehui kexueyuan jingji yanjiusuo, ed., 上海永安公司的产生, 发展和改造 (The birth, development, and transformation of Shanghai's Yong'an Company), 236.

21. Shanghai shehui kexueyuan jingji yanjiusuo, ed., 上海永安公司的产生, 发展和改造 (The birth, development, and transformation of Shanghai's Yong'an Company), 240–1. Yong'an included an annex, with two connecting bridges, that included a floor for leisure activities (游乐休闲场所). See Lian Lingling, 打造消费天堂: 百货公司与近代上海城市文化 (Creating a paradise for consumption: Department stores and modern urban culture in Shanghai), 169, 176.

22. For details, see Xin Zhongguo diyi dian de gushi bianweihui, ed., 新中国第一店的故事 (The story of New China's Number One Store) (Shanghai: Shanghai dianzi chuban youxian gongsi, 2012), 31. For brief histories of the counterparts in cities elsewhere in China during the Mao era, see Shangyebu

baihuoju, ed., 中国百货商业 (Chinese commerce), ch. 5. The state takeover of the Four Department Stores occurred at different paces; see Lien Ling-ling, "上海百货公司的社会主义改造，1949–1956" (The socialist transformation of Shanghai Department Store, 1949–1956), 333–72.

23. During the NPM, stores such as Yong'an had similarly responded to popular calls for the consumption of "national products" and the boycott of "foreign products" by featuring China-made "national products" in their windows while inside continuing to rely heavily on the sale of imports. Gerth, *China Made*, 152–3, and ch. 5 for Republican-era efforts to create commercial spaces for exclusively "national products."

24. Shanghai shehui kexueyuan jingji yanjiusuo, ed., 上海永安公司的产生，发展和改造 (The birth, development, and transformation of Shanghai's Yong'an Company), 242–7. Even when the store began to sell leisure activities to less affluent customers on its rooftop, the elevators took them directly to the roof, bypassing the floors with the products they could not afford and the customers with whom they seldom mixed.

25. Shanghai shehui kexueyuan jingji yanjiusuo, ed., 上海永安公司的产生，发展和改造 (The birth, development, and transformation of Shanghai's Yong'an Company), 288.

26. Li Ying, "Shops and Shoppers in Shanghai," *China Reconstructs*, vol. 13, no. 10 (1964), 49–50.

27. Shanghai shehui kexueyuan jingji yanjiusuo, ed., 上海永安公司的产生，发展和改造 (The birth, development, and transformation of Shanghai's Yong'an Company), 259.

28. "公私合营工业企业暂行条例" (Provisional regulations on public–private joint venture industries and enterprises), *RMRB*, September 6, 1954, 2; "关于'公司合营工业企业暂行条例'的说明（一九五四年九月二日政务院第二百二十三次政务会议通过）" (An explanation of the "provisional regulations" on public–private joint ventures in industries and enterprises [Adopted by the 223rd Administrative Council of the State Council on September 2, 1954]), *RMRB* September 6, 1954, 2. Like other capitalists, Guo received "interest" payments from the state and remained useful as a propaganda tool both in the late 1950s, when he publicly praised the superior consumer experience provided by socialism, and at the start of the Cultural Revolution, when his house was ransacked by Red Guards and its contents were used to teach the need for continued class struggle against capitalists (Chapter 6). See Denise Y. Ho, *Curating Revolution: Politics on Display in Mao's China* (Cambridge: Cambridge University Press, 2018), ch. 5.

29. Shangyebu shangye zuzhi yu jishuju商店橱窗陈列与内部布置 (Store window displays and interior decorations) (Beijing: Caizheng jingji chubanshe, 1955), 11–13.

30. Shangyebu shangye zuzhi yu jishuju,商店橱窗陈列与内部布置 (Store window displays and interior decorations), 39–49.

31. "百货业职工向顾客宣传" (Employees in department stores propagandize customers), *Wenhuibao*, July 21, 1950.

32. "橱窗宣传工作应该经常化" (Window promotion work should be regularized), *RMRB*, November 18, 1951, 4.

33. "橱窗宣传工作应该经常化" (Window promotion work should be regularized).

34. Ma Jianxiong (麻建雄), 武汉老橱窗 (Old window displays in Wuhan) (Wuhan: Wuhan chubanshe, 2013), 250.

35. "提高商业广告思想艺术水平，更好地为生产和消费者服务" (Raising the ideological and artistic standards of commercial advertising to better serve production and consumers), *JFRB*, August 4, 1959.

36. Ma Jianxiong (麻建雄), 武汉老橱窗 (Old window displays in Wuhan), 250.

37. Fan Tianyi (樊天益), "商店橱窗巡礼" (A tour of shop windows), *JFRB*, August 4, 1959.

38. Fan Tianyi (樊天益), "商店橱窗巡礼" (A tour of shop windows).

39. Fan Tianyi (樊天益), "商店橱窗巡礼" (A tour of shop windows).

40. On the ways industrial consumerism teaches people to experience the world as individuals, see Don Slater, *Consumer Culture and Modernity* (Oxford: Polity Press, 1997).

41. Shen Wenying, "一幅背季的电影广告" (An out-of-season movie advertisement), *RMRB*, June 28, 1953, 2.

42. Shanghaishi guanggao gongsi, ed., "关于服务质量与设计质量问题的调查报告" (Inspection report of issues of service and design quality in the advertising industry), SMA B123-5-78 (September 11, 1961).

43. "首都东安等商场 实行明码标价售货 西单等商场应切实做到明码交易" (Capital Dong'an Department Store and others implement a policy of having clearly marked prices on every product they sell; Xidan Department Store and others should similarly put prices on every good they sell), *RMRB*, February 7, 1950, 4. See also Nie Rongzhen, Zhang Youyu, and Wu Han, "北京市人民政府令,一九五〇年一月廿日, 兹制定"北京市公立（市）场管理暂行规则"公布" (Beijing government decree [January 1, 1950, the "Provisional Rules for Public Administration of Beijing Municipality" are promulgated]), *RMRB*, January 22, 1950, 6; "保护正当商业合法经营 市府颁布四项法令 取缔囤积居奇空头交易等非法行为" (To protect legitimate business operations, the municipal government issues four decrees to ban illegal activities such as hoarding), *RMRB*, January 22, 1950, 4.

44. Zi Fei, "苏州举办私营企业生产改进展览会的方法值得提倡" (The Suzhou way of holding an exhibition to promote nationwide how private firms improve their business worth), *RMRB*, December 9, 1951, 2.

45. Dong Qian, "规训与溢出: '新民晚报'与社会主义上海商业空间和商业文化建构 1949–1966" (Discipline and overflow: *Xinmin Evening News* and the construction of Shanghai's socialist business space and business culture 1949–1966), *Xinwen daxue*, no. 5 (2013), 1–14.

46. Kang Weizhong, "北京朝阳门菜市变了样" (Beijing's Chaoyang Gate Vegetable Market changes), *RMRB*, May 1, 1951, 7.

47. Hai Lan and Ye Shitao, "兴旺繁荣气象新: 记十年来我国市场的变化" (Prosperity and the new environment: Recalling ten years of changes in the market of our country), *RMRB*, September 24, 1959, 10.

48. Muqiao Xue, *China's Socialist Economy*, 20.

49. Chris Bramall, *Chinese Economic Development* (London: Routledge, 2009), 130–1, and his discussion of the political economy of the Great Leap more generally. For a detailed discussion on the prevention of urban famine at the expense of the countryside, see Felix Wemheuer, *Famine Politics in Maoist China and the Soviet Union* (New Haven: Yale University Press, 2014), 115–53.

50. Dorothy J. Solinger, *Chinese Business Under Socialism: The Politics of Domestic Commerce, 1949–1980* (Berkeley: University of California Press, 1984), ch. 4.

51. Muqiao Xue, *China's Socialist Economy*, 31–2, 42, 105–7. See also Hanchao Lu, *Beyond the Neon Lights: Everyday Shanghai in the Early Twentieth Century* (Berkeley: University of California Press, 1999); Robert W. Swallow, *Sidelights on Peking Life* (Peking: China Booksellers Ltd., 1927).

52. See, for instance, 中共上海市第一商业局委员会三反整风领导小组办公室 (Office of the Leading Group of the Three-Antis Rectification of the Committee of Shanghai First Business Bureau of the CCP), "局党委扩大会议有关党委官僚主义方面的综合材料" (Comprehensive materials on bureaucratic aspects of party committees for the expanded meeting of party committees), SMA B123-4-568 (July 31, 1960).

53. See Chris Bramall, *Industrialization of Rural China* (Oxford: Oxford University Press, 2007).

54. On the "culture of shortages" and the general shopping experience in the Soviet Union, see Julie Hessler, *A Social History of Soviet Trade: Trade Policy, Retail Practices, and Consumption, 1917–1953* (Princeton, NJ: Princeton University Press, 2004). Economist Dwight H. Perkins labels queues "de facto rations." For a discussion of all three ways to deal with shortages, see his *Market Control and Planning in Communist China* (Cambridge, MA: Harvard University Press, 1966), 177–97.

55. Hua Xinmin, "那过去的事情 – 回忆五十年代" (That bygone era: Remembering the 1950s), China News Digest, http://archives.cnd.org/HXWK/author/HUA-Xinmin/kd090911-4.gb.html. Archived August 15, 2017.

56. Greg MacGregor, "Shopper in China Has Long Wait," *New York Times*, June 25, 1957.

57. Hua Xinmin, "那过去的事情 – 回忆五十年代" (That bygone era: Remembering the 1950s).

58. Zhu Zemin, "过去是穷排队 现在是富排队天津太平庄街居民认清了买东西为什么要排队" (Formerly a queue of poverty, now a queue of wealth. Residents of Taipingzhuang Street in Tianjin understand why they queue to shop), *RMRB*, December 7, 1957, 4. Stores in the Soviet Union had made similar attempts to air grievances through complaint books, letters from readers published in newspapers, customer conferences, and other forms of structured feedback and participation. Amy E. Randall, *The Soviet Dream World of Retail Trade and Consumption in the 1930s* (New York: Palgrave Macmillan, 2008), 134–52.

59. Zhu Zemin, "过去是穷排队 现在是富排队天津太平庄街居民认清了买东西为什么要排队" (Formerly a queue of poverty, now a queue of wealth. Residents of Taipingzhuang Street in Tianjin understand why they queue to shop).

60. Wen Ying, "让社员们很快买到东西" (Allow cooperative members to make purchases swiftly), *RMRB*, June 5, 1954, 2.

61. Zhu Zemin, "过去是穷排队 现在是富排队天津太平庄街居民认清了买东西为什么要排队" (Formerly a queue of poverty, now a queue of wealth. Residents of Taipingzhuang Street in Tianjin understand why they queue to shop).

62. Sha Hang, "越过 '长蛇阵'" (Step over the "snake-like line"), *Hangzhou ribao*, March 2, 1958.

63. "北京市若干商店和公共场所采取措施, 大力消除顾客排队现象" (Measures taken by some shops and public places in Beijing to eliminate customer queuing), *RMRB*, February 11, 1958, 3.

64. Fixed investment in machinery, buildings, and technology rose to more than 31 percent of GDP. The all-out push for industrialization across the country included transferring labor out of the service sector, light industry, and the production of grain, the most fundamental consumer good. These workers were moved out of the service sector and into making goods for producers such as iron and steel production, often through the small-scale "backyard furnaces" set up around the country. Likewise, over one hundred million people worked in farmland water conservancy projects during the Great Leap. Bramall, *Chinese Economic Development*, 125; David Allen Pietz, *The Yellow River: The Problem of Water in Modern China* (Cambridge, MA: Harvard University Press, 2015), 207.

65. On the service industry during the Great Leap Forward, see Shangyebu jingji yanjiusuo, ed., 新中国商业三十年 (征求意见稿) (Thirty years of New China's business: Draft Soliciting Opinions) (Internal circulation, 1980), 95–6. On the state's framing of these policies to include the "emancipation"

of women from the household, see Ch'eng-chih Shih, *Urban Commune Experiments in Communist China* (Hong Kong: Union Research Institute, 1962), 99–104. On the construction of gender to further state extraction in China during the Mao era, there is no equivalent for China of Wendy Z. Goldman, *Women at the Gates: Gender and History in Stalin's Russia* (Cambridge: Cambridge University Press, 2002).

66. Xiong Yuezhi, ed., 上海通史,第12卷: 当代经济 (General history of Shanghai, Volume 12, The contemporary economy) (Shanghai: Shanghai renmin chubanshe, 1999), 202.

67. Shangyebu shangye jingji yanjiusuo, ed., 新中国商业史稿 (1949–1982) (Draft of New China's business history, 1949–1982) (Beijing: Zhongguo caizheng jingji chubanshe, 1984), 152; Shangyebu jingji yanjiusuo, ed., 新中国商业三十年 (Thirty years of New China's business).

68. "加强政治思想工作, 提高社会主义觉悟, 天桥百货商场职工举起大跃进旗帜, 减少人员一半, 实行一天一班顶到底 吸收商业工作的传统经验, 服务态度大改观" (Strengthening political and ideological work, improving socialist consciousness: The staff at Tianqiao Department Store raise the banner of the Great Leap Forward, reduce the number of personnel, implement one day and one class, absorb the traditional experience of commercial work, and greatly improve service attitudes), *RMRB*, February 14, 1958, 4.

69. Li Shuhua, "同家梁上大团圆" (Reunion in Tongjialiang), *Renmin wenxue*, no. 5 (May 30, 1960), 45–51.

70. Barry Naughton, *The Chinese Economy: Transitions and Growth* (Cambridge, MA: MIT Press, 2007), 80–1.

71. Riskin, *China's Political Economy*, 274.

72. For a typical example of official calls for service workers to implement the Commercial Leap Forward in stores, see "商业工作一定能跃进" (Commercial work can certainly make a Leap Forward), *RMRB*, February 14, 1958, 1.

73. See, for example, Jackie Sheehan, *Chinese Workers: A New History* (London: Routledge, 1998), 89–92.

74. "中共中央批转中共北京市委关于北京市天桥百货商场改革商业工作的报告" (The CCP Central Committee approves the work report of the Beijing Tianqiao Department Store on reform of commercial work submitted by the Beijing Municipal Committee of the CCP), *Beijing ribao*, April 19, 1958, republished in 大跃进中的北京天桥百货商场 (Beijing Tianqiao Department Store during the Great Leap Forward) (Beijing: Beijing chubanshe, 1958), 1–8. For a similar attempt in the Soviet Union in the 1930s to promote "cultured socialist trade," particularly better service attitudes, see Hessler, *A Social History of Soviet Trade*, 197–201.

75. "学'天桥'赶"天桥"许多城市商店订出跃进计划" (Learn from Tianqiao, Catch up with Tianqiao, many city stores set up a Great Leap plan), *RMRB*, February 26, 1958, 3. On additional efforts to extend Tianqiao into the countryside, see "'天桥'人在农村" ("Tianqiao" people in the countryside), *RMRB*, March 4, 1958, 3. On the official call for nationwide commercial workers to emulate Tianqiao, see "商业部和商业工会全国委员会联合发出号召商业职工们，都来响应天桥商场的革命倡议" (The Ministry of Commerce and the National Committee of the Commercial Trade Union jointly issue a call to business workers to respond to the revolutionary initiative of Tianqiao Department Store), *RMRB*, February 14, 1958, 1 and "商业工作一定能跃进" (Commercial work can certainly make a Leap Forward).

76. Shangyebu shangye jingji yanjiusuo, ed., 新中国商业史稿 (1949–1982) (Draft of New China's business history [1949–1982]), 175.

77. "'学天桥'赶"天桥"武汉丽丰百货商店" ("Learn from Tianqiao," "Catch up with Tianqiao": Wuhan's Lifeng Department Store), *RMRB*, February 18, 1958, 3.

78. "昆明赶天桥" (Kunming catches up with Tianqiao), *RMRB*, March 5, 1958, 3; Dong Shanyuan, "'天桥'散记" (Miscellaneous observations of "Tianqiao"), *RMRB*, March 20, 1958, 8.

79. Gansusheng Qingyangxian shangyeju, ed., "破旧立新，十大改革" (Destroy the old and establish the new, ten big reforms), in Shangyebu, ed., 商业红旗，上册 (The red flag of commerce, vol. 1) (Beijing: Renmin chubanshe, 1959), 177–8.

80. Dong Shanyuan, "天桥散记" (Miscellaneous observations of Tianqiao); "商业工作一定能跃进" (Commercial work can certainly make a Leap Forward). For this and other articles on efforts to reduce staff by making the store more "efficient," see the articles collected in Beijing chubanshe bianjibu, ed., 大跃进中的北京天桥百货商场 (Beijing Tianqiao Department Store in the Great Leap Forward) (Beijing: Beijing chubanshe, 1958). The book reprints articles from major newspapers and was intended to guide other stores into making similar commercial reforms. See especially, Zhonggong Beijing shiwei (Beijing Municipal Party Committee), ed., "北京市天桥百货商场改革商业工作的报告" (A report on the business reforms at Beijing Tianqiao Department Store), *Beijing ribao*, March 4, 1958; "中共中央批转中共北京市委关于北京市天桥百货商场改革商业工作的报告," (The CCP Central Committee approves the work report of the Beijing Tianqiao Department Store on reform of commercial work submitted by the Beijing Municipal Committee of the CCP).

81. Zhao Jialie and Lei Runming, "天桥百货商场圆满实现倡议 人员减少；销货额上升；库存量下降；资金周转快；服务态度好；售货员一班顶到底，还能愉快地休息" (Tianqiao Department Store has successfully implemented the reduction in the number of personnel; the sales volume has increased; the inventory has decreased; the capital turnover is fast; the service attitude is good; the salespeople work to the end and can rest happily), *RMRB*, April 6, 1958, 2; "加强政治思想工作，提高社会主义觉悟 天桥百货商场职工举起大跃进旗帜 减少人员一半，实行一天一班顶到底，吸收商业工作的传统经验，服务态度大改观" (Strengthening political and ideological work, enhancing socialist consciousness. The staff at Tianqiao Department Store raised the banner of the Great Leap Forward, reduced the number of personnel, implemented one day and one class, absorbed the traditional experience of commercial work, and greatly improved the service attitude).

82. Dong Shanyuan, "天桥散记" (Miscellaneous observations of Tianqiao).

83. For a brief history of the store, which was established in 1953 with eighty-four employees, see Shangyebu baihuoju, ed., 中国百货商业 (Chinese general commerce), 408–10.

84. "天桥百货商场职工举起大跃进旗帜" (Clerks at Tianqiao Department Store hold up the flag of the Great Leap Forward). For a complete list of vows made by clerks at Tianqiao, see "天桥百货商场服务公约" (Service compact of Tianqiao Department Store), originally published in *Beijing ribao*, February 9, 1958, and republished in 大跃进中的北京天桥百货商场 (Beijing Tianqiao Department Store during the Great Leap Forward), 83.

85. Tien Yuan, "Learn from Tienchiao, Emulate Tienchiao," *Women of China*, no. 4 (1958), 26–8.

86. Even state media reinforced this attitude, such as in a hit movie in which the protagonist's desire to be a hairdresser was opposed by her status-conscious husband. "女理发师" (Female hairdresser, 1962).

87. Tien Yuan, "Learn from Tienchiao, Emulate Tienchiao," (photo on p. 28).

88. Liu Di, "在'人人'之中" (Within the "All for one and one for all"), *RMRB*, May 25, 1958, 4; "解放街百货商店气象一新" (Things have been changed a lot in Liberation Street Department Store), *Hangzhou ribao*, March 10, 1958.

89. "顾客就是亲人" (Customers are our family members), *Hangzhou ribao*, May 9, 1958.

90. "中共中央批转中共北京市委关于北京市天桥百货商场改革商业工作的报告," (The CCP Central Committee approves the work report of the Beijing Tianqiao Department Store on reform of commercial work submitted by the Beijing Municipal Committee of the CCP).

91. This ideology is perhaps best encapsulated in the title of a *People's Daily* editorial published amidst the campaign: "人人为我，我为人人" (All for one and one for all), *RMRB*, March 15, 1958, 1.

92. "杭州棉布店里营业员的新态度" (New attitude of salesclerks at Hangzhou Cloth Store), *RMRB*, December 27, 1955, 2.

93. See Fu Dong, "一个积极为顾客需要服务的营业员" (A salesperson who actively serves the needs of customers), *RMRB*, May 17, 1953, 2.

94. Sichuansheng shangyeting, ed., "千方百计把方便送给顾客" (Take every means to make conveniences for customers), in Shangyebu, ed., 商业红旗 (日用工业品类) (The red flag of commerce [industrial consumer goods sector]) (Beijing: Gongren chubanshe, 1960), 105.

95. Sichuansheng shangyeting, ed., "不断跃进, 面貌一新的重庆'三八'百货商店" (Continuous leap forward, the appearance of a new Chongqing "March Eighth" Department Store), in Shangyebu, ed., 商业红旗 (日用工业品类) (The red flag of commerce [industrial consumer goods sector]), 98.

96. On policies whereby managers participated in factory production and workers participated in management, see Sheehan, *Chinese Workers: A New History*, 86–8.

97. Zhang Jibin, "让顾客称心如意" (Offer customers the best service), *Zhejiang ribao*, April 17, 1958.

98. On such complaint books in the Soviet Union, see Randall, *The Soviet Dream World of Retail Trade and Consumption in the 1930s*.

99. Dong Shanyuan, "'天桥'散记" (Miscellaneous observations of Tianqiao).

100. Han Guang, "天桥商场营业员深夜配前轴" (Tianqiao Department Store worker fixes the front axle for a driver late at night), *RMRB*, August 5, 1958, 6.

101. Quoted in Shangyebu baihuoju, ed., 中国百货商业 (Chinese general commerce), 408.

102. Dong Shanyuan, "天桥"散记 (Miscellaneous observations of Tianqiao); Song Dingyuan, "不让红旗褪色" (Keep the red flag from fading), *Hangzhou ribao*, December 6, 1958; Zhang Zhiqing, "能干的售货员" (A capable clerk), *RMRB*, August 11, 1958, 3.

103. For examples of provincial and municipal newspapers publishing such testimonials, see Fu Hengda, "'天桥' 之花在杭州结果" (The flowers of Tianqiao grow fruit in Hangzhou), *Zhejiang ribao*, April 17, 1958; "解放街商店服务态度顾客称好" (Customer praises service of Liberation Street Department Store), *Hangzhou ribao*, May 25, 1958.

104. On the advent of self-service retailing underway in the UK at the same time, see Dawn Nell et al., "Investigating Shopper Narratives of the Supermarket in Early Post-War England, 1945–75," *Oral History*, vol. 37, no. 1 (2009), 61–73.

105. Dong Zhongxin, Qi Guanhuai, and Jin Lianqing, "'解放街' 服务优良誉满全城" (Service on "Liberation Street" is well-known throughout the whole city), *Hangzhou ribao*, August 7, 1958.

106. Song Dingyuan, "不让红旗褪色" (Keep the red flag from fading).

107. On the way capitalism requires a steady supply of expropriated labor, especially of women, rather than simply a one-off "primitive accumulation," see Silvia Federici, *Caliban and the Witch: Women, the Body and Primitive Accumulation* (Brooklyn, NY: Autonomedia, 2004), and her subsequent work, *Revolution at Point Zero: Housework Reproduction and Feminist Struggle* (Brooklyn, NY: Autonomedia, 2012); and, on what David Harvey calls "accumulation by dispossession," see his *The New Imperialism* (Oxford: Oxford University Press, 2003), 137–82. For an introduction to forms of expropriation used to continue capitalist accumulation, see Nancy Fraser and Rahel Jaeggi, *Capitalism: A Conversation in Critical Theory* (Cambridge: Polity, 2018).

108. For an example of attempts to promote household labor in the formal economy, see Jacob Eyferth, *Eating Rice from Bamboo Roots: The Social History of a Community of Handicraft Papermakers in Rural Sichuan, 1920–2000* (Cambridge, MA: Harvard University Asia Center, 2009).

109. Hua Yi, "An Urban People's Commune in Chungking," *Women of China*, nos. 4–5 (April 5, 1960), 12–17. In addition, the CCP continued Republican-era expansions of the state into the running of households for the good of the nation. For instance, on Women's Day, March 8, 1956, the state initiated a campaign in 106 cities that instructed housewives that money "should be spent in a planned way and frugality cherished as a virtue." Chin Feng, "Good Housewife Campaign Sweeps the Country," *Women of China*, no. 3 (March 1957), 11.

110. Li Duanxiang, 城市人民公社运动研究 (Research on the urban People's Commune movement) (Changsha: Hunan renmin chubanshe, 2006), 153–8. In the effort to promote a collective consciousness, some communes took experiments to an extreme, socializing not only dining and childcare but childrearing more generally. See Luo Pinghan, "大锅饭": 公共食堂始末 ("The big rice bowl": The origin and end of public canteens) (Nanning: Guangxi renmin chubanshe, 2001), 82. Luo notes how these efforts to eliminate all forms of selfishness backfired. On the long history of communal dining as an element of socialism, see Felix Wemheurer, "Dining in Utopia: An Intellectual History of the Origins of the Chinese Public Dining Halls," in Matthias Middell and Felix Wemheuer, *Hunger and Scarcity under State-Socialism* (Leipzig: Leipziger Universitätsverlag, 2012), 277–302. For how the state thought communal dining would save female household labor and "bring new freedom," see Chen Lo-Kiang, "Get-Together Cooking Is Best," *Women of China* (February 1960), 13–15.

111. Yu Wenmin, "财贸战线上的红旗" (The red flags at the commercial frontline), *Shida jiaoxue*, December 24, 1958, 4. For examples of two other

women-run stores, see Hubeisheng Machengxian shangyeju, "五女商店人 人夸" (Everyone praises the five-women store) and Henansheng Zhongmouxian shangyeju, "十五好的中牟四女商店" (Fifteen good experiences in a Zhongmou store run by four women). Both articles are found in Shangyebu, ed., 商业红旗, 下册 (The red flag of commerce, vol. 3) (Beijing: Renmin chubanshe, 1959), 9–15 and 15–20. The latter store, for instance, was praised for being entirely run by only four women yet serving 50,000 people.

112. Xin Zhongguo diyi dian de gushi bianweihui, ed., 新中国第一店的故事 (The story of New China's Number One Store), 61.

113. Xin Zhongguo diyi dian de gushi bianweihui, ed., 新中国第一店的故事 (The story of New China's Number One Store), 60.

114. Earlier scholarship saw the shifts back and forth between greater and lesser state control over the economy as a battle between Mao and his opponents over two different "lines" of policies. But Teiwes and Sun demonstrate that there was a high degree of policy consensus at the top and, in any case, there was no such battle over policy that Mao promoted. Instead, Mao promoted some policies rather than others. Frederick C. Teiwes and Warren Sun, *China's Road to Disaster: Mao, Central Politicians, and Provincial Leaders in the Unfolding of the Great Leap Forward, 1955–1959* (Armonk, NY: M.E. Sharpe, 1999).

115. In the highly decentralized economy, the number of rationed products varied by location and time. Shandong province, for instance, was rationing 200 products by the end of 1962, before the number tapered off. For a brief overview of rationing during the Mao era in Shandong, see "山东 省省情资料库" (Shandong province provincial information database), http://lib.sdsqw.cn/bin/mse.exe?seachword=&K=b1&A=11&rec=20&run=13. Archived February 20, 2018. In Zhejiang province, there were four types of rations by the early 1960s: individual rations and ration IDs for basic necessities; industrial products; bonuses for providing additional products to the state; and special dispensation rations for soldiers, ethnic minorities, and those working in difficult conditions. Zhejiang baihuo gongsi, ed., 浙江 百货商业志 (Annals of Zhejiang department store commerce), 289–91. The state-run rationing and the need for ration coupons to buy many essential items and luxuries, such as the Three Great Things, is referred to throughout this book. However, because the topic is the best known and best studied, I have not examined it in detail here. See, for instance, Chen Mingyuan, 历 史的见证: 四十年票证和人民币史 (Historical witness: Forty years of ration coupons and the history of the Renminbi) (Beijing: Fenghuang chubanshe, 2009); Chen Chunfang, 上海票证故事 (Stories of Shanghai ration coupons) (Shanghai: Dongfang chuban zhongxin, 2009); Zhang

Shichun, 物质供应票证鉴赏与收藏 (Appreciation and collection of material supply rations) (Wuhan: Hubei renmin chubanshe, 2008). Ironically, the ration coupons have become collectors' items in contemporary China and, consequently, there is a market for publications on the topic.

116. Beijingshi difangzhi bianzuan weiyuanhui, ed., 北京志 商业卷 饮食服务 志 (Beijing gazetteer, commerce volume: Food and service sector) (Beijing: Beijing chubanshe, 2008), 371–72.

117. Beijingshi difangzhi bianzuan weiyuanhui, ed., 北京志 商业卷 饮食服 务志 (Beijing gazetteer, commerce volume: Food and service sector), 371.

118. Reproduced in Shanghai difangzhi (Shanghai gazetteer), "'炮轰' 南京路" ("Bombard" Nanjing Road), 上海通网, www.shtong.gov.cn/node2/node4/ node2249/huangpu/node36258/node62519/index.html. Archived May 19, 2014; Ma Weiyong, "从买票打菜到餐饮业繁荣" (From self-serving to the boom in the food business), *Xingtai ribao*, October 14, 2008.

119. Sheng Guilin, "回眸哈尔滨: 老外道的回忆 – 国营饭店" (Reviewing Harbin: Remembering a state-owned restaurant in Laowaidao), http://blog .sina.com.cn/s/blog_4c1959c001000e2k.html. Archived December 12, 2017.

120. Bi Jiarong, "南京财贸行业在动乱中的徘徊" (Lingering finance and trade in Nanjing during the time of chaos), in Zhuang Xiaojun and Xu Kangying, eds., 风雨同舟: 南京探索前进三十年 1949–1978 (Stand together through storm and stress: Thirty years of exploration and progress in Nanjing 1949–1978) (Beijing: Zhonggong dangshi chubanshe, 2002), 506–7. The Cultural Revolution revived earlier ideas on how the shopping experience was an opportunity for clerks and customers to help build socialism through frugal living. In August 1968, writer Hua Jiannan was a cadre on a group visit to Beijing. While there, he and his training group visited the town center to shop. At a fruit stall, Hua's friend asked the salesclerk to pick big pears for him and pointed to the specific ones he wanted. However, instead of complying, the salesperson informed him that she would not let him choose the biggest and best pears for himself because that would leave only small pears for other customers. He was told "people should not only think about themselves but should consider the interests of others." Pears, she continued, were sold in groups that included big and small ones; customers were not allowed to choose their own. Hua Jiannan, "学习班'记事" (Memories of the "Study Group"), *Remembrance*, no. 98 (2013), 76–9, http://prchistory.org/wp-content/uploads/2014/05/REMEMB RANCE_No98.pdf. Archived August 26, 2016.

121. Hu Yuanjie, "1967年'炮轰'南京路事件" (The "bombardment" of Nanjing Road in 1967), *Shiji*, no. 3 (2014), 28–9; Mao Zedong (毛泽东), "炮打司令部

(我的一张大字报) (一九六六年八月五日)" (Bombard the headquarters: My big-character poster of August 5, 1966), *RMRB*, August 5, 1967, 1 (published in *RMRB* on the one-year anniversary of the poster).

122. On inequalities among these different categories of workers and efforts by the privileged labor elite to exclude other workers, see Nara Dillon, *Radical Inequalities: China's Revolutionary Welfare State in Comparative Perspective* (Cambridge, MA: Harvard University Asia Center, 2015).

123. Shanghaishi geming weiyuanhui fandui jingjizhuyi lianluo zongbu (Shanghai Revolutionary Committee Against Economism) (上海市革命委员会反对经济主义联络总部), ed., 无产阶级文化大革命中上海反对经济主义大事记 (讨论稿) (1966.11–1967.3.15) (Primary events of Shanghai opposition to economism during the Great Proletarian Cultural Revolution [Draft for discussion]) (November 1966–March 15, 1967), March 17, 1967, in *WDGW*.

124. Shanghaishi geming weiyuanhui fandui jingjizhuyi lianluo zongbu (Shanghai Revolutionary Committee Against Economism (上海市革命委员会反对经济主义联络总部), ed., 无产阶级文化大革命中上海反对经济主义大事记 (讨论稿) (1966.11–1967.3.15) (Primary events of Shanghai opposition to economism during the Great Proletarian Cultural Revolution [Draft for discussion]) (November 1966–March 15, 1967).

125. Beijingshi difangzhi bianzuan weiyuanhui, ed., 北京志 商业卷 饮食服务志 (Beijing gazetteer, commerce volume: Food and service sector), 374.

126. Beijingshi difangzhi bianzuan weiyuanhui, ed., 北京志 商业卷 饮食服务志 (Beijing gazetteer, commerce volume: Food and service sector), 374.

Consumerism in the Cultural Revolution

1. As my discussion of consumerism throughout the Mao era suggests, the "cultural" part of the Cultural Revolution in fact began earlier. In contrast to the Cultural Revolution decade of 1966–76, I use "Cultural Revolution" to refer to the three years from 1966 until the official end at the CCP Ninth Congress in April 1969. On the complexities of dating the beginning and end of the Cultural Revolution, see Roderick MacFarquhar and Michael Schoenhals, *Mao's Last Revolution* (Cambridge, MA: Belknap Press of Harvard University Press, 2008).

2. "Decision of the Central Committee of the Chinese Communist Party Concerning the Great Proletarian Cultural Revolution (Adopted on August 8, 1966)," *Peking Review*, vol. 9, no. 33 (August 12, 1966), 6–11 and posted at www.marxists.org/subject/china/peking-review/1966/PR1966-33g.htm. Archived July 15, 2018.

3. The definitive overview of the Cultural Revolution, especially elite political maneuverings, is MacFarquhar and Schoenhals, *Mao's Last Revolution*. The

pool of potential targets within the CCP was large. On the eve of the Cultural Revolution, Mao had determined that at least a third of the party leadership throughout the country was untrustworthy. Jiaqi Yan and Gao, *Turbulent Decade: A History of the Cultural Revolution*, tr. D. W. Y Kwok (Honolulu: University of Hawai'i Press, 1996), 7.

4. The call to "Destroy the Four Olds" was then echoed in leading state and CCP newspapers and journals, including *Red Flag* (红旗), the primary CCP theoretical journal, signaling its endorsement at the highest levels of the party-state. See Guo Jian, Yongyi Song, and Yuan Zhou, *Historical Dictionary of the Chinese Cultural Revolution* (Lanham, MD: Scarecrow Press, 2006), 70–2.

5. For an introduction, see Jonathan Unger, "Grassroots Turmoil in China's Cultural Revolution: A Half-Century Perspective," 77th George E. Morrison Lecture, November 3, 2016, www.chinoiresie.info/grassroots-turmoil-in-chinas-cultural-revolution-a-half-century-perspective/. Archived July 18, 2018. For an overview history of the Red Guards, see MacFarquhar and Schoenhals, *Mao's Last Revolution*, 102–17.

6. MacFarquhar and Schoenhals, *Mao's Last Revolution*, 262.

7. On the Cultural Revolution outside of the major coastal cities, see, for instance, Yang Su, *Collective Killings in Rural China During the Cultural Revolution* (New York: Cambridge University Press, 2011); Melvyn C. Goldstein, Ben Jiao, and Tanzen Lhundrup, *On the Cultural Revolution in Tibet: The Nyemo Incident of 1969* (Berkeley: University of California Press, 2009).

8. In addition to the more conspicuous activities examined here, the initial years of the Cultural Revolution unintentionally spread consumerism in other ways. Most notably, the initial breakdown of state authority aided speculative activities, including buying and selling sewing machines, bicycles, wristwatches, radios, and other desired but often hard-to-acquire products. See Dongguanshi gongshang xingzheng guanliju, ed., 东莞市工商行政管理制 (Administrative records of industry and commerce in Dongguan) (Guangzhou: Guangdong renmin chubanshe, 2011), 190. Such unauthorized economic activity included collective enterprises. See, for instance, Jiangsusheng difangzhi bianzuan weiyuanhui, ed., 江苏省志: 工商行政管理志 (Jiangsu province: Administrative records of industry and commerce), 279–80. Others used the moment to establish mom-and-pop businesses. See 广州市志: 卷九(上) (Guangzhou City records: vol. 9, part 1) (Guangzhou: Guangzhou chubanshe, 1999), 681–4; "Wenzhoushi gongshang xingzheng guanlizhi" bianzuan weiyuanhui, ed., 温州市工商行政管理志 (Administrative records of industry and commerce of Wenzhou City) (Shanghai: Fudan daxue chubanshe, 1993), 77–8.

9. On the radical critiques of the Cultural Revolution, including contemporary doubts that the CCP was "building socialism," see Yiching Wu, *The Cultural*

Revolution at the Margins: Chinese Socialism in Crisis (Cambridge, MA: Harvard University Press, 2014).

10. Dating the start of the Cultural Revolution depends on one's focus. Most point to the formal notification to cadres across the country in a May 16, 1966, memo outlining Mao's ideas. Others have demonstrated that the origins are much more complex. See MacFarquhar and Schoenhals, *Mao's Last Revolution.*

11. Hung Wu, "Tiananmen Square: A Political History of Monuments," *Representations*, no. 35 (1991), 88.

12. The Red Terror was intended as a Communist retaliation for the White Terror that the KMT had inflicted on all those labeled "Communists" in Shanghai in 1927.

13. Zhang Pinghua, "张平化在湖南大学的讲话" (Speech by Zhang Pinghua at Hunan University), August 31, 1966, in *WDGW.*

14. Xu Qing and Guo Xiuru, "'文化大革命'在南京的发动" (The launch of the "Great Cultural Revolution" in Nanjing), in Zhuang Xiaojun and Xu Kangying, eds., 风雨同舟: 南京探索前进三十年1949–1978 (Stand together through storm and stress: Thirty years of exploration and progress in Nanjing, 1949–1978) (Beijing: Zhonggong dangshi chubanshe, 2002), 435.

15. Guo, Song, and Zhou, *Historical Dictionary of the Chinese Cultural Revolution*, 70–2.

16. MacFarquhar and Schoenhals, *Mao's Last Revolution*, 118. A Chinese blogger has compiled an exhaustive list of major sites destroyed across the country. See http://blog.sina.com.cn/s/blog_5ce15ce60100nude.html. Archived November 12, 2017. The list includes well-known examples of Red Guard destruction, such as the Old Summer Palace (Yuanming Yuan) site in Beijing and the Confucian temples and countless rare books and other artifacts in his hometown of Qufu by over 200 Red Guards from Beijing. But the webpage also includes many other sites that seldom appear in standard histories of the era. In Hunan province, the burial site of Emperor Yandi and its associated building were seriously damaged. In Anhui province, King Xiangyu's and his wife's temples and graves, which date back to 202 BCE, were all destroyed. In Huai'an County of Jiangsu province, the birthplace of Wu Cheng'en, author of the Chinese classic, *Pilgrimage to the West*, was pulled down because his book was deemed part of the Four Olds. In Xi'an, some one hundred halls associated with a famed center of Daoism were destroyed. See also Dahpon David Ho, "To Protect and Preserve: Resisting the Destroy the Four Olds Campaign, 1966–1967," in Joseph Esherick, et al., eds., *The Chinese Cultural Revolution as History* (Stanford: Stanford University Press, 2006), 64–95.

17. Zhang Pinghua, "张平化在湖南大学的讲话" (Speech by Zhang Pinghua at Hunan University), August 31, 1966.

18. "上海天津革命小将和商业职工向剥削阶级'四旧'发动总攻 挥起革命铁扫帚 横扫一切旧习俗" (Shanghai and Tianjin Red Guards and businesspeople launch an attack against the "Four Olds" of the exploiting classes to sweep away all old customs), *RMRB*, August 25, 1966, 2; "红卫兵在'全聚德'点起了革命烈火" (Red Guards set off a revolutionary fire in Quanjude), *RMRB*, August 25, 1966, 2.

19. "上海天津革命小将和商业职工向剥削阶级'四旧'发动总攻 挥起革命铁扫帚 横扫一切旧习俗" (Shanghai and Tianjin Red Guards and businesspeople launch an attack against the "Four Olds" of the exploiting classes to sweep away all old customs); Yan and Gao, *Turbulent Decade*, 73, which mentions destroy activities in other cities, including as far away from Beijing as Xinjiang, Tibet, and Inner Mongolia, where minority populations also participated in name changes, including ethnic-sounding personal and place names. For a photo of the East Wind Market with its new name, see Huang Shengmin, Ding Junjie, and Liu Yinghua, 中国广告图史 (An illustrated history of Chinese advertising) (Guangzhou: *Nanfang ribao* chubanshe, 2006), 268. Similarly, in the commercial center of Tianjin, near Binjiang Street, many stores changed their names to sound more revolutionary. For example, Zhongyuan Company became the Worker-Farmer-Soldier Market and businesses such as the Beiyang Cotton Mill changed its name to the Four News Cotton Mill.

20. "'红卫兵'的革命精神万岁!" (Long live the revolutionary spirit of the "Red Guards"), *Zhejiang ribao*, August 24, 1966, reprinted in Cheng Chao and Wei Haoben, eds., 浙江文革纪事 (1966.5–1976.10) (A chronicle of the Cultural Revolution in Zhejiang province [1966.5–1976.10]) (Hangzhou: Zhejiang fangzhi bianjibu, 1989) in *WDGW*.

21. Shangyebu shangye jingji yanjiusuo, ed., 新中国商业史稿 (1949–1982) (A draft history of commerce in New China [1949–1982]) (Beijing: Zhongguo caizheng jingji chubanshe, 1984), 316, 317.

22. 毛泽东主义学校(原二十六中)红卫兵(卫旗) (Red Guards of Maoism School [the original name of the school was the Beijing No. 26 Secondary School]), "破旧立新一百例" (100 ways to get rid of the old and to establish the new), August 1968, in *WDGW*. For a translation of the entire list, see Michael Schoenhals' *China's Cultural Revolution, 1966–1969: Not a Dinner Party* (Armonk, NY: M.E. Sharpe, 1996) 212–22.

23. "上海天津革命小将和商业职工向剥削阶级'四旧'发动总攻, 挥起革命铁扫帚, 横扫一切旧习俗" (Shanghai and Tianjin revolutionary Red Guards and commercial workers launch a general attack on the "four olds" of the exploiting class; wielding the revolutionary iron broom, they swept away all old customs), *RMRB*, August 25, 1966, 2; "一块'造反'去!" (Let's "rebel" together!); "'麻婆豆腐'易名记" ("Mapo tofu" renamed). These

articles are from *RMRB*, August 25, 1966, which printed a full page of news
reporting on Red Guard destroy activities in cities throughout China.

24. Reproduced in 上海市地方志 (*Shanghai Municipal Gazetteer*), "'炮轰' 南京路" ("Bombard" Nanjing Road), 上海通网, www.shtong.gov.cn/node2/node4/node2249/huangpu/node36258/node62519/index.html. Archived May 19, 2014.

25. "上海天津革命小将和商业职工向剥削阶级'四旧'发动总攻　挥起革命铁扫帚　横扫一切旧习俗" (Shanghai and Tianjin Red Guards and businesspeople launch an attack against the "Four Olds" of the exploiting classes to sweep away all old customs).

26. 上海市地方志 (*Shanghai Municipal Gazetteer*), "'红卫兵'闹市'扫四旧'" ("Red Guards" sweep away "Four-Olds"), 上海通网, www.shtong.gov.cn /node2/node4/node2249/huangpu/node36258/node62519/index.html. Archived November 12, 2017.

27. "上海天津革命小将和商业职工向剥削阶级'四旧'发动总攻　挥起革命铁扫帚　横扫一切旧习俗" (Shanghai and Tianjin Red Guards and businesspeople launch an attack against the "Four Olds" of the exploiting classes to sweep away all old customs). On the confusion among customers in Nanjing caused by the renaming of stores and their being painted in red, see Bi Jiarong, "南京财贸行业在动乱中的徘徊" (Lingering finance and trade in Nanjing during the time of chaos), in Zhuang Xiaojun and Xu Kangying, eds., 风雨同舟：南京探索前进三十年1949–1978 (Stand together through storm and stress: Thirty years of exploration and progress in Nanjing, 1949–1978), 506.

28. Reproduced in上海市地方志 (*Shanghai Municipal Gazetteer*), "'炮轰'南京路" ("Bombard" Nanjing Road).

29. Red Guard critics of advertising were similar to participants in the NPM who attacked advertisements for foreign products for promoting the desire for foreign products that enticed foreign capitalist powers (imperialists) into China. See Karl Gerth, *China Made: Consumer Culture and the Creation of the Nation* (Cambridge, MA: Harvard University Asia Center, 2003), 16 and throughout.

30. Even in the case of the *People's Daily*, there were some industrial and other advertisements until early 1970, although these had almost entirely vanished by the end of the Cultural Revolution. Liu Jialin, 新编中外广告通史, 2nd ed. (A general history of Chinese and world advertising) (Guangzhou: Ji'nan daxue chubanshe, 2004), 144.

31. Xie Jingyi, 毛泽东身边工作琐忆 (Memories of working alongside Mao Zedong) (Beijing: Zhongyang wenxian chubanshe, 2015), 168–9.

32. Xu Shanbin, "红色的海洋" (A sea of red), 现代阅读网, February 21, 2013, www.readit.com.cn/djwz/cjws/2013/02/65101.shtml. Archived November 12, 2017. For additional details, see Xu Shanbin, 证照中国 1966–1976: 共和国

特殊年代的纸上历史 (Authorizing China 1966–1976: A history of paper during the special period of the republic) (Beijing: Xinhua chubanshe, 2009), ch. 3.

33. Mao Zedong zhuyi xuexiao, "破旧立新一百例" (100 ways to get rid of the old and to establish the new).

34. Mao Zedong zhuyi xuexiao, "破旧立新一百例" (100 ways to get rid of the old and to establish the new); Cao Qianli, 红色官窑: 文革瓷器 (The red official kiln: Cultural Revolution porcelain) (Beijing: Tuanjie chubanshe, 2002), 17–74. Having pets was attacked as a bourgeois hobby, and pet stores were closed: Tianjin baihuo gongsi, ed., 天津市百货公司四十年史 (1949–1989) (Forty years of the Tianjin Department Store [1949–1989]) (Self-published and not intended for public circulation, 1989), 60.

35. Shangyebu shangye jingji yanjiusuo, ed., 新中国商业史稿 (1949–1982) (A draft history of commerce in New China [1949–1982]), 316.

36. Tianjin baihuo gongsi, ed., 天津市百货公司四十年史 (1949–1989) (Forty years of the Tianjin Department Store [1949–1989], 59–60.

37. Tianjin baihuo gongsi, ed., 天津市百货公司四十年史 (1949–1989) (Forty years of the Tianjin Department Store [1949–1989], 59–60.

38. Shangyebu shangye jingji yanjiusuo, ed., 新中国商业史稿 (1949–1982) (A draft history of commerce in New China [1949–1982]), 316.

39. Liang Xiaosheng, 一个红卫兵的自白 (Confessions of a Red Guard) (Beijing: Wenhua yishu chubanshe, 2006), 44–6. Liang and his friends later saw smoke rising four stories into the air and heard it was from a bonfire of hundreds of pairs of new Huili shoes from a Harbin department store. When the rumor began, Harbin Number One Department Store offered to exchange the offending Huili shoes. When the rumor faded, they resumed selling the shoes, which soon regained their popularity. Song Xiake (blog name), "回力球鞋的故事" (A story about Huili gym shoes). Sina Blog, posted July 31, 2013, http://blog.sina.com.cn/s/blog_633646eb0102e10h.html. Archived November 12, 2017.

40. Market capitalist countries provide many examples of this same power of consumerism to incorporate extreme subcultures attempting to create anti-consumerism. Indeed, the expansion of consumerism relies on the mainstreaming of subcultures for new fashion trends, consumer tastes, and further individualization through consumption. See Joseph Heath and Andrew Potter, *The Rebel Sell: Why the Culture Can't Be Jammed* (Toronto: HarperCollins, 2004).

41. Bi Jiarong, "南京财贸行业在动乱中的徘徊" (Lingering finance and trade in Nanjing during the time of chaos), 507.

42. Xu Qing and Guo Xiuru, "'文化大革命'在南京的发动" (The launch of the "Great Cultural Revolution" in Nanjing), 442.

43. Shangyebu shangye jingji yanjiusuo, ed., 新中国商业史稿 (1949–1982) (A draft history of commerce in New China [1949–1982]), 316.

44. Tianjin baihuo gongsi, ed., 天津市百货公司四十年史 (1949–1989) (Forty years of the Tianjin Department Store [1949–1989]), 59.

45. Shangyebu jingji yanjiusuo, ed., 新中国商业三十年 (Thirty years of commerce in New China) (Internal circulation, 1980), 97–103.

46. Xin Zhongguo diyi dian de gushi bianweihui, 新中国第一店的故事 (The story of New China's No. 1 Store) (Shanghai: Shanghai dianzi chuban youxian gongsi, 2012), 62–3.

47. Tianjin baihuo gongsi, ed., 天津市百货公司四十年史 (1949–1989) (Forty years of the Tianjin Department Store [1949–1989]), 59–60.

48. The term "A-Fei" appears to come from the American slang term "fly." Ye Shisun and Ye Jianing, 上海话外来语二百例 (200 loanwords in the Shanghai dialect) (Shanghai: Shanghai daxue chubanshe, 2015), 161.

49. Liang Xiaosheng, 一个红卫兵的自白 (Confessions of a Red Guard), 101–3.

50. Shangyebu shangye jingji yanjiusuo, ed., 新中国商业史稿 (1949–1982) (A draft history of commerce in New China [1949–1982]), 319. On service restrictions, see also Shangyebu jingji yanjiusuo, ed., 新中国商业三十年 (Thirty years of commerce in New China), 124–6.

51. Li Jingrong, "狂热　幻灭：红卫兵运动剪影" (Fanaticism and disillusionment: Silhouettes of the Red Guard movement), in Zhe Yongping, ed., 那个时代中的我们 (Ourselves at that time) (Huhehaote: Yuanfang chubanshe, 1998), 116–19. Sometimes the pressure to conform to the anti-bourgeois (or "socialist") fashion was subtler than an assault. The popular girl's style of wearing one's hair in braids became a target. At the time of the movement, Sun Libo was a fifteen-year-old middle-school student in Heilongjiang province when her school required all girls to cut their braids. Doing so was labeled a "political task." If a girl cut her braids, it confirmed she was part of the revolution; otherwise, it meant she opposed the Destroy movement. "I never liked short hair and was proud of my two long braids, which attracted attention whenever I went out. But now I felt I had no choice but to go to the hairdresser. . . . I cried as the hairdresser cut my braids." Sun Libo, "'破四旧'剪掉大辫子" (Cutting my long braids during the "Destroy the Four Olds"), *Laonian ribao*, October 19, 2012.

52. Gerth, *China Made*, ch. 2.

53. Sun Peidong, 时尚与政治：广东民众日常着装时尚 (1966–1976) (Fashion and politics: Everyday clothing fashions of the Guangdong masses [1966–1976]) (Beijing: Renmin chubanshe, 2013), 124.

54. Xu Youyu, then a middle-school student in Chengdu, was not a member of one of the Five Red Classes, so was not directly involved in the Destroy movement but he did have a chance to watch. One day, he saw a group of Red

Guards stop a young woman and lead her to their duty station. A few minutes later, she emerged with the legs of her pants shredded from top to bottom, so much so that she could barely walk. She was clearly ashamed. According to Xu, this was one of the most popular ways the Destroy movement was enacted, and it was repeated many times. Xu Youyu, "我在1966年" (Me in 1966), in Xu Youyu, ed., 1966: 我们那一代的回忆 (1966: Memories of our generation) (Beijing: Zhongguo wenlian chuban gongsi), 1988), 17–41.

55. Zheng Guanglu, "文革中成都的'破四旧'运动" (The "Destroy the Four Olds" movement during the Cultural Revolution in Chengdu). Reposted at https://tieba.baidu.com/p/49484013?red_tag=0801333644&traceid=. Archived April 22, 2019.

56. Hong Xia, "剃过光头" (Shaved bald), in Zhe Yongping (者永平), ed., 那个时代中的我们 (Ourselves at that time), 439–41.

57. Shan Shaojie, 毛泽东执政春秋 (The reign of Mao Zedong) (Taipei: Lianjing chubanshe, 2001), 433.

58. Antonia Finnane, *Changing Clothes in China: Fashion, History, Nation* (New York: Columbia University Press, 2008), 232.

59. Nimrod Baranovitch, *China's New Voices: Popular Music, Ethnicity, Gender, and Politics, 1978–1997* (Berkeley: University of California Press, 2003), 108; Emily Honig, "Maoist Mappings of Gender: Reassessing the Red Guards," in Susan Brownell and Jeffrey N. Wasserstrom, eds., *Chinese Femininities and Chinese Masculinities: A Reader* (Berkeley: University of California Press, 2002), 255–308.

60. Ding Shu, "追思节" (Pursuing Memorial Day), May 25, 2009. Originally in 民间历史 but reposted on www.edubridge.com/letter/dingshu_fumu.htm. Archived April 13, 2016.

61. Tina Mai Chen, "Film and Gender in Sino-Soviet Cultural Exchange, 1949–1969," in Thomas P. Bernstein and Hua-Yu Li, eds., *China Learns from the Soviet Union, 1949–Present* (Lanham, MD: Lexington Books, 2010), 429.

62. Shan Shaojie, 毛泽东执政春秋 (The reign of Mao Zedong), 433.

63. Finnane, *Changing Clothes in China*, 227.

64. "高举毛泽东思想的革命批判旗帜积极投入战斗" (Carry forward the revolutionary critique of Mao Zedong Thought and actively participate in the battle), *RMRB*, April 3, 1967, 1. Similar headlines appeared in the following days.

65. For instance, Red Guards charged that in 1963, on the eve of the Southeast Asia trip, Wang Guangmei took a chartered plane to Shanghai to have a special wardrobe made. What she could not find or have made in Shanghai, including her hat and silk stockings, she imported from Hong Kong. In 1966, she again went with Liu Shaoqi on state visits to

Pakistan and other countries and once again used official channels to buy nice clothing in Hong Kong. During her visit, she changed dresses, shoes, and handbags multiple times, including on a single day. The final bit of incriminating sartorial evidence: she changed her watchband to match the color of her clothes. As with so many officials and others attacked, the person of Wang became a Cultural Revolution "exhibit" intended to spread an antibourgeoisie message. Jinggangshan Corps Zhen Heilang of Tsinghua University, ed., 王光美究竟是什么货色 (Wang Guangmei, what sort of trash is she?), January 16, 1967. Booklet in *WDGW*.

66. MacFarquhar and Schoenhals. *Mao's Last Revolution*, 124. For Wang's interrogation beforehand, see Schoenhals, *China's Cultural Revolution, 1966–1969*, 101–16 (esp. 104–5).

67. Mao Zedong zhuyi xuexiao, "破旧立新一百例" (100 ways to get rid of the old and to establish the new).

68. "上海天津革命小将和商业职工向剥削阶级 '四旧'发动总攻 挥起革命铁扫帚 横扫一切旧习俗" (Shanghai and Tianjin Red Guards and businesspeople launch an attack against the "Four Olds" of the exploiting classes to sweep away all old customs).

69. Shangyebu jingji yanjiusuo, ed., 新中国商业三十年 (Thirty years of commerce in New China), 124–5. On the Red Guards in Shanghai enforcing the ban on the sale of famous brands, particularly alcohol and local delicacies, see 上海市地方志 (*Shanghai Municipal Gazetteer*), "'红卫兵'闹市'扫四旧'" ("Red Guards" sweep away the "Four-Olds" downtown), www.shtong.gov.cn/node2/node4/node2249/huangpu/node36258/node62519/index.html. Archived November 12, 2017.

70. Shangyebu shangye jingji yanjiusuo, ed., 新中国商业史稿 (1949–1982) (A draft history of commerce in New China [1949–1982]), 316.

71. For the experiences of one Beijing Red Guard inflicting such violence during ransackings, see Zhenhua Zhai, *Red Flower of China* (New York: SOHO, 1992), 91–100.

72. These statistics were printed in newspapers in the mid-1980s during a time of openness about these issues and are summarized in Wang Nianyi, 大动乱的年代 (A decade of great upheaval) (Zhengzhou: Henan renmin chubanshe, 1988), 71.

73. These totals are summarized in MacFarquhar and Schoenhals. *Mao's Last Revolution*, 117.

74. For brief overviews of these house ransackings, see Yan and Gao, *Turbulent Decade*, 76–81.

75. Tan Jiewen, "'抄家'述略" (A brief account of "home ransackings"), *Hunan wenshi*, no. 6 (2001), 74–5.

76. Liang Shuming, 梁漱溟自述 (An Autobiography of Liang Shuming) (Zhengzhou: Henan renmin chubanshe, 2004), 156–9. On that same day,

August 24, Gu Xiegang wrote in his diary that Red Guards searched the home of his neighbor, Jin Heqing (the aunt of the last emperor, Puyi), and confiscated many gold bars. Likewise, the actress Wu Ruiyan was driven away from her home. Gu Xiegang, 顾颉刚日记 (1964–1967) (Gu Xiegang's diary [1964–1967]) (Taipei: Lianjing chuban shiye gufen youxian gongsi, 2007), 10.516.

77. Gu Xiegang, 顾颉刚日记 (1964–1967) (Gu Xiegang's diary [1964–1967]), 10.516, 10.519.

78. Tan Jiewen, "'抄家'述略" (A brief account of "home ransackings"), 74–5. These examples also demonstrate the tacit state support for ransackings in the form of groups set in Beijing, Shanghai, and other places to process the seized goods. Denise Ho, *Curating Revolution: Politics on Display in Mao's China* (Cambridge: Cambridge University Press, 2018), 233–42. Here again the actions taken to catalog and preserve cultural artifacts contradicted the rhetoric of destruction.

79. Zhensheng Li, Robert Pledge, and Jacques Menasche, *Red-color News Soldier: A Chinese Photographer's Odyssey Through the Cultural Revolution* (London: Phaidon, 2003), 75. For photographs of the items, see pp. 114–15.

80. Daiyun Yue and Carolyn Wakeman, *To the Storm: The Odyssey of a Revolutionary Chinese Woman* (Berkeley: University of California Press, 1985), 168–70.

81. Li, Pledge, and Menasche, *Red-color News Soldier*, 137.

82. Jiangshanqiangu (blogger name of a retired cadre living in Nanjing but originally from Shenyang, where the story takes place), "往事回首: 我的第一辆自行车" (Recalling my first bicycle), http://jiangshanqiangu .blog.163.com/blog/static/18548737220138295155757/.   Archived November 12, 2017.

83. Liang Xiaosheng, 一个红卫兵的自白 (Confessions of a Red Guard), 131–5; Zhai, *Red Flower of China*, 94, includes the description of the author as a young Red Guard in Beijing who participated in house ransackings and recalls the tactile experience of bourgeois niceties such as silk and gold.

84. Yue and Wakeman, *To the Storm*, 171. For a broader discussion of these exhibitions, see Ho, *Curating Revolution*.

85. For photographs of one such modest exhibition of seized personal belongings, such as a Swiss watch and radio inside the home of a former landlord, and the long line of farmers from Acheng county in Heilongjiang lined up to visit the "landlord mansion" in rural Heilongjiang, see Li, Pledge, and Menasche, *Red-color News Soldier*, 52–4.

86. Yang Yaojian, "一个小学生的保皇与造反" (A primary student experiences rebellion), *Jiyi*, no. 4 (February 2, 2009), 48–51, http://prchistory.org/wp-

content/uploads/2014/05/REMEMBRANCE-No-14-2009年2月12日.pdf.
Archived August 26, 2016.

87. The CCP Central Committee finally stepped in on March 20, 1967, issuing: "关于在文化大革命运动中处理红卫兵抄家物资的几项规定" (Several provisions on dealing with properties confiscated by Red Guards during the Cultural Revolution).

88. Zhao Yuan, "'都在可破之列': '文革'中的私产与公物" ("Everything could be broken": Private property and public property in the "Cultural Revolution"), *The Paper*, www.thepaper.cn/newsDetail_forward_1261079. Archived November 12, 2017.

89. Tan Jiewen, "'抄家'述略" (A brief account of "home ransackings"), 74–5.

90. 上海市革命委员会反对经济主义联络总部 (The liaison headquarters of the Shanghai revolutionary committee against economism), ed., 无产阶级文化大革命中上海反对经济主义大事记 (讨论稿) (November 1966–March 15, 1967) (Primary events of Shanghai opposition to economism during the Great Proletarian Cultural Revolution [Draft for discussion]) (November 1966–March 15, 1967), March 17, 1967, in *WDGW*.

91. Guan Shengli, "屠鸽" (Killing a pigeon), in Zhe Yongping, ed., 那个年代中的我们 (Ourselves at that time), 20.

92. Fang Jihong, "公物还家" (Public property becomes private), in Zhe Yongping (者永平), ed., 那个年代中的我们 (Ourselves at that time), 462–3.

93. "One day, a staff member who was working in the storage showed me two valuable hand scrolls. One was Chairman Mao's calligraphy and the other was calligraphy by Chu Suiliang, one of the greatest calligraphers and politicians during the Tang dynasty. He also told me these were worth more than RMB 10,000 before the Cultural Revolution. Although I took these two for Ye Qun, it felt wrong, so I informed a staff member in the General Office of the Central Military Commission. A few days later, I was dismissed from her service and returned to my previous work unit." These excerpts are quoted in Zhang Jianqing, "林彪集团主要成员窃夺文物记" (The primary members of the Lin Biao clique stole cultural relics from the state), *Bainianchao*, no. 1 (2004), 49–54.

94. Similarly, Chen Boda and his secretary came to the office and removed items some 139 times. When they took antiques, they paid very little. Even Chen Boda admitted as much: "I should owe you [that is, the Heritage Management Office] several million RMB." Zhang Jianqing, "林彪集团主要成员窃夺文物记" (The primary members of the Lin Biao clique stole cultural relics from the state), 49–54. See also Denise Ho, "Revolutionizing Antiquity: The Shanghai Cultural Bureaucracy in the Cultural Revolution, 1966–1968," *The China Quarterly*, no. 207 (2011), 687–705.

95. Xie Quan, who was in Chengdu at the time, found that there was a new "second-hand book market" selling those books confiscated by Red Guards and books stolen from libraries. Xie Quan, 我在文化大革命中的经历 (My experience in the Cultural Revolution), in Xu Youyu, ed., 1966: 我们那一代的回忆 (1966: Memories of our generation), 154.

96. It remained on Huaihai Road until its demolition in 1992 to widen the road. "国营上海市贸易信托公司旧货商店启事" (State-Managed Second-Hand Store of the Shanghai Trade and Trust Company [advertisement]), *JFRB*, September 27, 1954. A documentary covers the basic history of the store and includes interviews with former workers and patrons: Shao Daxing (writer and director), 上海故事: 曾经的淮国旧 (Shanghai stories: The *Huaiguojiu*), documentary first broadcast on上海广播电视台. Posted online at http://shanghaistory.kankanews.com/movie/jingcaijiemushipin/184.html. Consulted January 30, 2016. All patrons quoted here come from this documentary. The name Huaiguojiu (Huai State Secondhand) was the abbreviated colloquial name for the "Huaihai Road State-Managed Second-Hand Store." *Huai* refers to the name of its location on Shanghai's prominent Huaihai Road in the former French concession, *Guo* indicates its status as a state-run store, and *jiu* informed people the store sold used products, i.e., *jiu huo*.

97. Shao Daxing (writer and director), 上海故事: 曾经的淮国旧 (Shanghai stories: The *Huaiguojiu*).

98. As noted, all patrons quoted here come from the documentary, Shao Daxing, writer and director, 上海故事: 曾经的淮国旧 (Shanghai stories: The *Huaiguojiu*).

99. Shao Daxing, writer and director, 上海故事: 曾经的淮国旧 (Shanghai stories: The *Huaiguojiu*).

100. Shen Jialu, "淮国旧,曾让我开眼界" (The Huaihai Store, The time it opened my eyes), *Shanghai wanba*, August 25, 2012.

101. Email correspondence with Cheng Linsun, August 27, 2016.

102. For an examination of one such case, see Jie Li, *Shanghai Homes: Palimpsests of Private Life* (New York: Columbia University Press, 2015).

103. For a discussion of the bloodline theory, see Wu, *The Cultural Revolution at the Margins*, ch. 3.

104. "回望淮国旧" (Recalling the Huaiguojiu), collected in Shanghai yingxiang gongzuoshi, ed., 百姓生活记忆: 上海故事 (Memories of people's life experiences: Shanghai stories) (Shanghai: Xuelin chubanshe, 2012), 145.

105. Xu Youyu, "我在1966年" (Me in 1966), 34–5.

106. He helped one of his classmates transport four confiscated square stools made of mahogany that his friend had bought for only RMB 2 each. See

Shao Daxing (writer and director), "上海故事: 曾经的淮国旧" (Shanghai stories: The *Huaiguojiu*).

107. Yu Yang, "浅析'京剧样板戏'音乐对京胡演奏的影响" (A brief analysis of the influences of "Peking model operas" on Jinghu performances), *Xijiang yue* (西江月), 2013.

108. Liu Zhenghui, "京胡的发展与制作 (六)" (The development and production of Jinghu [Part 6]), *Zhongguo jingju*, no. 11 (2005), 24.

109. Mobo Gao, *The Battle for China's Past: Mao and the Cultural Revolution* (London: Pluto Press, 2008), 21–2.

110. Dahpon David Ho, "To Protect and Preserve: Resisting the Destroy the Four Olds Campaign, 1966–1967," in Joseph Esherick, et al., eds., *The Chinese Cultural Revolution as History* (Stanford: Stanford University Press, 2006), 64–95.

111. Zhang Huicang, "我所亲历的毛主席八次接见红卫兵" (My personal experiences during Chairman Mao's eight Red Guard receptions), *Dangshi bocai*, no. 2 (2006), 32; Zhang Huicang and Mu An, "毛泽东八次接见红卫兵亲历记" (My personal memories of Mao Zedong's eight receptions of Red Guards), *Shidai wenxue*, no. 5 (2006), 32.

112. "毛主席和林彪周恩来等同志接见了学生代表并检阅了文化革命大军的游行" (Chairman Mao, Lin Biao, Zhou Enlai, and other comrades receive student representatives and inspect the Cultural Revolution mass parade), *RMRB*, August 19, 1966.

113. "解放军首次军衔制取消内幕" (The inside story of the PLA's canceling of its first military rank system), http://news.ifeng.com/a/20180801/59558112_0.shtml. Archived April 22, 2019.

114. Qi Mai (probably a pen name for a blogger who contributes to 民间历史网, 共识网), "文革琐记: 政治边缘处的众生相" (Remembrances of the Cultural Revolution: People at the political edge), *Minjian lishi* (no date), ed. 香港中文大学中国研究服务中心主办, http://mjlsh.usc.cuhk.edu.hk/Book.aspx?cid=4&tid=1670. Archived November 12, 2017.

115. Liu Yangdong, 红底金字: 六七十年代的北京孩子 (Gold characters on red: Beijing children in the 1960s and the 1970s) (Beijing: Zhongguo qingnian chubanshe, 2005), 268.

116. Qi Mai, "文革琐记: 政治边缘处的众生相" (Remembrances of the Cultural Revolution: People at the political edge).

117. Because real uniforms were difficult to acquire, most of those seen on the streets were homemade. Finnane, *Changing Clothes in China*, 227.

118. Sun Peidong, 时尚与政治: 广东民众日常着装时尚 (1966–1976) (Fashion and politics: Everyday clothing fashions of the Guangdong masses [1966–1976]), 120–1.

The Mao Badge Phenomenon as Consumer Fad

1. Edgar Snow, "A Reporter Got This Rare Interview with Chairman Mao in 1965, Even Though China Was Entirely Closed to the West," *The New Republic*, February 27, 1965, 17–23. This was not Mao's first expression of anxiety about youngsters. As he put it in about 1961, "The children of our cadres are a cause of discouragement. They lack experience of life and of society, yet their airs are considerable and they have a great sense of superiority. They have to be educated not to rely on their parents or martyrs of the past but entirely on themselves." *Reading Notes on the Soviet Text* Political Economy (1961–2), www.marxists.org/reference/archive/mao/s elected-works/volume-8/mswv8_64.htm. Archived August 12, 2014. A leading historian on the elite politics of the Mao era concludes that by the end of the 1950s, Mao's concern with the degeneration of the revolution was a "growing obsession." Roderick MacFarquhar, *The Origins of the Cultural Revolution*, 3 vols. (New York: Columbia University Press, 1974, 1983, 1997), 2.336.

2. For a full description of Mao's public and private meetings with Red Guards and a detailed schedule of the first rally, see Jiaqi Yan and Gao, *Turbulent Decade: A History of the Cultural Revolution*, tr. D. W. Y. Kwok (Honolulu: University of Hawai'i Press, 1996), 6–64; Gao Gao and Yan Jiaqi, "文化大革命"十年史: 1966–1976 (Ten Years of the "Great Cultural Revolution": 1966–1976) (Tianjin: Tianjin renmin chubanshe, 1986), 49.

3. Yarong Jiang and David Ashley, eds., *Mao's Children in the New China: Voices from the Red Guard Generation* (London: Routledge, 2000), 5.

4. Discussions of fads in histories of consumerism are surprisingly sparse. Although he does not address fads and their link to the expanding consumerism, Peter Stearns provides an overview of the expansion of consumerism through the endless creation of new needs as part of what he prefers to call "modernity" rather than industrial capitalism in Peter N. Stearns, *Satisfaction Not Guaranteed: Dilemmas of Progress in Modern Society* (New York: New York University Press, 2012), 213–54 and, globally, in Peter N. Stearns, *Consumerism in World History: The Global Transformation of Desire* (London: Routledge, 2006).

5. Sun Peidong shows that the Cultural Revolution decade had its own fashions, including the wearing of PLA uniforms. Sun Peidong, 时尚与政治: 广东民众日常着装时尚 (1966–1976) (Fashion and politics: Everyday fashion in Guangdong [1966–1976]) (Beijing: Renmin chubanshe, 2013), ch. 3.

6. "周恩来接见新疆大学'九·三'事件赴京汇报代表团" (Zhou Enlai meets with a delegation from Xinjiang University reporting on the events of "9.3") (October 28, 1966), *Xinjiang daxue geming zaofan tuan geming zaofan bao*, no. 6 (November 14, 1966) in *WDGW*.

7. Helen Wang, *Chairman Mao Badges: Symbols and Slogans of the Cultural Revolution*, British Museum Research Publication, no. 169 (London: British Museum Press, 2008), ch. 2. Wang's book accompanied the British Museum exhibition "Icons of Revolution: Mao Badges Then and Now" (April–September 2008). It is the single best overview of Mao badges. For a more analytical overview, see Melissa Schrift, *Biography of a Chairman Mao Badge: The Creation and Mass Consumption of a Personality Cult* (New Brunswick, NJ: Rutgers University Press, 2001). Clint Twist's website www .maozhang.net provides an excellent collection of badges with descriptions.

8. Wang Anting's catalogue of badges includes information (with examples) on badge fads before the Cultural Revolution. Wang Anting, ed., 毛泽东像章图谱 (An illustrated catalogue of Mao Zedong badges) (Beijing: Zhongguo shudian chubanshe, 1993). The Mao cult was one of the forces driving the desire – and compulsion – to own and display Mao badges and other Mao material culture. For an overview of the growth of the Mao cult, see Helmut Martin, *Cult and Canon: The Origins and Development of State Maoism* (Armonk, NY: M.E. Sharpe, 1982) and Daniel Leese, *Mao Cult: Rhetoric and Ritual in China's Cultural Revolution* (Cambridge: Cambridge University Press, 2011).

9. Xu Qiumei and Wu Jijin, "'文化大革命'时期的毛泽东像章" (Mao Zedong badges during the "Cultural Revolution"), *Dangshi zonglan*, no. 9 (2008), 51–2.

10. Wang, *Chairman Mao Badges*, 24.

11. Badge production was a response to the market slowdown in demand for the factory's original products, such as the "longevity lock," a traditional good-luck charm worn by newborn babies. "让毛主席的光辉普照全世界: 记北京红旗证章厂制作毛主席像章的故事" (Let the light of Chairman Mao brighten the whole world: The story of the Beijing Red Flag Badge Factory making Mao badges), *RMRB*, November 15, 1967, 2.

12. Even before the advent of the fad, Lin Biao had promoted other forms of devotion to Mao. He began with the PLA, overseeing, for instance, the compilation of Mao quotations as a PLA training manual. The manual became the *Quotations from Chairman Mao* (also known as the "Little Red Book"), of which more than a billion copies were in print when production peaked in 1971. The "Little Red Book" was the focus of another fad, as people vied to possess multiple copies and different versions. For a discussion of the origins of the *Quotations*, see Daniel Leese, "A Single Spark: Origins and Spread of the Little Red Book in China," in Alexander C. Cook, ed., *Mao's Little Red Book: A Global History* (Cambridge: Cambridge University Press, 2014), 23–42.

13. Lin's order mandated that soldiers wear both badges. "毛泽东思想光辉永远照耀全军胜利前进" (Mao Zedong Thought will forever shine to lead the entire army victoriously forward), *RMRB*, May 14, 1967, 13.

14. Note that "serve the people" was the same slogan the Commercial Leap had modified for its own purposes as "serve the consumer." See Chapter 5.

15. "Chinese women don't like fashionable dress, but like to dress like a soldier" was another popular Mao quotation that people sought out for their badges. It is yet another contradictory bit of evidence from the era that a slogan demonizing fashion sensibility occupied center stage in a fad involving personal appearance.

16. Dangdai Zhongguo shangye bianjibu, ed., 中华人民共和国商业大事记 (1958–1978) (A record of commercial activities in the People's Republic of China [1958–1978]) (Beijing: Zhongguo shangye chubanshe, 1990), 609–10.

17. Li Ping'an et al., eds., 陕西经济大事 *1949–1985* (Record of major events in Shaanxi's economy 1949–1985) (Xi'an: Sanqin chubanshe, 1987), 295–307.

18. Despite the focus of historical narratives on the pressure to conform, not everyone experienced the pressure in the same way or to the same degree. Two books that explore experiences beyond these conventional narratives are: Xueping Zhong, Zheng Wang, and Di Bai, *Some of Us: Chinese Women Growing Up in the Mao Era* (New Brunswick, NJ: Rutgers University Press, 2001); Mobo Gao, *The Battle for China's Past: Mao and the Cultural Revolution* (London: Pluto Press, 2008).

19. Red Guard circulars, for example, demanded that everyone own and carry with them copies of the *Quotations from Chairman Mao*, "studying their copies whenever possible." Mao Zedong zhuyi xuexiao, "破旧立新一百例" (100 ways to get rid of the old and to establish the new), August 1968, in *WDGW*.

20. Jin Dalu, 非常与正常: 上海'文革'时期的社会生活 (The extraordinary and the ordinary: Social life in Shanghai during the "Cultural Revolution"), 2 vols. (Shanghai: Shanghai cishu chubanshe, 2011), 2.177.

21. The early versions of the *Selected Works* were big volumes. Publishers reduced the size and weight of the pages in subsequent editions to make the volumes more portable. Editions that used dictionary-quality thin paper were smaller and lighter. Publishers also released smaller volumes of the *Quotations* to accommodate student preferences (easier to pack and carry) and fashions. According to one student at the time, those who only owned the largest, bulkiest versions of the *Selected Works* felt "ashamed." Qi Mai, "文革琐记: 政治边缘处的众生相" (Remembering the Cultural Revolution: People at the political edge), http://mjlsh.usc.cuhk.edu.hk/Book.aspx?cid=4&tid=1670. Archived November 12, 2017.

22. Xu Qiumei and Wu Jijin, "'文化大革命'时期的毛泽东像章" (Mao Zedong badges during the "Cultural Revolution"), 52.

23. Judy Manton, "Mao Badges – Graven Images?" *China Now*, no. 125 (Summer 1988), 8, www.sacu.org/maobadges.html. Archived September 7, 2018. The author lived in Guangzhou in 1972 at the end of the Mao badge fad.

24. Lu Na, 毛泽东像章收藏与鉴赏 (Collecting and appreciating Mao Zedong badges) (Beijing: Guoji wenhua chubanshe, 1993), 5–6, 14. One thorough but unsourced article suggests eight billion as the total number of badges produced: Xu Qiumei and Wu Jijin, "'文化大革命'时期的毛泽东像章" (Mao Zedong badges during the "Cultural Revolution"), 51–4.

25. On the prevalence of such gray market activities during the Mao era, see Chapters 1 and 6 as well as Zhang Xuebing, "中国计划经济时期的'地下经济'探析" (An analysis of the "underground economy" during the period of China's planned economy), *Zhonggong dangshi yanjiu*, no. 4 (2012), 39–48. On how such markets were an endemic part of "planned" economies generally, see János Kornai, *The Socialist System: The Political Economy of Communism* (Oxford: Clarendon Press, 2007).

26. Xu Qiumei and Wu Jijin, "'文化大革命'时期的毛泽东像章" (Mao Zedong badges during the "Cultural Revolution"), 51–4.

27. In Guangzhou, a small social-services work unit on Cherish the People Street made badges. But the smallest unit in the entire country to make its own badges may have been a single shift at the Baoding Electric Machinery Plant in Hebei province. Li Baolong, "行业最小单位: '班组'制作的毛主席像章" (Mao badge made by the smallest unit: A "shift"), *Baoding wanbao*, October 19, 2008.

28. Mo'ren, "文革时期我参观毛主席像章制造厂" (I visited a Mao badge factory during the Cultural Revolution), http://blog.sina.com.cn/s/blog_4 ca44b540100drhb.html. Consulted September 4, 2016.

29. Discussion and email exchange with Peter Zhou, Director, C. V. Starr East Asian Library, UC Berkeley, March 23, 2017.

30. Hua Jiannan, "'学习班'记事" (Memories of the "Study Group"), *Jiyi*, no. 7 (May 31, 2013), 76–9, http://prchistory.org/wp-content/uploads/2014/05/RE MEMBRANCE_No98.pdf. Archived March 24, 2017.

31. Chen Zhizhong, "'文革'时期像章描漆工艺" (Painting techniques used in making Mao badges during the "Cultural Revolution"), *Zhongguo shangbao*, December 8, 2001.

32. Joel Andreas, "Reconfiguring China's Class Order after the 1949 Revolution," in Yingjie Guo, ed., *Handbook on Class and Social Stratification in China* (Cheltenham: Edward Elgar, 2016), 21–43. Andreas' argument about the formation of this class is elaborated on in *Rise of the Red Engineers: The Cultural Revolution and the Origins of China's New Class* (Stanford: Stanford University Press, 2009).

33. Manton, "Mao Badges – Graven Images?" 8.

34. Qing Cha (blogger pseudonym), "伟大领袖毛主席像章" (Badges of the great leader Chairman Mao), http://blog.sina.com.cn/s/blo g_499a195d0100fg6q.html. Archived April 21, 2019.

35. Ken Ling, *Red Guard: From Schoolboy to "Little General" in Mao's China* (London: Macdonald, 1972), 286. See also Robert A. White, "Mao Badges and the Cultural Revolution," *International Social Science Review*, vol. 69 nos. 3–4 (1994), 53–70.

36. Ji Xudong, "毛澤東像章" (Mao Zedong badges), 大公报网 (Hong Kong), October 10, 2009.

37. Jin Dalu, 非常与正常: 上海'文革'时期的社会生活 (The extraordinary and the ordinary: Social life in Shanghai during the "Cultural Revolution"), 2.193.

38. "西安收藏家45年收藏毛泽东像章5万多种" (Over 45 years, Xi'an collector collects more than 50,000 kinds of Mao badges), www .chinanews.com/sh/2011/07–08/3166885.shtml. Archived April 26, 2019.

39. White, "Mao Badges and the Cultural Revolution," 53–70; Gordon A. Bennett and Ronald N. Monaperto, *Red Guard: The Political Biography of Dai Hsiao-ai* (Garden City, NY: Anchor Books, 1972); Robert Benewick and Stephanie Donald, "Badgering the People: Mao Badges, a Retrospective 1949–1995," in Robert Benewick, ed., *Belief in China: Art and Politics, Deities and Mortality* (Brighton: Green Centre for Non-Western Art and Culture at the Royal Pavilion, Art Gallery and Museums, 1996), 31.

40. White, "Mao Badges and the Cultural Revolution," 53–70.

41. Of these, mangos were the newest, most common, and used in the widest variety of ways, including to sell consumer goods. See Alfreda Murck, ed., *Mao's Golden Mangoes and the Cultural Revolution* (Zurich: Scheidegger & Spiess, 2013); Michael Dutton, "Mango Mao: Infections of the Sacred," *Public Culture*, vol. 16, no. 2 (2004), 161–87.

42. Yao Xiaoping, "疯狂的像章" (The badge craze), original article published in *Xin tiandi*, no. 6 (2011), 44–5 and reprinted online at http://lrtd.qikan.com /ArticleView.aspx?titleid=lrtd20110633. Consulted June 28, 2015.

43. Yuyang shanren (blogger name), "文革初期的倒卖毛主席像章活动" (The reselling of Chairman Mao badges at the beginning of the Cultural Revolution), http://blog.creaders.net/yuyangshanren/user_blog_diary.php?d id=182435. Archived April 13, 2019.

44. Yao Xiaoping, "疯狂的像章" (The badge craze), 44–5.

45. Robert Benewick, "Icons of Power: Mao Zedong and the Cultural Revolution," in Harriet Evans and Stephanie Donald, eds., *Picturing Power in the People's Republic: Posters of the Cultural Revolution* (Lanham, MD: Rowman & Littlefield, 1999), 131.

46. Contemporary collector Chen Xinji, who has more than 20,000 badges, owns badges made of metal, crystal, jade, white marble, bamboo, and silk. One badge, made of 24k gold made by the Shanghai Watch Factory, shows that non-designated badge factories used their machinery to make badges. Liu Yaohua and Liu Fangjie, "陈新记收藏毛主席像章2万枚" (Chen Xinji has collected 20,00 Mao badges), *Xinhua wang*, March 5, 2004 (initially published in *Guilin ribao*), http://news.xinhuanet.com/co llection/2004–03/05/content_1346043.htm. Consulted March 8, 2016. The range of objects adorned with Mao's image or quotations were even greater than the materials used for badges, including wine bottles, candy-paper, pillows, and so forth. See Leese, *Mao Cult*, 212–13.

47. Jicai Feng, *Voices from the Whirlwind: An Oral History of the Chinese Cultural Revolution* (New York: Pantheon Books, 1991), 211.

48. Mirroring the absurdity of many consumer fads, some badges were so big they were no longer wearable. Sun Maoxing recalled that the size of badges peaked in the spring of 1969 for the celebration of the Ninth National Party Congress, when work units such as the Shanghai Smelting Plant decorated a parade float with nine Mao badges, the largest "as big as a round banquet table." Sun Maoxing, "文革初期的毛主席像章" (Mao badges during the early Cultural Revolution), Sina blog posted November 12, 2012, http://blog.sina.com.cn/s/bl og_86a388020102wubi.html. Consulted August 17, 2016. Five workers at Hainan's Nongken Haikou Machinery Factory commemorated the congress by making the largest still-extant Mao badge, which is two meters (6.5 feet) in diameter. Fang Dong and Li Ying, "全国最大毛泽东像章现身 出自海口5 工人之手" (The biggest Mao badge found in Haikou; made by 5 factory workers), *Xinhua wang*, June 27, 2005, https://news.artron.net/20050627/n8120 .html. Archived April 26, 2019.

49. "Students" and "Red Guards" were often the same or at least hard to differentiate. I try to reserve "students" as a more general category of young people and "Red Guards" as a (large) subset of more actively involved students.

50. Suinian Liu and Qungan Wu, eds., *China's Socialist Economy: An Outline History (1949–1984)* (Beijing: Beijing Review, 1986), 343.

51. Roderick MacFarquhar and Michael Schoenhals, *Mao's Last Revolution* (Cambridge, MA: Belknap Press of Harvard University Press, 2008), 173, which discusses the attempts to end the Great Exchange.

52. Leese, *Mao Cult*, 139.

53. Jiang Jiangao, "韶山又兴'像章热'" (The "badge fad" is hot again in Shaoshan), *Nanfang chuang*, no. 1 (1993). Other popular sites included two in major cities: the Peasant Movement Institute in Guangzhou, where Mao and Zhou Enlai taught in 1925, and the birthplace of the

CCP in Shanghai. Rural locations included Yan'an, Mao's headquarters during most of World War II; Jinggangshan, symbol of the founding of Red Army; Ruijin, where the Communists fled after Nationalist troops chased them out of Jinggangshan; and Zunyi, where Mao rose to power during the Long March.

54. Travel was expensive, and the household registration system, imposed in 1958, made it impossible to obtain food rations outside of one's home area, thus making travel prohibitive for most Chinese. Along with the rustication of urban youth, the Great Exchange also served to teach participants about urban-rural inequalities.

55. Yuan Gao, *Born Red: A Chronicle of the Cultural Revolution* (Stanford: Stanford University Press, 1987), 120.

56. Liang Heng and Judith Shapiro, *Son of the Revolution* (New York: Knopf, 1983), 94, 104. Although I primarily rely on lesser-known memoirs, Liang and Shapiro's is one of the earliest memoirs by a Red Guard.

57. On the organization of Red Guard information networks, which helps explain how students were able to spread news of the Cultural Revolution around the country, see Michael Schoenhals, "China's 'Great Proletarian Information Revolution' of 1966–1967," in Jeremy Brown and Matthew D. Johnson, eds., *Maoism at the Grassroots: Everyday Life in China's Era of High Socialism* (Cambridge, MA: Harvard University Press, 2015), 230–58.

58. Yao Xiaoping, "疯狂的像章" (The badge craze), 44–5. The fair provided invaluable hard currency and was held uninterrupted throughout the Cultural Revolution decade, conducting US$21.4 billion in transactions, or 42 percent of the country's total foreign trade. Xin Jin, Karin Weber, and Jing Xu, "The China Import and Export (Canton) Fair: A Trade Show in Transformation," Proceedings of the International Convention Exposition Summit (ICES) (2008). Although Yao Xiaoping's experience was in 1966, photos show the same scenes two years later at the fair. See 中国出口商品交易会 (Special issue on the Chinese Export Commodities Fair) (Spring, April 15, 1968), 31, 35, 37–9, and 41–3.

59. He Yunhua, "文革期间的广交会" (The Canton Fair during the Cultural Revolution), 搜狐博客, http://hehouao.blog.sohu.com/162554454.html. Archived November 12, 2017. Demand for all kinds of Mao memorabilia ran high throughout the fair, which was attended by more than 6,000 visitors from around the world. The organizers accommodated demand by setting up a designated stall. The stall sold over 50,000 *Quotations from Chairman Mao* (毛主席语录), 7,500 sets of his *Selected Works* (毛泽东选集), countless photos of Mao, and over 230,000 badges. "我出口商品交易会政治经济双丰收" (The double bumper harvest in politics and economics of our export commodities trade fair), *RMRB*, November 18, 1966, 2. See also "反映我国社

会主义建设新成就的出口商品交易会" (Export Commodity Fair reflects new achievements in our country's socialist construction), in 中国出口商品交易会 (Chinese Export Commodities Fair), published as a supplement to *Jingji daobao*, April 15, 1968, 36–7. The catalog includes many photographs of people around the world reading Mao publications as well as a photo of a display of badges at the fair. It does not provide the number of Mao badges distributed overseas but it does mention that in the year from October 1966 to September 1967, the *Quotations from Chairman Mao* was translated into twenty-four languages and 1.3 million copies were distributed in 128 countries and regions. Mao badges were likely distributed through the same channels (see p. 37).

60. According to the Shanghai Reception Office (上海市接待各地革命学生办公室), the city officially accommodated more than four million visiting Red Guards, not including students hosted by relatives and other work units. Many were housed at Shanghai universities, such as the Shanghai Theater Academy (上海戏剧学院), whose 400 students were joined by 1,000 exchange students. Jin Dalu, 非常与正常：上海'文革'时期的社会生活 (The extraordinary and the ordinary: Social life in Shanghai during the "Cultural Revolution"), 1.64, 69.

61. Jin Dalu, 非常与正常：上海'文革'时期的社会生活 (The extraordinary and the ordinary: Social life in Shanghai during the "Cultural Revolution"), 1.74.

62. Liang and Shapiro, *Son of the Revolution*. See also Benewick, "Icons of Power," 125.

63. Xie was responsible for handling sensitive documents from 1959 to 1976. Xie Jingyi, 毛泽东身边工作琐忆 (Memories of working alongside Mao Zedong) (Beijing: Zhongyang wenxian chubanshe, 2015), 168–70.

64. Yuyang shanren (blogger name), "文革初期的倒卖毛主席像章活动" (The reselling of Chairman Mao badges at the beginning of the Cultural Revolution).

65. Yao Xiaoping, "疯狂的像章" (The badge craze). See also Zhang Yunsheng, 毛家湾纪实：林彪秘书回忆录 (A true account of Maojiawan: The memoirs of Lin Biao's secretary) (Beijing: Chunqiu chubanshe, 1988), 229.

66. Manton, "Mao Badges – Graven Images?"

67. "取缔纪念章交换场所 揪出了投机倒把分子" (Banning memorial badge exchanges, exposing speculators), *JFRB*, February 24, 1967. See also Jin Dalu, 非常与正常：上海'文革'时期的社会生活 (The extraordinary and the ordinary: Social life in Shanghai during the "Cultural Revolution"), 2.182.

68. Jung Chang, "Twentieth Century China Through Three Generations of Women," *India International Centre Quarterly*, vol. 31, no. 1 (July 2004), 23–31 (p. 29).

69. Schoenhals, "China's 'Great Proletarian Information Revolution' of 1966–1967," 252. Little wonder there were thriving markets for contraband and other books, as there was no shortage of supply: an estimated seven million library books from five provinces were pilfered, lost, or destroyed. MacFarquhar and Schoenhals, *Mao's Last Revolution*, 121.

70. Zhou also noted, however, that he knew of no such markets in his home town and thought that few people there would have been willing to risk extreme punishment for openly selling badges. Discussion and email exchange with Peter Zhou, Director, C. V. Starr East Asian Library, UC Berkeley, March 23, 2017.

71. Jin Dalu, 非常与正常: 上海'文革'时期的社会生活 (The extraordinary and the ordinary: Social life in Shanghai during the "Cultural Revolution"), 2.185; 上海市革命委员会反对经济主义联络总部 (The liaison headquarters of the Shanghai revolutionary committee against economism), ed., 无产阶级文化大革命中上海反对经济主义大事记 (讨论稿) (November 1966–March 15, 1967) (Primary events of Shanghai opposition to economism during the Great Proletarian Cultural Revolution [Draft for discussion]) (November 1966–March 15, 1967). March 17, 1967, in *WDGW*. By Spring Festival in 1967, there had been twelve big exchanges: five around Nanjing Road, Huangpi Road, and Shanxi Road in Huangpu District; others were around Beizhan train stations in Zhabei District, Caojiadu in Changning District, Tianqiao in Hongkou District, and so forth. Jin Dalu, 非常与正常: 上海'文革'时期的社会生活 (The extraordinary and the ordinary: Social life in Shanghai during the "Cultural Revolution"), 2.177, 184–5.

72. Jin Dalu, 非常与正常: 上海'文革'时期的社会生活 (The extraordinary and the ordinary: Social life in Shanghai during the "Cultural Revolution"), 2.180–3.

73. "坚决取缔纪念章交换场所" (Determinedly ban places for exchanging commemorative badges), *JFRB*, February 12, 1967. In case this argument was not persuasive enough, they also cited the traffic problems caused by such large crowds.

74. 上海市革命委员会反对经济主义联络总部 (The liaison headquarters of the Shanghai revolutionary committee against economism), ed., 无产阶级文化大革命中上海反对经济主义大事记 (讨论稿) (November 1966–March 15, 1967) (Primary events of Shanghai opposition to economism during the Great Proletarian Cultural Revolution [Draft for discussion]) (November 1966–March 15, 1967). March 17, 1967, in *WDGW*.

75. Jin Dalu, 非常与正常: 上海'文革'时期的社会生活 (The extraordinary and the ordinary: Social life in Shanghai during the "Cultural Revolution"), 2.184–5.

76. Jin Dalu, 非常与正常: 上海'文革'时期的社会生活 (The extraordinary and the ordinary: Social life in Shanghai during the "Cultural Revolution"), 2.186–7.

77. Judy Manton notes both the ban on trading as well as its widespread nonobservance. Manton, "Mao Badges – Graven Images?"

78. Jin Dalu, 非常与正常: 上海'文革'时期的社会生活 (The extraordinary and the ordinary: Social life in Shanghai during the "Cultural Revolution"), 2.184–5, 190–1.

79. Wang Yuli, "黑龙江像章厂建厂始末" (The rise and demise of the Heilongjiang Badge Factory), *Heilongjiang shizhi*, no. 24 (2011), 44–5. The author is president of the Red Collection Research Association of Heilongjiang Province (黑龙江省红色收藏研究会会长).

80. Wang Yuli, "黑龙江像章厂建厂始末" (The rise and demise of the Heilongjiang Badge Factory), 68.

81. The activities mentioned by Jiang include the loyalty dance; the recitation of Mao quotations; soldiers who wore badges and sewed a very large "loyalty" character onto their uniforms; and the Mao badges collected by individuals across the entire country. Moreover, he cited the custom that one could not simply "buy" a Mao book, badge, or poster but must use the verb "request," which he noted was the same term used in temples. Everywhere he looked, Jiang saw the construction of "Long Life Palaces" – public buildings such as conference and exhibition halls, including the one that housed the Canton Fair, or train stations that usually had giant banners proclaiming, "Long Live Chairman Mao." Yu Xiguang, ed., 位卑未敢忘忧国: "文化大革命"上书集 (Humble people do not forget their country: A collection of petitions from the Cultural Revolution) (Changsha: Hunan renmin chubanshe, 1989), 124.

82. Yin Jiamin, "文革时大学生上书毛泽东: 一句顶万句很荒谬" (A university student writes a letter to Mao Zedong during the Cultural Revolution: It is absurd to say Mao's one sentence is greater than ten thousand), http://news.ifeng.com/history/zhiqing/ziliao/detail_2013_02/26/22495744_0.shtml. Archived April 21, 2019. That same day, he was arrested, beaten, and put into a makeshift prison that work units and districts used to lock up "counter-revolutionaries" during the Cultural Revolution. See also "姜明亮等上中共中央, 毛泽东书" (Letter to the Central Committee of the Chinese Communist Party and Mao Zedong by Jiang Mingliang et al.), in Yu Xiguang, ed., 位卑未敢忘忧国:"文化大革命"上书集 (Humble people do not forget their country: A collection of petitions from the Cultural Revolution), 124–5, 128.

83. "萧瑞怡上毛泽东书" (Xiao Ruiyi's letter to Mao Zedong"), in Yu Xiguang, ed., 位卑未敢忘忧国:'文化大革命'上书集 (Humble people do not forget their country: A collection of petitions from the Cultural Revolution), 11–12.

84. This account comes from Han Suyin, the pen name of Elizabeth K.C. Comber; the badges read "毛泽东以永恒的激情从事工作" (Mao Zedong always works in a passionate way), in Deng Liqun, ed., 中外名人评说毛泽东 (Comments on Mao Zedong by famous Chinese and foreigners) (Beijing: Zhongyang minzu daxue chubanshe, 2003), 509–10. On June 11–12, 1969, Mao had inked "do so" on the document "关于宣传毛主席形象应注意的几个问题" (Several issues deserving attention when publicizing the image of Chairman Mao), submitted by the CCP Central Committee, which determined that badges and other memorabilia were wasteful. Pang Xianzhi and Feng Hui, eds., 毛泽东年谱 (1949–1976), 六卷 (A Chronicle of Mao Zedong [1949–1976], Volume 6) (Beijing: Zhongyang wenxian chubanshe, 2013), 6. 255–6.

85. Fang Houshu, "'文革'十年毛泽东著作、毛泽东像出版纪实" (Mao Zedong works and posters published during the ten years of Cultural Revolution), in Song Yuanfang, ed., 中国出版史料第三卷上册/现代部分 (Historical materials on publishing in China, vol. 3, part 1: Contemporary section) (Ji'nan: Shandong jiaoyu chubanshe, 2001), 234–5.

86. Zhou went on to suggest solutions: "People who have hundreds of badges should return them. Some of these people wear a different badge every day, which cheapens the idea of the badge ... and is incompatible with Mao Zedong Thought." According to Zhou, the fad was not only creating a shortage of raw materials to create planes, but also everyday necessities. Zhou Enlai, "周恩来在全国计划工作会议上谈党史历次路线斗争" (Zhou Enlai's speech at the National Planning Conference on the previous lines struggles in the history of the party) (March 24, 1969), in Zhou Liangxiao and Gu Juying, eds. 疯狂, 扭曲与堕落的年代之二:十年文革中首长讲话传信录 (Times of madness, distortion, and degradation [2]: Collected speeches by central party leaders during the ten years of the Cultural Revolution) (Hong Kong: Xindalu chubanshe, 2008), 595.

87. Zhou Jihou, 毛泽东像章之谜: 世界第九大奇观 (The mystery of the Mao badge: The ninth wonder of the world) (Taiyuan: Beiyue wenyi chubanshe, 1993), 76–7. The best evidence of the collapse comes from two sources. First, websites devoted to badge trading yield countless badges from 1966–9, only a handful of badges in 1970, and none in 1971 or 1972. Periodic searches in the summer of 2017 of two popular webpages for selling badges (www.997788.com and www.kongfz.com) yielded only three badges from 1970. Second, books compiled by collectors confirm this date as the end of the fad, including the observation by Zhou Jihou, who writes that he never saw a badge made in 1971.

88. Publication of Lin Biao's original Mao-cult project, *Quotations from Chairman Mao*, was temporarily halted to accommodate a design change

and the population was told to tear out the front pages of their copies to remove their association. Edgar Snow, "A Conversation with Mao Tse-tung," *Life*, vol. 70, no. 16 (April 30, 1971), 46-7. On the impact of the Lin Biao incident and the pullback from Mao as infallible, see MacFarquhar and Schoenhals, *Mao's Last Revolution*, ch. 12.

89. Xu Qiumei and Wu Jijin, "'文化大革命'时期的毛泽东像章" (Mao Zedong badges during the "Cultural Revolution"), 51-4. It is easy to imagine that the farther away from the seats of political power, the longer the badge fad continued. An American reporter in Inner Mongolia in 1973, for instance, reported seeing a display of 2,000 badges. Manton, "Mao Badges – Graven Images?"

90. "中央宣传部关于处理留存的'忠'字品的请示" (The Central Propaganda Department requests instructions on handling retained loyalty items), July 28, 1978. Published in Zhongyang xuanchuanbu bangongting, ed., 党的宣传工作文件选编 (Selected documents on party propaganda work) (Beijing: Zhonggong zhongyang dangxiao chubanshe, 1994), vol. 2 (1976–82): 609-10. This series of books was published for internal circulation among cadres in work units from the county level and above.

91. Zhao Juan, ed., "中共中央关于坚持'少宣传个人'的几个问题的指示" (The Central Committee of the Communist Party of China on problems related to supporting the policy of "less propaganda on individuals"), July 30, 1980, http://cpc.people.com.cn/GB/64162/71380/71387/71592/4854499.html. Archived November 12, 2017.

92. Fang Dong and Li Ying, "全国最大毛泽东像章现身 出自海口5工人之手" (Biggest Mao badge found in Haikou; Made by 5 factory workers), *Shanglü bao*, June 27, 2005. Reprinted online at https://news.artron.net/200 50627/n8120.htm. Archived April 26, 2019.

Afterword

1. Lili Cui, "Mao Badge Craze Returns to China," *Beijing Review*, vol. 36, no. 19 (May 10–16, 1993), 32–3; Yao Yanxi, "毛泽东像收藏漫谈" (The story of a Mao Zedong badge collection), *Zhejiang dang'an*, 50–3.

2. For a feature on the collector Wang Anting, see Luo Weiran, "闯入吉尼斯大全的'毛泽东像章'收藏家" (Mao Zedong badge collector is granted place in *Guinness Book of World Records*), *Zhongzhou jingu*, no. 2 (1997), 38–41. Wang edited one of the earliest and best books for collectors, with 400 pages. There are five or more badges from 1956 to 1968 on each page. See Wang Anting, ed., 毛泽东像章图谱 (An illustrated catalogue of Mao Zedong badges) (Beijing: Zhongguo shudian chubanshe, 1993).

3. Li Lin, "毛泽东像章的收藏初探" (A brief study of Mao Zedong badge collections), *Sichuansheng ganbu hanshou xueyuan xuebao*, no. 3 (2010), 40–3.

For a list of prominent Chinese Mao badge collectors and photos of parts of their collections, see www.wengewang.org/read.php?tid=19639. Archived April 21, 2019. Li Qitian, "红色收藏, 投资热流涌动" (Red collecting, a favorite investment activity), *Jinrong bolan*, no. 6 (2011), 70; Fang Xiang, "红色收藏热神州" (Red collecting is hot in China), *RMRB* (overseas edition), July 1, 2011, 15; Chen De, "海内外展出毛泽东像章二十余万枚" (Over 200,000 Mao Zedong badges exhibited inside and outside of China), www.chinanews.com/sh/news/2008/12–26/1503400.shtml. Archived November 12, 2017.

4. Luo Zhengyuan, Dong Zhigang, Liao Qin, and Zhang Fei, "韶山的'红色经济'热" (The "red economy" is flourishing in Shaoshan), *Guang'an ribao*, October 29, 2009; Yang Wenhua and Lin Yigang, "韶山旅游纪念品开发中的问题与对策" (The problem of and solution for the development of tourist souvenirs in Shaoshan), *Jingji tequ*, no. 11 (November 2007), 196–7.

5. Rather than change the framing of the political economy as "socialism," the official lengthy self-assessment by the CCP on the Mao era uses the term "mistakes" fifty times. See "Resolution on Certain Questions in the History of our Party since the Founding of the State," adopted by the Sixth Plenary Session of the Eleventh Central Committee of the Communist Party of China on June 27, 1981, www.marxists.org/subject/china/ documents/cpc/history/01 .htm. Consulted September 9, 2019.

6. Deng Xiaoping, "Building Socialism with a Specifically Chinese Character," excerpt from a talk with the Japanese delegation to the Second Session of the Council of Sino-Japanese Non-Governmental Persons, June 30, 1984, http://en .people.cn/dengxp/vol3/text/c1220.html. Archived December 26, 2017. In addition to Deng Xiaoping's "building socialism with Chinese characteristics," post-Mao variations of the "building socialism" formulation also include: Hu Jintao's "comprehensively building a moderately prosperous society" and, since 2006, "building a new socialist countryside."

7. The shift along the spectrum of capitalism toward greater private control over capital is especially obvious in the party's 2001 decision to admit capitalists into its ranks. See Bruce J. Dickson, including *Red Capitalists in China: The Party, Private Entrepreneurs and the Prospects for Political Change* (New York: Cambridge University Press, 2003) and *Wealth into Power: The Communist Party's Embrace of China's Private Sector* (New York: Cambridge University Press, 2008).

8. In 2017, for instance, Xi Jinping predicted that by 2050 China would be a "great modern socialist country." See "Xi warns party to tackle challenges as China moves into new 'modern socialist' era," *South China Morning Post*, October 18, 2017, www.scmp.com/news/china/policies-politics/article/21159 70/xi-lays-out-path-confident-new-era-china. Archived August 8, 2019.

9. Economist Peter Nolan critiques these views of a Chinese state-led economy as a unique economic threat in *Is China Buying the World?* (Cambridge: Polity Press, 2012).

10. Since the early 2000s, discussions of the "varieties of capitalism" have used a narrow range of institutions centering on private property and markets between "liberal market economies," such as the United States and the United Kingdom, and "coordinated market economies," including Germany and Sweden. See Peter A. Hall and David W. Soskice, *Varieties of Capitalism: The Institutional Foundations of Comparative Advantage* (Oxford: Oxford University Press, 2001) and the considerable literature generated thereafter.

Bibliography

Altehenger, Jennifer E. *Legal Lessons: Popularizing Laws in the People's Republic of China, 1949–1989*. Cambridge, MA: Harvard University Asia Center, 2018.

Andreas, Joel. "Reconfiguring China's Class Order after the 1949 Revolution." Pp. 21–43, in Yingjie Guo, ed. *Handbook on Class and Social Stratification in China*. Cheltenham: Edward Elgar, 2016.

Andreas, Joel. *Rise of the Red Engineers: The Cultural Revolution and the Origins of China's New Class*. Stanford: Stanford University Press, 2009.

Arnold, David. *Everyday Technology: Machines and the Making of India's Modernity*. Chicago: University of Chicago Press, 2013.

"把上海的天空保护起来" (Protect the Shanghai sky). Pp. 132–40, in Zhongguo renmin jiefangjun Shanghai jingbeiqu zhengzhibu, Zhonggong Shanghai shiwei dangshi yanjiushi 中国人民解放军上海警备区政治部, 中共上海市委党史研究室, eds. 警备大上海 (Guard great Shanghai). Shanghai: Shanghai yuandong chubanshe, 1994.

Ball, Alan M. *Russia's Last Capitalists: The Nepmen, 1921–1929*. Berkeley: University of California Press, 1987.

Baranovitch, Nimrod. *China's New Voices: Popular Music, Ethnicity, Gender, and Politics, 1978–1997*. Berkeley: University of California Press, 2003.

Barber, John and Mark Harrison, eds. *The Soviet Defence-Industry Complex from Stalin to Khrushchev*. Basingstoke: Macmillan, 2000.

Barnett, A. Doak. *Communist China: The Early Years, 1949–55*. New York: Praeger, 1964.

Baum, Richard and Frederick C. Teiwes. *Ssu-Ch'ing: The Socialist Education Movement of 1962–1966*. Berkeley: Center for Chinese Studies, University of California, 1968.

Bays, Daniel H. *A New History of Christianity in China*. Malden, MA: Wiley-Blackwell, 2012.

Beckert, Sven. *Empire of Cotton: A Global History*. New York: Alfred A. Knopf, 2014.

Beijing chubanshe bianjibu 北京出版社编辑部, ed. 大跃进中的北京天桥百货商场 (Beijing Tianqiao Department Store in the Great Leap Forward). Beijing: Beijing chubanshe, 1958.

Beijing huace bianji weiyuanhui 北京画册编辑委员会, ed. 北京 (Beijing). Beijing: Beijing huace bianji weiyuanhui, 1959.

Beijingshi difangzhi bianzuan weiyuanhui 北京市地方志编纂委员会, ed. 北京志 商业卷 饮食服务志 (Beijing gazetteer, commerce volume: Food and service sector). Beijing: Beijing chubanshe, 2008.

Benedict, Carol. *Golden-Silk Smoke: A History of Tobacco in China, 1550–2010.* Berkeley: University of California Press, 2011.

Benewick, Robert. "Icons of Power: Mao Zedong and the Cultural Revolution." Pp. 123–37, in Harriet Evans and Stephanie Donald, eds. *Picturing Power in the People's Republic: Posters of the Cultural Revolution.* Lanham, MD: Rowman & Littlefield, 1999.

Benewick, Robert and Stephanie Donald. "Badgering the People: Mao Badges, A Retrospective 1949–1995." Pp. 28–39, in Robert Benewick, ed. *Belief in China: Art and Politics, Deities and Mortality.* Brighton: Green Centre for Non-Western Art and Culture at the Royal Pavilion, Art Gallery and Museums, 1996.

Bennett, Gordon A. *Yundong: Mass Campaigns in Chinese Communist Leadership.* Berkeley: Center for Chinese Studies, University of California, 1976.

Bennett, Gordon A. and Ronald N. Montaperto. *Red Guard: The Political Biography of Dai Hsiao-ai.* Garden City, NY: Anchor Books, 1972.

Bernstein, Thomas P. "Introduction: The Complexities of Learning from the Soviet Union." Pp. 1–23, in Thomas P. Bernstein and Hua-Yu Li, eds. *China Learns from the Soviet Union, 1949–Present.* Lanham, MD: Lexington Books, 2010.

Bernstein, Thomas P. "Mao Zedong and the Famine of 1959–1960." *The China Quarterly,* no. 186 (2006), 421–45.

Bernstein, Thomas P. *Up to the Mountains and Down to the Villages: The Transfer of Youth from Urban to Rural China.* New Haven: Yale University Press, 1977.

Bi Jiarong 毕家镕. "南京财贸行业在动乱中的徘徊" (Lingering finance and trade in Nanjing during the time of chaos). Pp. 506–12, in Zhuang Xiaojun 庄小军 and Xu Kangying 徐康英, eds. 风雨同舟: 南京探索前进三十年 1949–1978 (Stand together through storm and stress: Thirty years of exploration and progress in Nanjing 1949–1978). Beijing: Zhonggong dangshi chubanshe, 2002.

Bijker, Wiebe E. *Of Bicycles, Bakelites, and Bulbs: Toward a Theory of Sociotechnical Change.* Cambridge, MA: MIT Press, 2002.

Bo Fen 伯奋. 好莱坞: 电影帝国 (Hollywood: Cinematic imperialism). Shanghai: Hufeng chubanshe, 1951.

Bonnell, Victoria E. *Iconography of Power: Soviet Political Posters under Lenin and Stalin.* Berkeley: University of California Press, 1997.

Bossen, Laurel and Hill Gates. *Bound Feet, Young Hands: Tracking the Demise of Footbinding in Village China.* Stanford: Stanford University Press, 2017.

Bourdieu, Pierre. *Distinction: A Social Critique of the Judgement of Taste,* tr. Richard Nice. Cambridge, MA: Harvard University Press, 1984.

Bramall, Chris. *Chinese Economic Development.* London: Routledge, 2009.

Bramall, Chris. *Industrialization of Rural China.* Oxford: Oxford University Press, 2007.

Bray, Francesca. *Technology and Gender: Fabrics of Power in Late Imperial China.* Berkeley: University of California Press, 1997.

Brewer, John and Roy Porter, eds. *Consumption and the World of Goods.* London: Routledge, 1994.

Brown, Jeremy. *City versus Countryside in Mao's China: Negotiating the Divide.* New York: Cambridge University Press, 2012.

Brown, Jeremy and Paul G. Pickowicz., eds. *Dilemmas of Victory: The Early Years of the People's Republic of China.* Cambridge, MA: Harvard University Press, 2010.

Brown, Kate. *Plutopia: Nuclear Families, Atomic Cities, and the Great Soviet and American Plutonium Disasters.* Oxford: Oxford University Press, 2013.

Buick, Adam and John Crump. *State Capitalism: The Wages System under New Management.* Basingstoke: Macmillan, 1986.

Cao Qianli 草千里. 红色官窑: 文革瓷器 (The red official kiln: Cultural Revolution porcelain). Beijing: Tuanjie chubanshe, 2002.

Castells, Manuel. "Collective Consumption and Urban Contradictions in Advanced Capitalism." Pp. 107–29, in Ida Susser, ed. *The Castells Reader on Cities and Social Theory.* Oxford: Blackwell, 2002.

Ceplair, Larry. *Anti-Communism in Twentieth-Century America: A Critical History.* Santa Barbara: Praeger, 2011.

Ch'en, Yün et al. *Ch'en Yün's Strategy for China's Development: A Non-Maoist Alternative.* Armonk, NY: M.E. Sharpe, 1983.

Chan, Anita and Jonathan Unger. "Grey and Black: The Hidden Economy of Rural China." *Pacific Affairs*, vol. 55, no. 3 (Fall 1982), 452–71.

Chan, Anita, Richard Madsen, and Jonathan Unger. *Chen Village: Revolution to Globalization*, 3rd ed. Berkeley: University of California Press, 2009.

Chan, Sylvia. "The Image of a 'Capitalist Roader' – Some Dissident Short Stories in the Hundred Flowers Period." *The Australian Journal of Chinese Affairs*, no. 2 (July 1979), 77–102.

Chan, Wellington K. K. "Personal Styles, Cultural Values and Management: The Sincere and Wing On Companies in Shanghai and Hong Kong, 1900–1941." *Business History Review*, vol. 70, no. 2 (1996), 141–66.

Chan, Wellington K. K. "Selling Goods and Promoting a New Commercial Culture: The Four Premier Department Stores on Nanjing Road, 1917–1937." Pp. 19–36, in Sherman Cochran, ed. *Inventing Nanjing Road: Commercial Culture in Shanghai, 1900–1945.* Ithaca, NY: East Asia Program, Cornell University, 1999.

Chang, Jung. "Twentieth Century China Through Three Generations of Women." *India International Centre Quarterly*, vol. 31, no. 1 (July 2004), 23–31.

Chase-Dunn, Christopher K., ed. *Socialist States in the World-System.* Beverly Hills: Sage Publications, 1982.

Chattopadhyay, Paresh. *Marx's Associated Mode of Production: A Critique of Marxism.* New York: Palgrave Macmillan, 2016.

Chen Boda 陈伯达. "不要乱打原来的企业机构" (Don't throw into disarray the existing structure of capitalist enterprises). Pp. 17–29, in 中国人民解放军入城政策 (Policies regarding the takeover of cities by the People's Liberation Army). Hankou: Xinhua shudian, 1949.

Chen Chi-hua. "Films for the People." *People's China*, vol. 24, no. 10 (December 16, 1953), 10–13.

Chen Chunfang 陈春舫. 上海票证故事 (Stories of Shanghai ration coupons). Shanghai: Dongfang chuban zhongxin, 2009.

Chen, Feng. *Economic Transition and Political Legitimacy in Post-Mao China: Ideology and Reform.* Albany: State University of New York Press, 1995.

Chen Jian. *China's Road to the Korean War: The Making of the Sino-American Confrontation.* New York: Columbia University Press, 1994.

Chen Jian. "The Chinese Communist 'Liberation' of Tibet, 1949–51." Pp. 160–83, in Jeremy Brown and Paul G. Pickowicz, eds. *Dilemmas of Victory: The Early Years of the People's Republic of China.* Cambridge, MA: Harvard University Press, 2010.

Chen Jian. *Mao's China and the Cold War.* Chapel Hill: University of North Carolina Press, 2001.

Chen Lo-Kiang. "Get-Together Cooking Is Best." *Women of China*, no. 2 (February 1960), 13–15.

Chen Mingyuan. 陈明远, 历史的见证: 四十年票证和人民币史 (Historical witness: Forty years of ration coupons and the history of the Renminbi). Beijing: Fenghuang chubanshe, 2009.

Chen, Theodore H. E. and Wen-hui C. Chen. "The 'Three Anti' and 'Five Anti' Movements in Communist China." *Pacific Affairs*, vol. 26, no. 1 (1953), 4–5.

Chen, Tina Mai. "Dressing for the Party: Clothing, Citizenship, and Gender-Formation in Mao's China." *Fashion Theory*, vol. 5, no. 2 (2001), 143–71.

Chen, Tina Mai. "Film and Gender in Sino-Soviet Cultural Exchange, 1949–1969." Pp. 421–45, in Thomas P. Bernstein and Hua-Yu Li, eds. *China Learns from the Soviet Union, 1949–Present.* Lanham, MD: Lexington Books, 2010.

Chen, Tina Mai. "International Film Circuits and Global Imaginaries in the People's Republic of China, 1949–57." *Journal of Chinese Cinemas*, vol. 3, no. 2 (2009), 149–61.

Chen, Tina Mai. "Proletarian White and Working Bodies in Mao's China." *positions: east asia, cultures critiques*, vol. 11, no. 2 (2003), 361–93.

Chen, Tina Mai. "Propagating the Propaganda Film: The Meaning of Film in Chinese Communist Party Writings, 1949–1965." *Modern Chinese Literature and Culture*, vol. 15, no. 2 (Fall 2003), 154–93.

Chen, Xin-zhu J. "China and the US Trade Embargo, 1950–1972." *American Journal of Chinese Studies*, vol. 13, no. 2 (2006), 169–86.

Chen Yilin 陈毅林. "三块手表" (Three watches). *Wenshi yuekan*, no. 12 (December 2008), 68.

Chen Yu 陈煜. 中国生活记忆: 建国60年民生往事 (Recollections of life in China: 60 years of everyday happening since the establishment of the state). Beijing: Zhongguo qinggongye chubanshe, 2009.

Chen Zhengqing. "Socialist Transformation and the Demise of Private Entrepreneurs: Wu Yunchu's Tragedy." *European Journal of East Asian Studies*, vol. 13, no. 2 (2014), 240–61.

Cheng, Tiejun and Mark Selden. "The Construction of Spatial Hierarchies: China's *Hukou* and *Danwei* Systems." Pp. 23–50, in Timothy Cheek and Tony Saich, eds. *New Perspectives on State Socialism in China*. Armonk, NY: M.E. Sharpe, 1997.

Chernyshova, Natalya. *Soviet Consumer Culture in the Brezhnev Era*. London: Routledge, 2013.

Cheung, Tai Ming. *Fortifying China: The Struggle to Build a Modern Defense Economy*. Ithaca, NY: Cornell University Press, 2009.

Chin Feng. "Good Housewife Campaign Sweeps the Country." *Women of China*, no. 3 (March 1957), 10–12.

Chou Ping-kun. "The 1947 Boycott of U.S. Goods." *China Reconstructs*, vol. 14, no. 1 (1965), 40–2.

Chu Chan-liang. "Fountain Pens for Everyone." *China Reconstructs*, vol. 13, no. 4 (April 1964), 26–7.

Ciarlo, David. *Advertising Empire: Race and Visual Culture in Imperial Germany*. Cambridge, MA: Harvard University Press, 2011.

Clark, Paul. *Chinese Cinema: Culture and Politics Since 1949*. Cambridge: Cambridge University Press, 1987.

Clayton, David. *Imperialism Revisited: Political and Economic Relations between Britain and China, 1950–54*. New York: St. Martin's Press, 1997.

Clunas, Craig. *Superfluous Things: Material Culture and Social Status in Early Modern China*. Honolulu: University of Hawai'i Press, 2004.

Coble, Parks M. *Chinese Capitalists in Japan's New Order: The Occupied Lower Yangzi, 1937–1945*. Berkeley: University of California Press, 2003.

Coble, Parks M. *The Shanghai Capitalists and the Nationalist Government, 1927–1937*, 2nd ed. Cambridge, MA: Council on East Asian Studies, Harvard University, 1986.

Cochran, Sherman. *Big Business in China: Sino-Foreign Rivalry in the Cigarette Industry, 1890–1930*. Cambridge, MA: Harvard University Press, 1980.

Cochran, Sherman. "Marketing Medicine and Advertising Dreams in China, 1900–1950." Pp. 62–97, in Wen-hsin Yeh, ed. *Becoming Chinese: Passages to Modernity and Beyond*. Berkeley: University of California Press, 2000.

Cochran, Sherman, ed. *The Capitalist Dilemma in China's Communist Revolution*. Ithaca, NY: East Asia Program, Cornell University, 2015.

Coderre, Laurence. "A Necessary Evil: Conceptualizing the Socialist Commodity under Mao." *Comparative Studies in Society and History*, vol. 61, no. 1 (2019), 23–49.

The Common Program and Other Documents of the First Plenary Session of the Chinese People's Political Consultative Congress. Peking: Foreign Languages Press, 1950.

The Constitution of the People's Republic of China. Peking: Foreign Languages Press, 1954.

Cox, Randi. "All This Can Be Yours! Soviet Commercial Advertising and the Social Construction of Space, 1928–1956." Pp. 125–62, in Evgeny Dobrenko and Eric Naiman, eds. *The Landscape of Stalinism: The Art and Ideology of Soviet Space.* Seattle: University of Washington Press, 2003.

Croll, Elisabeth. "Marriage Choice and Status Groups in Contemporary China." Pp. 175–97, in James L. Watson, ed. *Class and Social Stratification in Post-Revolution China.* Cambridge: Cambridge University Press, 1984.

Crossick, Geoffrey and Serge Jaumain, eds. *Cathedrals of Consumption: The European Department Store, 1850–1939.* Aldershot: Ashgate, 1999.

Crowley, David and Susan E. Reid. "Style and Socialism: Modernity and Material Culture in Post-War Eastern Europe." Pp. 1–17, in Susan Emily Reid and D. J. Crowley, eds. *Style and Socialism: Modernity and Material Culture in Post-War Eastern Europe.* Oxford: Berg, 2000.

Cui, Lili. "Mao Badge Craze Returns to China." *Beijing Review,* vol. 36, no. 19 (May 10–16, 1993), 32–3.

"Dangdai Zhongguo" congshu bianjibu "当代中国"丛书编辑部, ed. 当代中国的轻工业 (Light industry in contemporary China), 2 vols. Beijing: Zhongguo shehui kexue chubanshe, 1986.

Dangdai Zhongguo shangye bianjibu 当代中国商业编辑部, ed. 中华人民共和国商业大事记 (1958–1978) (A record of commercial activities in the People's Republic of China [1958–1978]). Beijing: Zhongguo shangye chubanshe, 1990.

Davies, Robert Bruce. *Peacefully Working to Conquer the World: Singer Sewing Machines in Foreign Markets, 1854–1920.* New York: Arno Press, 1976.

Davin, Delia. *Woman-Work: Women and the Party in Revolutionary China.* Oxford: Clarendon Press, 1976.

Day, Richard. "Preobrazhensky and the Theory of the Transition Period." *Soviet Studies,* vol. 27, no. 2 (1975), 196–219.

"Decision of the Central Committee of the Chinese Communist Party Concerning the Great Proletarian Cultural Revolution (Adopted on August 8, 1966)." *Peking Review,* vol. 9, no. 33 (August 12, 1966), 6–11. www.marxists.org/subject/china/peking-review/1966/PR1966–33g.htm. Archived July 15, 1918.

De Grazia, Victoria. *Irresistible Empire: America's Advance through Twentieth-Century Europe.* Cambridge, MA: Belknap Press of Harvard University Press, 2005.

Deng Pu 邓普. 美帝侵略上海的罪证 (Evidence of the US imperialist invasion of Shanghai). Beijing: Shijie zhishi chubanshe, 1950.

Deng Xiaoping. "Building Socialism with a Specifically Chinese Character." Excerpt from a talk with the Japanese delegation to the Second Session of the Council of Sino-Japanese Non-Governmental Persons, June 30, 1984. http://en.people.cn/dengxp/vol3/text/c1220.html. Archived December 26, 2017.

Diamant, Neil Jeffrey. *Revolutionizing the Family: Politics, Love, and Divorce in Urban and Rural China, 1949–1968.* Berkeley: University of California Press, 2000.

Dickson, Bruce J. *Red Capitalists in China: The Party, Private Entrepreneurs and the Prospects for Political Change.* New York: Cambridge University Press, 2003.

Dickson, Bruce J. *Wealth into Power: The Communist Party's Embrace of China's Private Sector*. New York: Cambridge University Press, 2008.

Dikötter, Frank. *The Cultural Revolution: A People's History, 1962–1976*. New York: Bloomsbury Press, 2017.

Dillon, Nara. *Radical Inequalities: China's Revolutionary Welfare State in Comparative Perspective*. Cambridge, MA: Harvard University Asia Center, 2015.

Ding Shu 丁抒. "追思节" (Pursuing Memorial Day). May 25, 2009. Originally published in 民间历史, but reposted on www.edubridge.com/letter/dingshu_fumu.htm. Archived April 13, 2016.

Dittmer, Lowell. *Liu Shao-ch'i and the Chinese Cultural Revolution: The Politics of Mass Criticism*. Berkeley: University of California Press, 1974.

Djilas, Milovan. *The New Class: An Analysis of the Communist System*. New York: Praeger, 1957.

Dong Qian 董倩. "规训与溢出: '新民晚报'与社会主义上海商业空间和商业文化建构 1949–1966" (Discipline and overflow: *Xinmin Evening News* and the construction of Shanghai's socialist business space and business culture 1949–1966), *Xinwen daxue*, no. 5 (2013), 1–14.

Dongguanshi gongshang xingzheng guanliju 东莞市工商行政管理局, ed. 东莞市工商行政管理志 (Administrative records of industry and commerce in Dongguan). Guangzhou: Guangdong renmin chubanshe, 2011.

Donnithorne, Audrey. *China's Economic System*. London: Allen & Unwin, 1967.

Dunham, Vera S. *In Stalin's Time: Middleclass Values in Soviet Fiction*, enlarged and updated ed. Durham, NC: Duke University Press, 1990.

Dutton, Michael. "Mango Mao: Infections of the Sacred." *Public Culture*, vol. 16, no. 2 (2004), 161–87.

Eckstein, Alexander. *China's Economic Revolution*. New York: Cambridge University Press, 1977.

Esfehani, Amir Moghaddass. "The Bicycle's Long Way to China: The Appropriation of Cycling as a Foreign Cultural Technique (1860–1940)." Pp. 94–102, in Nicholas Clayton and Andrew Ritchie, eds. *Cycle History 13, Proceedings of the 13th International Cycling History Conference*. San Francisco: Van der Plas Publications, 2003.

Evans, Harriet. "The Language of Liberation: Gender and *Jiefang* in Early Chinese Communist Discourse." Pp. 193–220, in Jeffrey N. Wasserstrom, ed. *Twentieth-Century China: New Approaches*. London: Routledge, 2003.

Evans, Harriet and Stephanie Donald, eds. *Picturing Power in the People's Republic: Posters of the Cultural Revolution*. Lanham, MD: Rowman & Littlefield, 1999.

Ewen, Stuart. *All Consuming Images: The Politics of Style in Contemporary Culture*. New York: Basic Books, 1988.

Ewen, Stuart. *Captains of Consciousness: Advertising and the Social Roots of the Consumer Culture*. New York: McGraw-Hill, 1976.

Eyferth, Jacob. "Beyond the Maoist Commodity: Material Life in Rural China, 1950–1980." Paper presented at the workshop, "Material Culture in Maoist China," King's College London, May 18, 2019.

Eyferth, Jacob. *Eating Rice from Bamboo Roots: The Social History of a Community of Handicraft Papermakers in Rural Sichuan, 1920–2000*. Cambridge, MA: Harvard University Asia Center, 2009.

Fang Houshu 方厚枢. "'文革'十年毛泽东著作、毛泽东像出版纪" (Mao Zedong works and posters published during the ten years of Cultural Revolution). Pp. 215–36, in Song Yuanfang 宋原放, ed. 中国出版史料第三卷 上册: 现代部分 (Historical materials on publishing in China, vol. 3, part 1: Contemporary section). Ji'nan: Shandong jiaoyu chubanshe, 2001.

Fang Jihong 方继红. "公物还家" (Public property becomes private). Pp. 462–63, in Zhe Yongping 者永平, ed. 那个年代中的我们 (Ourselves at that time). Huhehaote: Yuanfang chubanshe, 1998.

Federici, Silvia. *Caliban and the Witch: Women, the Body and Primitive Accumulation*. Brooklyn, NY: Autonomedia, 2004.

Federici, Silvia. *Revolution at Point Zero: Housework Reproduction and Feminist Struggle*. Brooklyn, NY: Autonomedia, 2012.

Feng, Jicai. *Voices from the Whirlwind: An Oral History of the Chinese Cultural Revolution*. New York: Pantheon Books, 1991.

Feng Xiaocai. "Between Class Struggle and Family Loyalty: The Mobilization of Businessmen's Wives and Children during the Five Antis Movement." *European Journal of East Asian Studies*, vol. 13, no. 2 (2014), 284–304.

Feng Xiaocai. "Rushing toward Socialism: The Transformation and Death of Private Business Enterprises in Shanghai, 1949–1956." Pp. 240–58, in William C. Kirby, ed. *The People's Republic of China at 60: An International Assessment*. Cambridge, MA: Harvard University Asia Center, 2011.

Feng Xiaocai 冯筱才. "社会主义的边缘人: 1956 年前后的小商小贩改造问题" (The marginalized people of socialism: The transformation of small business hawkers circa 1956). *Zhongguo dangdai shi yanjiu*, no. 3 (August 2011), 3–45.

Feng Xiaocai 冯筱才. "一九五八年至一九六三年中共自由市场政策研究" (A study of the free market policy of the CPC from 1958 to 1963). *Zhonggong dangshi yanjiu*, no. 2 (2015), 38–53.

Finnane, Antonia. *Changing Clothes in China: Fashion, History, Nation*. New York: Columbia University Press, 2008.

Finnane, Antonia and Peidong Sun. "Textiles and Apparel in the Mao Years: Uniformity, Variety, and the Limits of Autarchy." Pp. 16–43, in Wessie Ling and Simona Segre-Reinach, eds. *Making Fashion in Multiple Chinas: Chinese Styles in the Transglobal Landscape*. London: I.B. Tauris, 2018.

Fitzpatrick, Sheila. *The Cultural Front: Power and Culture in Revolutionary Russia*. Ithaca, NY: Cornell University Press, 1992.

Fitzpatrick, Sheila. *Everyday Stalinism: Ordinary Life in Extraordinary Times, Soviet Russia in the 1930s*. New York: Oxford University Press, 1999.

Fraser, Nancy and Rahel Jaeggi. *Capitalism: A Conversation in Critical Theory*. Cambridge: Polity, 2018.

Frazier, Mark W. *The Making of the Chinese Industrial Workplace: State, Revolution, and Labor Management*. New York: Cambridge University Press, 2002.

Friend, Robert C. "What Is It Like to Go Shopping in China?" *China Reconstructs*, vol. 13, no. 4 (1964), 31–3.

Fürst, Juliane. "The Importance of Being Stylish: Youth, Culture and Identity in Late Stalinism." Pp. 209–30, in Juliane Fürst, ed. *Late Stalinist Russia: Society Between Reconstruction and Reinvention*. London: Routledge, 2006.

Gabriel, Satyananda J. *Chinese Capitalism and the Modernist Vision*. London: Routledge, 2006.

Ganshin, G. and T. Zazerskaya. "Pitfalls Along the Path of 'Brotherly Friendship' (A Look at the History of Soviet-Chinese Relations)." *Far Eastern Affairs*, no. 6 (1994), 63–70.

Gansusheng Qingyangxian shangyeju 甘肃省青阳县商业局, ed. "破旧立新，十大改革" (Destroy the old and establish the new, ten big reforms). Pp. 177–78, in Shangyebu (商业部), ed. 商业红旗，上册 (The red flag of commerce, vol. 1). Beijing: Renmin chubanshe, 1959.

Gao Gao 高皋 and Yan Jiaqi 严家其. "文化大革命"十年史: 1966–1976 (Ten Years of the "Great Cultural Revolution": 1966–1976). Tianjin: Tianjin renmin chubanshe, 1986.

Gao Hongtao 高洪涛. "我们对'大众电影'方向的看法" (Our view of the direction of *Mass Films*). *Zhongguo dianying zazhi*, no. 12 (1958), 52.

Gao, James Z. "A Call of the Oases: The 'Peaceful Liberation' of Xinjiang, 1949–53." Pp. 184–204, in Jeremy Brown and Paul G. Pickowicz, eds. *Dilemmas of Victory: The Early Years of the People's Republic of China*. Cambridge, MA: Harvard University Press, 2010.

Gao, James Z. *The Communist Takeover of Hangzhou: The Transformation of City and Cadre, 1949–1954*. Honolulu: University of Hawai'i Press, 2004.

Gao, Mobo. *The Battle for China's Past: Mao and the Cultural Revolution*. London: Pluto Press, 2008.

Gao Wangling 高王凌. 中国农民反行为研究 (1950–1980) (Research on the counter-strategies of Chinese peasants [1950–1980]). Hong Kong: Zhongwen daxue chubanshe, 2013.

Gao Yuan. *Born Red: A Chronicle of the Cultural Revolution*. Stanford: Stanford University Press, 1987.

Gardner, John. "The *Wu-Fan* Campaign in Shanghai: A Study in the Consolidation of Urban Control." Pp. 477–539, in A. Doak Barnett, ed. *Chinese Communist Politics in Action*. Seattle: University of Washington Press, 1969.

Garon, Sheldon. "Luxury is the Enemy: Mobilizing Savings and Popularizing Thrift in Wartime Japan." *Journal of Japanese Studies*, vol. 26, no. 1 (Winter 2000), 41–78.

Ge Kai 葛凯 (Karl Gerth). "社会主义中国与消费主义的妥协" (The contradictions between socialist China and consumerism). *Huadong shifan daxue*, no. 4 (Winter 2013), 1–7.

Gebhardt, Eike and Andrew Arato, eds. *The Essential Frankfurt School Reader*. New York: Continuum, 2007.

Gershenkron, Alexander. *Economic Backwardness in Historical Perspective*. Cambridge, MA: Belknap Press of Harvard University Press, 1962.

Gerth, Karl. *As China Goes, So Goes the World: How Chinese Consumers Are Transforming Everything.* New York: Hill and Wang, 2010.

Gerth, Karl. *China Made: Consumer Culture and the Creation of the Nation.* Cambridge, MA: Harvard University Asia Center, 2003.

Gerth, Karl. "Compromising with Consumerism in Socialist China: Transnational Flows and Internal Tensions in 'Socialist Advertising'." *Past & Present*, no. 218 (Spring 2013), 203–32.

Gerth, Karl. "Make Some Get Rich First: State Consumerism and Private Enterprise in the Creation of Postsocialist China." Pp. 449–73, in Juliane Fürst, Silvio Pons, and Mark Selden, eds. *Cambridge History of Communism. Vol. III, Endgames. Late Communism in Global Perspective, 1968 to the Present.* Cambridge: Cambridge University Press, 2017.

Gerth, Karl. "Wu Yunchu and the Fate of the Bourgeoisie and Bourgeois Lifestyles under Communism." Pp. 175–202, in Sherman Cochran, ed. *The Capitalist Dilemma in China's Communist Revolution.* Ithaca, NY: East Asia Program, Cornell University, 2015.

Gittings, John. *Survey of the Sino-Soviet Dispute: A Commentary and Extracts from the Recent Polemics, 1963–1967.* Oxford: Oxford University Press, 1968.

Glickman, Lawrence B. *A Living Wage: American Workers and the Making of Consumer Society.* Ithaca, NY: Cornell University Press, 1997.

Gluckstein, Ygael. *Mao's China: Economic and Political Survey.* Boston: Beacon Press, 1957.

Godley, Andrew. "Global Diffusion of the Sewing Machine, 1850–1914." *Research in Economic History*, vol. 20 (2001), 1–46.

Godley, Andrew. "Selling the Sewing Machine Around the World: Singer's International Marketing Strategies, 1850–1920." *Enterprise and Society*, vol. 7, no. 2 (2006), 266–313.

Goffman, Erving. *The Presentation of Self in Everyday Life.* Woodstock, NY: Overlook Press, 1973.

Goldman, Wendy Z. *Women at the Gates: Gender and History in Stalin's Russia.* Cambridge: Cambridge University Press, 2002.

Goldstein, Melvyn C., Ben Jiao, and Tanzen Lhundrup. *On the Cultural Revolution in Tibet: The Nyemo Incident of 1969.* Berkeley: University of California Press, 2009.

Gooderham, Peter, "The Komsomol and Worker Youth: The Inculcation of 'Communist Values' in Leningrad during NEP." *Soviet Studies*, vol. 34, no. 4 (1982), 506–28.

Gordon, Andrew. "Selling the American Way: The Singer Sales System in Japan, 1900–1938." *Business History Review*, vol. 82, no. 4 (2008), 671–99.

Gronow, Jukka. *The Sociology of Taste.* London: Routledge, 1997.

Gronow, Jukka and Sergey Zhuravlev. *Fashion Meets Socialism: Fashion Industry in the Soviet Union After the Second World War.* Helsinki: Finnish Literature Society, 2014.

Gu Hua. *A Small Town Called Hibiscus*, tr. Gladys Yang. Beijing: Foreign Languages Press, 1983.

Gu Xiegang 顾颉刚. 顾颉刚日记 (1964–1967) (Gu Xiegang's diary [1964–1967]). Taipei: Lianjing chuban shiye gufen youxian gongsi, 2007.

Guan, Datong. *The Socialist Transformation of Capitalist Industry and Commerce in China*. Peking: Foreign Languages Press, 1960.

Guan Shengli 关圣力. "屠鸽" (Killing a pigeon). Pp. 20–4, in Zhe Yongping 者永平, ed. 那个年代中的我们 (Ourselves at that time). Huhehaote: Yuanfang chubanshe, 1998.

广州市志: 卷九(上) (Guangzhou City records: vol. 9, part 1). Guangzhou: Guangzhou chubanshe, 1999.

Guffey, Elizabeth E. *Posters: A Global History*. London: Reaktion Books, 2015.

Guo Jian, Yongyi Song, and Yuan Zhou. *Historical Dictionary of the Chinese Cultural Revolution*. Lanham, MD: Scarecrow Press, 2006.

Hall, Peter A. and David W. Soskice. *Varieties of Capitalism: The Institutional Foundations of Comparative Advantage*. Oxford: Oxford University Press, 2001.

Han Jianwen 罕见闻. "'大众电影' 的封面和封底" (The cover page and back page of *Mass Films*). *Zhongguo dianying zazhi*, no. 12 (1958), 52–3.

Han Suyin 韩素英. "毛泽东以永恒的激情从事工作" (Mao Zedong always works in a passionate way). Pp. 509–10, in Deng Liqun 邓力群, ed. 中外名人评说毛泽东 (Comments on Mao Zedong by famous Chinese and foreigners). Beijing: Zhongyang minzu daxue chubanshe, 2003.

Hanson, Philip. *Advertising and Socialism: The Nature and Extent of Consumer Advertising in the Soviet Union, Poland, Hungary, and Yugoslavia*. London: Macmillan, 1974.

Harrison, Mark, ed. *Guns and Rubles: The Defense Industry in the Stalinist State*. New Haven: Yale University Press, 2008.

Harvey, David. *The New Imperialism*. Oxford: Oxford University Press, 2003.

Haug, Wolfgang Fritz. *Critique of Commodity Aesthetics: Appearance, Sexuality, and Advertising in Capitalist Society*. Minneapolis: University of Minnesota Press, 1986.

He, Donghui. "Coming of Age in the Brave New World: The Changing Reception of the Soviet Novel, *How the Steel Was Tempered*, in the People's Republic of China." Pp. 393–420, in Thomas P. Bernstein and Hua-Yu Li, eds. *China Learns from the Soviet Union, 1949–Present*. Lanham, MD: Lexington Books, 2010.

Heath, Joseph and Andrew Potter. *The Rebel Sell: Why the Culture Can't Be Jammed*. Toronto: HarperCollins, 2004.

Heinrich, Michael. *An Introduction to the Three Volumes of Karl Marx's Capital*. New York: Monthly Review Press, 2012.

Henansheng Zhongmouxian shangyeju 河南省中某县商业局. "十五好的中牟四女商店" (Fifteen good experiences in a Zhongmou store run by four women). Pp. 15–20, in Shangyebu 商业部, ed. 商业红旗下册 (The red flag of commerce, vol. 3). Beijing: Renmin chubanshe, 1959.

Herlihy, David V. *Bicycle: The History*. New Haven: Yale University Press, 2006.

Herndon, Neil. "Effective Ethical Response: A New Approach to Channel Stakeholder Needs for Ethical Behavior and Socially Responsible Conduct." *Journal of Marketing Channels*, vol. 13, no. 1 (2006), 1, 63–78.

Hershatter, Gail. *The Gender of Memory: Rural Women and China's Collective Past.* Berkeley: University of California Press, 2011.

Hessler, Julie. *A Social History of Soviet Trade: Trade Policy, Retail Practices, and Consumption, 1917–1953.* Princeton, NJ: Princeton University Press, 2004.

Ho, Dahpon David. "To Protect and Preserve: Resisting the Destroy the Four Olds Campaign, 1966–1967." Pp. 64–95, in Joseph Esherick et al., eds. *The Chinese Cultural Revolution as History.* Stanford: Stanford University Press, 2006.

Ho, Denise. *Curating Revolution: Politics on Display in Mao's China.* Cambridge: Cambridge University Press, 2018.

Ho, Denise. "Revolutionizing Antiquity: The Shanghai Cultural Bureaucracy in the Cultural Revolution, 1966–1968." *The China Quarterly*, no. 207 (2011), 687–705.

Hochschild, Arlie Russell. *The Managed Heart: Commercialization of Human Feeling.* Berkeley: University of California Press, 1983.

Hong Xia 洪霞. "剃过光头" (Shaved bald). Pp. 439–41, in Zhe Yongping 者永平, ed. 那个时代中的我们 (Ourselves at that time). Huhehaote: Yuanfang chubanshe, 1998.

Honig, Emily. "Maoist Mappings of Gender: Reassessing the Red Guards." Pp. 258–68, in Susan Brownell and Jeffrey N. Wasserstrom, eds. *Chinese Femininities and Chinese Masculinities: A Reader.* Berkeley: University of California Press, 2002.

Howlett, Jonathan J. "'The British Boss Is Gone and Will Never Return': Communist Takeovers of British Companies in Shanghai (1949–1954)." *Modern Asian Studies*, vol. 47, no. 6 (2013), 1941–76.

Hsia Kung. "Producing Goods for the Peasants." *China Reconstructs*, vol. 13, no. 11 (1964), 18–20.

Hu Yuanjie 胡远杰. "1967 年'炮轰'南京路事件" (The "bombardment" of Nanjing Road in 1967). *Shiji*, no. 3 (2014), 28–9.

Hua Jiannan 华建南. "'学习班'记事" (Memories of the "Study Group"). *Remembrance*, no. 7 (May 31, 2013), 76–83. http://prchistory.org/wp-content/uploads/2014/05/REMEMBRANCE_No98.pdf. Archived August 26, 2016.

Hua Yi. "An Urban People's Commune in Chungking." *Women of China*, nos. 4–5 (April 5, 1960), 12–17.

Huang Shengmin 黄升民, Ding Junjie 丁俊杰, and Liu Yinghua 刘英华, eds. 中国广告图史 (An illustrated history of Chinese advertisements). Guangzhou: Nanfang ribao chubanshe, 2006.

Huang Zongjiang 黄宗江, ed. 美国电影: 帝国主义的侵略工具 (American films: Tools of imperialist invasion). Nanjing: Jiangnan chubanshe, 1951.

Huang Zongjiang 黄宗江. "美国电影毒在那里" (Where is the poison in American films?). Pp. 1–19, in Nanjing wenlian dianyingbu 南京文联电影部, ed. 美国电影: 帝国主义的侵略工具 (American films: Tools of imperialist invasion). Nanjing: Jiangnan chubanshe, 1951.

Hubeisheng Machengxian shangyeju 湖北省麻城县商业局. "五女商店人人夸" (Everyone praises the five-women store). Pp. 9–15, in Shangyebu 商业部, ed. 商业红旗, 下册 (The red flag of commerce, vol. 3). Beijing: Renmin chubanshe, 1959.

Huff, Gregg. "Finance for War in Asia and Its Aftermath." Pp. 56–93, in Michael Geyer and J. Adam Tooze, eds. *The Cambridge History of the Second World War: Volume 3, Total War: Economy, Society and Culture*. Cambridge: Cambridge University Press, 2015.

"回望淮国旧" (Recalling the Huaiguojiu). Pp. 138–48, in 上海影像工作室, ed. 百姓生活记忆: 上海故事 (Memories of people's life experiences: Shanghai stories). Shanghai: Xuelin chubanshe, 2012.

Hung, Chang-tai. *Mao's New World: Political Culture in the Early People's Republic*. Ithaca, NY: Cornell University Press, 2011.

Hung, Ho-fung. *The China Boom: Why China Will Not Rule the World*. New York: Columbia University Press, 2016.

Ilf, Ilya and Eugenii Petrov. *Little Golden America: Two Famous Soviet Humorists Survey These United States*, tr. Charles Malamuth. New York: Farrar & Rinehart, Inc., 1937.

Ironside, Kristy. "Khrushchev's Cash-and-Goods Lotteries and the Turn Toward Positive Incentives." *The Soviet and Post-Soviet Review*, vol. 41, no. 3 (2014), 296–323.

Jersild, Austin. "Socialist Exhibits and Sino-Soviet Relations, 1950–60." *Cold War History*, vol. 18, no. 3 (2018), 275–89.

Ji Zhifeng 冀志枫. "制毒大本营, 好莱坞的剖视" (The basecamp of poison: An analysis and observation of Hollywood). Pp. 27–8, in Nanjing wenlian dianyingbu 南京文联电影部, ed. 美国电影: 帝国主义的侵略工具 (American films: Tools of imperialist invasion). Nanjing: Jiangnan chubanshe, 1951.

Jiang Jiangao 江建高. "韶山又兴'像章热'" (The "badge fad" is hot again in Shaoshan). *Nanfang chuang*, no. 1 (1993).

"姜明亮等上中共中央, 毛泽东书" (Letter to the Central Committee of the Chinese Communist Party and Mao Zedong by Jiang Mingliang et al.). Pp. 121–31, in Yu Xiguang 余习广, ed. 位卑未敢忘忧国: "文化大革命"上书集 (Humble people do not forget their country: A collection of petitions from the Cultural Revolution). Changsha: Hunan renmin chubanshe, 1989.

Jiang, Yarong and David Ashley, eds. *Mao's Children in the New China: Voices from the Red Guard Generation*. London: Routledge, 2000.

Jiang Yigao 江义高. "'倒卖'粮票换手表" ("Speculating" on grain ration coupons for a wristwatch). *Longmeizhen*, no. 10 (2009), 39–43.

Jiangsusheng difangzhi bianzuan weiyuanhui 江苏省地方志编纂委员会, ed. 江苏省志: 工商行政管理志 (Jiangsu province: Administrative records of industry and commerce). Nanjing: Jiangsu guji chubanshe, 1995.

Jin Dalu 金大陆. 非常与正常: 上海 "文革"时期的社会生活 (The extraordinary and the ordinary: Social life in Shanghai during the "Cultural Revolution"). 2 vols. Shanghai: Shanghai cishu chubanshe, 2011.

Jin, Xin, Karin Weber and Jing Xu. "The China Import and Export (Canton) Fair: A Trade Show in Transformation." *Proceedings of the International Convention Exposition Summit* (ICES) (2008).

Johnson, Matthew D. "International and Wartime Origins of the Propaganda State: The Motion Picture in China, 1897–1955." PhD dissertation, University of California, San Diego, 2008.

Joseph, William A. *The Critique of Ultra-Leftism in China, 1958–1981.* Stanford: Stanford University Press, 1984.

"局党委扩大会议有关党委官僚主义方面的综合材料"　　　(Comprehensive materials on the bureaucratic aspects of party committees for the expanded meeting of party committees). SMA B123-4-568 (July 31, 1960).

Kaldor, Mary. *The Imaginary War: Understanding the East–West Conflict.* Oxford: Blackwell, 1990.

Kaple, Deborah. "Agents of Change: Soviet Advisers and High Stalinist Management in China, 1949–1960." *Journal of Cold War Studies*, vol. 18, no. 1 (2016), 5–30.

Kaple, Deborah A. *Dream of a Red Factory: The Legacy of High Stalinism in China.* New York: Oxford University Press, 1994.

Kelly, Catriona. *Refining Russia: Advice Literature, Polite Culture, and Gender from Catherine to Yeltsin.* Oxford: Oxford University Press, 2001.

Kern, Stephen. *The Culture of Time and Space 1880–1918.* Cambridge, MA: Harvard University Press, 1983.

Kirby, William C. "The Chinese War Economy." Pp. 185–212, in James C. Hsiung and Steven I. Levine, eds. *China's Bitter Victory: The War with Japan, 1937–1945.* Armonk, NY: M.E. Sharpe, 1992.

Kirby, William C. "Continuity and Change in Modern China: Economic Planning on the Mainland and on Taiwan, 1943–1958." *The Australian Journal of Chinese Affairs*, no. 24 (July 1990), 121–41.

Kirby, William C. "The Nationalist Regime and the Chinese Party-State, 1928–1958." Pp. 211–37, in Merle Goldman and Andrew Gordon, eds. *Historical Perspectives on Contemporary East Asia.* Cambridge, MA: Harvard University Press, 2000.

Klein, Naomi. *No Logo: Taking Aim at the Brand Bullies.* New York: Picador, 1999.

Klochko, Mikhail A. *Soviet Scientist in Red China*, tr. Andrew MacAndrew. New York: Praeger, 1964.

Knight, Nick. "Introduction: Soviet Marxism and the Development of Mao Zedong's Philosophical Thought." Pp. 3–83, in Nick Knight, ed. *Mao Zedong on Dialectical Materialism: Writings on Philosophy*, 1937. Armonk, NY: M.E. Sharpe, 1990.

Knight, Nick. "Mao Zedong on the Chinese Road to Socialism, 1949–1969." Pp. 217–47, in Nick Knight, *Rethinking Mao: Explorations in Mao Zedong's Thought.* Lanham, MD: Lexington Books, 2007.

Kocka, Jürgen. *Capitalism: A Short History*, tr. Jeremiah M. Riemer. Princeton, NJ: Princeton University Press, 2016.

Koeber, Chuck. "The Social Reorganization of Time: The 'Great Speedup' and the Transformation of Time and Work Discipline." *Humanity & Society*, vol. 41, no. 2 (2017), 143–57.

Köll, Elisabeth. *Railroads and the Transformation of China*. Cambridge, MA: Harvard University Press, 2019.

Kong, Hanbing. "The Transplantation and Entrenchment of the Soviet Economic Model in China." Pp. 153–66, in Thomas P. Bernstein and Hua-Yu Li, eds. *China Learns from the Soviet Union, 1949–Present* Lanham, MD: Lexington Books, 2010.

Kornai, János. *The Socialist System: The Political Economy of Communism*. Oxford: Clarendon Press, 2007.

Kozlov, Denis and Eleonary Gilbourd. *The Thaw: Soviet Society and Culture during the 1950s and 1960s*. Toronto: University of Toronto Press, 2013.

Kurlantzick, Joshua. *State Capitalism: How the Return of Statism Is Transforming the World*. New York: Oxford University Press, 2016.

Laermans, Rudi. "Learning to Consume: Early Department Stores and the Shaping of the Modern Consumer Culture (1860–1914)." *Theory, Culture & Society*, vol. 10, no. 4 (November 1993), 79–102.

Lakoff, George. *The Political Mind: A Cognitive Scientist's Guide to Your Brain and Its Politics*. New York: Penguin, 2009.

Landsberger, Stefan R. *Chinese Propaganda Posters: From Revolution to Modernization*. Armonk, NY: M.E. Sharpe, 1995.

Landsberger, Stefan R. "'Life as It Ought to Be': Propaganda Art of the PRC." *IIAS Newsletter*, no. 48 (Summer 2008), 27.

Landsberger, Stefan R. and Marien van der Heijden. *Chinese Propaganda Posters: The IISH-Landsberger Collections*. Munich: Prestel, 2009.

Landsman, Mark. *Dictatorship and Demand: The Politics of Consumerism in East Germany*. Cambridge, MA: Harvard University Press, 2005.

Lary, Diana. *China's Civil War: A Social History, 1945–1949*. New York: Cambridge University Press, 2015.

Lasch, Christopher. *The Culture of Narcissism: American Life in an Age of Diminishing Expectations*. New York: Warner Books, 1980.

Lebowitz, Michael A. *The Socialist Alternative: Real Human Development*. New York: Monthly Review Press, 2010.

Lebowitz, Michael A. *The Socialist Imperative: From Gotha to Now*. New York: Monthly Review Press, 2015.

Ledovsky, Andrei. "Two Cables from Correspondence between Mao Zedong and Joseph Stalin." *Far Eastern Affairs*, no. 6 (2000), 89–96.

Lee, Leo Ou-fan. *Shanghai Modern: The Flowering of a New Urban Culture in China, 1930–1945*. Cambridge, MA: Harvard University Press, 1999.

Leese, Daniel. *Mao Cult: Rhetoric and Ritual in China's Cultural Revolution*. Cambridge: Cambridge University Press, 2011.

Leese, Daniel. "A Single Spark: Origins and Spread of the Little Red Book in China." Pp. 23–42, in Alexander C. Cook, ed. *Mao's Little Red Book: A Global History*. Cambridge: Cambridge University Press, 2014.

Leiss, William et al. *Social Communication in Advertising: Persons, Products, and Images of Well-Being.* Toronto: Methuen, 1986.

Lenin, Vladimir. "An Essential Condition of the Bolsheviks' Success." In *"Left-Wing" Communism: An Infantile Disorder* (1920). www.marxists.org/archive/lenin/works/1920/lwc/cho2.htm. Archived March 28, 2018.

Levine, Steven I. *Anvil of Victory: The Communist Revolution in Manchuria, 1945–1948.* New York: Columbia University Press, 1987.

Lewis, John Wilson and Litai Xue. *China Builds the Bomb.* Stanford: Stanford University Press, 1988.

Li, Danhui and Yafeng Xia. *Mao and the Sino-Soviet Split, 1959–1973: A New History.* Lanham, MD: Lexington Books, 2018.

Li Dong 李动. "永远的歼 6" (The eternal J-6). Pp. 348–50, in Shanghai difangzhi bangongshi 上海地方志办公室, ed. 人民军队中的上海兵 (Shanghai soldiers in the People's Army). Shanghai: Shanghai renmin chubanshe, 2013.

Li Duanxiang 李端祥. 城市人民公社运动研究 (Research on the urban People's Commune movement). Changsha: Hunan renmin chubanshe, 2006.

Li, Hua-Yu. "Instilling Stalinism in Chinese Party Members: Absorbing Stalin's *Short Course* in the 1950s." Pp. 107–30, in Thomas P. Bernstein and Hua-Yu Li, eds. *China Learns from the Soviet Union, 1949–Present.* Lanham, MD: Lexington Books, 2011.

Li, Hua-Yu. *Mao and the Economic Stalinization of China, 1948–1953.* Lanham, MD: Rowman & Littlefield, 2006.

Li, Jie. *Shanghai Homes: Palimpsests of Private Life.* New York: Columbia University Press, 2015.

Li Jingrong 李景荣. "狂热 幻灭: 红卫兵运动剪影" (Fanaticism and disillusionment: Silhouettes of the Red Guard movement). Pp. 116–19, in Zhe Yongping 者永平, ed. 那个时代中的我们 (Ourselves at that time). Huhehaote: Yuanfang chubanshe, 1998.

Li Lin 李琳. "毛泽东像章的收藏初探" (A brief study of Mao Zedong badge collections). *Sichuansheng ganbu hanshou xueyuan xuebao*, no. 3 (2010), 40–3.

Li, Mingjiang. *Mao's China and the Sino-Soviet Split: Ideological Dilemma.* London: Routledge, 2012.

Li Pao-kuang. "Speaking of Women's Clothing." *Women of China*, no. 1 (Spring 1956), 22–3.

Li Ping'an 李平安 et al., eds. 陕西经济大事 1949–1985 (Record of major events in Shaanxi's economy 1949–1985). Xi'an: Sanqin chubanshe, 1987.

Li Qitian 李启天. "红色收藏, 投资热流涌动" (Red collecting, a favorite investment activity). *Jinrong bolan*, no. 6 (2011), 68–70.

Li Ruojian 李若建. 虚实之间: 20世纪50年代中国大陆谣言研究 (Between fact and fiction: An analysis of rumors in China during the 1950s). Beijing: Shehui kexue wenxian chubanshe, 2011.

Li Shuhua 李叔华. "同家梁上大团圆" (Reunion in Tongjialiang). *Renmin wenxue*, no. 5 (May 30, 1960), 45–51.

Li Xiaojun 李晓军. 牙医史话: 中国口腔卫生文史概览 (A narrative history of dentistry: An overview of Chinese dental hygiene). Hangzhou: Zhejiang daxue chubanshe, 2014.

Li, Yan. *China's Soviet Dream: Propaganda, Culture, and Popular Imagination.* London: Routledge, 2018.

Li Ying. "Shops and Shoppers in Shanghai." *China Reconstructs*, vol. 13, no. 10 (1964), 49–51.

Li Zhensheng, Robert Pledge, and Jacques Menasche. *Red-color News Soldier: A Chinese Photographer's Odyssey Through the Cultural Revolution.* London: Phaidon, 2003.

Liang Heng and Judith Shapiro. *Son of the Revolution.* New York: Knopf, 1983.

Lian Lingling (Lien Ling-ling) 连玲玲. 打造消费天堂: 百货公司与近代上海城市文化 (Creating a paradise for consumption: Department stores and modern urban culture in Shanghai). Beijing: Shehui kexue wenxian chubanshe, 2018.

Lian Lingling (Lien Ling-ling) 連玲玲. "上海百货公司的社会主义改造, 1949–1956 (The socialist transformation of Shanghai Department Store, 1949–1956). Pp. 333–72, in Hsieh Kuo-hsing 謝國興, ed. 改革与改造, 冷战初期两岸的粮食, 土地与工商业变革 (Reform and reconstruction: The transformation of rice supplies, land reform, and industry and commerce in early Cold War Mainland China and Taiwan). Taipei: Institute of Modern History, Academia Sinica, 2010.

Liang Shuming 梁漱溟. 梁漱溟自述 (An autobiography of Liang Shuming). Zhengzhou: Henan renmin chubanshe, 2004.

Liang Xiaosheng 梁晓声. 一个红卫兵的自白 (Confessions of a Red Guard). Beijing: Wenhua yishu chubanshe, 2006.

Lin, Cyril Chihren. "The Reinstatement of Economics in China Today." *The China Quarterly*, no. 85 (1981), 1–48.

Lin Qihong. *Social Life of the Chinese (in Peking).* Peking: China Booksellers, 1928.

Ling, Ken. *Red Guard: From Schoolboy to "Little General" in Mao's China.* London: Macdonald, 1972.

Liu, Alan P. L. *Communications and National Integration in Communist China.* Berkeley: University of California Press, 1975.

Liu Dishan 柳迪善. "苏联电影在中国: 五十年代的考察" (Soviet movies in China: An examination of the 1950s). *Dianying yishu*, no. 4 (2008), 55–60.

Liu Jialin 刘家林. 新编中外广告通史 (A general history of Chinese and world advertising). Guangzhou: Ji'nan daxue chubanshe, 2004.

Liu Shanling 刘善龄. 西洋风: 西洋发明在中国 (Wind from the West: Western inventions in China). Shanghai: Shanghai guji chubanshe, 1999.

Liu Shaoqi 刘少奇. "刘少奇关于 '四清' '五反'蹲点问题的报告" (Liu Shaoqi's report on the issue of the "four clean-ups" and the "five antis"), September 16, 1964. In 批判资料: 中国赫鲁晓夫刘少奇反革命修正主义言论集 (1958.6–1967.7). Beijing: Renmin chubanshe ziliaoshi, September 1967.

Liu, Shaw-tong. *Out of Red China*, tr. Jack Chia and Henry Walter. New York: Duell, Sloan, and Pearce, 1953.

Liu Suinian and Wu Qungan, eds. *China's Socialist Economy: An Outline History (1949–1984)*. Beijing: Beijing Review, 1986.

Liu Yajuan 刘亚娟. "国家与都市之间: 上海劳模形象建构与流变的个案研究 (1949–1963)" (Between the state and the metropolis: A case study of the construction and change in the image of Shanghai model laborers, 1949–1963). *Zhonggong dangshi yanjiu*, no. 5 (2016), 68–78.

Liu Yangdong 刘仰东. 红底金字: 六七十年代的北京孩子 (Gold characters on red: Beijing children in the 1960s and the 1970s). Beijing: Zhongguo qingnian chubanshe, 2005.

Liu Zhenghui 刘正辉. "京胡的发展与制作 (六)" (The development and production of Jinghu [Part 6]). *Zhongguo jingju*, no. 11 (2005), 24, plus photos.

Lu, Hanchao. *Beyond the Neon Lights: Everyday Shanghai in the Early Twentieth Century*. Berkeley: University of California Press, 1999.

Lu, Hanchao. "Bourgeois Comfort under Proletarian Dictatorship: Home Life of Chinese Capitalists before the Cultural Revolution." *Journal of Social History*, vol. 52, no. 1 (2018), 74–100.

Lu Na 鲁娜. 毛泽东像章收藏与鉴赏 (Collecting and appreciating Mao Zedong badges). Beijing: Guoji wenhua chubanshe, 1993.

Lu Xiangbo 鲁湘伯. "图说早期国产表的发展轨迹和时代烙印" (The picture shows the development of early domestic watches and the brands at that time). *Zui shijian* (May 2016), 26–35.

Lü, Xiaobo and Elizabeth J. Perry, eds. *Danwei: The Changing Chinese Workplace in Historical and Comparative Perspective*. Armonk, NY: M.E. Sharpe, 1997.

Luo Hanping 罗汉平. "东北解放区1947年土改中的'砍挖运动'" (The "chopping and digging campaign" during Land Reform in the liberated districts of Northeast China in 1947). *Shiji qiao*, no. 4 (2004), 31–3.

Luo Pinghan 罗平汉. "大锅饭": 公共食堂始末 ("The big rice bowl": The origins and end of the public canteens). Nanning: Guangxi renmin chubanshe, 2001.

Luo Weiran 罗未然. "闯入'吉尼斯大全'的'毛泽东像章'收藏家'" (Mao Zedong badge collector is granted place in *Guinness Book of World Records*). *Zhongzhou jingu*, no. 2 (1997), 38–41.

Luthi, Lorenz M. *The Sino-Soviet Split: Cold War in the Communist World*. Princeton, NJ: Princeton University Press, 2008.

Lutze, Thomas D. *China's Inevitable Revolution: Rethinking America's Loss to the Communists*. New York: Palgrave Macmillan, 2007.

Luxemburg, Rosa. *The Accumulation of Capital*, tr. Agnes Schwarzschild. London: Routledge, 2003.

Ma Jianxiong 麻建雄. 武汉老橱窗 (Old window displays in Wuhan). Wuhan: Wuhan chubanshe, 2013.

MacFarquhar, Roderick. *The Origins of the Cultural Revolution*, 3 vols. New York: Columbia University Press, 1974, 1983, 1997.

MacFarquhar, Roderick and Michael Schoenhals. *Mao's Last Revolution*. Cambridge, MA: Belknap Press of Harvard University Press, 2008.

MacGregor, Greg. "Shopper in China Has Long Wait." *New York Times*, June 25, 1957.

Manton, Judy. "Mao Badges – Graven Images?" *China Now*, no. 125 (Summer 1988), 8–9.

Mao Dechuan 毛德传. "国民党军修建利用岱山机场的前前后后" (The complete story of the KMT army's building of and using the Daishan airport for military purposes). Pp. 13–19, in Zhongguo renmin zhengzhi xieshang huiyi, Zhejiangsheng Daishanxian weiyuanhui wenshi ziliao weiyuanhui 中国人民政治协商会议, 浙江省岱山县委员会文史资料委员会, eds. 岱山文史资料 (Daishan historical materials) (1991).

Mao Tse-tung, *On the People's Democratic Dictatorship*, 3rd ed. Peking: Foreign Languages Press, 1950.

Mao Zedong. "Analysis of the Classes in Chinese Society," March 1926. Pp. 1.13–19, in *Selected Works of Mao Tse-tung*. Peking: Foreign Languages Press, 1965.

Mao Zedong. "The Chinese Revolution and the Chinese Communist Party," December 1939. Pp. 2: 305–31, in *Selected Works of Mao Tse-tung*. Peking: Foreign Languages Press, 1965.

Mao Zedong. "On Coalition Government," April 24, 1945. Pp. 3.255–320, in *Selected Works of Mao Tse-tung*. Peking: Foreign Languages Press, 1965.

Mao Zedong 毛泽东. "同民建和工商联负责人的谈话" (Conversation with the principals of the China Democratic National Construction Association and the Federation of Industry and Commerce). February 7, 1956. *Dang de wenxian*, no. 6 (1998), 8–10.

Mao Zedong. *A Critique of Soviet Economics*, tr. Moss Roberts. New York: Monthly Review, 1977.

Mao Zedong. "Let Us Unite and Clearly Distinguish Ourselves and the Enemy," August 4, 1952. Pp. 5.80, in *Selected Works of Mao Tse-tung*. Beijing: Foreign Languages Press, 1977.

Mao Zedong. "On New Democracy," January 1940. Pp. 2: 339–82, in *Selected Works of Mao Tse-tung*. Peking: Foreign Languages Press, 1965.

Mao Zedong. *Report from Xunwu*, tr. Roger R. Thompson. Stanford: Stanford University Press, 1990.

Mao Zedong. "Talks at the Hangzhou Conference (Draft Transcript)," January 3–4, 1958. Pp. 377–91, in Roderick MacFarquhar, Timothy Cheek, and Eugene Wu, eds. *The Secret Speeches of Chairman Mao: From the Hundred Flowers to the Great Leap Forward*. Cambridge, MA: Council on East Asian Studies, Harvard University, 1989.

Marchand, Roland. *Advertising the American Dream: Making Way for Modernity, 1920–1940*. Berkeley: University of California Press, 1985.

Martin, Helmut. *Cult and Canon: The Origins and Development of State Maoism*. Armonk, NY: M.E. Sharpe, 1982.

Marx, Karl. *Capital: A Critique of Political Economy*, 3 vols., tr. Ben Fowkes. London: Penguin Books, 1990–2.

Marx, Karl. "Critique of the Gotha Programme" (1875), www.marxists.org/archive/marx/works/1875/gotha/ch01.htm. Archived July 9, 2018.

Marx, Karl. *Grundrisse: Foundations of the Critique of Political Economy*, tr. Martin Nicolaus. New York: Vintage Books, 1973.

Marx, Karl. *Theories of Surplus Value*. Moscow: Progress Publishers, 1968, 2.519, reproduced at www.massline.org/PolitEcon/crises/Crisesoi.htm. Archived November 12, 2018.

McCord, Edward A. *The Power of the Gun: The Emergence of Modern Chinese Warlordism*. Berkeley: University of California Press, 1993.

McCrossen, Alexis. *Marking Modern Times: A History of Clocks, Watches, and Other Timekeepers in American Life*. Chicago: University of Chicago Press, 2013.

McDougall, Bonnie S. *Mao Zedong's "Talks at the Yan'an Conference on Literature and Art": A Translation of the 1943 Text with Commentary*. Ann Arbor: Center for Chinese Studies, University of Michigan, 1980.

McGuire, Elizabeth. *Red at Heart: How Chinese Communists Fell in Love with the Russian Revolution*. New York: Oxford University Press, 2018.

McKendrick, Neil, John Brewer, and J.H. Plumb. *The Birth of a Consumer Society: The Commercialization of Eighteenth-Century England*. Bloomington: Indiana University Press, 1982.

McNeill, William H. *The Pursuit of Power: Technology, Armed Force, and Society since AD 1000*. Oxford: Basil Blackwell, 1983.Meng Liye 孟犁野. "从农村来的一封信" (A letter from the countryside). *Dianying yishu*, no. A2 (1956), 73.

美帝怎样摧残我工商业 (How US imperialism destroyed our country's industry and commerce). Beijing: Shiyue chubanshe, 1950.

Messaris, Paul. *Visual Persuasion: The Role of Images in Advertising*. Thousand Oaks, CA: Sage Publications, 1997.

Meyskens, Covell. *Mao's Third Front: The Militarization of Cold War China*. Cambridge: Cambridge University Press, 2020.

Mi Ruo 米若. "'上影画报' 的方向是什么?" (What is the direction of *Shanghai Film Pictorial?*). *Zhongguo dianying zazhi*, no. 10 (1958), 71–2.

Millar, James R. "The Little Deal: Brezhnev's Contribution to Acquisitive Socialism." *Slavic Review*, vol. 44, no. 4 (1985), 694–706.

Min, Anchee, Jie Zhang, and Duoduo. *Chinese Propaganda Posters*. Cologne: Taschen, 2008.

Mitter, Rana. *Forgotten Ally: China's World War II, 1937–1945*. Boston: Houghton Mifflin Harcourt, 2013.

Murck, Alfreda, ed. *Mao's Golden Mangoes and the Cultural Revolution*. Zurich: Scheidegger & Spiess, 2013.

Muscolino, Micah S. *Ecology of War in China: Henan Province, the Yellow River, and Beyond, 1938–1950*. Cambridge: Cambridge University Press, 2015.

Naughton, Barry. *The Chinese Economy: Transitions and Growth*. Cambridge, MA: MIT Press, 2007.

Naughton, Barry. "The Third Front: Defence Industrialization in the Chinese Interior." *The China Quarterly*, no. 115 (1988), 351–86.

Naughton, Barry and Kellee S. Tsai, eds. *State Capitalism, Institutional Adaptation, and the Chinese Miracle*. Cambridge: Cambridge University Press, 2015.

Nell, Dawn et al. "Investigating Shopper Narratives of the Supermarket in Early Post-War England, 1945–75." *Oral History*, vol. 37, no. 1 (2009), 61–73.

Ni Ping 倪萍. "上海牌手表" (Shanghai wristwatches). P. 39, in Wang Xiaozhen 王晓真, ed. 商品的故事 (Stories about merchandise). Guangzhou: Nanfang ribao chubanshe, 2000.

Nolan, Peter. *Is China Buying the World?* Cambridge: Polity Press, 2012.

Nove, Alec. *An Economic History of the U.S.S.R., 1917–1991*, 3rd ed. Harmondsworth: Penguin, 1992.

Oakley, Peter. "Ticking Boxes: (Re)Constructing the Wristwatch as a Luxury Object." *Luxury*, vol. 2. no. 1 (2015), 41–60.

Ogle, Vanessa. *The Global Transformation of Time: 1870–1950*. Cambridge, MA: Harvard University Press, 2015.

Oi, Jean C. *State and Peasant in Contemporary China: The Political Economy of Village Government*. Berkeley: University of California Press, 1991.

Osokina, Elena. *Our Daily Bread: Socialist Distribution and the Art of Survival in Stalin's Russia, 1927–1941*, ed. Kate Transchel, tr. Kate Transchel and Greta Bucher. Armonk, NY: M.E. Sharpe, 2001.

Pang Xianzhi 逄先知 and Feng Hui 冯蕙, eds. Zhonggong zhongyang wenxian yanjiushi 中共中央文献研究室, eds. 毛泽东年谱 (1949–1976), 六卷 (A chronicle of Mao Zedong [1949–1976], Volume 6). Beijing: Zhongyang wenxian chubanshe, 2013.

Pang Xianzhi 逄先知 and Jin Chongji 金冲及, eds. 毛泽东传, 1949–1976 (The life of Mao Zedong, 1949–1976). Beijing: Zhongyang wenxian chubanshe, 2003.

Parker, Geoffrey. *The Military Revolution: Military Innovation and the Rise of the West, 1500–1800*, 2nd ed. Cambridge: Cambridge University Press, 2016.

Patterson, Patrick Hyder. *Bought and Sold: Living and Losing the Good Life in Socialist Yugoslavia*. Ithaca, NY: Cornell University Press, 2011.

Patterson, Patrick Hyder. "Truth Half Told: Finding the Perfect Pitch for Advertising and Marketing in Socialist Yugoslavia, 1950–1991." *Enterprise & Society: The International Journal of Business History*, vol. 4, no. 2 (2003), 179–225.

Peng, Kuang-hsi. *Why China Has No Inflation*. Peking: Foreign Languages Press, 1976.

Perkins, Dwight H. *Market Control and Planning in Communist China*. Cambridge, MA: Harvard University Press, 1966.

Perry, Elizabeth J. "Masters of the Country? Shanghai Workers in the Early People's Republic." Pp. 59–79, in Jeremy Brown and Paul G. Pickowicz, eds. *Dilemmas of Victory*. Cambridge, MA: Harvard University Press, 2007.

Perry, Elizabeth J. and Li Xun, *Proletarian Power: Shanghai in the Cultural Revolution*. Boulder, CO: Westview Press, 1997.

Pickowicz, Paul G. *Marxist Literary Thought in China: The Influence of Ch'ü Ch'iu-pai*. Berkeley: University of California Press, 1981.

Pietz, David Allen. *The Yellow River: The Problem of Water in Modern China*. Cambridge, MA: Harvard University Press, 2015.

Pilling, Geoffrey. *Marx's Capital: Philosophy and Political Economy*. London: Routledge & Kegan Paul, 1980.

Po I-po [Bo Yibo]. "Industry's Tasks in 1959." *Peking Review*, no. 1 (1959), 9–11.

Po I-po [Bo Yibo]. *The Polemic on the General Line of the International Communist Movement*. Peking: Foreign Languages Press, 1965.

Postone, Moishe. *Time, Labor, and Social Domination: A Reinterpretation of Marx's Critical Theory*. Cambridge: Cambridge University Press, 1993.

Preobrazhenskiĭ, E. A. and Donald A. Filtzer. *The Crisis of Soviet Industrialization: Selected Essays*. White Plains, NY: M.E. Sharpe, 1979.

Priestley, K. E. "The Sino-Soviet Friendship Association." *Pacific Affairs*, vol. 25, no. 3 (1952), 287–92.

Putnam, Tim. "The Sewing Machine Comes Home." Pp. 269–83, in Barbara Burman, ed. *The Culture of Sewing: Gender, Consumption and Home Dressmaking*. New York: Berg, 1999.

Qi Weiping 齐卫平 and Wang Jun 王军. 关于毛泽东'超英赶美'思想演变阶段的历史考察. (Historical research on the formation and development of Mao Zedong's Thought of "surpassing Great Britain and catching up with the United States"). *Shixue yuekan*, no. 2 (2002), 66–71.

Qin Benli 钦本立. 美帝经济侵华史 (A history of the American imperialist economic invasion of China). Beijing: Shijie zhishi chubanshe, 1950.

Qingdaoshi shizhi bangongshi, 青岛市志办公室, ed. 青岛市志: 轻工业志建材工业志 (Qingdao annals: Light industry/building materials industry). Beijing: Xinhua chubanshe, 2000.

Que Wen 阙文 et al. 抗美援朝畫冊: 第二冊 (Resist America and Aid Korea album: Volume 2). Beijing: Renmin meishu chubanshe, 1951.

Radchenko, Sergey. "The Rise and the Fall of the Sino-Soviet Alliance 1949–1989." Pp. 243–68, in N. Naimark, S. Pons, and S. Quinn-Judge, eds. *The Cambridge History of Communism*. Cambridge: Cambridge University Press, 2017.

Radchenko, Sergey. *Two Suns in the Heavens: The Sino-Soviet Struggle for Supremacy, 1962–1967*. Washington, DC: Woodrow Wilson Press and Stanford: Stanford University Press, 2009.

Randall, Amy E. *The Soviet Dream World of Retail Trade and Consumption in the 1930s*. New York: Palgrave Macmillan, 2008.

Reid, Susan E. "Cold War in the Kitchen: Gender and the De-Stalinization of Consumer Taste in the Soviet Union under Khrushchev." *Slavic Review*, vol. 61, no. 2 (2002), 211–52.

Resnick, Stephen A. and Richard D. Wolff. *Class Theory and History: Capitalism and Communism in the U.S.S.R.* New York: Routledge, 2002.

Resnick, Stephen A. and Richard D. Wolff. *Knowledge and Class: A Marxian Critique of Political Economy*. Chicago: University of Chicago Press, 1987.

Rhoads, Edward J. M. "Cycles of Cathay: A History of the Bicycle in China." *Transfers*, vol. 2, no. 2 (Summer 2012), 95–120.

Richman, Barry M. *Industrial Society in Communist China: A Firsthand Study of Chinese Economic Development and Management, with Significant Comparisons with Industry in India, the U.S.S.R., Japan, and the United States*. New York: Random House, 1969.

Riskin, Carl. *China's Political Economy: The Quest for Development since 1949.* Oxford: Oxford University Press, 1988.

Rohlf, Gregory. "The Soviet Model and China's State Farms." Pp. 197–230, in Thomas P. Bernstein and Hua-Yu Li, eds. *China Learns from the Soviet Union, 1949–Present.* Lanham, MD: Lexington Books, 2011.

Rosdolsky, Roman. *The Making of Marx's "Capital,"* tr. Pete Burgess. London: Pluto, 2004.

Sanchez-Sibony, Oscar. *Red Globalization: The Political Economy of the Soviet Cold War from Stalin to Khrushchev.* Cambridge: Cambridge University Press, 2014.

Schoenhals, Michael. *China's Cultural Revolution, 1966–1969: Not a Dinner Party.* Armonk, NY: M.E. Sharpe, 1996.

Schoenhals, Michael. "China's 'Great Proletarian Information Revolution' of 1966–1967." Pp. 230–58, in Jeremy Brown and Matthew D. Johnson, eds. *Maoism at the Grassroots: Everyday Life in China's Era of High Socialism.* Cambridge, MA: Harvard University Press, 2015.

Schoenhals, Michael. *Doing Things with Words in Chinese Politics: Five Studies.* Berkeley: Institute of East Asian Studies, University of California, 1992.

Schor, Juliet B. *The Overspent American: Why We Want What We Don't Need.* New York: HarperPerennial, 1999.

Schram, Stuart R. "Mao Tse-tung and the Theory of the Permanent Revolution, 1958–1969." *The China Quarterly*, no. 46 (1971), 221–44.

Schram, Stuart R. "Mao Tse-tung's Thought from 1949 to 1976." Pp. 1–104, in John King Fairbank and Roderick MacFarquhar, eds. *The Cambridge History of China, vol. 14: The People's Republic of China, part 2: Revolutions Within the Chinese Revolution, 1966–1982.* Cambridge: Cambridge University Press, 1991.

Schram, Stuart R., ed. *Mao Zedong Unrehearsed: Talks and Letters, 1956–71.* Harmondsworth: Penguin, 1974.

Schrift, Melissa. *Biography of a Chairman Mao Badge: The Creation and Mass Consumption of a Personality Cult.* New Brunswick, NJ: Rutgers University Press, 2001.

Schudson, Michael. *Advertising, The Uneasy Persuasion: Its Dubious Impact on American Society.* New York: Basic Books, 1986.

Scott, James C. "Everyday Forms of Resistance." Pp. 3–33, in Forrest D. Colburn, ed. *Everyday Forms of Peasant Resistance.* Armonk, NY: M.E. Sharpe, 1989.

Scott, James C. *Weapons of the Weak: Everyday Forms of Peasant Resistance.* New Haven: Yale University Press, 1985.

Selden, Mark. *The Political Economy of Chinese Socialism.* Armonk, NY: M.E. Sharpe, 1988.

Service, Robert. *Trotsky: A Biography.* Cambridge, MA: Belknap Press of Harvard University Press, 2009.

Shai, Aron. *The Fate of British and French Firms in China, 1949–54: Imperialism Imprisoned.* Basingstoke: Macmillan, 1996.

Shan Shaojie "商标工作座谈会纪要" (An outline of the trademark working meeting). SMA, Document 2 B170-1-1079 (February 6, 1964).

Shan Shaojie 单少杰. 毛泽东执政春秋 (The reign of Mao Zedong). Taipei: Lianjing chubanshe, 2001.

Shan Shaojie 山东省日用机械工业制 1915–1985 (Records of the Shandong everyday goods machinery industry, 1915–1985). Shandong: Shandongsheng riyong jixie gongye gongsi, 1988.

Shanghai baihuo gongsi. Shanghai shehui kexueyuan jingji yanjiusuo, Gongshang xingzheng guanliju 上海百货公司, 上海社会科学院经济研究所, 上海市工商行政管理局, eds. 上海近代百货商业史 (A history of modern department store commerce in Shanghai). Shanghai: Shanghai shehui kexue chubanshe, 1988.

"上海解放初期警备工作的日日夜夜" (Days and nights of garrison work in the early days of Shanghai's Liberation). Pp. 9–41, in Zhongguo renmin jiefangjun Shanghai jingbeiqu zhengzhibu, Zhonggong Shanghai shiwei dangshi yanjiushi 中国人民解放军上海警备区政治部, 中共上海市委党史研究室, eds. 警备大上海 (Guard great Shanghai). Shanghai: Shanghai yuandong chubanshe, 1994.

Shanghai qinggongye zhi bianzuan weiyuanhui 上海轻工业志编纂委员会, ed. 上海轻工业志 (Shanghai light industry annals). Shanghai: Shanghai shehui kexue chubanshe, 1996.

Shanghai shehui kexueyuan jingji yanjiusuo 上海社会科学院经济研究所, ed. 上海永安公司的产生, 发展和改造 (The birth, development, and transformation of Shanghai's Yong'an Company). Shanghai: Shanghai renmin chubanshe, 1981.

"上海市电影局" (Shanghai municipal movie office). SMA, B170-1-1149 (March 22, 1965).

"上海市广告公司, 关于服务质量与设计质量问题的调查报告" (Inspection report of issues of service and design quality in the advertising industry). SMA B123-5-78 (September 11, 1961).

"商业广告" (Commercial advertising). SMA B135-1-551 (1957).

Shangyebu baihuo ju 商业部百货局, ed. 中国百货商业 (Chinese general commerce). Beijing: Beijing daxue chubanshe, 1989.

Shangyebu jingji yanjiusuo 商业部经济研究所, ed. 新中国商业三十年 (征求意见稿) (Thirty years of New China's business) (Draft Soliciting Opinions). Internal circulation, 1980.

Shangyebu shangye jingji yanjiusuo 商业部商业经济研究所, ed. 新中国商业史稿 (1949–1982) (Draft of New China's business history, 1949–1982). Beijing: Zhongguo caizheng jingji chubanshe, 1984.

Shangyebu shangye zuzhi yu jishuju 商业部商业组织与技术局, ed. 商店橱窗陈列与内部布置 (Store window displays and interior decorations). Beijing: Caizheng jingji chubanshe, 1955.

Shao Wenguang. *China, Britain and Businessmen: Political and Commercial Relations, 1957*. Basingstoke: Macmillan, 1991.

Sheehan, Jackie. *Chinese Workers: A New History*. London: Routledge, 1998.

Shen Kuiyi. "Publishing Posters Before the Cultural Revolution." *Modern Chinese Literature and Culture*, vol. 12, no. 2 (Fall 2000), 177–202.

Shen Kun 沈琨. "老县城记" (Memories of my county), in 沈琨文集: 散文卷4 (The collected works of Shen Kun: Prose, Volume 4). Beijing: Zuojia chubanshe, 2012.

Shen, Zhihua and Guy Alitto. "A Historical Examination of the Issue of Soviet Experts in China: Basic Situation and Policy Changes." *Russian History*, vol. 29, nos. 2/4 (2002), 377–400.

Shen Zhihua 沈志华. 苏联专家在中国 *(1948–1960)* (Soviet Experts in China, 1948–1960). Beijing: Zhongguo guoji guangbo chubanshe, 2003.

Sheng, Michael M. "Mao Zedong and the Three-Anti Campaign (November 1951 to April 1952): A Revisionist Interpretation." *Twentieth-Century China*, vol. 32, no. 1 (2006), 56–80.

Shih, Ch'eng-chih. *Urban Commune Experiments in Communist China*. Hong Kong: Union Research Institute, 1962.

十年宣传画选集 (A selection of propaganda posters during the ten years). Shanghai: Shanghai meishu chubanshe, 1960.

Sichuansheng shangyeting 四川省商业厅, ed. "不断跃进, 面貌一新的重庆'三八'百货商店" (Continuous leap forward, the appearance of a new Chongqing "March Eighth" Department Store). P. 98, in Shangyebu 商业部, ed. 商业红旗 (日用工业品类) (The red flag of commerce [industrial consumer goods sector]). Beijing: Gongren chubanshe, 1960.

Sichuansheng shangyeting 四川省商业厅, ed. "千方百计把方便送给顾客" (Take every means to make conveniences for customers). P. 105, in Shangyebu (商业部), ed. 商业红旗 (日用工业品类) (The red flag of commerce [industrial consumer goods sector]). Beijing: Gongren chubanshe, 1960.

Sidalin 斯大林 (Joseph Stalin). 苏联社会主义经济问题 (Economic problems of socialism in the USSR). Beijing: Renmin chubanshe, 1952. Also published in *Xuexi*, no. 8 (November 1952), 3–27.

Siegelbaum, Lewis H. *Cars for Comrades: The Life of the Soviet Automobile*. Ithaca, NY: Cornell University Press, 2008.

Slater, Don. *Consumer Culture and Modernity*. Oxford: Polity Press, 1997.

Smith, John. *Imperialism in the Twenty-first Century: Globalization, Super-Exploitation, and Capitalism's Final Crisis*. New York: Monthly Review Press, 2016.

Smith, Stephen A. "Introduction: Towards a Global History of Communism." Pp. 1–34, in S. A. Snow, Edgar. "A Conversation with Mao Tse-tung." *Life*, vol. 70, no. 16 (April 30, 1971), 46–7.

Smith, Stephen A., ed. *The Oxford Handbook of the History of Communism*. Oxford: Oxford University Press, 2013.

Snow, Edgar. "A Reporter Got This Rare Interview with Chairman Mao in 1965, Even Though China Was Entirely Closed to the West." *The New Republic*, February 27, 1965, 17–23.

So, Bennis Wai-yip. "The Policy-Making and Political Economy of the Abolition of Private Ownership in the Early 1950s: Findings from New Materials." *The China Quarterly*, no. 171 (2002), 682–703.

Solinger, Dorothy J. *Chinese Business Under Socialism: The Politics of Domestic Commerce, 1949–1980*. Berkeley: University of California Press, 1984.

Stalin, Joseph V. *Economic Problems of Socialism in the U.S.S.R.* Peking: Foreign Languages Press, 1972.

Stalin, Joseph V. *Problems of Leninism*. Moscow: Foreign Languages Publishing House, 1953.

Starr, John Bryan. "Conceptual Foundations of Mao Tse-Tung's Theory of Continuous Revolution." *Asian Survey*, vol. 11, no. 6 (1971), 610–28.

Stearns, Peter N. *Consumerism in World History: The Global Transformation of Desire*. London: Routledge, 2006.

Stearns, Peter N. *Satisfaction Not Guaranteed: Dilemmas of Progress in Modern Society*. New York: New York University Press, 2012.

Stitziel, Judd. *Fashioning Socialism: Clothing, Politics, and Consumer Culture in East Germany*. Oxford: Berg, 2005.

Stone, David R. *Hammer and Rifle: The Militarization of the Soviet Union, 1926–1933*. Lawrence: University Press of Kansas, 2000.

Stranahan, Patricia. *Molding the Medium: The Chinese Communist Party and Liberation Daily*. London: Routledge, 2015.

Su Feng 苏峰. "改革开放初期北京安置待业青年与多种经济形式的起步" (The arrangements for youth waiting for employment in Beijing and the beginning of various economic forms during the early reform and opening-up). *Dangdai Zhongguo shi yanjiu*, vol. 24, no. 4 (2017), 50–62.

Su Shimei 苏士梅. 中国近现代商业广告史 (A history of modern and contemporary advertising in China). Kaifeng: Henan daxue chubanshe, 2006.

Su Xiu 苏秀. 我的配音生涯 (My career doing voiceovers). Shanghai: Wenhui chubanshe, 2005.

Su, Yang. *Collective Killings in Rural China During the Cultural Revolution*. New York: Cambridge University Press, 2011.

Sun Peidong 孙沛东. "视听暴力: '九评'的生产传播及红卫兵一代的记忆" (Audiovisual violence: The production and transmission of the nine commentaries and memories of the Red Guard generation). *Sixiang*, no. 35 (2018), 43–91.

Sun Peidong 孙沛东. 时尚与政治: 广东民众日常着装时尚 (1966–1976) (Fashion and politics: Everyday clothing fashions of the Guangdong masses [1966–1976]). Beijing: Renmin chubanshe, 2013.

Swallow, Robert W. *Sidelights on Peking Life*. Peking: China Booksellers Ltd., 1927.

Swayne, Elizabeth. "Soviet Advertising: Communism Imitates Capitalism." Pp. 93–103, in C. H. Sandage and Vernon Fryburger, eds. *The Role of Advertising*. Homewood, IL: R. D. Irwin, 1960.

Tan Jiewen 谭解文. "'抄家'述略" (A brief account of "home ransackings"). *Hunan wenshi*, no. 6 (2001), 74–5.

Tang, Jianzhong and Laurence J. C. Mao. "Evolution of Urban Collective Enterprises in China." *The China Quarterly*, no. 104 (1985), 614–40.

Tang, Peter S. H. *Communist China Today*, 2 vols. New York: Praeger, 1957–58.

Taylor, Philip M. *Munitions of the Mind: A History of Propaganda from the Ancient World to the Present Age*, 3rd ed. Manchester: Manchester University Press, 2003.

Teiwes, Frederick C. and Warren Sun. "China's New Economic Policy under Hua Guofeng: Party Consensus and Party Myths." *China Journal*, no. 66 (July 2011), 1–23.

Teiwes, Frederick C. and Warren Sun. *China's Road to Disaster: Mao, Central Politicians, and Provincial Leaders in the Unfolding of the Great Leap Forward, 1955–1959*. Armonk, NY: M.E. Sharpe, 1999.

Thai, Philip. *China's War on Smuggling: Law, Economic Life, and the Making of the Modern State, 1842–1965*. New York: Columbia University Press, 2018.

Thaxton, Ralph A. *Catastrophe and Contention in Rural China: Mao's Great Leap Forward: Famine and the Origins of Righteous Resistance in Da Fo Village*. Cambridge: Cambridge University Press, 2008.

Thaxton, Ralph A. *Salt of the Earth: The Political Origins of Peasant Protest and Communist Revolution*. Berkeley: University of California Press, 1997.

Thompson, E. P. "Time, Work-Discipline, and Industrial Capitalism." *Past & Present*, no. 38 (December 1967), 56–97.

Thompson, Thomas N. *China's Nationalization of Foreign Firms: The Politics of Hostage Capitalism, 1949–57*. Baltimore: School of Law, Occasional Papers/Reprint Series in Contemporary Asian Studies, University of Maryland, 1979.

Tian Fanghua 天方画 [pseudonym]. "谈'浪费美学'" (Let's talk about the "aesthetics of wastefulness"). *Zhongguo dianying*, no. 3 (1958), 68.

Tianjin baihuo gongsi 天津市百货公司, ed. 天津市百货公司四十年史 (1949–1989) (Forty years of the Tianjin Department Store [1949–1989]). Self-published and not intended for public circulation, 1989.

"天桥百货商场服务公约" (Service compact of Tianqiao Department Store). *Beijing ribao*, February 9, 1958, republished in Beijing chubanshe bianjibu 北京出版社编辑部, ed. 大跃进中的北京天桥百货商场 (Beijing Tianqiao Department Store during the Great Leap Forward). Beijing: Beijing chubanshe, 1958.

Tien, Yuan. "Learn from Tienchiao, Emulate Tienchiao." *Women of China*, no. 4 (1958), 26–8.

Timasheff, Nicholas S. *The Great Retreat: The Growth and Decline of Communism in Russia*. New York: E.P. Dutton, 1946.

Trentmann, Frank. *Empire of Things: How We Became a World of Consumers, from the Fifteenth Century to the Twenty-First*. New York: HarperCollins Publishers, 2016.

Trentmann, Frank. "Introduction." Pp. 1–19 in Trentmann, ed. *Oxford Handbook of the History of Consumption*. Oxford: Oxford University Press, 2012.

Tsai, Weipin. *Reading Shenbao: Nationalism, Consumerism and Individuality in China, 1919–37*. London: Palgrave Macmillan, 2010.

Twitchell, James B. *Adcult USA: The Triumph of Advertising in American Culture*. New York: Columbia University Press, 1996.

Unger, Jonathan. "Grassroots Turmoil in China's Cultural Revolution: A Half-Century Perspective." 77th George E. Morrison Lecture, November 3, 2016. www.chinoiresie.info/grassroots-turmoil-in-chinas-cultural-revolution-a-half-century-perspective/. Archived July 18, 2018.

van de Ven, Hans. "The Military in the Republic." *The China Quarterly*, no. 150 (June 1997), 352–74.

Van Fleit Hang, Krista. *Literature the People Love: Reading Chinese Texts from the Early Maoist Period (1949–1966)*. New York: Palgrave Macmillan, 2013.

Veblen, Thorstein. "The Economic Theory of Woman's Dress." *The Popular Science Monthly*, vol. 46 (1894), 198–205.

Vokov, Vadim. "The Concept of *kul'turnost'*: Notes on the Stalinist Civilizing Process." Pp. 210–30, in Sheila Fitzpatrick, ed. *Stalinism: New Directions*. London: Routledge, 2000.

Volland, Nicolai. *Socialist Cosmopolitanism: The Chinese Literary Universe, 1945–1965*. New York: Columbia University Press, 2017.

Wakeman, Frederic, Jr. "'Cleanup': The New Order in Shanghai." Pp. 21–58, in Jeremy Brown and Paul G. Pickowicz, eds. *Dilemmas of Victory*. Cambridge, MA: Harvard University Press, 2007.

Walder, Andrew G. *China under Mao: A Revolution Derailed*. Cambridge, MA: Harvard University Press, 2015.

Walder, Andrew G. *Communist Neo-Traditionalism: Work and Authority in Chinese Industry*. Berkeley: University of California Press, 1986.

Walder, Andrew G. "Property Rights and Stratification in Socialist Redistributive Economies." *American Sociological Review*, vol. 57 (1992), 524–39.

Wallerstein, Immanuel. *The Capitalist World-Economy: Essays*. Cambridge: Cambridge University Press, 1979.

Wang Anting 王安廷, ed. 毛泽东像章图谱 (An illustrated catalogue of Mao Zedong badges). Beijing: Zhongguo shudian chubanshe, 1993.

Wang Chenlong 王辰龙. "男青年们的花衬衫" (Young men's colorful shirts). *Jiari 100 tian*, no. 9 (September 18, 2009).

Wang Haibo 汪海波, comp. 中华人民共和国工业经济史 (A history of the industrial economy of the People's Republic of China). Taiyuan: Shanxi jingji chubanshe, 1998.

Wang, Helen. *Chairman Mao Badges: Symbols and Slogans of the Cultural Revolution*. British Museum Research Publication, no. 169. London: British Museum Press, 2008.

Wang Nianyi 王年一. 大动乱的年代 (A decade of great upheaval). Zhengzhou: Henan renmin chubanshe, 1988.

Wang Qianli 汪千里, ed. 缝纫机 (Sewing machines). Beijing: Zhongguo caizheng jingji chubanshe, 1964.

Wang Yuli 王玉利. "黑龙江像章厂建厂始末" (The rise and demise of the Heilongjiang Badge Factory). *Heilongjiang shizhi*, no. 24 (2011), 44–5.

Wang, Zheng. *Finding Women in the State: A Socialist Feminist Revolution in the People's Republic of China, 1949–1964*. Berkeley: University of California Press, 2017.

Weathersby, Kathryn. "Stalin, Mao, and the End of the Korean War." Pp. 90–116, in Odd Arne Westad, ed. *Brothers in Arms: The Rise and Fall of the Sino–Soviet Alliance, 1945–1963*. Washington, DC: Woodrow Wilson Center Press and Stanford: Stanford University Press, 1998.

Wei Zichu 魏子初. 美帝在华经济侵略 (The US imperialist economic invasion of China). Beijing: Renmin chubanshe, 1951.

"为大批生产的药品不能宣传广告的通知" (A notice stating that pharmaceutical products that have not yet been massively manufactured should not be promoted through advertisements). SMA B123-4-556 (April 17, 1959).

Wemheuer, Felix. "Dining in Utopia: An Intellectual History of the Origins of the Chinese Public Dining Halls." Pp. 277–302, in Matthias Middell and Felix Wemheuer, eds. *Hunger and Scarcity under State-Socialism*. Leipzig: Leipziger Universitätsverlag, 2012.

Wemheuer, Felix. *Famine Politics in Maoist China and the Soviet Union*. New Haven: Yale University Press, 2014.

"Wenzhoushi gongshang xingzheng guanlizhi" bianzuan weiyuanhui "温州市工商行政管理志"编纂委员会, ed. 温州市工商行政管理志 (Administrative records of industry and commerce of Wenzhou City). Shanghai: Fudan daxue chubanshe, 1993.

West, Philip. *Yenching University and Sino-Western Relations, 1916–1952*. Cambridge, MA: Harvard University Press, 1976.

Westad, Odd Arne. *Decisive Encounters: The Chinese Civil War, 1946–1950*. Stanford: Stanford University Press, 2003.

Westad, Odd A. *The Global Cold War: Third World Interventions and the Making of Our Time*. Cambridge: Cambridge University Press, 2005.

Werner, Jake. "Global Fordism in 1950s Urban China." *Frontiers of History in China*, vol. 7, no. 3 (September 2012), 415–41.

White, Robert A. "Mao Badges and the Cultural Revolution." *International Social Science Review*, vol. 69, nos. 3–4 (1994), 53–70.

Whyte Martin K. and William L. Parish. *Urban Life in Contemporary China*. Chicago: University of Chicago Press, 1984.

Wickeri, Philip L. *Seeking the Common Ground: Protestant Christianity, the Three-Self Movement, and China's United Front*. Maryknoll, NY: Orbis Books, 1988.

Wilson, Verity. "Dress and the Cultural Revolution." Pp. in 167–86, in Valerie Steele and John S. Major, eds. *China Chic: East Meets West*. New Haven: Yale University Press, 1999.

Witke, Roxane. *Comrade Ch'iang Ching*. Boston: Little, Brown, 1977.

Wolff, Charles., Jr. "China's Capitalists Join the Party." *New York Times*, August 13, 2001.

Wu, Guoguang. "Command Communication: The Politics of Editorial Formulation in the *People's Daily*." *The China Quarterly*, no. 137 (March 1994), 194–211.

Wu Hanren 吴汉仁 and Bai Zhongqi 白中琪. 双城故事 从上海到台北的一次文化平移 (Stories of two cities: A cultural shift from Shanghai to Taipei). Shanghai: Shanghai wenhua chubanshe, 2014.

Wu, Hung. "Tiananmen Square: A Political History of Monuments." *Representations*, no. 35 (1991), 84–117.

Wu Lengxi 吴冷西. 十年论战: 1956–1966 中苏关系回忆录 (A decade of polemics: A memoir of Sino-Soviet relations between 1956 and 1966). Beijing: Zhongyang wenxian chubanshe, 1999.

Wu Renshu 巫仁恕. 品味奢华: 晚明的消费社会与士大夫 (A taste of luxury: Consumer culture in the late Ming dynasty and scholar-officials). Beijing: Zhonghua shuju, 2008.

Wu Xiaobo 吴晓波. 历代经济变革得失 (The successes and failures of economic reforms in history). Hangzhou: Zhejiang daxue chubanshe, 2016.

Wu, Yiching. *The Cultural Revolution at the Margins: Chinese Socialism in Crisis.* Cambridge, MA: Harvard University Press, 2014.

Xiang, Lanxin. *Recasting the Imperial Far East: Britain and America in China, 1945–1950.* Armonk, NY: M.E. Sharpe, 1995.

Xiang Xiaomi 项小米. 记忆洪荒 (A flood of memories). Beijing: Beijing chubanshe, 2013.

Xiao Ling 肖玲. " 件花旗袍引起的风波" (Controversy over a flowered *qipao*). *Zhongguo funü*, no. 4 (April 1956), 18–19.

"萧瑞怡上毛泽东书" (Xiao Ruiyi's letter to Mao Zedong"). Pp. 11–12, in Yu Xiguang 余习广, ed. 位卑未敢忘忧国: "文化大革命"上书集 (Humble people never forget their country: A collection of petitions from the Cultural Revolution) Changsha: Hunan renmin chubanshe, 1989.

Xiao, Zhiwei. "Anti-Imperialism and Film Censorship During the Nanjing Decade, 1927–1937." Pp. 35–58, in Sheldon Hsiao-peng Lu, ed. *Transnational Chinese Cinemas: Identity, Nationhood, Gender.* Honolulu: University of Hawai'i Press, 1997.

Xiao, Zhiwei. "The Expulsion of American Films from China, 1949–1950." *Twentieth Century China*, vol. 30, no. 1 (November 2004), 64–81.

Xie Chenjian 谢沉见. "'三转一响': 我们那个年代的时尚故事" (The three things that go "round and the one that makes a sound": Stories about fashion from our times). *Minjian wenhua luntan*, no. 21 (May/June 2000), 28–31.

Xie Jingyi 谢静宜. 毛泽东身边工作琐忆 (Memories of working alongside Mao Zedong). Beijing: Zhongyang wenxian chubanshe, 2015.

Xie Quan 解全. 我在文化大革命中的经历 (My experience in the Cultural Revolution). Pp. 145–69, in Xu Youyu 徐友渔, ed. 1966: 我们那一代的回忆 (1966: Memories of our generation). Beijing: Zhongguo wenlian chuban gongsi, 1988.

Xin Zhongguo diyi dian de gushi bianweihui 新中国第一店的故事编委会, ed. 新中国第一店的故事 (The story of New China's Number One Store). Shanghai: Shanghai dianzi chuban youxian gongsi, 2012.

Xiong Yuezhi 熊月之, ed. 上海通史, 第11卷: 当代政治 (General history of Shanghai: Volume 11, Contemporary politics). Shanghai: Shanghai renmin chubanshe, 1999.

Xu Bin 徐斌. "'地下经济'的顽强生存与民营企业的先发优势" (The tenacious survival of the "underground economy" and the first-mover advantages of privately owned enterprises). *Shangye jingji yu guanli*, no. 1 (2010), 51–60, 68.

Xu Hualong 徐华龙. 上海服装文化史 (A history of Shanghai clothing culture). Shanghai: Dongfang chuban zhongxin, 2010.

Xu Lin 徐琳. "从我国社会主义建设实践看消灭城乡差别, 工农差别和体力劳动与脑力劳动差别的问题" (Seeing the inequalities between urban and rural areas, workers and peasants, and manual and mental labor in the practice of socialist construction in China). *Jiaoxue yu yanjiu* (1959), 23–40.

Xu Muzhi 徐牧之. 这就是美國 (This is America). Shanghai: Dadong shuju, 1951.

Xu Ping 徐平. "军版'布拉吉'" (The military version of the "bulaji"). *Junying wenhua tiandi* (January 2018), 37–8.

Xu Qing 许青 and Guo Xiuru 郭秀茹. "'文化大革命'在南京的发动" (The launch of the "Great Cultural Revolution" in Nanjing). P. 435, in Zhuang Xiaojun 庄小军 and Xu Kangying 徐康英, eds. 风雨同舟: 南京探索前进三十年 1949–1978 (Stand together through storm and stress: Thirty years of exploration and progress in Nanjing, 1949–1978). Beijing: Zhonggong dangshi chubanshe, 2002.

Xu Qiumei 徐秋梅 and Wu Jijin 吴继金. "'文化大革命'时期的毛泽东像章" (Mao Zedong badges during the "Great Cultural Revolution"). *Dangshi zonglan*, no. 9 (2008), 51–6.

Xu Shanbin 许善斌. 证照中国 1966–1976: 共和国特殊年代的纸上历史 (Authorizing China 1966–1976: A history of paper during the special period of the republic). Beijing: Xinhua chubanshe, 2009.

Xu Tao 徐涛. 自行车与近代中国 (Bicycles and modern China). Shanghai: Shanghai renmin chubanshe, 2015.

Xu Youyu 徐友渔. "我在1966年" (Me in 1966). Pp. 297–330, in Xu Youyu 徐友渔, ed. 1966: 我们那一代的回忆 (1966: Memories of our generation). Beijing: Zhongguo wenlian chuban gongsi), 1988.

Xue Muqiao. *China's Socialist Economy*. Beijing: Foreign Languages Press, 1981.

Xue Muqiao 薛暮桥, Su Xing 苏星, and Lin Zili 林子力. 中国国民经济的社会主义改造 (The Socialist Transformation of the national economy in China). Beijing: Renmin chubanshe, 1959.

Yan, Jiaqi and Gao Gao. *Turbulent Decade: A History of the Cultural Revolution*, tr. D. W. Y. Kwok. Honolulu: University of Hawai'i Press, 1996.

Yan Mingfu 阎明复. 亲历中苏关系: 中央办公厅翻译组的十年 (1957–1966) (A personal account of Sino-Soviet relations: A decade in the Translation Group of the General Office of the CCP Central Committee). Beijing: Zhongguo renmin daxue chubanshe, 2015.

Yang, Jisheng. *Tombstone: The Untold Story of Mao's Great Famine*. London: Penguin Books, 2013.

Yang Kuisong 杨奎松. "1952 年上海 '五反' 运动始末" (The entire story of Shanghai's 5-Anti campaign in 1952). *Shehui kexue*, no. 4 (2006), 5–30.

Yang Kuisong 杨奎松. 毛泽东与莫斯科的恩恩怨怨 (Gratitude and resentment between Mao Zedong and Moscow), 4th ed. Nanchang: Jiangxi renmin chubanshe, 1999.

Yang, Kuisong and Sheng Mao. "Unafraid of the Ghost: The Victim Mentality of Mao Zedong and the Two Taiwan Strait Crises in the 1950s." *China Review*, vol. 16, no. 1 (Spring 2016), 1–34.

Yang Tianliang 杨天亮. "上海四大百货公司" (Shanghai's four great department stores). Pp. 353–8, in Xin Ping 忻平, Hu Zhenghao 胡正豪, and Li Xuechang 李学昌, eds. 民国社会大观 (A comprehensive view of society in the Republic of China). Fuzhou: Fujian renmin chubanshe, 1991.

Yang Wenhua 杨文华 and Lin Yigang 林移刚. "韶山旅游纪念品开发中的问题与对策" (The problem of and solution for the development of tourist souvenirs in Shaoshan). *Jingji tequ*, no. 11 (November 2007), 196–7.

Yang Yaojian 杨耀健. "一个小学生的保皇与造反" (A primary student experiences rebellion). *Wangshi*, no. 4 (February 2, 2009), 48–51. http://prchistory.org/wp-content/uploads/2014/05/REMEMBRANCE-No-14–2009年2月12日.pdf. Archived August 26, 2016.

Yao Xiaoping 姚小平. "疯狂的像章" (The badge craze), *Xin tiandi*, no. 6 (2011), 44–5.

Yao Yanxin 姚炎鑫. "毛泽东像收藏漫谈" (The story of a Mao Zedong badge collections). *Zhejiang dang'an* (March 2015), 50–3.

Ye Shisun 叶世荪 and Ye Jianing 叶佳宁. 上海话外来语二百例 (200 loanwords in the Shanghai dialect). Shanghai: Shanghai daxue chubanshe, 2015.

Yeh, Wen-hsin. *Shanghai Splendor: Economic Sentiments and the Making of Modern China, 1843–1949*. Berkeley: University of California Press, 2007.

Yen, Ching-hwang. "Wing-on and the Kwok Brothers: A Case of Pre-war Chinese Entrepreneurs." Pp. 47–65, in Kerrie L. MacPherson, ed. *Asian Department Stores*. Surrey: Curzon, 1998.

"一位劳模的美丽记忆" (Beautiful memories of a model worker). Pp. 128–37, in Shanghai yingxiang gongzuo shi 上海影像工作室, ed. 百姓生活记忆：上海故事 (Memories of people's life experiences: Shanghai stories). Shanghai: Xuelin chubanshe, 2012.

Yu, Frederick T. C. *Mass Persuasion in Communist China*. New York: Praeger, 1964.

Yu Guangyuan 于光远. "反对资产阶级的进攻，坚持工人阶级的领导权" (Resist the attacks by the bourgeois class, determinedly uphold the leadership of the working class). *Xuexi zazhi* (January 1952), 13–18.

Yu Miin-ling 余敏玲. "從高歌到低唱：蘇聯群眾歌曲在中國" (From singing loud to singing low: Soviet mass songs in China). *Zhongyang yanjiuyuan jindaishi yanjiusuo jikan* (Academia Sinica), no. 53 (September 2006), 149–91.

Yu Miin-ling. "Learning from the Soviet Union: CPC Publicity and Its Effects – A Study Centered on the Sino-Soviet Friendship Association." *Social Sciences in China*, vol. 26, no. 2 (2005), 100–11.

Yu Wenmin 于文敏. "财贸战线上的红旗" (The red flags at the commercial frontline). *Shida jiaoxue* (December 24, 1958), 4.

Yu Xiguang 余习广, ed. 位卑未敢忘忧国: "文化大革命"上书集 (Humble people do not forget their country: A collection of petitions from the Cultural Revolution) Changsha: Hunan renmin chubanshe, 1989.

Yu Yang 于洋. "浅析'京剧样板戏'音乐对京胡演奏的影响" (A brief analysis of the influences of "Peking model operas" on Jinghu performances). *Xijiang yue* (西江月), 2013.

Yue Daiyun and Carolyn Wakeman. *To the Storm: The Odyssey of a Revolutionary Chinese Woman*. Berkeley: University of California Press, 1985.

Zang Jian. "The Soviet Impact on 'Gender Equality' in China in the 1950s." Pp. 259–74, in Thomas P. Bernstein and Hua-Yu Li, eds. *China Learns from the Soviet Union, 1949–Present*. Lanham, MD: Lexington Books, 2010.

Zhai, Zhenhua. *Red Flower of China*. New York: SOHO, 1992.

Zhang Di 张谛. "中国第一块手表诞生记" (The birth of China's first watch). 河东区文史资料选辑,第17辑 (Collection of cultural and historical materials on Hedong District, vol. 17). Tianjin: Tianjinshi Hedongqu weiyuanhui xuexi wenshi ziliao weiyuanhui, 2005.

Zhang Huicang 张辉灿. "我所亲历的毛主席八次接见红卫兵" (My personal experiences during Chairman Mao's eight Red Guard receptions). *Dangshi bocai*, no. 2 (2006), 32–7.

Zhang Huicang 张辉灿 and Mu An 慕安. "毛泽东八次接见红卫兵亲历记" (My personal memories of Mao Zedong's eight receptions of Red Guards). *Shidai wenxue*, no. 5 (2006), 164–8.

Zhang Huihu 张辉虎. "戴六块表的坏人" (The bad guy with six watches on his wrists). Pp. 40–1, in Wang Xiaozhen 王晓真, ed. 商品的故事 (Stories about merchandise). Guangzhou: Nanfang ribao chubanshe, 2000.

Zhang Jianqing 章涧青. "林彪集团主要成员窃夺文物记" (The primary members of the Lin Biao clique stole cultural relics from the state). *Bainianchao*, no. 1 (2004), 49–54.

Zhang Jishun 张济顺. 远去的都市: 1950 年代的上海 (A city displaced: Shanghai in the 1950s). Beijing: Shehui kexue wenxian chubanshe, 2015.

Zhang, Jishun. "Cultural Consumption and Popular Reception of the West in Shanghai, 1950–1966." *The Chinese Historical Review*, vol. 12, no. 1 (Spring 2005), 97–126.

Zhang Ming 张鸣. "执政的道德困境与突围之道: 三反五反运动解析" (The moral dilemma of being in power and the ways out: The "Three Antis" and "Five Antis" campaigns). *Ershiyi shiji*, no. 92 (2005), 46–58.

Zhang, Qi and Mingxing Liu. *Revolutionary Legacy, Power Structure, and Grassroots Capitalism under the Red Flag in China*. Cambridge: Cambridge University Press, 2019.

Zhang Qi 章奇 and Liu Mingxing 刘明兴. 权力结构、政治激励和经济增长 基于浙江民营经济发展经验的政治经济学分析 (Power structure, political incentives, and economic growth: A political economy analysis based on the experiences of Zhejiang's private economic development). Shanghai: Gezhi chubanshe, 2016.

Zhang Shichun 张世春. 物质供应票证鉴赏与收藏 (Appreciation and collection of material supply rations). Wuhan: Hubei renmin chubanshe, 2008.

Zhang, Shu Guang. *Beijing's Economic Statecraft during the Cold War, 1949–1991*. Washington, DC: Woodrow Wilson Center Press and Baltimore: Johns Hopkins University Press, 2014.

Zhang, Shu Guang. *Mao's Military Romanticism: China and the Korean War, 1950–1953*. Lawrence: University Press of Kansas, 1995.

Zhang Shuoguo 张硕果. "解放初期上海电影发行放映初探 (1949–1952)" (A preliminary study on the distribution of movies in Shanghai during the early years of Liberation [1949–1952]). *Dianying yishu*, no. 1 (2008), 95–102.

Zhang, Xinxin and Ye Sang. *Chinese Profiles*. Beijing: Chinese Literature, 1986.

Zhang Xuebing 张学兵. "中国计划经济时期的'地下经济'探析" (An analysis of the "underground economy" during the period of China's planned economy). *Zhonggong dangshi yanjiu*, no. 4 (2012), 39–48.

Zhang, Yingjin. *Chinese National Cinema*. New York: Routledge, 2004.

"中央转发北京市委关于三反斗争的报告的批语" (January 5, 1952) (Comments and instructions of the Central Committee on transmitting the report by the Beijing Municipal Committee on the struggle against the Three-Antis). January 5, 1952, Pp. 3.21–2, in 建国以来毛泽东文稿 (Mao Zedong's manuscripts since the founding of the state). Beijing: Zhongyang wenxian chubanshe, 1989.

Zhang Yunsheng 张云生. 毛家湾纪实: 林彪秘书回忆录 (A true account of Maojiawan: The memoirs of Lin Biao's secretary). Beijing: Chunqiu chubanshe, 1988.

Zhao Dexin 赵德馨, ed. 湖北省志工业志稿: 轻工业) (Hubei province annals: Light industry). Beijing: Zhongguo qinggongye chubanshe, 1994.

Zhao Yuan 赵园. "'都在可破之列': '文革'中的私产与公物" ("Everything could be broken": Private property and public property in the "Cultural Revolution"). *The Paper*. www.thepaper.cn/newsDetail_forward_1261079. Archived November 12, 2017.

Zhejiang baihuo gongsi 浙江百货公司, ed. 浙江百货商业志 (Annals of Zhejiang department store commerce). Hangzhou: Zhejiang renmin chubanshe, 1990.

Zhong, Xueping, Zheng Wang, and Di Bai. *Some of Us: Chinese Women Growing Up in the Mao Era*. New Brunswick, NJ: Rutgers University Press, 2001.

"中共中央批转中共北京市委关于北京市天桥百货商场改革商业工作的报告" (The CCP Central Committee approves the work report of the Beijing Tianqiao Department Store on reform of commercial work submitted by the Beijing Municipal Committee of the CCP), republished in Beijing chubanshe bianjibu 北京出版社编辑部, ed. 大跃进中的北京天桥百货商场 (Beijing Tianqiao Department Store during the Great Leap Forward). Beijing: Beijing chubanshe, 1958.

Zhonggong zhongyang wenxian yanjiushi 中共中央文献研究室, ed. 建国以来重要文献选编 (A selection of major documents since the founding of the state). Beijing: Zhongyang wenxian chubanshe, 1997–8.

Zhonggong zhongyang 中共中央. "关于在文化大革命运动中处理红卫兵抄家物资的几项规定" (Several provisions on dealing with properties confiscated by Red Guards during the Cultural Revolution). March 20, 1967. Available on many sites, including: www.360doc.com/content/14/1126/13/1909 6873_428196989.shtml. Archived November 12, 2017.

Zhongguo guowyuyuan, Zhishi qingniian shangshan xiaxiang lingdao xiaozu bangongshi 中国国务院, 知识青年上山下乡领导小组办公室, ed. 全国城镇知识青年上山下乡统计资料, 1962–1979. Beijing, 1981.

"中央宣传部关于处理留存的'忠'字品的请示" (The Central Propaganda Department requests instructions on handling retained loyalty items). July 28, 1978. Pp. 609–10, in Zhongyang xuanchuanbu bangongting 中央宣传部办公厅, ed. 党的宣传工作文件选编 (1976–1982) (Selected documents on party propaganda work [1976–1982]). Beijing: Zhonggong zhongyang dangxiao chubanshe, 1994.

"中央宣传部关于禁止用毛主席字拼凑商标的通知" (Notice of the Central Propaganda Department on prohibiting using Chairman Mao's calligraphy in the creation of trademarks). April 4, 1964. P. 491, in Zhongyang xuanchuanbu bangongting 中央宣传部办公厅, ed. 党的宣传工作文件选编 (1949–1966) (Selected documents of party propaganda work [1949–1966]). Beijing: Zhonggong zhongyang dangxiao chubanshe, 1994.

Zhou Enlai 周恩来. "周恩来在全国计划工作会议上谈党史历次路线斗争" (Zhou Enlai's speech at the National Planning Conference on the previous lines struggles in the history of the party). March 24, 1969. P. 595, in Zhou Liangxiao 周良霄 and Gu Juying 顾菊英, eds. 疯狂, 扭曲与堕落的年代之二: 十年文革中首长讲话传信录 (Times of madness, distortion, and degradation [2]: Collected speeches by central party leaders during the ten years of the Cultural Revolution). Hong Kong: Xindalu chubanshe, 2008.

Zhou Enlai 周恩来. "社会主义改造与国家资本主义" (Socialist Transformation and state capitalism). September 11, 1953. Pp. 253–7, in Zhonggong zhongyang wenxian yanjiushi 中共中央文献研究室, ed. 周恩来统一战线文选 (Selected writings by Zhou Enlai on the United Front). Beijing: Renmin chubanshe, 1984.

Zhou Jihou 周继厚. 毛泽东像章之谜: 世界第九大奇观 (The mystery of the Mao Zedong badge: The ninth wonder of the world). Taiyuan: Beiyue wenyi chubanshe, 1993.

Zhou, Kate Xiao. *How the Farmers Changed China: Power of the People.* Boulder, CO: Westview Press, 1998.

Zhou, Xun. *Forgotten Voices of Mao's Great Famine, 1958–1962: An Oral History.* New Haven: Yale University Press, 2014.

Zhou, Xun. *The Great Famine in China, 1958–1962: A Documentary History.* New Haven: Yale University Press, 2012.

Zhu Zhanliang 朱展良. "上海轻工业名牌产品初探" (A brief analysis of Shanghai light industry brand products). *Shanghai jingji yanjiu*, no. 9 (September 1981), 7–11.

Zuo Xuchu 左旭初, ed. 民国商标图典 (An illustrated book of trademarks in modern China). Shanghai: Shanghai jinxiu wenzhang chubanshe, 2013.

Zweig, David. *Agrarian Radicalism in China, 1968–1981*. Cambridge, MA: Harvard University Press, 1989.

Index

as form of advertising, 128
marketing of, 121
Soviet promoted, 76, 81
US banned, 121, 125
First Five-Year Plan (1953–7), 69
Fitzpatrick, Sheila, 242, 244, 271
Five-Antis campaign of 1962–6, 164, 171
Five Star brand watches, 15, 50
Flying Dragon brand bicycles, 19
Flying Pigeon brand bicycles, 18, 20, 35, 211
Forever brand bicycles, 19, 20
Forward brand watches, 16
Four News, 169
Four Olds, 169, *See also* Destroy movement;
    Tianqiao campaign
Fraser, Nancy, 238, 307
Frazier, Mark W., 262
Fujian, 207
furniture, 99, 128, 185, 187, 188, 190, 193, 195

Gabriel, Satyananda J., 265
Gansu, 153
Gao Yuan, 214
gender equality. *See* socialism: attributes of
Germany, 15, 19, 44, 51, 122, 187, 336
Gershenkron, Alexander, 254
gifts, 27, 29, 32, 33, 34, 35, 63, 93, 97, 202, 209, 223,
    See also bribery
"Give me back the planes," 224
Glickman, Lawrence B., 233
Gluckstein, Ygael, 278
gray economy, 31–8, *See also* institutional
    arrangements of capitalism: shifts along
    spectrum; state consumerism: policies
    backfire
    and badge fad, 215, 219–22
    and collective enterprises, 311
    and gender, 246
    and Great Leap Forward shortages, 147
    and movie tickets, 130
    and used products, 192
    defined, 248
    in Cultural Revolution, 311
    recent scholarship on, 239
    tacit state approval of, 31, 33, 35, 36, 54, 163, 166
    unauthorized production in, 95–6, 205–8, 221
Great Exchange Program, 213–18, 328, *See also*
    Cultural Revolution; fashion; state
    consumerism: policies backfire
Great Leap Famine. *See* famine
Great Leap Forward. *See also* Tianqiao campaign
    and gray economy, 147
    and queues, 147
    and service sector, 153–9
    and shopping, 147–50

elimination of peddlers, 147
impact on advertising, 115
impact on product availability and quality, 147
impact on Sino-Soviet relations, 94
resistance to state extractions, 70
shift in institutional arrangements, 94
transfer of agricultural labor to factories, 146
transfer of industrial workers to agriculture
    after, 71
transfer of service workers to production, 151
unremunerated labor in, 94, 153–9, 160–1, 302
"Great Retreat," 77
Gronow, Jukka, 275
Gu Hua, 55
Guan Weixun, 190
Guangzhou
    badge production in, 326
    badge redistribution in, 204
    Five-Antis campaign in, 62, 63
    privileged place of production and
        consumption, 16, 22, 33, 38, 142, 215, 216
    Red Guards in, 181
    tourist destination, 328
Guangzhou brand watches, 40
Guards On the Railway Line, 84
Guizhou, 96
Guo Linshuang, 137–9
Guo Moruo, 158

haggling, 144–6, *See also* socialist commerce
Hainan, 328
Hangzhou, 83, 127, 158, 160, 175
Haolai/Hawley Pharmaceutical Company, 103
Harbin, 36, 142, 165, 179, 180, 198, 222, 315
hard work and frugal living, ethos of. *See also* state
    consumerism
    alternative phrasings of, 46
    and compulsion to consume, 32, 37, 217
    and criticism of extravagances, 28
    and frugality collars, 162
    and Japan, 254
    cadres expected to abide by, 42, 44, 58
    equated with socialism, 8, 11, 63, 117, 126,
        129, 203
    fashion manifests, 82
    impact on department stores, 137
    imposed in countryside, 64–71
    in Cultural Revolution, 309
    in Great Leap Forward, 153–9
    in wartime, 255
    in window displays, 141, 143
    PLA as exemplars of, 42
    popular embrace of, 10
    Shanghai as antithesis of, 42
    shifts away from, 89

Shen Kuiyi, 119, 133
Shen Wenying, 143
Shenbao, 103, 104
Shengjia brand sewing machines, 22
Shenyang, 59
Shenyang Glass Measurement Device
  Factory, 206
shortages, 32, 34, 58, 115, 134, 136, 147, 162, 198, 281
Sichuan Restaurant, 174
Sincere Department Store (Xianshi), 136
Singer brand sewing machines, 22, 246
Singer Corporation, 14
Smith, Adam, 65
Snow, Edgar, 200, 226
social consumption. *See also* hard work and frugal
    living, ethos of; state consumerism
  and socialist realism, 118
  and the Soviet Union, 118
  as the opposite of "bourgeois" consumerism,
    44, 101, 102, 238
  defined, 5, 238
  examples of, 6, 12, 101, 117
  GDP worship, 289
  used in advertising, 109
socialism. *See also* Chinese Communist Party:
    terms used by; institutional arrangements of
    capitalism; state capitalism
  and "mistakes" of Mao era, 335
  and inequalities, 2, 8, 230
  and social relations of production, 41–3, 44, 55,
    71, 133, 185
  and unremunerated labor, 160–1
  as catch-all label for state policies, 2, 7, 65, 72,
    102, 113, 121, 134, 147, 164, 237
  attributes of, 5, 7, 41, 50, 52, 66, 70, 81, 119, 133,
    231, 236
  challenges to state definitions of, 66, 67, 70,
    76, 81, 92, 102, 103, 110, 121, 169, 170, 175–8,
    180, 223–4, 227, 285
  defined as transition stage to communism, 2,
    4, 11, 17, 44, 50, 56, 74, 77, 97, 98, 132,
    234, 239
  equated with industrialization, 12
  equated with Soviet Union, 74
  negation of capitalism, 5
  qualified with "actually existing" or "state," 7
socialist advertising. *See* advertising
socialist China. *See* Mao era
socialist commerce, 135–40, *See also* department
    stores; service sector; Tianqiao campaign
  additional experiments, 162
  and open shelves, 158–60
  and state priorities, 167
  and window displays, 139–44
  attempts to eliminate haggling, 144–6

catch-all label for state policies, 237
complaints about, 149
contrasted with capitalist commerce, 113,
  133–4, 142
in Cultural Revolution, 164–6, 175, 183
political implications of, 134, 142, 164
socialist commodities. *See* commodities
socialist construction. *See* socialism: as catch-all
    for state policies
Socialist Education Campaign, 97, 164, 171
socialist profit, 133
socialist smiles, 134
Socialist Transformation. *See also* Chinese
    Communist Party: terms used by;
    expropriation; institutional arrangements,
    shifts in; ownership, four arrangements;
    state capitalism
  and haggling, 145
  and payments to capitalists, 193
  and state ownership, 52, 55, 64, 106, 125
  as part of state capitalism, 233
  defined, 256
  equated with socialism, 54, 69, 133
  incomplete, 95, 113, 122, 147, 248
  shifts in class power, 207
  synonym for state capitalist expropriation, 51
socialist window displays. *See* window displays
socialistic policies. *See also* fashion; hard work
    and frugal living, ethos of; socialist
    commerce; state consumerism
  and haggling, 144–6
  challenged as insufficient, 175–8
  defined, 7
  in advertising, 102, 109, 117
  in brand names, 174
  in media images, 122
  in propaganda images, 118
  in window displays, 139–44
  justified with socialist language, 3
  manifest in fashion, 81–2, 91, 195–8
  street peddlers, 146
Song Binbin, 195, 196
Song Qingling, 84, 183
Soviet experts in China, 79
Soviet Union. *See also* negation of revolution;
    state capitalism
  Chinese visitors to, 89, 93
  cloth exports to China, 84–8
  consumerism in, 80, 107, 270
  critiques of advertising, 113
  different models within, 270
  exhibitions in China, 80
  fashion in China, 81–8, 182
  films, 121, 124
  inequalities accepted, 4, 244